NEW YORK RANGERS
BY THE
NUMBERS

NEW YORK RANGERS

BY THE

NUMBERS

*A Complete Team History
of the Broadway Blueshirts by Uniform Number*

MARK ROSENMAN AND HOWIE KARPIN

Foreword by Kenny Albert

SPORTS
PUBLISHING

Sports Publishing books may be purchased in bulk at special discounts
for sales promotion, corporate gifts, fund-raising, or educational purposes.
Special editions can also be created to specifications. For details, contact the
Special Sales Department, Sports Publishing, 307 West 36th Street, 11th Floor,
New York, NY 10018 or sportspubbooks@skyhorsepublishing.com.

Sports Publishing® is a registered trademark of Skyhorse Publishing, Inc.®,
a Delaware corporation.

Visit our website at www.sportspubbooks.com.

10 9 8 7 6 5 4 3 2 1

Library of Congress Cataloging-in-Publication Data is available on file.

Cover design by Tom Lau
Cover photo credit: AP Images

Print ISBN: 978-1-68358-177-2
Ebook ISBN: 978-1-68358-178-9

Printed in the United States of America

Mark:

This book is dedicated to Marv Albert,
who allowed me to see my first Ranger game
on the radio. I was hooked with the very first
"He shoots, he scores!"

Howie:

I dedicate this book to Ruth and Sidney Karpin,
my late mother and father.

My dad took me to my first hockey game
at the old Madison Square Garden
over 50 years ago and I've been
a huge fan ever since.

CONTENTS

FOREWORD BY KENNY ALBERT

I've been a passionate hockey fan since I was very young and was very familiar with jersey numbers, especially the New York Rangers' numbers.

When I was fourteen years old, I got an opportunity to be the official statistician for New York Rangers' radio broadcasts. The play-by-play announcer just happened to be my dad, Marv Albert. The relationship did not make it any easier for me, as I still needed to put the work in. With the fast-paced play and continuous substitutions on the ice, recognizing the players by their jersey numbers became an integral part of the job.

In 1990, I began my professional broadcasting career as the play-by-play announcer for the Baltimore Skipjacks (a minor-league affiliate of the Washington Capitals). Five years later, I was named the radio voice of the Rangers and have been on the job ever since. I've been privileged to be a TV play-by-play announcer for NHL games, but radio is where you really need to recognize the numbers that are worn by the players on the ice.

Recognizing the sweater numbers that encompass the Rangers' glorious history is what *New York Rangers by the Numbers* is all about. Throughout the proud history of the Rangers' franchise, the sweater numbers have always inspired historical references, trivia questions, and fond memories for their loyal fan base.

Seven Ranger numbers (for eight players) hang in the rafters at Madison Square Garden, but they will be joined by one more in the 2017–18 season.

From #1 Eddie Giacomin to #99 Wayne Gretzky and every number in-between, the glorious history of a proud franchise is told in this book through the single and double digits that graced the Ranger sweater. Mark Rosenman and Howie Karpin went deep into the archives to unearth everyone and anyone who ever wore the Ranger uniform throughout the ninety-year history of the franchise.

It is said that "a picture tells a thousand words," but a sweater number tells a thousand stories.

—**Kenny Albert**

#1: "EDDIE, EDDIE, EDDIE"

Ed Giacomin

NYR Debut: October 24, 1965 (vs. Montreal Canadiens, lost 4–3)

Regular Season Games with NYR: 538

Playoff Games with NYR: 65

Also wore: #23 and #30

Thirty-eight goaltenders have worn #1 for the New York Rangers, but Eddie Giacomin's #1 is one of seven retired numbers (for eight players, soon to be joined by Jean Ratelle's #19) that hang in the rafters at Madison Square Garden.

Hockey Hall of Famer Frank Patrick created a numerical system to identify players' positions on the ice that debuted in the Pacific Coast Hockey League beginning with the 1911–12 season.

Patrick numbered the players from the-goal-out, so the goaltender was #1.

Giacomin's career began as a nineteen-year-old with the Washington Presidents of the Eastern Amateur Hockey League in 1958. He played in the final four games of the season and won all of them, which assured him a spot on next year's team. The following season, the franchise moved to Clinton, New York, and became the Comets. Giacomin was hired as an assistant trainer and back-up goaltender, but later that season was sent to the Providence Reds of the American Hockey League.

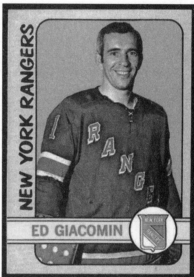

Eddie Giacomin was the second Ranger to have his number retired.

Topps trading cards used per the courtesy of The Topps Company, Inc.

During his five years in Providence, Giacomin caught the eye of a Ranger scout who tipped off head coach Emile Francis about the "acrobatic" goaltender. In May of 1965, the Rangers acquired Giacomin from Providence in exchange for four minor leaguers including backup goalie Marcel Paille who also wore #1 and had played seven years for the Rangers.

On October 24, 1965, Giacomin made his Rangers' and National Hockey League debut at Madison Square Garden against the Montreal Canadiens and lost, 4–3, but it was the beginning of an 11-year career in New York.

It was a struggle for Giacomin early on in his Rangers' tenure. The fans were impatient with the twenty-six-year-old's inconsistent play, so they booed him and rode him pretty hard. But as he kept at it, Giacomin started to develop as a goaltender and so did the fans' affection for him.

From the 1965–1966 through the 1969–70 seasons, Giacomin led the NHL in games played. His workload decreased in the 1970–71 season, but with good reason as he shared the Vezina Trophy with Gilles Villemure (who wore #30).

Giacomin never won a Stanley Cup with the Rangers, but he helped them get there in 1972 against the Boston Bruins. Giacomin, who had injured his knee in the Rangers' semifinal, four-game sweep of Chicago, was awful in Game One as he yielded 6 goals on 28 shots.

After being replaced by Villemure in Game Two, Giacomin returned to the net and won Game Three. His knee acted up again in a Game Four loss and he did not play for the remainder of the series as the Rangers lost in six.

October 29, 1975, is marked as an infamous date in Ranger history. It was the day that Giacomin was placed on waivers and claimed by the Detroit Red Wings. The Red Wings' first game after making the claim was against the Rangers at Madison Square Garden.

November 2 became a memorable night in Garden history as Giacomin started the game in a Red Wings uniform. The crowd gave him a raucous and prolonged standing ovation, and actually rooted for him over the home team throughout the game. Detroit won the game, 6–4.

Giacomin's #1 became the second number to be retired by the team (Rod Gilbert's #7 was first) on March 15, 1989. He was inducted into the Hockey Hall of Fame in 1987.

Lorne "Gump" Worsley

> **NYR Debut:** October 9, 1952 (at Detroit Red Wings, lost 5–2)
> **Regular Season Games with NYR:** 582
> **Playoff Games with NYR:** 20

Lorne "Gump" Worsley began his Hall of Fame career with the Rangers in 1952, when he captured the Calder Memorial Trophy as the National Hockey League's Rookie of the Year.

A high school friend gave Worsley the nickname of "Gump" because he bore a facial resemblance to a comic strip character named "Andy Gump." The 5-foot-7, 180-pounder hated playing with a mask and was one of the last NHL goaltenders to play without one.

The Montreal native posted a 13–29–8 record for a Rangers team that won a total of 17 games in the 1952–53 season.

After a successful first season, Worsley came to camp out of shape and lost his starting job to Johnny Bower. When a reporter questioned Worsley about his conditioning and accused him of carrying around a "beer belly,"

Photo from the public domain.

Lorne's nickname comes from comic strip character Andy Gump.

the goalie responded, "I do not have a beer belly. I only drink Seagram's VO and ginger ale."

With Worsley in net, the Rangers made the playoffs four times. In the 1956, five-game, semifinal loss to the Montreal Canadiens, Worsley went 0–3. The next season, the Rangers once again lost the semifinals in five to Montreal, but Worsley got his first postseason win.

Worsley would play in two more series for the Rangers. In the 1958 postseason, Worsley won two games but the Rangers dropped a six-game, semifinal series to Boston. Four years later, the Rangers were ousted by the Toronto Maple Leafs in six games with Worsley getting his final two postseason victories in a Rangers sweater.

On June 4, 1963, the Rangers and Canadiens swung a memorable seven-player deal. The Rangers traded Worsley, along with left wingers Dave Balon and Len Ronson, and right wing Leon Rochefort to Montreal in exchange for Hall of Fame goaltender Jacques Plante, left wing Don Marshall, and center Phil Goyette.

Worsley was inducted into the Hockey Hall of Fame in 1980.

Chuck Rayner

NYR Debut: November 3, 1945 (at Toronto Maple Leafs, won 4–1)

Regular Season Games with NYR: 376

Playoff Games with NYR: 18

Chuck Rayner did not begin his Hall of Fame career with the Rangers, although it did start with a New York team that played their home games at Madison Square Garden.

In 1939, Rayner signed a free agent contract with the New York Americans and played 12 games for them in the 1940–41 season. The Americans were the third expansion team in the National Hockey League and the second to be based in the United States.

The team changed its name to the Brooklyn Americans for the 1941–42 season, and Rayner played 36 games that season and won 13 of their 16 total wins.

After serving three years in World War II, Rayner signed with the Rangers, who were a last place team that won a total of 13 games in the 1945–46 season. Rayner won 12 but lost a league high 21 games in his first season with the "Broadway Blueshirts."

Rayner was a workhorse in net, as he played 58 of 60 games in the 1946–1947 season. He won 22 and lost 30 games, yet led the league with five shutouts and posted a respectable 3.05 goals against average (which was fourth-best in the league that season).

Head coach Frank Boucher wanted to lessen the workload on Rayner, so "Sugar" Jim Henry was brought back for the 1947–48 season to share the goaltending duties. Boucher alternated the goalies on a game-by-game basis. He went even further by alternating the goaltenders in-game with switches every five minutes. The team carried just one pair of goalie gloves so there was a "ritual" when the change was made. "Frank switched us every third line or so," Rayner explained. "When I skated off to the bench and 'Sugar Jim' came on the ice, we would meet at the blue line so we could exchange gloves in front of 15,000 fans." Rayner would end up suffering a broken cheekbone during the season, so Henry finished as the starting goalie.

Rayner was adept with his stick which made him somewhat of an offensive threat. While playing with the Royal Canadian Armed Forces team, Rayner skated the length of the ice and scored a goal. In the late 1940s, Boucher utilized Rayner's offensive skills by occasionally using him on the power play. "I'd only come out half way up to the blue line. It only happened four or five times," Rayner said.

Rayner led a surprising Ranger team into the Stanley Cup Final against the Detroit Red Wings in 1950. The Blueshirts finished under .500, but Rayner sparkled in 69 of 70 games to lead the team to a surprising playoff berth as he captured the Hart Trophy as the NHL's Most Valuable Player.

Rayner carried the Rangers to a seventh and deciding game, but they ended up losing 4–3 in double overtime.

In 1953, Rayner injured his knee and lost his starting job to "Gump" Worsley. He played in the Western Hockey and Western International Hockey League before ending his pro career.

Rayner was inducted into the Hockey Hall of Fame in 1973.

Dave Kerr

NYR Debut: December 16, 1934 (vs. Boston Bruins, won 2-1)
Regular Season Games with NYR: 324
Playoff Games with NYR: 32

Dave Kerr is one of four goaltenders in franchise history to have won a Stanley Cup.

Kerr beat the Toronto Maple Leafs, 3–2, in overtime of Game Six of the 1940 Stanley Cup Final to give the Rangers their third Cup victory in franchise history. The Toronto native had an added bonus of beating his hometown Maple Leafs.

During the regular season, Kerr had a 19-game unbeaten streak (14–0–5) and won the Vezina Trophy as the league's best goaltender with a 1.54 goals against average, to go along with 8 shutouts.

The Rangers sent cash to the Montreal Maroons in December of 1934 to acquire the Toronto native.

Kerr was the only goaltender in franchise history to start every game for five consecutive seasons, from 1936–41 (during that time the league played a 48-game schedule), and he only missed one game as a Ranger between 1934 and 1941.

With his acrobatic and athletic style of goaltending, Kerr became an immediate fan favorite. In practice, Kerr would lay his goal stick across the goal mouth in front of the goal line while he did splits to take away the lower portion. Kerr's hands would be free to catch his teammates' practice shots and he would dare them to beat him, but it was a rarity when they did.

Kerr became the second hockey player ever featured on the cover of *Time* magazine (see Lorne Chabot later in this chapter). On March 18, 1938,

5

an illustration of Kerr (drawn by noted illustrator S. J. Woolf), defending his net in his Ranger blue sweater, was featured.

In the 1940 Stanley Cup, the Rangers won three overtime games. In Game One at Madison Square Garden, rookie center Alf Pike's goal at 15:30 of overtime gave the Rangers a 2–1 win. The Rangers won Game Two at the Garden but, because of a scheduling conflict with the circus, the last four games were played in Toronto. The Maple Leafs won Games Three and Four to tie the series, but the Rangers won Game Five in double overtime on Muzz Patrick's goal.

In Game Six, the Leafs took a 2–0 lead with a little under five minutes gone in the second period, but Kerr slammed the door shut from there. In the third period, center Neil Colville and Pike scored, in a span of one minute and 53 seconds, to tie the game. Bryan Hextall's goal at 2:07 of overtime clinched the Cup victory.

Kerr retired after the 1940–41 season.

John Ross Roach

NYR Debut: November 15, 1928 (at Detroit Cougars, won 2–0)
Regular Season Games with NYR: 180
Playoff Games with NYR: 21

When the Rangers began the 1928–29 season, they had a new starting goaltender.

The Rangers swung a one-for-one deal when they sent their starting goalie Lorne Chabot to the Toronto Maple Leafs for twenty-eight-year-old John Ross Roach. The 5-foot-5, 130-pound goaltender was a Stanley Cup champion with the Toronto St. Patricks in 1922. His diminutive size led to the nickname "Little Napoleon."

The Ontario native had a successful first season in New York, beginning with opening night, when he debuted with a 2–0 shutout of the Detroit Cougars. In his initial Ranger season, Roach set single season franchise records for the lowest goals against average (1.48) and shutouts (13).

In the 1929 Stanley Cup Playoffs, Roach had a 0.97 goals against average with three shutouts, but was outplayed in the Finals by Boston rookie goaltender Cecil "Tiny" Thompson to give the Bruins their first Stanley Cup victory. (Note: the final series was a best-of-three.)

Roach would start every game for the next three seasons, and the Rangers made the playoffs in every one of his four with the team.

In the 1930 playoffs, the Rangers faced the Montreal Canadiens for the first time in postseason play in a best-of-three, semifinal series. Game One became the longest game in the history of the thirteen-year-old National Hockey League. Canadiens' right wing Gus Rivers beat Roach 6:52 into the fourth overtime to give Montreal a 2–1 win. The game at the Montreal Forum ended at 12:45 a.m. The Canadiens completed the sweep with a 2–0 win in Game Two in New York.

Roach's tenure ended after getting swept by the Toronto Maple Leafs in the 1932 Stanley Cup Final. In three games, Roach gave up 27 goals. In October of 1932, Roach was sold to the Detroit Red Wings and was named a first team All-Star in his first season in Motown.

Glen Hanlon

NYR Debut: January 9, 1983 (vs. New Jersey Devils, won 4–3)
Regular Season Games with NYR: 138
Playoff Games with NYR: 12

On January 4, 1983, the Rangers sent defenseman Andre Dore to the St. Louis Blues in exchange for right winger Vaclav Nedomansky and veteran goaltender Glen Hanlon.

The soon to be twenty-six-year-old netminder had already logged seven years of NHL experience when he came to New York.

The 1983–84 season was Hanlon's best in Broadway Blue. He won 28 games, and was the starting goaltender against the four-time champion New York Islanders in a best-of-five divisional semifinal series.

The Rangers had a 2–1 series lead, but lost Game Four to set up a fifth and deciding game at Nassau Coliseum.

Hanlon and the Rangers trailed 2–1 with time running out in the third period when Don Maloney tied the game in the final minute to send the game into overtime. The Rangers had an opportunity to put an end to the Islanders' four-year reign as Stanley Cup champions. In overtime, Hanlon robbed Islanders' center Bob Bourne on a backhand shot from in close with a gorgeous glove save. Less than a minute after Islanders' goaltender Billy Smith robbed Rangers' center Bob Brooke on a breakaway, Islanders' defenseman Ken Morrow beat Hanlon from the right face-off circle to end the game and the series with a 3–2 win.

In July of 1986, the Rangers traded Hanlon along with two draft picks to the Detroit Red Wings for three players including center Kelly Kisio. Hanlon played the final five seasons of his career in Detroit.

"Sugar" Jim Henry

NYR Debut: November 1, 1941 (at Toronto Maple Leafs, won 4–3)
Regular Season Games with NYR: 109
Playoff Games with NYR: 6
Also wore: #20

In the 1941–42 season, Rangers rookie goaltender "Sugar" Jim Henry set a franchise record by winning a league-leading 29 games. (Henrik Lundqvist broke the mark in the 2005–06 season with 30 wins.)

The Rangers finished in first place with 60 points, three ahead of the Toronto Maple Leafs. Henry finished second in the vote for the Calder Trophy to his teammate, right winger Grant Warwick, who had 16 goals and 33 points in 44 games.

The Winnipeg, Manitoba, native recalled his nickname derived from his boyhood days. When he would go next door to visit some girls, Henry said they would "dip my soother in a sugar bowl, so the girls gave me the name 'Sugar.' Then I couldn't get rid of it."

Rangers' general manager Frank Boucher was looking for a replacement for the retired Dave Kerr so he signed the twenty-one-year-old as a free agent in October of 1941.

After his outstanding first season, Henry served in the military for the next three years. Unfortunately, he was not the same when he returned to the NHL in 1945. Henry split time in the next three seasons between the Rangers and their top minor league affiliate at New Haven, Connecticut.

In October of 1948, the Rangers traded Henry to the Chicago Black Hawks for goaltender Emile Francis and left winger Alex Kaleta.

Marcel Paille

NYR Debut: October 31, 1957 (at Boston Bruins, won 3–0)
Regular Season Games with NYR: 107
Playoff Games with NYR: 0
Also wore: #23

Marcel Paille was a solid goaltender who was a victim of his times.

The Quebec native played in an era that featured a plethora of all-time great goaltenders like Johnny Bower and Jacques Plante. With only six teams in the National Hockey League carrying just a single goaltender, many good net-minders never got a chance to shine.

In his rookie season of 1957–58, Paille played in 33 games as he backed up the starter Gump Worsley, but spent most of the season with the Providence Reds of the American Hockey League.

In the minors, Paille became almost legendary. In 1959, he joined the Springfield Indians of the AHL and led them to three consecutive Calder Cup trophies, emblematic of the league championship. Paille played 765 games in a record 15 seasons in the AHL and won a total of four Calder Cup Trophies.

Andy Aitkenhead

NYR Debut: November 10, 1932 (at Montreal Maroons, won 4–2)
Regular Season Games with NYR: 106
Playoff Games with NYR: 10

For a player whose career was limited to three seasons, Andy Aitkenhead made quite an impact during that time. In his rookie season of 1932–33, Aitkenhead led the Rangers to their second Stanley Cup championship.

The Rangers finished third in the American Division of the NHL, but wins over the Montreal Canadiens and Detroit Red Wings set up a rematch with the Toronto Maple Leafs who swept them in the previous year's finals. Thanks to Aitkenhead, who had two shutouts and was 6–1 in the playoffs, the Rangers avenged their loss with a three-games-to-one series victory.

The twenty-eight-year-old, who was born in Glasgow, Scotland, and nicknamed the "Glasgow Gobbler," played every game in his first two seasons. Despite his success, Aitkenhead caused some concern when his behavior began to become neurotic. Reportedly, he would obsess greatly over games afterward in the locker room. The situation got to a point that management gave up on him.

Aitkenhead played only 10 games in his final NHL season of 1934–35. He finished his pro career by playing five more seasons with Portland of the PCHL.

Doug Soetaert

NYR Debut: December 19, 1975 (at Atlanta Flames, lost 8–3)
Regular Season Games with NYR: 103
Playoff Games with NYR: 0
Also wore: #33 and #31

Photo courtesy of Ken Tash.

Soapy also wore #31 and #33 as a Ranger.

With their second round pick in the 1975 amateur draft, the Rangers selected a 6-foot goaltender out of the Western Canada Junior Hockey League.

Doug Soetaert, who was nicknamed "Soapy," got off to a rough start in his Rangers career as he was pummeled by the Atlanta Flames 8–3 in his NHL debut. He went 2–2 in his first season as he shuffled back and forth between New York and the New Haven Nighthawks, the Rangers' AHL affiliate.

The Edmonton, Alberta, native spent his career on a shuttle as he had to compete for playing time with goalies like John Davidson and Wayne Thomas. In his first two seasons, Soapy played in 52 games but some of those were in a relief role.

In the 1980–81 season, Soetaert (who wore numbers 33 and 31 that season) played 39 games and finished with a 16–16–7 record. The Rangers made the playoffs, but Soetaert backed up Steve Baker and did not play in any games.

Following that season, Soetaert was traded to the Winnipeg Jets for a third round pick in the 1983 entry draft. He returned to the Rangers as a free agent for the 1986–87 season and played in 13 games.

Jacques Plante

> **NYR Debut:** October 9, 1963 (at Chicago Black Hawks, lost 3–1)
> **Regular Season Games with NYR:** 98
> **Playoff Games with NYR:** 0

Hall of Famer Jacques Plante was famous for being the first goaltender to regularly wear a mask in the National Hockey League, but he was also a part of one of the biggest swaps in Rangers history (see Worsley earlier in Chapter One).

Plante was a six-time Vezina Trophy winner, including five in a row from 1956–60. He played a total of 11 seasons in Montreal.

In his second game as a Ranger, the Quebec native faced his old team at the Montreal Forum. Following his trade to New York, Plante, in a published report, said "Montreal was on the way down," Jean Beliveau was "growing old," and Bernie "Boom Boom" Geoffrion "couldn't shoot anymore."

Spurred on by the comments, the Canadiens unloaded 59 shots on Plante en route to a 6–2 thrashing.

Plante's first win in a Rangers sweater came four days after the Montreal fiasco as he blanked the Detroit Red Wings at Madison Square Garden, 3–0. He followed that up with a 5–1 win over the Boston Bruins at MSG.

In his first season with the Broadway Blueshirts, Plante played in 65 of 70 games and had all 22 Ranger wins, but the team failed to make the playoffs.

Photo from the public domain.

Jacques was part of one of biggest Rangers trade in franchise history.

On November 1, 1959, Plante, while playing for Montreal, took a shot squarely in the face from Rangers' right winger Andy Bathgate. After leaving the ice for medical attention, he returned and made history by wearing a mask for the first time.

The Hall of Famer retired after the 1964–65 season, but returned three years later to play for the expansion St. Louis Blues in their second season.

Ken McAuley

> **NYR Debut:** October 30, 1943 (at Toronto Maple Leafs, lost 5–2)
> **Regular Season Games with NYR:** 96
> **Playoff Games with NYR:** 0

What Marv Throneberry was to the New York Mets, goaltender Ken McAuley was to the Rangers.

In his first season, McAuley won a total of six games while allowing a record-setting 310 goals for the season and a GAA of 6.24. The most infamous game was in Detroit on January 23, 1944, when the Red Wings destroyed McAuley and the Rangers 15–0. A 16th goal was scored, but did not count because it didn't beat the buzzer.

In his second and final season, McAuley improved to 11 wins but the Rangers wound up in last place once again.

Wayne Thomas

NYR Debut: October 15, 1977 (Rangers at Montreal Canadiens, lost 5–0)

Regular Season Games with NYR: 94

Playoff Games with NYR: 1

Also wore: #33

Photo courtesy of Ken Tash.

Wayne Thomas also served as an assistant coach for Rangers.

In October of 1977, Rangers general manager John Ferguson claimed goaltender Wayne Thomas on waivers from the Toronto Maple Leafs.

The 6-foot-2 Ottawa native backed up starting goaltender John Davidson in the 1977–78 season. Thomas wore #33 and had only 12 wins in his first season, but four of those were shutouts.

After Davidson suffered a concussion in Game Two of their preliminary round playoff against the Buffalo Sabres, Thomas started and lost the deciding Game Three, 4–1. It would be his only postseason appearance as a Ranger.

Thomas appeared in 53 more games for the Rangers. He retired in 1981, and became an assistant coach with the team for four seasons, from 1982–85.

Lorne Chabot

NYR Debut: November 27, 1926 (at Montreal Canadiens, won 2–0)

Regular Season Games with NYR: 80

Playoff Games with NYR: 8

Being 6-foot-1 and 185 pounds was not a prototypical goaltender's physique, but Lorne Chabot was not just a physical specimen.

Chabot was a nimble and athletic goaltender who caught the eye of a young Conn Smythe when he was leading the Port Arthur Ports to two consecutive Allan Cups, emblematic of the championship of the Manitoba Senior Hockey League in 1925 and 1926.

The Rangers signed Chabot as a free agent in September of 1926.

Even though he was not Jewish, there was an attempt to market Chabot as "Chabotsky" to appeal to the Jewish fans in New York. The Montreal-born Chabot rejected this proposition outright.

In his second season, Chabot played all 44 games and led the Rangers into the Stanley Cup Final vs. the Montreal Maroons. During that season, Chabot was reportedly approached by gamblers (some reports said it was an "old-time boxer") with a proposition to "throw" a game, but the Ranger goaltender immediately reported the encounter to general manager and head coach Lester Patrick, and nothing else came of it.

With the circus in New York, the five-game series was played entirely in Montreal.

The Maroons won the first game. In the second, Chabot was injured late in the second period of a then scoreless game. The Ranger goaltender was hit in the left eye as the result of a shot from Montreal's Nels Stewart. Goalies did not wear masks then, and Chabot was bleeding all over the ice. He was rushed to the hospital for medical attention and the officials decided to end the period and take a break for the third.

With no backup goaltender on the roster, Patrick lobbied to use Ottawa star goaltender Alex Connell, who was in the stands, but Montreal refused. The forty-four-year-old Patrick, who was a defenseman as a player, inserted himself as the goalie.

Thirty seconds into the third period, right winger Bill Cook gave the Rangers a 1–0 lead, but with a little over five minutes left in regulation, Stewart tied the game to force overtime. Rangers center Frank Boucher then scored at 7:05 of sudden death overtime to give the Blueshirts a 2–1 win.

Chabot was done for the series, so Patrick acquired goaltender Joe Miller on loan from the New York Americans. Miller lost the third game but won the final two to give the Rangers a stunning Cup victory.

Chabot's eye injury became a concern for the Rangers, so they traded him to the Toronto Maple Leafs in October of 1928 for goaltender John Ross Roach.

Chabot became the first hockey player ever featured for a cover story in *Time* magazine. On February 11, 1935, he was pictured in a Black Hawks sweater defending the net.

During an 11-year career, he had 201 wins and 71 shutouts while his 2.03 GAA is the fourth best in NHL history.

Johnny Bower

NYR Debut: October 8, 1953 (at Detroit Red Wings, lost 4–1)
Regular Season Games with NYR: 77
Playoff Games with NYR: 0

In July of 1953, the Rangers acquired twenty-nine-year-old goaltender Johnny Bower from Cleveland of the American Hockey League. Bower had toiled in the minors for nine seasons until he finally got a chance in New York.

In his first season, Bower played every minute of every game, as he replaced an out of shape "Gump" Worsley and won 29 games, but the Rangers missed the playoffs. During that season, the 5-foot-11 goaltender posted five shutouts.

Bower came to camp overweight the next season and lost his starting job to the younger Worsley. He was sent to the minors and, over the next two seasons, played only seven more games for the Rangers. In 1957, he was traded back to Cleveland but was claimed by Toronto in the 1958 Inter-League Draft.

Bower would go on to play 12 years with the Maple Leafs where he would win the Stanley Cup four times, along with two Vezina trophies. The Saskatchewan native was inducted into the Hockey Hall of Fame in 1976.

Jim Franks

NYR Debut: November 26, 1942 (at Chicago Black Hawks, won 2–1)
Regular Season Games with NYR: 23
Playoff Games with NYR: 0

Saskatchewan-born Jim Franks was considered a "mercenary."

In 1942, the Rangers needed a goaltender as "Sugar" Jim Henry was summoned for military duty during World War II. After the club used a combination of Lionel Bouvrette and Steve Buzinski to begin the season in Henry's absence, the Rangers acquired Franks on loan from the Detroit Red Wings.

Franks would only win five of his 23 games in the 1942–43 season, which ended when he suffered a broken wrist.

Emile "The Cat" Francis

NYR Debut: December 19, 1948 (vs. Montreal Canadiens, won 3–2)

Regular Season Games with NYR: 22

Playoff Games with NYR: 0

Also wore: #16

Emile Francis made his Rangers legacy as their head coach and longtime general manager, but he was first associated with the hockey club as a young goaltender.

Francis got his nickname, "The Cat," when he was playing junior hockey in Moose Jaw, Saskatchewan, because a local sportswriter wrote he was "quick as a cat in goal."

Francis is also credited with introducing the goalie glove to the game. The Saskatchewan-born Francis was a baseball fan, so he used that passion to fashion a new glove for goaltenders. The old glove was a standard five fingers with very little webbing. Francis complained that anytime he caught a puck his hand would be filled with bruises. The goalie secured a first baseman's mitt and had the trainer

The Cat played 22 games as a goalie, with 654 as the team's head coach.

Photo from the public domain.

take the cuff off of an old hockey glove and sew it onto the baseball glove. Francis used the glove without a problem in the minors, but it became an issue when he debuted in the National Hockey League.

15

During the pregame warmups before a game in Detroit, Red Wings head coach Jack Adams complained to referee King Clancy about the glove. Eventually, Francis had a meeting with NHL president Clarence Campbell who allowed him to use the glove. According to Francis, "the story got out and within a month, all the sporting goods companies were making those goal gloves. I should have copyrighted the idea."

In October of 1948, Francis was traded from Chicago to the Rangers where he played a total of 22 games over a four-year period.

In 1965, Francis, who was already an assistant general manager, was made the full-time GM and head coach. In his first season behind the bench, the Rangers missed the playoffs. It would be the only time during his ten-year tenure that they would not make a postseason berth.

Francis ceded his head coaching duties to Bernie "Boom Boom" Geoffrion for the 1968–69 season, but the Hall of Famer was forced to resign midway through the season due to health issues. Francis went back behind the bench for the remainder of the season. The Rangers made the playoffs but lost a four-game quarterfinal sweep to the eventual Stanley Cup champion Montreal Canadiens.

In 1972, Francis guided the team to the Stanley Cup Final vs. the Boston Bruins, but lost in six games.

Francis gave up the coaching duties for a second time in 1973 when he handed the reins to former Ranger Larry Popein. The team was struggling and there were reports of discontent so Francis once again took over behind the bench. "The Cat" led the team to a quarterfinal series win over Montreal but they lost a tough, seven-game semifinal series to the eventual champion Philadelphia Flyers.

In Francis's final season, the Rangers lost a best-of-three preliminary round to the upstart New York Islanders. The final game went 11 seconds into overtime before Islanders' left winger J. P. Parise scored the winning goal that ended the season and essentially Francis's career with the Rangers.

The Rangers fired Francis in January of 1976. He went on to become the general manager and head coach of the St. Louis Blues until 1983 when he joined the Hartford Whalers' front office. Francis was elected to the Hockey Hall of Fame in 1982 as a contributor.

Bill Beveridge

NYR Debut: January 28, 1943 (at Chicago Black Hawks, lost 10–1)
Regular Season Games with NYR: 17
Postseason Games with NYR: 0

In the 1936–37 Stanley Cup Semifinals the Rangers defeated the Montreal Maroons, two games to none to advance to the Final where they lost to Detroit. Montreal's goaltender was Bill Beveridge.

Six years later, Beveridge would be tending goal for the Rangers.

Goalie Jimmy Franks was injured so the Rangers acquired the thirty-three-year-old Beveridge on loan from Cleveland of the American Hockey League. Beveridge did not fare so well in his debut in late January, being hammered in a 10–1 loss to the Black Hawks in Chicago. He did record the only Rangers shutout of the season when he blanked the Maple Leafs in Toronto.

Beveridge is in the record books for being the first goaltender to allow an opposing player to score a hat trick in a single period, which happened on November 20, 1934. While tending goal for the St. Louis Eagles, Beveridge allowed Maple Leafs winger Harvey Jackson to score four goals in the third period of a 5–2 loss.

The following goaltenders played less than 15 games with NYR:

Jack McCartan

NYR Debut: March 6, 1960 (vs. Detroit Red Wings, won 3–1)
Regular Season Games with NYR: 12
Playoff Games with NYR: 0

Al Rollins

NYR Debut: February 20, 1960 (at Montreal Canadiens, tie 3–3)
Regular Season Games with NYR: 10
Playoff Games with NYR: 0

Steve Buzinski

NYR Debut: October 31, 1942 (at Toronto Maple Leafs, lost 7–2)
Regular Season Games with NYR: 9
Playoff Games with NYR: 0

Hal Winkler

NYR Debut: November 16, 1926 (vs. Montreal Maroons, won 1–0)
Regular Season Games with NYR: 8
Playoff Games with NYR: 0

Doug Stevenson

NYR Debut: February 11, 1945 (vs. Montreal Canadiens, lost 4–3)

Regular Season Games with NYR: 4

Playoff Games with NYR: 0

Lorne Anderson

NYR Debut: March 19, 1952 (vs. Boston Bruins, won 6–4)

Regular Season Games with NYR: 3

Playoff Games with NYR: 0

Marcel Pelletier

NYR Debut: October 28, 1962 (vs. Chicago Black Hawks, lost 5–3)

Regular Season Games with NYR: 2

Playoff Games with NYR: 0

Joe Schaefer

NYR Debut: February 17, 1960 (vs. Chicago Black Hawks, lost 5–1)

Regular Season Games with NYR: 2

Playoff Games with NYR: 0

Bruce Gamble

NYR Debut: February 11, 1959 (vs. Boston Bruins, lost 5–3)

Regular Season Games with NYR: 2

Playoff Games with NYR: 0

Lionel Bouvrette

NYR Debut: March 18, 1943 (at Montreal Canadiens, lost 6–3)

Regular Season Games with NYR: 1

Playoff Games with NYR: 0

Bob DeCourcy

NYR Debut: November 12, 1947 (vs. Boston Bruins, lost 8–2)

Regular Season Games with NYR: 1

Playoff Games with NYR: 0

Dave Dryden

NYR Debut: February 3, 1962 (at Toronto Maple Leafs, lost 4–1)

Regular Season Games with NYR: 1

Playoff Games with NYR: 0

Bert Gardiner

NYR Debut: March 22, 1936 (at Boston Bruins, lost 3–1)

Regular Season Games with NYR: 1

Playoff Games with NYR: 6

Percy Jackson

NYR Debut: November 15, 1934 (at Detroit Red Wings, lost 8–2)

Regular Season Games with NYR: 1

Playoff Games with NYR: 0

Julian Klymkiw

NYR Debut: October 11, 1958 (at Detroit Red Wings, lost 3–0)

Regular Season Games with NYR: 1

Playoff Games with NYR: 0

Harry Lumley

NYR Debut: December 23, 1943 (at Detroit Red Wings, lost 5–3)

Regular Season Games with NYR: 1

Playoff Games with NYR: 0

Dan Olesevich

NYR Debut: October 21, 1961 (at Detroit Red Wings, 4–4 tie)

Regular Season Games with NYR: 1

Playoff Games with NYR: 0

Joe Miller

NYR Debut: April 10, 1928 (at Montreal Maroons, Game Three of Stanley Cup Finals, lost 2–0)

Regular Season Games with NYR: 0

Playoff Games with NYR: 3

Gordie Bell

NYR Debut: March 22, 1956 (at Montreal Canadiens, Game Two of Stanley Cup Semifinals, won 4–2)

Regular Season Games with NYR: 0

Playoff Games with NYR: 2

#2: 2 GREAT ONES

Brian Leetch

NYR Debut: February 29, 1988 (vs. St Louis, won 5–2)

Regular Season Games with NYR: 1,129

Playoff Games with NYR: 82

The 1986 NHL Entry Draft became a seminal moment in franchise history. The Rangers used their first round pick and the ninth overall to select a player who is arguably the greatest to ever wear the Ranger sweater. American-born Brian Leetch went on to have a spectacular 17-year career with the Rangers that featured a Calder Trophy as the top rookie; two Norris Trophies as the top defenseman in the NHL, a Conn Smythe Trophy as the Playoff MVP, and a Stanley Cup championship.

Before joining the Rangers, Leetch played a year at Boston College and was the Team USA Captain for the 1988 Winter Olympic Games in Calgary, Alberta. He played all six games while nursing

Photo by Håkan Dahlström via Wikimedia Commons.

Won Calder, Conn Smythe, Norris, and Stanley Cup winner.

a knee injury. Eight days after the United States' team was eliminated without a medal, Leetch made his NHL debut at Madison Square Garden against the St. Louis Blues. Leetch recorded his first NHL point, an assist on a Kelly Kisio goal, as the Rangers won 5–2.

Leetch was a great two-way player who excelled with the puck. His skating and stick-handling ability made him an offensive force on the back line and he was particularly adept at running the point on the power play. Leetch had a knack for keeping pucks in the offensive zone and keeping power plays alive.

In the 1988–89 season, the 6-foot, 185-pound defenseman put up some impressive numbers. Leetch scored a rookie record 23 goals and totaled 71 points to win the Calder Trophy as the NHL's top rookie. In 1991–92, Leetch won the first of his two Norris Trophies as the top defenseman in the league. He recorded a league record 80 assists en route to a 102-point season, making him the fourth defenseman in history to reach the triple-digit milestone.

With the arrival of Hall of Famer Mark Messier in 1991, Leetch's play shifted into another gear. The uniting of the two all-time greats culminated in the 1994 Stanley Cup championship that ended a 54-year "drought." Messier's winning pedigree rubbed off on Leetch who became the first American-born player to win the Conn Smythe Trophy with a playoff performance for the ages. During the Rangers run to the Cup, Leetch scored 11 goals and added 23 assists for 34 points in 23 games.

Leetch made his mark on franchise history with two memorable seventh game goals. In an epic Eastern Conference Final series against the New Jersey Devils, Leetch scored the first goal of Game Seven with a patented move. Leetch was being checked by Devils winger Bill Guerin as he was skating near the left corner and appeared to be heading behind the net. He suddenly put on the brakes and with a "spin-o-rama" move, he back-handed the puck past Hall of Fame goaltender Martin Brodeur. With the Stanley Cup and the 54-year gap without a Cup on the line against the Vancouver Canucks in Game Seven, Leetch scored the first goal of the game into an open net off a nice feed from Sergei Zubov and a secondary assist from Messier, who once referred to Leetch as "the greatest Ranger of all time."

In 1995, Leetch suffered through an injury-plagued season and the Rangers were swept in the Conference Semifinals as their quest for a second straight Stanley Cup fell short. Leetch had nine goals during the regular season but scored a total of six goals in 10 playoff games. He nearly beat the Flyers single-handedly in Game Two as he became the ninth defenseman in Stanley Cup playoff history to score a hat trick.

Leetch won his second Norris Trophy in 1997 as he scored 20 goals and was a first team All-Star for a second time. The Rangers faced the Flyers again, this time in the Eastern Conference Finals, but lost in five games. Leetch had 2 goals and 8 assists in 15 games, but it would mark his final postseason appearance in a Ranger sweater.

The Rangers missed the playoffs for the next six seasons and were on their way to a seventh. On March 3, 2004, Rangers general manager Glen Sather shocked the hockey world by dealing Leetch to the Toronto Maple Leafs on his thirty-sixth birthday.

Leetch played in only 15 games for Toronto. After the 2004–05 season was cancelled due to a labor dispute, Leetch became a free agent and signed with the Boston Bruins for one season. Despite receiving numerous contract offers, Leetch officially retired from the NHL on May 24, 2007.

On January 24, 2008, Leetch's #2 became the fifth number to be retired in Rangers history.

Brad Park

NYR Debut: October 23, 1968 (vs. Oakland Seals, won 6–1)
Regular Season Games with NYR: 465
Playoff Games with NYR: 64

Brad Park was a victim of bad timing.

Park played in an era that was dominated by Hall of Famer Bobby Orr. During his Ranger tenure, Park finished as a runner up to Orr a total of four times for the Norris Trophy.

Historic trade made Park a Bruin.

Photo courtesy of Mark Rosenman.

The 6-foot, 200-pound defenseman was a talented skater and stick handler who provided an offensive dimension from the back line that a Ranger team had never seen before.

The Rangers made the Toronto native their first pick and second overall in the 1966 NHL Amateur Draft. Park played 17 games with Buffalo of the American Hockey League before being summoned to join the Rangers.

From the moment he first stepped on the ice in 1968, the Rangers knew they had something special. Park played 54 games in his first season and scored 26 points (3 goals, 23 assists). Park's first NHL goal came against the Boston Bruins at Madison Square Garden on February 23, 1969, as part of a 9–0 rout. The goal hit the post and went in past Bruins' goaltender Eddie Johnston. Park finished third in the voting for the Calder Trophy. Montreal swept a four-game series from the Rangers in the Stanley Cup Quarterfinals, but the twenty-year-old had his first two postseason assists.

In the 1971–72 season, Park scored 24 goals and scored 73 points to lead the Rangers into the Stanley Cup Final against Orr and the Boston Bruins. Orr won the Conn Smythe Trophy and led the Bruins to their second Stanley Cup title in three seasons but Park's skills were on full display in Game Three. The Rangers were down two games to none when they hosted Game Three at Madison Square Garden. Park scored 2 goals and added 2 assists to lead the Rangers to a 5–2 win.

Park's best year in Broadway Blue was when he scored 25 goals and 82 points in the 1973–74 season. In the 1974 Stanley Cup Semifinals against the Philadelphia Flyers, the Rangers trailed two games to none and hosted Game Three at the Garden. The Flyers had a 3–1 lead midway through the second period, but the Rangers rallied to tie the game heading to the third. Park scored the go-ahead goal on the power play and the Rangers went on to a 5–3 win. Park totaled 3 goals and 2 assists, but it wasn't enough as the Rangers lost in seven games.

In 1975, the Rangers conducted a "housecleaning." The team was struggling and management felt a shakeup was needed. On October 29, popular goaltender Ed Giacomin was placed on waivers and claimed by Detroit (see Chapter One: Ed Giacomin). Nine days later, Rangers general manager Emile Francis engineered a historic five-player trade with the Bruins. Park, thirty-five-year-old center Jean Ratelle and minor league defenseman Joe Zanussi were sent to Boston in exchange for thirty-three-year-old All-Star center and Hall of Famer Phil Esposito and defenseman

Carol Vadnais. The irony of the trade is that Park became teammates with the player that he played "second fiddle" to during his 8-year career with the Rangers.

Park was inducted into the Hockey Hall of Fame in 1988.

Tom Laidlaw

NYR Debut: October 9, 1980 (at Boston Bruins, lost 7–2)

Regular Season Games with NYR: 510

Playoff Games with NYR: 48

Tom Laidlaw is the answer to a Ranger trivia question. Who was the last Ranger to wear #2 before Brian Leetch?

Laidlaw was the Rangers' sixth-round pick out of Northern Michigan in the 1978 NHL Amateur Draft. Laidlaw played all 80 games in his rookie year of 1980–81. He scored 6 goals and added 23 assists. In the 1981 Stanley Cup Playoffs, Laidlaw scored his first postseason goal. The Rangers hosted the Los Angeles Kings in Game Four of the best-of-five preliminary round. They were leading the series two games to one and had a chance to eliminate Los Angeles as they headed to the third period tied at 3–3. Ron Duguay won a faceoff and passed the puck to Laidlaw who blasted it past Kings goalie Mario Lessard.

The Ontario-born Laidlaw became known as a durable and physical defenseman who wasn't afraid to drop the gloves. In his first four years in New York he missed only two games. After seven years with the Rangers, Laidlaw was traded to the Kings in March of 1987.

Laidlaw retired after the 1989–90 season and became a player agent.

Art Coulter

NYR Debut: January 16, 1936 (vs. Toronto Maple Leafs, won 1–0)

Regular Season Games with NYR: 287

Playoff Games with NYR: 37

Also wore: #17

Hall of Fame defenseman Art Coulter came to the Rangers via a trade with the Chicago Black Hawks in January of 1936.

Coulter turned out to be a very good acquisition. The 5-foot-11, 185-pound physical specimen was a good puck handler and was tough as nails. When

Photo from the public domain.

One of four Rangers captains to win the Stanley Cup.

original team Captain Bill Cook retired, Coulter began wearing the "C" on his Ranger sweater beginning with the 1937–38 season.

The Hall of Famer is one of four Rangers to have worn the "C" when the team won a Stanley Cup. In the 1940 Stanley Cup Playoffs, Coulter was a physical presence as he piled up 21 penalty minutes and got into a few scrums with the Boston Bruins and Toronto Maple Leafs in the two playoff series. In Game One of the Final against Toronto at Madison Square Garden, Coulter scored the first goal of the game and the Rangers went on to a 2–1 win in overtime. Coulter and the Rangers won the Stanley Cup when they beat Toronto 3–2 in overtime of Game Six on a goal by Bryan Hextall.

Coulter played two more seasons with the Rangers. In 1942, he joined the United States Coast Guard where he played for its team during World War II. Coulter was elected to the Hockey Hall of Fame in 1974.

Frank Eddolls

NYR Debut: October 16, 1947 (at Montreal Canadiens, won 2–1)
Regular Season Games with NYR: 260
Playoff Games with NYR: 13

Defenseman Frank Eddolls was part of one of the great trades in Rangers' franchise history. On August 19, 1947, the Rangers acquired center Buddy O'Connor and Eddolls from the Montreal Canadiens in exchange for defenseman Hal Laycoe and left wingers Joe Bell and George Robertson. The two additions helped the Rangers make the Stanley Cup Playoffs for the first time in six seasons. O'Connor won the Lady Byng and Hart Trophies and was named the fifth captain in team history in 1949.

Eddolls became the sixth captain in 1950 and was part of the team that lost the Finals to the Detroit Red Wings in seven games. The twenty-eight-year-old native of Quebec did not get on the score sheet against Detroit but he was a steady defenseman for five years with the Rangers. After his playing career ended in 1952, Eddolls became the head coach of the Chicago Black Hawks for one season.

Wayne Hillman

NYR Debut: February 6, 1965 (at Boston Bruins, lost 3–2)
Regular Season Games with NYR: 219
Playoff Games with NYR: 6

Wayne Hillman's claim to fame with the Rangers is that he was brought to New York as part of a controversial trade that sent team captain and long-time Ranger Camille "The Eel" Henry to Chicago.

At 6-foot-1, Hillman was a physical defenseman. He had his best season in New York in the 1965–66 season when he scored 3 goals and added 17 assists for a career high 20 points in 68 games.

Earl Seibert

NYR Debut: November 12, 1931 (at Montreal Canadiens, won 4–1)
Regular Season Games with NYR: 219
Playoff Games with NYR: 6
Also wore: #21

Compared to most of his fellow defensemen in the National Hockey League, Earl Seibert was a giant.

Seibert was a 6-foot-2, 198-pound physical defenseman who helped the Rangers win the 1933 Stanley Cup championship. The twenty-year-old was acquired from Springfield of the Canadian-American Hockey League in 1931. During his time in Springfield, Seibert suffered a concussion. He began to wear a helmet on a regular basis, making him the first to do so.

Seibert played his first four years with the Rangers and paired with Hall of Famer Ching Johnson to form one of the most rugged duos of "back liners" in the league.

As tough as he was on the ice, Rangers management found Seibert tough to deal with off the ice. Oliver Seibert, Earl's father and a Hockey Hall of Famer, engaged in some acrimonious negotiations with the front office over a new contract. The Rangers tired of this process and traded Seibert to Chicago in 1936. Seibert was inducted into the Hockey Hall of Fame in 1963, two years after his father.

Ivan Irwin

NYR Debut: November 5, 1953 (at Montreal Canadiens, lost 4–3)
Regular Season Games with NYR: 151
Playoff Games with NYR: 5

At 6-foot-2, Ivan Irwin was known as "Ivan the Terrible" for his pugilistic skills and his rugged play as an NHL defenseman. Irwin began his career in Montreal and played one season with the Canadiens before the twenty-six-year-old was dealt to the Rangers in 1953.

Irwin was not a very good skater and lacked offensive skills but his role was as an enforcer. The Chicago-born defenseman got regular ice time in his first two seasons with the Rangers. He also got regular time in the penalty box. During his four-year tenure with the Rangers, Irwin accumulated 214 minutes of penalty time.

Irwin made his name by standing up to the Canadiens, particularly Hall of Famer and all-time great Maurice "The Rocket" Richard. In October of 1954, Irwin fought Richard in the third period during a 7–1 loss in Montreal. The year before, Irwin was on the ice when a nasty stick swinging incident occurred during a scrum against Montreal. "Ivan the Terrible" had to be held back after Montreal Hall of Famer and future Ranger Bernie "Boom Boom" Geoffrion hit Ranger rookie Ron Murphy in the face.

Doug Harvey

NYR Debut: October 11, 1961 (at Boston Bruins, won 6–2)
Regular Season Games with NYR: 151
Playoff Games with NYR: 6

Hall of Famer Doug Harvey put together an impressive 19-year National Hockey League career. Three of those years were spent in a Ranger sweater.

Harvey was already a six-time Stanley Cup winner and six-time Norris Trophy winner when he joined the Rangers in 1961.

By the time the 1960–61 season ended, the Rangers had missed the playoffs three years running. Head coach Alf Pike was fired and the Rangers made an inquiry into Harvey's availability with an additional offer to make the defenseman the head coach. On June 13, 1961, the Rangers acquired the thirty-six-year-old Harvey from the Canadiens for defenseman "Leapin' Lou" Fontinato.

In his first season in New York, Harvey won his seventh Norris Trophy and finished second in the voting for the Hart Trophy as the Rangers made the playoffs for the first time in four seasons. Harvey did not want to be a coach anymore so he yielded the position to general manager Muzz Patrick who went behind the bench. Harvey was left unprotected in the June 1963 NHL Intra-League Draft and played one more season with the Rangers. Three years later, he joined the Detroit Red Wings as a forty-two-year-old and finished his career with the St. Louis Blues. Harvey was inducted into Hockey's Hall of Fame in 1973.

Jack "Red" Bownass

> **NYR Debut:** December 10, 1958 (vs. Detroit Red Wings, lost 2–1)
> **Regular Season Games with NYR:** 76
> **Playoff Games with NYR:** 0
> **Also wore:** #15 for the 1961–62 season

Jack Bownass played 80 games in the National Hockey League, 76 of those with the Rangers. Bownass toiled in the minor leagues for ten years before joining the Montreal Canadiens for his other four NHL games.

The Rangers selected him from the Montreal Royals of the Quebec Senior Hockey League in the 1958 NHL Inter-League Draft. Bownass scored 3 goals and 7 assists for 10 points during his three years with the Rangers.

Hal Laycoe

> **NYR Debut:** January 16, 1946 (at Boston Bruins, lost 3–2)
> **Regular Season Games with NYR:** 75
> **Playoff Games with NYR:** 0
> **Also wore:** #17 in his first season

Saskatchewan-born Hal Laycoe played his first two seasons in New York, but his most notable moment with the Rangers came in a game against the Montreal Canadiens in 1947. Laycoe was involved in a wild brawl at Madison Square Garden that produced a benches-clearing brawl and four different major fights.

After the 1946–47 season, Laycoe was traded to Montreal (see Frank Eddolls earlier in the chapter).

Alex Gray

NYR Debut: November 17, 1927 (vs. Ottawa Senators, won 3–2)

Regular Season Games with NYR: 43

Playoff Games with NYR: 9

Right winger Alex Gray was one of two Rangers in franchise history to have worn the #2 but was not a defenseman.

Gray, who was born in Scotland, joined the Rangers in their second season of existence in 1927, and was part of the team that won the franchise's first Stanley Cup championship.

The 5-foot-7, 170-pound defenseman scored 7 goals in the regular season and added a postseason goal to help the Rangers defeat the Pittsburgh Pirates in the quarterfinals of the American Division of the National Hockey League.

After beating Boston in the semis, the Rangers won the best-of-five Final against Toronto to capture their first ever Stanley Cup championship. After one season, Gray was traded to the Maple Leafs along with goaltender Lorne Chabot for left wing Melville "Butch" Keeling and goalie John Ross Roach.

Reg Mackey

NYR Debut: November 16, 1926 (vs. Montreal Maroons, won 1–0)

Regular Season Games with NYR: 34

Playoff Games with NYR: 1

Reg Mackey was an original New York Ranger. Mackey, who was known as an excellent skater with the ability to score goals, has the dubious distinction of having played 34 games with the expansion Rangers in 1926–27 while not scoring a point. Mackey was acquired in October of 1926 via a trade with the Vancouver Maroons of the Western Hockey League.

Joe Jerwa

NYR Debut: December 14, 1930 (vs. Detroit Falcons, won 3–0)

Regular Season Games with NYR: 33

Playoff Games with NYR: 4

Joe Jerwa has the distinction of being the first Polish-born player in the NHL. In 1913, Jerwa moved to North America and began his pro career in the Alberta Senior League in 1926.

The Rangers acquired Jerwa from the Vancouver Lions of the Pacific Coast Hockey League in 1930. He split his first season with the Rangers and the Springfield Indians of the Canadian American Hockey League. In 33 games, Jerwa scored four goals and added seven assists while compiling 72 minutes in penalties. Jerwa's brother Frank also played in the NHL. In 1931, the Rangers traded Jerwa to Boston where he would play with his younger brother.

Vern Ayres

> **NYR Debut:** November 10, 1935 (at Detroit Red Wings, 1–1 tie)
> **Regular Season Games with NYR:** 28
> **Playoff Games with NYR:** 0

Vern Ayres was a giant of a man who used his 6-foot-2, 220-pound size to forge a 6-year NHL career. He was a slow and plodding skater who could be beaten by quicker opponents but he was one of the most feared body checkers in the league. Ayres once broke Hall of Famer and Toronto Maple Leafs' left winger Harvey "Busher" Jackson's ribs with a hard check.

Ayres was claimed by the Rangers from the St. Louis Eagles in the 1935 Dispersal Draft. He split time with the Rangers and the Springfield Ramblers during his one season in New York.

John Mahaffy

> **NYR Debut:** December 19, 1943 (vs Detroit Red Wings, won 6–2)
> **Regular Season Games with NYR:** 28
> **Playoff Games with NYR:** 0

Diminutive center John Mahaffy could be compared today to Mats Zuccarello. Mahaffy was a 5-foot-7 offensive dynamo who scored 29 points in 28 career games as a Ranger. He was also the only other non-defenseman in franchise history to have worn the #2. The Montreal native was loaned to the Rangers for the 1943–44 season but it was Mahaffy's misfortune that he was sent to the Rangers from the Canadiens. Montreal went on to win the Stanley Cup that season while the Rangers finished in last place with a franchise worst record of 6–39–5 for 17 points.

Jocelyn Guevremont

NYR Debut: October 10, 1979 (at Toronto Maple Leafs, won 6–3)

Regular Season Games with NYR: 20

Playoff Games with NYR: 0

By the time defenseman Jocelyn Guevremont joined the Rangers in 1979, he was on the final leg of his 10-year career.

The Montreal native spent four seasons in Vancouver and five with the Buffalo Sabres, who traded him to the Rangers (for future considerations). Guevremont was known for owning one of the hardest shots from the point in the National Hockey League.

The twenty-eight-year-old saw limited playing time in New York, which did not sit well with the veteran defenseman. Guevremont was sent to the Rangers affiliate in New Haven where he played 36 games, but he was not on the playoff roster due to an injury.

The following players played less than 20 games with NYR:

Jim Morrison - defenseman

NYR Debut: October 5, 1960 (vs. Boston Bruins, won 2–1)

Regular Season Games with NYR: 19

Playoff Games with NYR: 0

Ian "Crash" Cushenan - defenseman

NYR Debut: October 7, 1959 (at Chicago Black Hawks, lost 5–2)

Regular Season Games with NYR: 17

Playoff Games with NYR: 0

Tommy "Moose" Dewar - defenseman

NYR Debut: October 30, 1943 (at Toronto Maple Leafs, lost 5–2)

Regular Season Games with NYR: 9

Playoff Games with NYR: 0

Harry "Huddy" Bell - defenseman

NYR Debut: March 23, 1947 (vs. Chicago Black Hawks, lost 4–3)

Regular Season Games with NYR: 1

Playoff Games with NYR: 0

#3: 3 ALSO HAS A RETIREE

Harry Howell

NYR Debut: October 18, 1952 (at Toronto Maple Leafs, lost 4–3)
Regular Season Games with NYR: 1160
Playoff Games with NYR: 34

Harry Howell wore #3 on a Rangers sweater for 17 seasons and is arguably one of the greatest players in franchise history.

The Rangers took notice of Howell's talent at an early age. Teams could draft players at a young age back then and, thanks to a "reserve list" (different from a reserve clause because players were not necessarily under contract), they would have total control of a player who would not have any options. When he became sixteen years old, Howell expressed a desire to play junior hockey. Rangers' general manager Frank Boucher called Howell and grant-

First Ranger to play in 1000 games.

Photo from the public domain, via Wikimedia Commons.

ed his request with one stipulation: "You have to play in Guelph, because you've been on our Reserve List since you were fourteen."

Howell began the 1952–53 season with the Guelph Biltmores of the Ontario Hockey Association, but it wasn't long before the nineteen-year-old defenseman was called up to the Rangers. In his first game, at Maple Leaf Gardens in Toronto, Howell scored his first NHL goal on his first shot. The young defenseman was told that he would only play one game and would go back to Guelph, but he was told to join the team in New York and never went back.

It took four years before Howell would play in a playoff game. During his 17 years in New York, the Rangers missed the playoffs ten times and never played in a Stanley Cup Final. In the 1966–67 season, Howell had a career high 40 points (12 goals, 28 assists) and won the Norris Trophy as the league's best defenseman. In 1955, the twenty-two-year-old Howell was named the youngest team captain in history. He would wear the "C" for two seasons and was one of the most popular Rangers. From 1965–67 he was named the winner of the Ranger fan club's "Frank Boucher Award."

In January of 1967, Howell became the first Ranger to play in 1000 games. On January 25, 1967, the Rangers commemorated the event by holding "Harry Howell Night" at Madison Square Garden. The day before, New York City Mayor John Lindsay honored Howell with a medal of the City of New York. During the ceremony, in front of family and friends, Howell received numerous gifts including a new car. It was the first time that the Rangers organization had honored a player in such fashion.

Howell played two more seasons with the Rangers, though the latter was plagued by a back injury. The thirty-six-year-old needed to have spinal fusion surgery on his back if he wanted to continue playing. After the operation, the Rangers felt Howell should not play anymore. General manager Emile Francis offered the veteran defenseman a front office job, but Howell was not ready to give up his playing career. The Rangers granted Howell's request to be traded to a West Coast team, and sold him to the Oakland Seals in June of 1969.

Howell, who holds the franchise record with 1,160 games played, was inducted into the Hockey Hall of Fame in 1979. In February 2009, the Rangers retired Howell's #3 in a dual ceremony with Andy Bathgate's #9.

James "Jeep" Patrick

NYR Debut: March 7, 1984 (at Minnesota North Stars, lost 6–3)
Regular Season Games with NYR: 671
Playoff Games with NYR: 63

His surname was synonymous with hockey royalty, but even though he was not related to Frank or Lester Patrick, James Patrick put his own stamp on the Rangers.

James Patrick was a steady two-way defenseman who played 11 years with the Rangers. Patrick was the Rangers' first pick, ninth overall, in the 1981 NHL Entry Draft. Before joining the Rangers, the twenty-year-old defenseman played on the Canadian Olympic Team that finished fourth in the 1984 Winter Games at Sarajevo.

In his second NHL game in his hometown of Winnipeg, Patrick had 3 assists as the Rangers beat the Jets 6–5 in overtime. Patrick scored 8 goals and added 28 assists in his first full season, and his production steadily increased over the next three years. His first taste of the Stanley Cup playoffs ended with a bitter defeat. Patrick and the Rangers had a chance to end the New York Islanders' four-year run as Stanley Cup Champions, but were beaten in a fifth and deciding game in overtime.

The Rangers made the playoffs in eight of Patrick's ten seasons, but the furthest they went was to the Prince of Wales Conference Finals in 1986 where they lost to the Montreal Canadiens in five games. Were it not for Patrick, the Rangers may not have even made the playoffs that season. In the penultimate regular season game against the Washington Capitals, Patrick scored with 16 seconds left to tie the game and the point put the Rangers into the playoffs.

Patrick played for eight different coaches in New York before Mike Keenan was hired in 1993. The new head man was not a big fan of Patrick's game, and it showed as the veteran defenseman was benched for 7 of the team's first 13 games. On November 2, he was traded along with center Darren Turcotte to the Hartford Whalers for right winger Steve Larmer, left winger Nick Kypreos, and defenseman Barry Richter.

Ott Heller

NYR Debut: January 28, 1932 (vs. Boston Bruins, lost 4–1)
Regular Season Games with NYR: 647
Playoff Games with NYR: 61
Also wore: #14

The #3 hangs in the rafters at Madison Square Garden for Hall of Famer Harry Howell, but it could just as well have been hoisted there for Ott Heller. One of the most underrated players in Rangers history, Heller combined physicality with skating ability to produce a steady defenseman who played his entire 15-year NHL career with the Blueshirts. Heller signed as a free agent in 1929, and spent his first two years with the Rangers affiliate in Springfield.

Heller gave a demonstration of his skill in the 1932 playoffs. In Game Three of the semifinals against Montreal, Heller went the length of the ice to score the only goal of the game.

Heller is one of a handful of Rangers who have played on more than one Stanley Cup-winning team. In the 1933 Stanley Cup Final, Heller scored two goals to help the Rangers win their second Cup championship with a four-game sweep of the Toronto Maple Leafs. In Game Two of the 1940 Cup Final, Heller had the lone assist on the game-winning goal that was the second goal of Bryan Hextall's hat trick.

Heller became the third captain in franchise history when he wore the "C" from 1943–46. Following his final season in 1946, Heller held the franchise record for games played with 646.

Michal Rozsival

NYR Debut: October 5, 2005 (at Philadelphia Flyers, won 5–3)

Regular Season Games with NYR: 432

Playoff Games with NYR: 31

Also #33

Photo by Keith Allison from Owings Mills, USA, via Wikimedia Commons.

Scored double overtime game-winner in 2007 ECSF.

A lot was expected of Michal Rozsival when he signed as a free agent in 2005. The twenty-seven-year-old made his reputation as a two-way defenseman during his first four seasons in the National Hockey League with the Pittsburgh Penguins. Rozsival was signed, in part, because he was a teammate of Rangers' left winger Jaromir Jagr, (a fellow Czechoslovakian) when both played with the Penguins.

Throughout his Rangers career, Rozsival had a "love/hate" relationship with the fans that were noted for their cynicism.

Rozsival's signature moment as a Ranger came in the 2007 Stanley Cup Playoffs. The Rangers advanced to the Eastern Conference Semifinals and were trailing the Buffalo Sabres two games to none. Game Three went to a second overtime. Rozsival, who had been playing with a sore knee, scored at 16:43 of the second overtime to give the Rangers a 2–1 win. The Rangers were back in the series but eventually lost in six games.

After the Rangers fired head coach Tom Renney in February of 2009, Rozsival's game took a steady decline under hard-driving coach John

Tortorella. In January of 2011, Rozsival was traded to the Phoenix Coyotes in exchange for left winger Wojtek Wolski.

Ivan "Ching" Johnson

NYR Debut: November 16, 1926 (vs. Montreal Maroons, 1–0; Franchise's first game)
Regular Season Games with NYR: 405
Playoff Games with NYR: 55

"Ching" Johnson was a Hall of Fame player who was an original Ranger. Johnson was 5-foot-11, 210 pounds, and was the Rangers' first "enforcer." He played 10 of his 11 seasons in the NHL with the Rangers. In his final season of 1937–38, Johnson played his home games at Madison Square Garden but as a member of the New York Americans.

Johnson's hard hits and physical style made him a fan favorite and earned him the nickname of "Ivan the Terrible." The nickname "Ching" stuck as a result of Johnson's cooking prowess. Johnson and his friends would go on camping trips in the summer in Alberta, Canada, and would bring along a cook. Usually, a man of Chinese descent would be hired. With the idea of saving money, Johnson volunteered to handle the cooking chores.

In 1928, Johnson was the stalwart of the Rangers' defense corps that helped win the Stanley Cup. In Game Two of the semifinals vs. the Boston Bruins, Johnson was cut in the mouth with a stick. He left the ice, got patched up, and returned within a relatively short time to help the Rangers advance to the Final against the Montreal Maroons. The native of Winnipeg, Manitoba, was all over the ice against Montreal. The hits just kept on coming. Johnson and his partner Taffy Abel were cited for their hard hits. The game story in the *Montreal Gazette* claimed the Rangers went over the line with "dirty play." The quote read, ". . . stepped into the Maroons with abandon and frequently to the annoyance of both the Maroon players and supporters, many of whom believe that the Ranger guard with their body checks, are skating into opposition, in other words charging rather than body checking." The Rangers captured the Cup in five games, and Johnson's play was cited as one of the reasons.

In 1932, Johnson led the Rangers to a first-place finish in the "American Division" and finished second in the voting for the Hart Trophy, emblematic of the Most Valuable Player in the National Hockey League. The following season, Johnson was a first-team All-Star and part of a Stanley Cup-winning team for a second time. "Ivan the Terrible" retired in 1937, but the thirty-nine-year-old played one more season with the New York Americans. Johnson was inducted into the Hockey Hall of Fame in 1958.

Tom Poti

NYR Debut: March 21, 2002 (at Ottawa Senators, won 5–2)
Regular Season Games with NYR: 231
Playoff Games with NYR: 4
Also wore: #16

In March of 2002, Brian Leetch was thirty-four years old and in the twilight of his career. The Rangers needed a defenseman so they traded promising young right winger Mike York and a draft pick to the Edmonton Oilers for twenty-four-year-old defenseman Tom Poti and left winger Rem Murray.

York scored 58 goals and was popular with the fans during his three years with the Rangers, so Poti was under pressure from the start. Many die-hards were not in favor of the trade. As his time with the Rangers wore on, the fans became so frustrated with the 6-foot-3, 190-pound defenseman that they began to boo him every time he touched the puck.

In 2006, the Rangers made the playoffs for the first time in seven seasons. The Worcester, Massachusetts native did not record a point as the Rangers were swept in four games by the New Jersey Devils, which only added fuel to the ire of the fans. It was also the end of his disappointing tenure in New York. Poti's contract was up and the Rangers did not renew his deal, so he signed a free agent contract with the rival New York Islanders in 2006.

Dave Farrish

NYR Debut: October 6, 1976 (vs. Minnesota North Stars, won 6–5)
Regular Season Games with NYR: 217
Playoff Games with NYR: 10

Dave Farrish was a highly regarded young prospect because of what he accomplished in three seasons with the Sudbury Wolves of the Ontario Junior Hockey League. Beginning with the 1973–74 season as a seventeen-year-old, Farrish scored 11 goals and had 20 assists in 58 games. During the next two seasons with Sudbury, Farrish scored 46 goals and 93 assists.

The Rangers made the nineteen-year-old their second-round pick and the 24th overall in the 1976 NHL Amateur Draft. If anything, Farrish was durable as he only missed 23 games during his three seasons with the Rangers.

Kim Johnsson

NYR Debut: October 1, 1999 (at Edmonton Oilers, 1–1 OT tie)

Regular Season Games with NYR: 151

Playoff Games with NYR: 0

Kim Johnsson is probably best known for being one of the pieces that went back to Philadelphia in 2001 for Hall of Famer Eric Lindros.

The Rangers selected the defenseman in the 1994 NHL Entry Draft. In 1999, he was named the winner of the Lars-Erik Sjoberg Award which is emblematic of the top rookie in the Rangers' training camp. In the second of his two seasons, Johnsson scored five goals with four coming on the power play.

In August of 2001, the Rangers acquired Lindros from the Flyers in exchange for Johnsson, Jan Hlavac, Pavel Brendl, and a draft pick. Johnsson also played for the Minnesota Wild and Chicago Blackhawks during a 10-year NHL career.

Ron Harris

NYR Debut: November 29, 1972 (at Los Angeles Kings, 2–2 tie)

Regular Season Games with NYR: 146

Playoff Games with NYR: 24

Ron Harris played parts of four seasons with the Rangers but in that short time he had provided some memorable moments. The Rangers acquired the veteran defenseman from the Atlanta Flames in a deal for young center Curt Bennett. Harris was a tough, hard-nosed defenseman who would lay out players with fierce, but legal, body checks.

Harris's best moments with the Rangers came in the 1974 Stanley Cup Playoffs. Even though the Rangers failed to win the Cup, Harris had two game-winning goals, including one in overtime. In Game Five of the quarterfinals against the Montreal Canadiens, Harris scored the game-winning goal at 4:07 of overtime to give the Rangers a 3–2 lead in the series which they eventually won in six games.

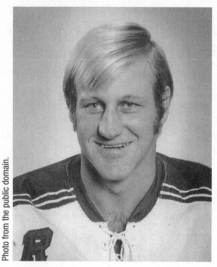

Photo from the public domain.

Harris had two game-winning goals in 1974 Stanley Cup Finals.

In the semifinals against the Philadelphia Flyers, Harris was credited with the game-winning goal to give the Rangers a series-tying win in Game Six. During that series, Harris engaged in a personal battle with Bob "Hound Dog" Kelly, one of the Flyers' many enforcers on the 1974 team. Flyers head coach Fred Shero (who was a former Ranger and would later become their head coach) used Kelly to distract Harris with his physical play. After Kelly leveled Ranger rookie Jerry Butler with a hard hit in Game Two, Harris got even in Game Three with a hip check that put Kelly out for the rest of the playoffs.

Harris's NHL and Rangers career ended when he suffered a career-ending knee injury against the New York Islanders in October of 1975.

Fred Shero

NYR Debut: October 16, 1947 (at Montreal Canadiens, won 2–1)
Regular Season Games with NYR: 145
Playoff Games with NYR: 13

His legacy was made as a head coach in two cities, but Fred Shero spent his playing career with the Rangers. Shero is famous for being the head coach of the Philadelphia Flyers, who won back-to-back Stanley Cup Championships in 1974 and 1975. He was also the Rangers' head coach in 1979, when they upset the favored New York Islanders in the Eastern Conference Finals to advance to the Stanley Cup Finals.

In December of 1949, Shero fought Hall of Famer Gordie Howe. Reportedly, the outcome was a draw. Shero was a part of the Ranger team that went to the 1950 Stanley Cup Final, but lost the seventh and deciding game in double overtime to the Detroit Red Wings. His NHL career ended after that game and after a couple of more seasons in the minors, Shero began a coaching career in 1958 with the St. Paul Saints of the International Hockey League.

"Freddy the Fog," as Shero was known, was behind the bench when the Philadelphia Flyers won their first Stanley Cup in 1974. After the 1977–78 season, Shero resigned with one year left on his contract.

The Rangers would pay a hefty price to sign Shero, who was a brilliant strategist and motivator. A $100,000 indemnity fee and a #1 draft pick was sent to the Flyers for the right to hire Shero for the 1978–79 season.

The upset of the Islanders was the high point of Shero's Rangers coaching career. After losing to Montreal in the Finals, Shero had the Rangers back in the playoffs in 1980, but they were eliminated in the quarterfinals by Shero's old team, the Flyers, in five games.

Lost as a Ranger player and as a head coach in Stanley Cup Finals.

Photo from the public domain, via Wikimedia Commons.

The low point was the beginning of the 1980–81 season. The Rangers got off to a 4–13–3 start. Shero took the fall, and was fired in November.

Shero was elected to the Hockey Hall of Fame as a "builder" in 2013.

Tim Horton

NYR Debut: March 4, 1970 (vs. Detroit Red Wings, lost 2–0)
Regular Season Games with NYR: 93
Playoff Games with NYR: 19

Everyone has heard of the donut shops that bear his name throughout Canada, but Tim Horton also compiled a 27-year, Hall of Fame playing career in the National Hockey League that included two seasons with the Rangers.

Horton spent twenty years with the Toronto Maple Leafs before he was traded to the Rangers in March of 1970. Even at forty years old, the veteran defenseman had an impact on the Rangers. In his first game at Madison Square Garden, Horton logged nearly 40 minutes of ice time. In Game Two of the East Division Semifinals against the Boston Bruins, Horton had a goal and an assist but the Rangers lost the game and the series in six games.

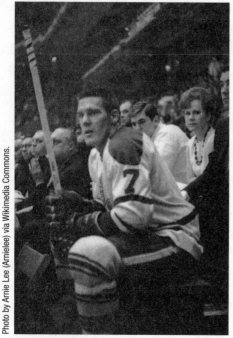

Photo by Arnie Lee (Arnielee) via Wikimedia Commons.

Played 20 years with Maple Leafs prior to two with the Rangers.

In the 1971 Stanley Cup Semi-finals against the Chicago Black Hawks, Horton had the secondary assist on Pete Stemkowski's famous triple-overtime goal to win Game Six.

The Ontario native was a very strong man. Former Ranger Vic Hadfield told a story in the book (*In Loving Memory: A Tribute to Tim Horton*) of how Horton (who was nicknamed "Superman") used his brute strength to pull off a prank. The Rangers returned late from a road game and stayed in a hotel right across from Madison Square Garden. Hadfield said, "It was an old hotel, never very busy. We were getting on the elevator to go up to our rooms late one night, and there was a Coke machine on one of the floors. So Timmy, being as strong as he was, picked up this big six-foot Coke machine, towed it on to the elevator, and pushed the down button. Sure enough the Coke machine made it down to the main level. It would've taken fifteen of those guys to move it back, whereas Timmy could do it all by himself."

Horton had planned to retire after the 1970–71 season. With that in mind, the Rangers left Horton unprotected and he was selected by the Pittsburgh Penguins in the Intra-League Draft. Horton played one year with the Penguins and then two more with the Buffalo Sabres. Horton, who became a multi-million dollar entrepreneur, was tragically killed in a one-car accident in February of 1974. He was inducted, posthumously, into the Hockey Hall of Fame in 1977.

Scot Kleinendorst

NYR Debut: December 20, 1982 (vs. Pittsburgh Penguins, won 6–3)
Regular Season Games with NYR: 53
Playoff Games with NYR: 6

The Rangers used a fifth-round pick in the 1980 NHL Amateur Draft to select American-born defenseman Scot Kleinendorst. The native of Grand Rapids, Minnesota, joined the Rangers for the remainder of the 1982–83 season. The 6-foot-3, 215-pound defenseman suffered through an injury-plagued second season in New York. He appeared in 23 games during the regular season and missed the 1984 Stanley Cup Playoff loss to the Islanders. After the season, Kleinendorst was traded to the Hartford Whalers in exchange for right winger Blaine Stoughton.

Gary Doak

NYR Debut: November 24, 1971 (vs. St. Louis Blues, won 8–3)
Regular Season Games with NYR: 49
Playoff Games with NYR: 12

Defenseman Gary Doak was a fearless shot blocker and suffered many injuries as a result of that style of play.

The Rangers acquired Doak from the Vancouver Canucks as part of a five-player trade in November of 1971. The Goderich, Ontario-born defenseman came to the Rangers at the right time as the team qualified for the Stanley Cup Finals, where they lost in six games to the Boston Bruins. Following the season, the Rangers traded Doak to the Detroit Red Wings.

The following players played less than 20 games with NYR:

Stan Neckar - defenseman

NYR Debut: December 2, 1998 (at New York Islanders, won 3–2)
Regular Season Games with NYR: 18
Playoff Games with NYR: 0

Leo Reise Sr. - defenseman

NYR Debut: February 6, 1930 (vs. Detroit Cougars, 1–1 OT tie)
Regular Season Games with NYR: 14
Playoff Games with NYR: 4
Also wore: #4

Fern Perrault - left wing

NYR Debut: February 18, 1948 (vs. Detroit Red Wings, lost 3–1)

Regular Season Games with NYR: 3

Playoff Games with NYR: 0

Note: Perrault is the only non-defenseman in Rangers history to wear #3.

#4: 4 OF A KIND

Ron Greschner

NYR Debut: November 3, 1974 (vs. Buffalo Sabres, lost 4–3)

Regular Season Games with NYR: 982

Playoff Games with NYR: 84

For a player who was chosen 32nd overall in the 1974 NHL Amateur Draft, Ron Greschner did pretty well for himself.

Greschner played his entire 16-year career in New York and had four seasons where he scored 20 or more goals. The nineteen-year-old was coming off a 103-point season for the New Westminster Bruins of the Western Canadian Junior Hockey League. He began the 1974–75 season with the Rangers' farm team in Providence and played seven games before being called up by GM Emile Francis as the Rangers' defense corps was besieged by injury.

The Saskatchewan native was told he would be heading back to New Westminster once the injured players got healthy, but he never played another game in the minors.

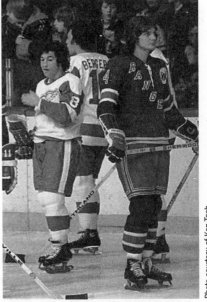

"Young" Greschner played his entire 16-year career as a Ranger.

Greschner was a two-way defenseman who was blessed with size (6-foot-2, 205 pounds) and skating ability. He was also a terrific puck handler.

Greschner scored his first NHL goal on December 8, 1974, in a 3–3 tie against the Montreal Canadiens. Trailing 1–0 in the first period, Greschner's shot caromed off Canadiens' defenseman and Hall of Famer Jacques Lemaire's skate to beat Hall of Fame goaltender Ken Dryden. In his rookie season, Greschner scored 8 goals and 37 points while finishing fifth in the voting for the Calder Trophy.

Greschner was a key component of the 1979 team that lost to the Montreal Canadiens in the Stanley Cup Final. In 18 games, Greschner had 7 goals and 5 assists. In Game Two of the quarterfinals against Philadelphia, Greschner scored 2 goals—including the game winner—that evened the Series at a game apiece. The Rangers went on to eliminate the Flyers in five games.

In the semifinals against the New York Islanders, Greschner scored a goal in the Rangers' Game Five win that gave them a three games to two lead in the series. In the series-clinching Game Six, Greschner scored the game winner on the power play as the Rangers eliminated the Islanders with a 2–1 win. Greschner took a pass from left wing Don Maloney and blasted a shot from just inside the blue line to beat Islanders goaltender Glenn "Chico" Resch on the glove side.

The 1980–81 season marked a turning point in Greschner's durability as a player. In his first seven seasons, he played less than 70 games only once. In his final nine seasons, he played more than 70 games just once as injuries began to curtail his availability. Despite all that, Greschner wore the captain's "C" from October of 1986 to December of 1987.

Greschner took to New York like a duck to water. He embraced the night life and was a partner with Ranger teammates Ron Duguay and Phil Esposito in a restaurant called "Sticks." Greschner was frequently seen in the company of glamorous models. Eventually he married one. In 1983, Greschner wed supermodel Carol Alt. The marriage lasted 18 years until they were divorced in 2001.

Greschner was thirty-five years old in his final season of 1989–90. He played 55 games and scored his final goal on January 8, 1990, in a 7–5 loss to the Pittsburgh Penguins at Madison Square Garden.

Longtime and beloved Rangers color analyst Bill Chadwick respectfully referred to the defenseman as "young Greschner" in tribute to his longevity with the Blueshirts.

Arnie Brown

NYR Debut: October 12, 1964 (at Boston Bruins, won 6–2)
Regular Season Games with NYR: 460
Playoff Games with NYR: 18

Defenseman Arnie Brown came to the Rangers in one of the biggest trades in team history.

In February of 1964, the Rangers sent popular right wing and Hall of Famer Andy Bathgate along with center Don McKenney to the Toronto Maple Leafs for left wing Dick Duff, right wings Bob Nevin and Bill Collins, defenseman Rod Seiling and Brown.

Brown made the team out of training camp in 1964 and played 58 games in his first season of 1964–65. The twenty-three-year-old was mostly a "stay-at-home" defenseman, but he began to show some offensive skill beginning with the 1967–68 season when he had 25 assists.

In the 1969–70 season, Brown had his best season in a Rangers sweater as he scored 15 goals and added 21 assists. He also played a key role as the Rangers qualified for the playoffs on the final day of the regular season in one of the most bizarre conclusions in NHL history.

The Rangers, who trailed Montreal by two points in the standings, hosted the Detroit Red Wings at Madison Square Garden in an afternoon matinee while the Canadiens played a night game in Chicago against the Black Hawks. If the Rangers won and the Canadiens lost, the teams would be tied in points but Montreal had the tiebreaker advantage with five more goals scored. The Rangers not only had to win, they needed to put the puck in the net as much as possible.

And they did. The Rangers fired 65 shots at Red Wings goalie Roger Crozier and scored a 9–5 win to put the pressure on Montreal. After the Rangers built a 9–3 lead, head coach Emile Francis pulled goaltender Ed Giacomin to try and score a few more goals. Left wing Dave Balon had a hat trick and Brown was the other offensive star with four assists, including three on the first three Ranger goals.

Montreal merely needed to score five goals and they would make the playoffs regardless of if they won or lost. Trailing 5–2 in the third period, the Canadiens pulled goaltender Rogie Vachon and gave up five empty-net goals to blow the game open and put the Rangers in the playoffs.

In the Eastern Conference Semifinal series against the Boston Bruins, Brown had four assists in the first four games. Unfortunately, he suffered a knee injury during the series. Brown missed the remainder of the playoffs and was never the same as he underwent numerous surgeries on both of his knees after the initial injury.

In February of 1971, Brown was traded to the Red Wings where he played parts of two seasons. In October of 1972, Brown became the first former Ranger to play for the New York Islanders. Brown finished his pro career by spending the 1974–75 season in the World Hockey Association with the Michigan Stags/Baltimore Blades and the Vancouver Blazers.

Bill Gadsby

NYR Debut: November 24, 1954 (vs. Boston Bruins, 2–2 tie)
Regular Season Games with NYR: 457
Playoff Games with NYR: 16

When twenty-seven-year-old defenseman Bill Gadsby came to the Rangers, he had already put together an impressive NHL career, but it almost never got started.

As a twelve-year-old, Gadsby and his mother were returning to Canada from England on the ocean liner *Athenia* when it was sunk by a German U-Boat at the outset of World War II. Both were rescued after spending several hours in a lifeboat off the Irish coast. It was reported that 100 of the 1400 passengers and crew perished in the attack.

Gadsby was a physical and sometimes reckless player. In his first ever NHL game for the Chicago Black Hawks, he received 12 stitches—which was a portent of things to come. The defenseman became famous for the numerous injuries and the number of stitches he took during his 20-year career.

After parts of nine seasons with the Black Hawks, Gadsby was traded to the Rangers in November of 1954. Gadsby joined a Ranger team that already had future Hall of Famers "Gump" Worsley, Andy Bathgate, and Harry Howell.

Gadsby's most memorable moment in a Rangers sweater occurred on March 13, 1955, in a game against the Toronto Maple Leafs. The rugged defenseman landed a crushing but legal open-ice check on Maple Leafs and Hall of Fame defenseman Tim Horton (who would become a Ranger in 1970) late in the second period that resulted in a broken right leg and jaw. "It scared the hell out of me, seeing the blood coming out of Tim's mouth and ear," Gadsby said during a November 2012 interview with the *Montreal Gazette*. "I thought he was dead. Thank God it wasn't a dirty check."

In the 1958–59 season, Gadsby was a first team All-Star and was second in the voting for the Norris Trophy. During his time in New York, Gadsby played in five NHL All-Star games and was a three-time, first team All-Star.

In February of 1960, Gadsby was packaged as part of a deal to bring Detroit Red Wings defenseman Red Kelly to New York. The deal broke down when Kelly refused to report to the Rangers. Gadsby was eventually traded to Detroit in June of 1961 and finished his career with the Red Wings before retiring after the 1965–66 season.

Alex Shibicky

NYR Debut: January 28, 1936 (vs. Montreal Canadiens, won 3–2 OT)

Regular Season Games with NYR: 324

Playoff Games with NYR: 39

Hall of Famer Bobby Hull may have brought the slap shot into vogue, but Rangers' winger Alex Shibicky may have been the first to employ it as an offensive weapon.

The Winnipeg native signed with the Rangers as a free agent in 1934. The twenty-one-year-old joined the Rangers after playing 28 games with the Philadelphia Ramblers of the Canadian-American Hockey League. Shibicky's NHL debut was overshadowed by another player who was making his debut in a Rangers uniform: Hall of Famer Howie Morenz. Morenz, who was acquired two days previous from Montreal, scored a goal in his first game

Photo from the public domain.

Shibicky(r) was productive with the Colville Brothers.

as the Rangers beat his old team, the Canadiens, 3–2 in overtime before a reported 11,000 fans at Madison Square Garden.

Shibicky played his entire 8-year career with the Rangers and was one of their first snipers. He scored 110 goals including a career-high 24 in the 1938–39 season.

The Rangers winger was an accurate shooter who developed a slap shot by watching former Ranger Bill Cook. In the late 1930s, Shibicky combined with Mac and Neil Colville to form a productive trio with the Rangers.

Shibicky proved to be a clutch player, and that was never more evident than in the 1940 Stanley Cup Playoffs. In the semifinals against the Boston Bruins, he assisted on the only goal of Game Five and then scored the game winner in Game Six as the Rangers advanced to the Final against the Toronto Maple Leafs.

Early in Game Three of Cup Finals, Shibicky broke his leg. He missed Game Four but returned for Game Five and played a key role in helping the

Rangers take a 3–2 lead in the series. Shibicky set up the first goal of the game that the Rangers eventually won in overtime. In the clinching Game Six, Shibicky had 2 assists in the third period as the Rangers tied the game at two before winning the game and the Cup in overtime on Bryan Hextall's memorable overtime goal.

Shibicky missed three seasons from 1942–1945 while serving in the Canadian Army during World War II. He returned for one final season in 1945, splitting time with the Rangers and Providence Reds. The following season, Shibicky played with the New Haven Ramblers before retiring in 1947.

Michael Del Zotto

NYR Debut: October 2, 2009 (at Pittsburgh Penguins, lost 3–2)

Regular Season Games with NYR: 292

Playoff Games with NYR: 32

Photo by Robert Kowal via Wikimedia Commons.

Made his Ranger debut at age 19.

The Rangers thought highly enough of Michael Del Zotto that they chose him with their first-round pick and the 20th overall in the 2008 NHL Entry Draft. The youngster was projected to be an offensive defenseman when he debuted with the Rangers in 2009 as a nineteen-year-old.

In the second game of his career, Del Zotto became the second-youngest defenseman in franchise history to score a game-winning goal when he got the pivotal tally against the Ottawa Senators. In his first season of 2009–10, Del Zotto scored 9 goals with 28 assists and finished 8th in voting for the Calder Trophy (top rookie), while being named to the NHL All-Rookie team.

In the 2011–12 season, Del Zotto looked like he was on his way to a productive career. The twenty-one-year-old scored 10 goals with 31 assists. On March 30, Del Zotto scored two goals in the third period to lead the Rangers past the Montreal Canadiens, 4–1.

In the playoffs, Del Zotto scored the game-winning goal in Game Seven of the Eastern Conference Semifinals as the Rangers eliminated the Washington Capitals with a 2–1 win.

When head coach John Tortorella was fired in May of 2013 and replaced by Alain Vigneault, the change did not help Del Zotto. The new head coach was not a fan, and Del Zotto's Ranger career ended on January 22, 2014, when he was traded to the Nashville Predators for defenseman Kevin Klein.

Kevin Lowe

NYR Debut: December 15, 1992 (vs. Calgary Flames, lost 3–0)

Regular Season Games with NYR: 217

Playoff Games with NYR: 42

Beginning with the acquisition of Hall of Famer Mark Messier in 1991, Rangers' general manager Neil Smith began a trend where he imported available players from the five-time Stanley Cup Champion Edmonton Oilers to enhance the Blueshirts' chances of winning a Cup in New York.

Before the 1992–93 season, Oilers defenseman Kevin Lowe was holding out for a new contract. Smith worked out a deal with Edmonton general manager Glen Sather (who later became the Rangers GM) and acquired Lowe for winger Roman Oksiuta and a draft pick.

In the 1994 Stanley Cup Playoffs, Lowe scored a goal in the first round, four-game sweep of the New York Islanders but that was his only point of the postseason. His contribution was not measured on the score sheet but rather how he enabled Conn Smythe Trophy (top playoff performer) winner Brian Leetch to perform at a top level while Lowe was the stay-home defenseman who was steady in his own end.

Lowe was in uniform for some of the greatest games in franchise history. His experience and calm demeanor helped the Rangers overcome a 3–2 series deficit in the epic Eastern Conference Final series against the New Jersey Devils. There was Mark Messier's guarantee and hat trick in Game Six followed by the thrilling double overtime win in Game Seven.

On June 14, 1994, the Rangers beat the Vancouver Canucks 3–2 in Game Seven to clinch their first Stanley Cup championship in 54 years. Lowe celebrated for the sixth time in his career.

Lowe played two more seasons with the Rangers before becoming an unrestricted free agent in 1996. He re-signed with the Oilers and played two more seasons. Lowe became the Oilers head coach for the 1999–2000 season. After Sather left for the Rangers in 2000, Lowe became Edmonton's general manager.

Hy Buller

NYR Debut: October 14, 1951 (at Chicago Black Hawks, lost 3–2)
Regular Season Games with NYR: 179
Playoff Games with NYR: 0

In the 1951–52 season, Rangers rookie defenseman Hy Buller had a fabulous first season. The twenty-five-year-old set an NHL record for most points (35) by a rookie defenseman, made the NHL All-Star second team, and finished second in the voting for the Calder Trophy. He was also named the team's Most Valuable Player.

Buller began his NHL career as a seventeen-year-old with the Detroit Red Wings in 1943. He got a chance at such a young age because many players were serving their countries during World War II. After parts of two seasons in Detroit, Buller spent seven years in the American Hockey League with the Hershey Bears and Cleveland Barons.

The Rangers bought Buller and Wally Hergesheimer for cash and a host of minor leaguers. Buller was nicknamed "The Blueline Blaster" for having one of the league's hardest shots.

Buller played for the Rangers for three years and retired after the 1953–54 season. He was known for being the lone player of Jewish heritage in the league at the time. Buller was inducted into the International Jewish Sports Hall of Fame in 2017.

Albert Langlois

NYR Debut: October 11, 1961 (at Boston Bruins, won 6–2)
Regular Season Games with NYR: 173
Playoff Games with NYR: 6

At 6-feet and over 200 pounds, Al Langlois was a rugged defenseman who was acquired from the Montreal Canadiens, where he won three Stanley Cups, in exchange for defenseman John Hanna.

Langlois did not hesitate to throw his body around, but he could also play in the offensive end. He scored 13 goals in his Rangers career, but his signature moment came in his first season with the club.

In the final weeks of the 1961–62 season, the Rangers led the Detroit Red Wings by one point for the fourth and final playoff spot, when the clubs met for an important game at the Olympia. Hall of Famer Gordie Howe scored his 30th goal of the season as the Wings took a 4–2 lead early in the third period. The Rangers stormed back and scored three goals within a span of 2:18 that was capped off by Langlois's seventh goal of the season as they went on to a 5–4 win that gave them a three-point cushion. The Rangers went on to qualify for the playoffs.

In February of 1964, the Rangers traded Langlois to the Detroit Red Wings. He was sent to the Boston Bruins in 1965 where he became the last player to wear #4 before Hall of Famer Bobby Orr.

Wally Stanowski

> **NYR Debut:** October 14, 1948 (at Montreal Canadiens, 1–1 tie)
> **Regular Season Games with NYR:** 146
> **Playoff Games with NYR:** 0

During his seven-year career with the Toronto Maple Leafs, defenseman Wally Stanowski played in 60 playoff games and won four Stanley Cups. During his three-year career with the Rangers, he did not play in a single playoff game, partly due to a quirk of fate.

Stanowski was a superb skater who was nicknamed "The Whirling Dervish." He reportedly received the moniker as a result of an incident during a game against the Boston Bruins in February of 1948 in Toronto. Bruins goaltender Frank Brimsek was hit by a shot and was cut. With only one goaltender on the roster, the Bruins were given ten minutes to get him stitched up and back on the ice. During that time, Maple Leafs head coach Hap Day told Stanowski to get on the ice and warm up. The defenseman had not seen any ice time up to that point. Stanowski leisurely skated around twice and went to sit down. Day yelled at him to stay out there and warm up properly. Stanowski reportedly began executing a brilliant series of skating maneuvers, including loops and spins, which inspired the arena organist to start accompanying him with a musical backdrop. The local crowd got into it as well and began a rhythmic clap.

You could make the argument that Stanowski was a good luck charm but his luck ran out when he joined the Rangers for the 1948–49 season after being dealt from the Leafs in a six-player deal. The Winnipeg native was one of four players to play all 60 games, but the Rangers missed the playoffs. In the 1949–50 season, Stanowski played 37 games because he tore cartilage in his knee during the second half of the season. The injury cost him the entire postseason that included the Rangers' Game Seven loss to Detroit in the Finals.

Stanowski played one season in the American Hockey League before retiring from pro hockey.

Rene Trudell

> **NYR Debut:** February 6, 1946 (at Chicago Black Hawks, lost 6–2)
> **Regular Season Games with NYR:** 129
> **Playoff Games with NYR:** 5

When World War II ended, not many veterans could make it back to the National Hockey League. One who did make it back was 5-foot-9 right winger Rene Trudell.

The twenty-seven-year-old played most of the 1945–46 season with the New York Rovers of the Eastern Amateur Hockey League, but he made his NHL debut with the Rangers in February 1946 and scored three goals in 16 games. His best year came in his third and final season of 1947–48, when he scored 13 goals.

Trudell did not get on the scoresheet during the Rangers' loss to the Detroit Red Wings in the 1948 Stanley Cup Semifinals. After the season, he was traded to the Toronto Maple Leafs as part of a five-player deal.

Clarence "Taffy" Abel

> **NYR Debut:** November 16, 1926 (vs. Montreal Maroons, won 1–0)
> **Regular Season Games with NYR:** 111
> **Playoff Games with NYR:** 17

Defenseman Clarence Abel was not only an original New York Ranger, he was the first American-born player to play regularly in the National Hockey League.

The Sault Ste. Marie, Michigan, native made his mark with the 1924 United States Olympic Hockey team that won a silver medal. The 6-foot-1, 225-pound Abel frequently played with 5-foot-11, 210-pound Hall of Famer Ching Johnson. The two men combined for 435 pounds on the backline.

Abel was a huge contributor to the 1928 Stanley Cup-winning team. His only goal of the postseason helped the Rangers eliminate the Pittsburgh Pirates in the American Quarterfinals. In the memorable second game of the Finals against the Montreal Maroons, goaltender Lorne Chabot was injured early in the second period. Forty-five-year-old manager and coach

Lester Patrick put the pads on and took over but, thanks to the combination of Abel and Johnson, Montreal did not even get close to the heroic replacement. The physical play of the Rangers' defense pair keyed the franchise's first Stanley Cup victory.

In April of 1929, Abel was sold to the Chicago Black Hawks where he helped that franchise win its first Stanley Cup in 1934. Abel, who, alphabetically, is the first name on the franchise's all-time roster, was a member of the inaugural class of the United States Hockey Hall of Fame in 1973.

Bob Dill

NYR Debut: January 6, 1944 (vs. Detroit Red Wings, lost 5–0)
Regular Season Games with NYR: 76
Playoff Games with NYR: 0

At 5-foot-8, twenty-three-year-old Bob Dill was a small defenseman by National Hockey League standards, but he was also an outstanding American-born athlete who nearly played major league baseball.

Despite his size, Dill was a physical defenseman and instigator who made a name for himself by being a top antagonist against Montreal Canadiens' Hall of Famer Maurice "The Rocket" Richard. The rivalry between the two was played out in a 2005 French-Canadian film entitled, *The Rocket: The Legend of Rocket Richard* that featured former Ranger Sean Avery as Dill and Canadian actor Roy Dupuis as Richard.

Dill was a star baseball player for the AAA Minneapolis Millers whose alumni included Ted Williams and Willie Mays. The New York Giants sought Dill's services but the Rangers squashed the deal.

After the 1944–45 season, Dill was sent to the Rangers' affiliate at St. Paul in the United States Hockey League, where he played five seasons. Dill was inducted into the United States Hockey Hall of Fame in 1979.

Kevin Hatcher

NYR Debut: October 1, 1999 (at Edmonton Oilers, 1–1 tie)
Regular Season Games with NYR: 74
Playoff Games with NYR: 0

Going into the 1999–2000 season, the Rangers were looking to replace physical defenseman Jeff Beukeboom, who had recently announced his retirement. On the day of the season opener, team president and general manager Neil Smith acquired veteran defenseman and unrestricted free agent Kevin Hatcher in exchange for defenseman Peter Popovic.

When Hatcher joined the team for the season opener, it was almost like one of "the Hatfields" going over to join "the McCoys." The Detroit native played ten years with the Washington Capitals and three with the Pittsburgh Penguins before joining the home team. Here was one of the visiting players who drew the wrath of Ranger fans, but who would now have to support him.

The 6-foot-4, 230-pound Hatcher was known for a blistering slap shot that made him a major threat on the power play, but his only season in New York was a disappointment as he scored only two power play goals and four overall. By the time he came to the Rangers, Hatcher was thirty-three years old and a 13-year veteran, which may have been a reason why his physical play was lessening.

Aaron Ward

> **NYR Debut:** October 5, 2006 (vs. Washington Capitals, won 5–2)
> **Regular Season Games with NYR:** 60
> **Playoff Games with NYR:** 0

Unfortunately for Aaron Ward, the most notable moment of his Rangers career was how it ended.

The free agent defenseman was already a three-time Stanley Cup winner (two with Detroit, one with Carolina) when he signed with the Rangers. As the season developed, it became apparent that Ward was not what the team hoped for.

An alleged incident with captain Jaromir Jagr may have sped up Ward's departure. Reportedly, the two had a heated exchange on the bench during a 3–2 loss in Tampa Bay in early February 2007. The writing was on the wall when head coach Tom Renney benched Ward in the Rangers' last game before the trade deadline.

On February 27, Ward was traded to the Boston Bruins for defenseman Paul Mara.

Albert "Babe" Siebert

> **NYR Debut:** November 10, 1932 (at Montreal Maroons, won 4–2)
> **Regular Season Games with NYR:** 56
> **Playoff Games with NYR:** 8

For a player that played less than 60 games with the Rangers, left wing/ defenseman and Hall of Famer Babe Siebert could not have had better timing. Siebert played the first seven years of his NHL career with the Montreal Maroons and won a Stanley Cup in 1926.

In July of 1932, Siebert was dealt to the Rangers. The twenty-nine-year-old scored one goal in the Stanley Cup playoffs, but he helped the Rangers hoist the Cup for the second time in franchise history. Siebert was traded to the Bruins in December of 1933.

Siebert was preparing to be the head coach of the Montreal Canadiens for the upcoming 1939–40 season when he tragically died in August of 1939, drowning while swimming with his two children in Lake Huron.

Greg de Vries

NYR Debut: October 10, 2003 (at Minnesota Wild, lost 1–0)
Regular Season Games with NYR: 53
Playoff Games with NYR: 0

Greg de Vries was a well-traveled defenseman who played with six teams during a 13-year career. The Sundridge, Ontario, native began his NHL career with the Edmonton Oilers in 1995. In 1998, he was traded twice within 23 days before signing a free agent contract with the Rangers for the 2003–04 season. After 53 games, de Vries was traded to the Ottawa Senators for defenseman Karel Rachunek and left winger Alexandre Giroux.

Chris Tamer

NYR Debut: November 25, 1998 (at Buffalo Sabres, lost 4–2)
Regular Season Games with NYR: 52
Playoff Games with NYR: 0

Defenseman Chris Tamer became a Ranger as part of one of the most memorable trades in team history. The Rangers sent right wing Alexei Kovalev and center Harry York to Pittsburgh for Tamer, center Sean Pronger, and center Petr Nedved, who returned for a second stint with the team. The Dearborn, Michigan, native was claimed by the Atlanta Thrashers in the 1999 NHL Expansion Draft.

Gord Davidson

NYR Debut: October 31, 1942 (at Toronto Maple Leafs, lost 7–2)
Regular Season Games with NYR: 51
Playoff Games with NYR: 0

By a quirk of fate, World War II was partly responsible for allowing defenseman Gord Davidson to get his shot with the Rangers. The Stratford, Ontario–born Davidson was ineligible for the Canadian military because he had flat feet. NHL rosters had many openings due to the war. Davidson was playing with the New York Rovers, the Rangers' minor league affiliate in the East Coast Hockey League, when he was brought up for the 1942–43 season. He played 35 games and then 16 in the following season before being dealt to the Buffalo Bisons of the American Hockey League.

Harold Starr

NYR Debut: December 25, 1934 (vs. New York Americans, won 3–1)
Regular Season Games with NYR: 49
Playoff Games with NYR: 4

Harold Starr was a steady defenseman who would do whatever it took to help his team win. That included playing goalie. Starr was with the Montreal Maroons when starting goaltender Norm Smith was injured in the third period of a game in which they were already trailing 5–1. Starr volunteered to go between the pipes and stopped all three shots he faced. The Ottawa native was a versatile athlete who helped the Ottawa Rough Riders of the Canadian Football League win the coveted Grey Cup in 1925 and 1926.

In December of 1934, the Maroons sold Starr's rights to the Rangers. The steady defenseman would not initiate any fisticuffs, but he did not back away either. Starr added some grit to the Rangers' back line where he played parts of two seasons.

Brad Brown

NYR Debut: October 7, 2000 (at Atlanta Thrashers, won 2–1)
Regular Season Games with NYR: 48
Playoff Games with NYR: 0

Brad Brown was a 6-foot-4 defenseman and former first-round pick of the Montreal Canadiens who made a short stop in New York. Right before the start of the 2000–01 season, the Rangers acquired Brown and right wing Michal Grosek from the Chicago Blackhawks for future considerations. Brown played a little over half of the season before he signed with the Minnesota Wild as a free agent.

Hib Milks

NYR Debut: November 12, 1931 (at Montreal Canadiens, won 4–1)
Regular Season Games with NYR: 48
Playoff Games with NYR: 7

Left winger Hib Milks can best be described as a hockey nomad. Milks began his NHL career in 1925 with the Pittsburgh Pirates. Financial woes forced the franchise to move within the state where they became the Philadelphia Quakers. The team folded after one season and Milks was acquired by the Rangers in the 1931 NHL dispersal draft. The Quebec native played all 48 games in the 1931–32 season and all seven in the Stanley Cup Playoffs where the Rangers lost in the Final to the Toronto Maple Leafs.

Larry Brown

NYR Debut: December 11, 1969 (at Boston Bruins, lost 2–1)
Regular Season Games with NYR: 46
Playoff Games with NYR: 11

Larry Brown began his NHL career with the Rangers, left the team, and then came back—all in the span of a little over three months.

Brown played 15 games for the Rangers in the 1969–70 season. On October 31, he was traded to Detroit for center Pete Stemkowski. Ninety-four days later, the Red Wings sent Larry Brown back to the Rangers along with center Bruce MacGregor for defenseman Arnie Brown (no relation), center Tom Miller, and defenseman Mike Robitaille. Brown played 31 games in the 1970–71 season. He was claimed by the Philadelphia Flyers in the 1971 NHL Entry Draft.

Frank Peters

NYR Debut: November 11, 1930 (at Philadelphia Quakers, won 3–0)
Regular Season Games with NYR: 43
Playoff Games with NYR: 4

Frank Peters has the dubious distinction of having played in the second-most career games in NHL history without scoring a point. Peters played 43 games in the 1930–31 season for the Rangers without notching his name on the score sheet, second to Detroit Red Wings defenseman Gord Strate, who did not score a point in 61 career games. The Rouses Point, New York–native also played in four playoff games with the Rangers and also failed to score a point.

Vic Ripley

NYR Debut: December 21, 1933 (vs. Ottawa Senators, 0–0 tie)
Regular Season Games with NYR: 38
Playoff Games with NYR: 2

Left winger Vic Ripley is credited with the Rangers' only goal scored in the 1934 Stanley Cup Playoffs. The format was a little different in that era. The quarterfinals were decided by what team scored the most goals in two games. Following a scoreless tie in Game One, the Montreal Maroons won Game Two, 2–1, to win the series. Ripley scored the first goal of the game but Maroons' right winger Earl Robinson scored two unanswered goals to eliminate Ripley and the Rangers. Ripley played four games with the Rangers before he was traded to the St. Louis Eagles in November of 1934.

Adam Clendening

NYR Debut: October 13, 2016 (vs. New York Islanders, won 5–3)
Regular Season Games with NYR: 31
Playoff Games with NYR: 0

Defenseman Adam Clendening was in and out of the lineup during his one season with the Rangers. The native of Niagara Falls, New York, scored two goals in 31 games. In late February, Clendening's second and final goal of the season tied a game against New Jersey late in the third period. The Rangers went on to beat the Devils in overtime.

Clendening played out his contract after the season.

Harry "Yip" Forster

> **NYR Debut:** November 14, 1929 (at Montreal Maroons, won 2–1)
>
> **Regular Season Games with NYR:** 31
>
> **Playoff Games with NYR:** 0

At 6-foot-6 and just under 200 pounds, Harry "Yip" Forster was a mountain of a man on skates. The Rangers signed Forster in September of 1927, but the Toronto Maple Leafs claimed they had the rights to the twenty-two-year-old who was born in Guelph, Ontario. The NHL helped broker a deal and Forster became the property of the Rangers. Despite his large size, Forster received only 10 minutes of penalty time and did not score a point during his one season in New York. After the season, Forster was traded to the Boston Bruins for defenseman Bill Regan.

The following played less than 20 games with NYR:

Ron Ingram - defenseman

> **NYR Debut:** February 16, 1964 (vs. Toronto Maple Leafs, won 4–2)
>
> **Regular Season Games with NYR:** 19
>
> **Playoff Games with NYR:** 0

Randy Legge - defenseman

> **NYR Debut:** November 19, 1972 (vs. Pittsburgh Penguins, lost 5–3)
>
> **Regular Season Games with NYR:** 12
>
> **Playoff Games with NYR:** 0

Erik Reitz - defenseman

> **NYR Debut:** February 3, 2009 (vs. Atlanta Thrashers, lost 2–1, SO)
>
> **Regular Season Games with NYR:** 11
>
> **Playoff Games with NYR:** 0

Bert Marshall - defenseman

> **NYR Debut:** March 10, 1973 (at Pittsburgh Penguins, won 5–4)
>
> **Regular Season Games with NYR:** 8
>
> **Playoff Games with NYR:** 6

Maxim Galanov - defenseman

NYR Debut: April 4, 1998 (at New York Islanders, lost 3–0)

Regular Season Games with NYR: 6

Playoff Games with NYR: 0

Bob Wood

NYR Debut: March 25, 1951 (at Chicago Black Hawks, won 5–2)

Regular Season Games with NYR: 1

Playoff Games with NYR: 0

CHAPTER 5: COOKIN' WITH FIVE

Bill Cook

> **NYR Debut:** November 16, 1926 (vs. Montreal Maroons, won 1–0)
>
> **Regular Season Games with NYR:** 474
>
> **Playoff Games with NYR:** 46

Right winger Bill Cook is arguably one of the greatest players in Rangers history. Cook was an original Ranger who won two Stanley Cups during his 11-year career in New York. The Hall of Famer was the first Rangers' captain, and owned that title throughout his entire Rangers' tenure.

Bill Cook played on a line (known as "the Bread Line") that

The Bread Line (l-r) Bill Cook, Frank Boucher, and Bun Cook.

featured three Hall of Famers and is widely regarded as on one of the greatest lines in NHL history. Bill's younger brother, Fred, who was nicknamed "Bun," played left wing while Frank Boucher was at center.

In his very first game and the first in the franchise's history, Cook provided a taste of things to come. A reported crowd of 13,000 was on hand at Madison Square Garden as the Rangers hosted the defending Stanley Cup Champion Montreal Maroons. Late in the second period, "Bun" Cook set up his brother, Bill, who beat Maroons' goaltender Clint Benedict for the only goal of the game to give the Rangers a 1–0 win. The Rangers had a second goal nullified by an offside, but Cook's tally proved to be enough. The game featured the Rangers' first fighting major when Boucher got into a scrap with Montreal's Bill Phillips. Both were assessed major penalties and fined $15.

In his first season, Cook led the league with 33 goals and 37 assists, but finished second to Montreal Canadiens' defenseman Herb Gardiner for the Hart Trophy as the league's Most Valuable Player. The Rangers won the American Division but lost in the Stanley Cup Semifinals to the Boston Bruins in a two-game sweep.

The elder Cook led the Rangers to the 1928 Stanley Cup Finals where they faced the Montreal Maroons. In their five-game triumph, "the Bread

Line" accounted for all five Rangers goals. Boucher had four including an overtime winner in Game Two. The other goal came from Bill Cook to open the scoring in Game Two. It was also the Rangers' first goal of the Finals after they were shut out in Game One.

Cook was developing a reputation for being a clutch player. In the 1932 Stanley Cup Semifinals against Montreal, Bill Cook assisted on "Bun" Cook's game-winning goal in triple overtime of Game Two. The Rangers went on to beat the Canadiens but lost the Final to the Toronto Maple Leafs. Bill Cook acquitted himself very well in the three-game sweep by scoring a goal and adding two assists.

In the 1933 Stanley Cup Playoffs, Cook, who led the NHL with 28 goals and 50 points during the regular season, scored 3 goals and 2 assists in 8 games as the Rangers won their second championship. Cook had the signature moment of his career in the Final.

The Rangers avenged the previous year's loss to the Maple Leafs as they beat Toronto, three games to one. Bill Cook capped off the victory by scoring the game-winning goal in overtime of Game Four. The winning goal was scored as the Rangers were on a 5-on-3 power play. Cook was in the corner when he took a feed from Butch Keeling and put it past former Ranger goaltender Lorne Chabot.

Cook was named a first-team All-Star for three consecutive years, including the first ever All-Star team in 1931. He holds the franchise record for the most career hat tricks (11) and most points (5) in one period. On March 12, 1933, Cook scored a hat trick and added two assists in the third period of an 8–2 win against the New York Americans at Madison Square Garden.

Cook retired after playing just 21 games in the 1936–37 season. He went on to coach the Cleveland Barons in the American Hockey League before becoming the Rangers head coach for the final 47 games of the 1951–52 season. Cook coached the Rangers for one more season before being replaced by former linemate Frank Boucher.

Cook became the first Ranger alumni inducted into the Hockey Hall of Fame in 1952.

Dan Girardi

NYR Debut: January 27, 2007 (at Philadelphia Flyers, won 2–1)
Regular Season Games with NYR: 788
Playoff Games with NYR: 122
Also wore: #46

In July 2006, the Rangers signed an un-drafted free agent named Dan Girardi. The defenseman went on to a solid 11-year career with the Rangers.

Girardi was known for his durability as he played in at least 80 games from 2007–15.

The Ontario native became a steady presence in the defensive zone but also had some offensive moments.

In the 2012 Stanley Cup Playoffs, Girardi scored the game-winning goal in Game Seven of the Eastern Conference Quarterfinal against the Ottawa Senators. With the game tied at one, midway through the second period,

Undrafted free agent played 788 regular season games as a Ranger.

Girardi was left wide open in the slot and beat Senators goaltender Craig Anderson for the game winner in a 2–1 victory.

In the run to the 2014 Stanley Cup Final, Girardi played in all 25 games. Unfortunately, Girardi's turnover in overtime of Game One of the Final led to the game-winning goal.

In the 2014–15 season, Girardi continued to be durable as he played in all 82 games, but it would be the last year that he would do so. He had just turned thirty years old and his play began to deteriorate in the next two seasons.

After a dismal 2016–17 campaign, Girardi played out his contract and signed with the Tampa Bay Lightning.

Carol Vadnais

NYR Debut: November 12, 1975 (vs. Chicago Black Hawks, 4–4 tie)
Regular Season Games with NYR: 485
Playoff Games with NYR: 54
Also wore: #2

Carol Vadnais is best known in Ranger lore as one of the pieces of the epic trade in November of 1975 with the Boston Bruins. The Rangers sent Hall of Famers Brad Park and Jean Ratelle along, with defenseman Joe Zanussi to the Boston Bruins in exchange for Vadnais and Hall of Famer and five-time NHL scoring champion Phil Esposito.

Photo courtesy of Mark Rosenman.

Part of blockbuster trade with Bruins.

The deal sent shock waves throughout both fanbases. Reportedly, the switch boards at Madison Square Garden, Boston Garden, and the National Hockey League offices in Montreal lit up like Christmas trees.

The thirty-year-old Vadnais was known as a power play specialist and played on two Stanley Cup-winning teams in Montreal and Boston, but his defensive skills had eroded and the Bruins fans were giving him a hard time because of it. He had a solid first year with the Rangers as he scored 20 goals with 30 assists in 64 games.

In the 1978–79 season, Vadnais, then thirty-three years old, was a veteran who helped lead a young corps of Rangers' defensemen which included twenty-two-year-old Dave Maloney, twenty-four-year-old Ron Greschner, and twenty-two-year-old Mike McEwen.

Vadnais played well in the 1979 Stanley Cup Playoffs as the Rangers advanced to the Finals where they lost in five to his former team, the Canadiens. The Montreal native had two goals and nine assists in 18 playoff games. In the next three seasons, Vadnais's career took a downward turn as he scored only 11 goals in that span. After a while, he became a target for fans who used him to voice their displeasure with his defensive play and lack of production.

Vadnais's Ranger career ended when the New Jersey Devils selected him in the 1982 NHL Waiver Draft.

Barry "Bubba" Beck

NYR Debut: November 3, 1979 (at Colorado Rockies, lost 7–2)

Regular Season Games with NYR: 415

Playoff Games with NYR: 49

Also wore: #3

It became the calling cry for a generation of Ranger fans. "Shoot the puck Barry, shoot the puck."

A 6-foot-3 defenseman, Barry Beck came to the Rangers in November of 1979 with a lot of expectations. The Rangers had a need for a big, physical, all-around defenseman, and so they acquired Beck from the Colorado Rockies as part of a four-for-one deal. Left winger Pat Hickey, right winger Lucien Deblois, and defensemen Mike McEwen and Dean Turner were sent to Colorado along with future considerations.

During Beck's tenure, the fans sometimes became frustrated with his indecision in the offensive zone, prompting the call for him to shoot the puck.

"Bubba," as he was affectionately referred to, arrived in New York right at the time that the New York Islanders were beginning their Stanley Cup run in the 1980s. The Vancouver native was facing enormous pressure to not only lead the Rangers but to also beat their hated rivals who

Photo courtesy of Ken Tash.

Shoot the puck Barry!

were becoming a dynasty. Beck got his first taste of the rivalry in the 1981 Stanley Cup Semifinals. The Rangers advanced to meet the Islanders after a six-game, quarterfinal win against the St. Louis Blues. In that series, Beck scored three goals with five assists, so the anticipation became even greater that the Rangers could knock off the defending champions. Unfortunately for Beck and the Rangers, they were swept in four games. Beck scored one goal in Game Four, but by that time it was too late.

That's kind of how it went for Beck. Over the next three seasons, the Islanders ended the Rangers' season in the playoffs and Beck took most of the blame for the losses. In his final playoff series with the Rangers, Beck had one assist in a three-game sweep at the hands of the Philadelphia Flyers.

At twenty-three years old, Beck became the Rangers' second youngest captain. He held the honor for five seasons and played in three NHL All-Star games during his seven years in New York. His best season with the Rangers was his first when he scored 14 goals and had a career high 45 assists in 61 games.

"Bubba" was plagued by a recurring shoulder injury in the 1984–85 season. The ailment eventually forced him to retire after the 1985–86 season.

Beck tried to make a comeback with the Los Angeles Kings three years later, but that lasted only one season.

Jack Evans

NYR Debut: March 15, 1949 (at Boston Bruins, lost 4–2)

Regular Season Games with NYR: 407

Playoff Games with NYR: 16

Also wore: #16, #3, and #20

Persistence paid off for Jack "Tex" Evans.

The 6-foot, 185-pound defenseman was born in the United Kingdom, but moved to Alberta a short time afterward. Evans did not begin to speak English until he started school. As he got older, he developed a Southern drawl which led his teammates to call him "Cowboy" and then "Tex."

Evans was a hard-nosed, no nonsense defenseman who split time between the Rangers and the minors for the first six years of his career. It wasn't until the 1955–56 season that Evans became a top-six defenseman. He proved to be very durable as he played in 70 games in each of his final three seasons with the Rangers.

Evans established a reputation as someone who was not to be challenged by the opposition, as evidenced by his penchant for spending time in the penalty box. When he became a regular with the Rangers, he averaged over 100 minutes in penalties.

In June of 1958, Evans was claimed by the Chicago Black Hawks in the NHL Intra-League Draft.

Mac Colville

NYR Debut: January 28, 1936 (at Montreal Canadiens, won 3-2)

Regular Season Games with NYR: 353

Playoff Games with NYR: 40

Twenty-year-old right winger Mac Colville couldn't have picked a better game to make his NHL debut. The game was at Madison Square Garden against the Montreal Canadiens. It also marked the Rangers' debut of Hall of Famer Howie Morenz, who was acquired from the Chicago Black Hawks two days prior. Morenz played 12 seasons with the Montreal Canadiens and was making his Blueshirt debut against his old team. Colville had an unheralded first game, but the Rangers beat Montreal 3–2 in overtime. The Edmonton, Alberta, native scored his first NHL goal against the Detroit Red Wings in his tenth NHL game.

In his second season, Mac Colville was joined on a line with his older brother Neil and left winger Alex Shibicky. The line began to click and culminated in a run for the 1940 Stanley Cup. The trio produced 21 points (7 goals, 14 assists) as the Rangers won their third Cup.

Mac Colville set the tone for the playoffs by scoring all three of his playoff goals in the first two games of the semifinals against the Boston Bruins. In the Finals against Toronto, Colville got the primary assist on brother Neil's goal to give the Rangers a 1–0 lead in Game Five. The Rangers went on to a 2–1 win in overtime to take a 3–2 lead in the series en route to winning in six games.

In the 1940–41 season, Colville tied a career high with 14 goals. The following season, he tied his career high for a third time but was one of the players who served in World War II and missed the next three seasons.

When Colville returned to the league, he began playing defense and was not the same player, scoring only seven goals in the 1945–46 season. The next season was his last as the thirty-one-year-old played only 14 games.

Larry Cahan

NYR Debut: October 12, 1956 (at Chicago Black Hawks, won 3–0)
Regular Season Games with NYR: 303
Playoff Games with NYR: 14
Also wore: #2

At 6-foot-2, Larry Cahan could have been the model for the kid's game "Rock 'em, Sock 'em Robots." Cahan never met a fight he didn't like to get involved with.

The Rangers claimed the defenseman from the Toronto Maple Leafs in the 1956 NHL Intra-League Draft. The native of Fort William, Ontario, gave the Rangers a much-needed physical presence on the back line. Cahan took on such noted tough guys as Boston's Ted Green and Detroit's Gordie Howe. In a December 1963 game, he incurred a major, a misconduct, and a game misconduct penalty after he fought with Montreal's Jacques Laperriere and Jean Claude Tremblay at the same time.

Cahan was loaned to the Vancouver Canucks of the Western Hockey League for two seasons before he returned to the Rangers for the 1961–62 season. He was later claimed by the Oakland Seals in the 1967 Expansion Draft and was involved in an infamous incident in NHL history. On January 13, 1968, Cahan combined with defense partner Ron Harris for a clean hit on Minnesota North Stars rookie center Bill Masterton who fell to the ice and hit his head. Masterton suffered serious brain damage and tragically died two days later.

Cahan later went on to play with the Los Angeles Kings and the Chicago Cougars of the World Hockey Association.

Ulf Samuelsson

NYR Debut: October 7, 1995 (at Hartford Whalers, lost 2–0)

Regular Season Games with NYR: 287

Playoff Games with NYR: 26

Photo b Håkan Dahlström via Wikimedia Commons.

Spent four seasons as a player and five as an assistant coach for Rangers.

While he played with the Pittsburgh Penguins, defenseman Ulf Samuelsson was one of the most hated players to hit the ice at Madison Square Garden. The tide turned when he was traded from the Penguins, along with high scoring winger Luc Robitaille, to the Rangers for center Petr Nedved and defenseman Sergei Zubov.

The Swedish-born Samuelsson carried a reputation for being one of the dirtiest players in hockey. In the 1991 Stanley Cup Playoffs, he injured Bruins winger Cam Neely with a knee-on-knee hit. Neely was never the same after that incident. In 1995, Samuelsson was on the receiving end of a dirty play. Toronto Maple Leafs winger and former Ranger Tie Domi was suspended for eight games after he sucker punched Samuelsson in the face. Domi claimed Samuelsson called him a "dummy" to provoke him into the altercation.

Following the 1998–99 season, Samuelsson was traded to the Detroit Red Wings for two draft choices. Beginning in 2011, Samuelsson served five seasons as an assistant coach with the Rangers.

Dale Rolfe

NYR Debut: March 3, 1971 (vs. California Golden Seals, won 8–1)

Regular Season Games with NYR: 244

Playoff Games with NYR: 50

Defenseman Dale Rolfe will forever be known as the focal point of one of the most infamous events in Rangers' franchise history.

Despite being 6-foot-4, Rolfe was not known as a physical defenseman. He was a good puck handler and could shoot, but never took advantage of his size to fulfill the expectations that were placed on him as a nineteen-year-old when he debuted with the Boston Bruins in the 1959–60 season. That lack of physicality reared its ugly head on May 5, 1974, in the seventh game of the Stanley Cup Semifinals against the Philadelphia Flyers.

The Flyers were a tough team that was known as the "Broad Street Bullies" for their physical style of play.

Was focal point of one of most infamous Rangers moment.

Photo from the public domain.

The teams were scoreless mid-way through the first period at the Philadelphia Spectrum when a scrum developed near the Ranger net. Noted tough guy Dave "The Hammer" Schultz began to fight with Rolfe. The bout was so one sided that if it was taking place in a boxing ring, it wouldn't have lasted as long as it did. For 45 seconds, Schultz unleashed a furious storm of punches that landed all over Rolfe's face. Despite the fact that the Rangers scored a goal less than two minutes later to take a 1–0 lead, the fight turned the game and the series. The Flyers scored three unanswered goals and went on to the Finals with a 4–3 win.

The Rangers were criticized for their lack of a response and developed a reputation for being soft, but defenseman Brad Park, who was on the ice at the time, refuted that claim. "You have to understand that there's a third man in rule," Park said during a recent interview. "This is the first period, if you jump in as a third man, you're tossed for the game."

Park said Schultz wanted to fight him. "Schultz had come through to fight me and I had my gloves off and I was ready for him," Park said, "and Dale just grabbed him and then from there, Schultz started throwing punches and I came to Dale's help and he looked at me. He knew it was a third man in, he said 'Stay out of it.'"

Rolfe played one more season for the Rangers.

Buddy O'Connor

> **NYR Debut:** October 16, 1947 (at Montreal Canadiens, won 2–1)
>
> **Regular Season Games with NYR:** 238
>
> **Playoff Games with NYR:** 18

Center Buddy O'Connor was one of the smallest players in NHL history, but he couldn't have had a bigger debut season for the Rangers.

The Hall of Famer was acquired from the Montreal Canadiens in exchange for four players in the summer of 1947. The 142-pound O'Connor scored a career high 60 points (24 goals, 36 assists) and became the first Ranger to win the Hart Trophy as the League's Most Valuable Player of the 1947–48 season. The popular Irishman from Quebec also captured the Lady Byng Memorial Trophy for the player who demonstrates the "best type of sportsmanship."

O'Connor, who won two Stanley Cups with Montreal, helped the Rangers end a five-season drought without making the playoffs in 1948. He was also the captain of the Ranger team that went to the 1950 Stanley Cup Final and lost to Toronto.

Eddie Shack

> **NYR Debut:** October 8, 1958 (at Chicago Black Hawks, 1–1 tie)
>
> **Regular Season Games with NYR:** 141
>
> **Playoff Games with NYR:** 0
>
> **Also wore:** #6

The classic Billy Joel song "The Entertainer" may have been based on the career of left winger Eddie Shack.

Shack joined the Guelph Biltmores of the Ontario Junior Hockey League as a fifteen-year-old for the 1952–53 season. After five years with Guelph, the left winger joined the Providence Reds, the Rangers' farm team in the

American Hockey League, for the 1957–58 season before joining the big club in October of 1958.

Shack was known for his magnetic personality and some legendary fights throughout the years. In an AHL game, Shack had a fight with Larry Zeidel who was one of the toughest players in the league. Both players were ejected and came out to watch the rest of the game from the stands. When Shack and Zeidel spotted each other, they resumed the fisticuffs.

It was Shack's showmanship that earned him the moniker of "The Entertainer." He had an ability to relate to the fans with some of his on-ice antics, and was considered one of the greatest ambassadors the sport has ever seen.

After playing parts of three seasons in New York, Shack was traded to the Detroit Red Wings for Red Kelly and Billy McNeill. When both players refused to report to the Rangers, the deal was nullified. After playing 12 games in the 1960–61 season, Shack was traded to the Toronto Maple Leafs for left wingers Pat Hannigan and Johnny Wilson.

Leo Reise Jr.

NYR Debut: October 9, 1952 (at Detroit Red Wings, lost 5–3)
Regular Season Games with NYR: 131
Playoff Games with NYR: 0

Leo Reise Jr. followed in the footsteps of his father, Leo Sr., when he joined the Rangers in 1952. The elder Reise played the final 14 games of his eight-year NHL career with the Rangers in 1930.

The younger Reise made his bones with the Detroit Red Wings. In the 1950 Stanley Cup Semifinals against the Toronto Maple Leafs, the defenseman scored two overtime goals. The first playoff goal came in double overtime to win the pivotal Game Four and tie the series at two games apiece. The second was the game winner in the seventh and deciding game. Detroit went on to beat the Rangers in the Finals and win the Stanley Cup.

Reise Jr. represented the Rangers in the 1953 All-Star Game. In the 1953–54 season, he played in all 70 games and retired after the season.

Bernie "Boom Boom" Geoffrion

NYR Debut: October 19, 1966 (at Chicago Black Hawks, lost 6–3)
Regular Season Games with NYR: 117
Playoff Games with NYR: 5

After fourteen years with the Montreal Canadiens and two years removed from playing, Hall of Fame right winger Bernie "Boom Boom" Geoffrion played the final two seasons of his fabulous NHL career with the Rangers.

The Quebec native was a six-time Stanley Cup winner with the Canadiens. In the 1960–61 season, Geoffrion captured the Hart Trophy as the MVP and the Art Ross Trophy as the leading scorer in league. He was known as "Boom Boom" because of his dynamic slap shot.

Following the 1963–64 season, Geoffrion retired, partly due to an arrangement he allegedly made with Canadiens owner David Molson. According to Geoffrion, Molson told him to go to the minors and coach the Quebec Aces for two seasons and then he would be promoted to run the Canadiens from behind the bench. Hall of Famer Toe Blake had just come off his seventh Stanley Cup win and was not going anywhere, so an irate Geoffrion decided to launch a comeback with the Rangers.

Geoffrion had an assist in his first game with the Rangers, but missed time in the early portion of the 1966–67 season due to a rib injury. "Boom Boom" scored his first Ranger goal in late October in a loss against the Detroit Red Wings.

On November 12, 1966, Geoffrion returned to the Forum for the first time as an opposing player. He received a thunderous standing ovation from the crowd of over 15,000 fans. "I'm against their team now, but Montreal fans haven't forgotten," Geoffrion told the *Montreal Gazette* after the game. Geoffrion made his return a memorable one as he scored a goal and added three assists to lead the Rangers past the Canadiens, 6–3. "Boom Boom" capped off his night with a breakaway goal in the third period that beat former Ranger and Canadiens goaltender "Gump" Worsley. Despite scoring two goals in the playoffs, Geoffrion and company were eliminated by the Canadiens in a four-game sweep.

Geoffrion's final game was in Game One of the 1968 Stanley Cup Playoffs against the Chicago Black Hawks. An ulcer that plagued him at the end of the regular season resurfaced and put him out for the remainder of the playoffs. It also spelled the end of his career.

Normand Rochefort

NYR Debut: October 6, 1988 (at Chicago Blackhawks, 2–2 tie)
Regular Season Games with NYR: 112
Playoff Games with NYR: 10

Normand Rochefort's Rangers career got cut short before it ever really started. He played in only 11 games in the 1988–89 season because of a knee injury. Rochefort needed reconstructive surgery on his right knee and missed three months before he returned for one game. Rochefort did not make his 1989–90 season debut until January. The Quebec native was never the same player after the injury.

Rochefort's Ranger career came to an end after the 1991–92 season. Normand's uncle, Leon, was a right winger for the Rangers for parts of two seasons in the early 1960s.

Matt Cullen

> **NYR Debut:** October 6, 2006 (vs. Washington Capitals, won 5–2)
> **Regular Season Games with NYR:** 80
> **Playoff Games with NYR:** 10

Matt Cullen's 19-year career featured a stopover with the Rangers for the 2006–07 season. Cullen was coming off a Stanley Cup win with the Carolina Hurricanes in 2006 when he signed a four-year free agent contract with the Rangers. Cullen scored 16 goals and added 25 assists with the Rangers while playing in 80 of 82 games.

During the playoffs, Cullen had a goal and an assist in the four-game sweep of the opening round against the Atlanta Thrashers. After the season, the Rangers traded him back to Carolina in exchange for two players and a third-round draft pick.

Stephane Quintal

> **NYR Debut:** October 1, 1999 (at Edmonton Oilers, 1–1 tie)
> **Regular Season Games with NYR:** 75
> **Playoff Games with NYR:** 0

Defenseman Stephane Quintal, who is one of two Rangers in franchise history whose last name begins with the letter Q, picked the right opponent to frustrate in his only season with the Blueshirts.

In five games against the New York Islanders in the 1999–2000 season, the veteran defenseman had a goal and three assists. In mid-October, the Rangers and Islanders were tied at two late in the third period when Quintal scored with less than three minutes left for the go-ahead goal in a 4–2 win. The thirty-one-year-old was placed on waivers after the season and was claimed by the Chicago Blackhawks.

Larry Sacharuk

NYR Debut: December 9, 1972 (at New York Islanders, won 4–1)

Regular Season Games with NYR: 75

Playoff Games with NYR: 0

Also wore: #3, #4, and #26

Photo courtesy of Ken Tash.

Only defenseman in professional hockey history to score 50 goals in a season.

Larry Sacharuk, who was known as an offensive defenseman, was the Rangers' third of three first-round picks and 21st overall in the 1972 NHL Amateur Draft. Unfortunately for Sacharuk, the Rangers already had an offensive defenseman in Brad Park.

Sacharuk played 64 games during the 1972–73 season for the Rangers' American Hockey League affiliate at Providence. The twenty-year-old was brought up for a short stint in December and scored one goal in eight games. In the 1975–76 season, Sacharuk had 6 goals and 7 assists in 42 games.

Sacharuk was traded away to the St. Louis Blues in August of 1974, but was dealt back to the Rangers in October of 1975. Sacharuk has the distinction of being the only defenseman in professional hockey history to score 50 goals in a season. He accomplished the feat as a nineteen-year-old in the Western Canada Junior Hockey League with the Saskatoon Blades.

Doug Robinson

NYR Debut: February 6, 1965 (at Boston Bruins, lost 3–2)

Regular Season Games with NYR: 73

Playoff Games with NYR: 0

Left winger Doug Robinson came to the Rangers from the Chicago Black Hawks as part of a six-player deal that sent popular Camille Henry to the

Windy City. Robinson made his NHL debut with Chicago and played 40 games in the 1964–65 season before he was traded to the Rangers in February.

Robinson finished the season in New York with 22 points in 21 games. The 6-foot-2 winger played only one game in the 1966–67 season as he spent most of the time with the Rangers' American Hockey League affiliate in Baltimore. Robinson was claimed by the Los Angeles Kings in the 1967 NHL Expansion Draft.

Jari Gronstrand

NYR Debut: October 23, 1987 (vs. Chicago Blackhawks, won 7–3)
Regular Season Games with NYR: 62
Playoff Games with NYR: 0

The Finnish defenseman played 62 games with the Rangers and scored all three of his goals within a six-day period. Gronstrand was acquired from the Minnesota North Stars right before the start of the 1987–88 season. After one season, he was traded to the Quebec Nordiques and then played with the New York Islanders for two seasons after being claimed off the waiver wire.

Fred Hunt

NYR Debut: October 28, 1944 (at Toronto Maple Leafs, lost 2–1)
Regular Season Games with NYR: 44
Playoff Games with NYR: 0

During his two-year NHL career, right winger Fred Hunt played all of his home games at Madison Square Garden, despite having played only one season with the Rangers. Hunt is one of those players who spent time with both the New York Americans and the Rangers.

Hunt played 15 games with the Americans during the 1940–41 season and made his debut against the Rangers at the Garden. After spending time in the minors, mostly with the Buffalo Bisons of the American Hockey League, he joined the Rangers for the 1944–45 season. Hunt scored 13 goals in 44 games for the Rangers.

Peter Andersson

NYR Debut: October 14, 1992 (vs. New Jersey Devils, won 6–1)
Regular Season Games with NYR: 39
Playoff Games with NYR: 0

Defenseman Peter Andersson was a fourth-round selection of the Rangers in the 1983 NHL Entry Draft. The twenty-seven-year-old spent most of the early years of his pro career playing in his native Sweden.

Andersson played 31 games during the 1992–93 season but he was benched for much of the 1993–94 season. In only his fifth game of the season, Andersson's shorthanded goal proved to be the game winner as the Rangers beat the Quebec Nordiques, 5–2. Andersson played three more games with the Rangers before he was traded to the Florida Panthers for a draft choice.

The following played less than 25 games with NYR:

Gus Mancuso - right wing

NYR Debut: January 21, 1943 (at Toronto Maple Leafs, lost 7–4)
Regular Season Games with NYR: 21
Playoff Games with NYR: 0

Bill Ezinicki - right wing

NYR Debut: February 12, 1955 (vs. Boston Bruins, 5–5 tie)
Regular Season Games with NYR: 16
Playoff Games with NYR: 0

Charlie Sands - right wing

NYR Debut: October 30, 1943 (at Toronto Maple Leafs, lost 5–2)
Regular Season Games with NYR: 9
Playoff Games with NYR: 0

Roger Leger - defenseman

NYR Debut: November 25, 1943 (at Boston Bruins, lost 6–2)
Regular Season Games with NYR: 9
Playoff Games with NYR: 0

Dale Purinton - defenseman

NYR Debut: April 9, 2000 (vs. Philadelphia Flyers, lost 4–1)
Regular Season Games with NYR: 5
Playoff Games with NYR: 0
Also wore: #45

Hank D'Amore - center

NYR Debut: January 13, 1944 (vs. Chicago Black Hawks, lost 5–2)

Regular Season Games with NYR: 4

Playoff Games with NYR: 0

Ron Howell - defenseman

NYR Debut: December 25, 1954 (at Montreal Canadiens, lost 4–1)

Regular Season Games with NYR: 4

Playoff Games with NYR: 0

Also wore: #21

Ulf Sterner - left wing

NYR Debut: January 27, 1965 (vs. Boston Bruins, won 5–2)

Regular Season Games with NYR: 4

Playoff Games with NYR: 0

Bill Sweeney - center

NYR Debut: November 8, 1959 (at Detroit Red Wings, 3–3 tie)

Regular Season Games with NYR: 4

Playoff Games with NYR: 0

The following three players wore #5 in one regular season game as a Ranger:

Tony Demers - right wing

NYR Debut: February 24, 1944 (vs. Detroit Red Wings, 3–3 tie)

Lloyd Mohns - defenseman

NYR Debut: January 9, 1944 (vs. Montreal Canadiens, lost 6–5)

Mel Read - center

NYR Debut: December 25, 1946 (vs. Montreal Canadiens, won 2–0)

#6: A MOST POPULAR NUMBER

Fred "Bun" Cook

> **NYR Debut:** November 16, 1926 (vs. Montreal Maroons, won 1–0)
> **Regular Season Games with Rangers:** 433
> **Playoff Games with Rangers:** 46

A total of 45 players have worn the #6 in Ranger history, led by Hall of Famer Fred "Bun" Cook, the older brother of Hall of Famer Bill Cook.

Like Bill, Fred "Bun" Cook was an original Ranger. In their very first game together and the first in franchise history, Bill scored the winning goal while "Bun" got the assist (see Chapter Five).

Bun Cook's career mirrored his brother's. They played on the same line with Hall of Fame center Frank Boucher that became known as the "Bread Line." "Bun" who played left wing, was a goal scorer like his brother, but added a combination of speed and physical play to the ice. Bun was also an adept passer and strong in the corners. The brothers' career numbers were similar as well. Bill finished with 229 goals and 138 assists in 474 games, while Bun compiled 154 goals and 139 assists in 433 games during his 11 years with the team.

Bun Cook's hustling and sometimes reckless style caught the attention of some of New York's celebrities, including TV host and newspaper columnist Ed Sullivan. "When Bun Cook is hot, he is one of the most amazing players in hockey," Sullivan wrote in the *New York Graphic*. It was one of the first times that a professional hockey player in New York received such recognition.

In the 1929–30 season, Bun scored a career-high 24 goals and was named a second team All-Star. He scored two goals in one playoff game but the Rangers were eventually eliminated by Montreal in the Stanley Cup Semifinals. His best output in the playoffs was in 1932 when he scored eight points (6 goals, 2 assists) in seven games. He also scored a triple-overtime goal to beat the Canadiens in Game Two of their semifinal series that the Rangers went on to win three games to one. In the Stanley Cup-winning year of 1933, Bun Cook scored two goals in the playoffs.

Cook's physical style began to catch up to him. He was thirty-one years old in the 1934–35 season when he scored 13 goals in his final productive season. A throat infection and an arthritic condition limited Cook to 26 games in the 1935–36 season, his last with the Rangers. Cook tried to come back with the Rangers but was sold to the Boston Bruins in September of 1936. It would mark the first and only time that Bun Cook would not be playing on the same team as his brother Bill.

The Kingston, Ontario, native is widely credited with introducing the drop pass and was elected to the Hockey Hall of Fame, posthumously, in 1995.

Neil Colville

> **NYR Debut:** November 19, 1935 (vs. Detroit Red Wings, 2–2 OT tie)
> **Regular Season Games with Rangers:** 464
> **Playoff Games with Rangers:** 26

Center Neil Colville was part of another successful brother combination that played with the Rangers. Along with his younger brother, Mac, the Colvilles were key members of the 1940 Stanley Cup-winning team. Playing on a line with left winger Alex Shibicky, the Colvilles became part of one of the most productive lines in NHL history.

Neil Colville was signed as a free agent in 1935 and played his entire 12-year NHL career with the Rangers. Team executive Lester Patrick was high on Neil Colville, but not so much on his brother Mac. However, Patrick instructed original Ranger Murray Murdoch, who was still a player at the time, to travel to Edmonton and, if need be, sign Mac as well.

Neil Colville was tied for the lead in scoring in the 1940 Stanley Cup Playoffs with 9 points (2 goals, 7 assists led the playoffs), and helped lead the Rangers to their third Stanley Cup Championship.

After Colville served two years as a navigator in the Royal Canadian Air Force during World War II, he adjusted his game to become a defenseman (as his brother Mac did) when he returned to the Rangers for the 1944–45 season. As a back liner, Neil Colville, who became the Rangers captain in 1945, was a second team All-Star in the 1947–48 season.

Colville retired after the 1948–49 season and became the Rangers head coach in 1950. After failing to make the playoffs, Colville coached only 23 games in the next season. Reportedly stomach ulcers forced him to step down. Colville was inducted into the Hockey Hall of Fame in 1967.

Darius Kasparaitis

> **NYR Debut:** October 9, 2002 (at Carolina Hurricanes, won 4–1)
> **Regular Season Games with Rangers:** 215
> **Playoff Games with Rangers:** 2

Darius Kasparaitis walked a fine line between being physical and dirty. The feisty Kasparaitis had an ability to infuriate the opposition while providing a spark for his team.

The New York Islanders made the Lithuanian-born defenseman their first-round pick and the fifth overall in the 1992 NHL Entry Draft. After being traded to Pittsburgh and then an 11-game stint with the Colorado Avalanche, Kasparaitis signed a six year, $25.5 million deal with the Rangers in July of 2002. The thirty-year-old was being brought in to add some grit and toughness to a team that had missed the playoffs five consecutive years running. So after all the times that Kasparaitis incurred the wrath of the die-hard Ranger fans, he was now wearing the home uniform.

Unfortunately for Kasparitis and the Rangers, the fans never totally warmed up to him. The team failed to make the playoffs in Kasparaitis's first three seasons. He was thirty-four years old when he reported to the 2005 training camp out of shape. Kasparaitis was sent to the Hartford Wolf Pack (the Rangers AHL affiliate) at mid-season and played only 24 games with the big club. Ironically, the Rangers made the playoffs and the defenseman played in two of those games.

Manny Malhotra

> **NYR Debut:** October 10, 1998 (at Montreal Canadiens, lost 7–1)
> **Regular Season Games with Rangers:** 206
> **Playoff Games with Rangers:** 0

The Rangers made 6-foot-2 center Manny Malhotra the seventh overall pick of the 1998 NHL Entry Draft but, unfortunately, he never lived up to his press clippings. The eighteen-year-old was projected to be a solid, two-way player who was very fast, good on face offs, and proficient on the penalty killing unit.

Malhotra won the Lars-Erik Sjoberg award as the "Best Rookie in Training Camp," and made the team and scored 8 goals in 73 games in his first season of 1998–99. Despite his status as a No. 1 pick, head coach John Muckler felt Malhotra would never be more than a third-line player. Muckler reportedly clashed with general manager Neil Smith over Malhotra's playing time. In his second season, Malhotra played only 27 games and split time with the Rangers' AHL affiliate in Hartford.

The young center was not developing as the team had hoped, and was being benched on a regular basis. In the 2000–01 season, he once again split time with the Rangers and the Hartford Wolf Pack. Muckler was replaced as head coach by Ron Low, but things didn't get better for Malhotra.

The Rangers' front office, which was now led by general manager Glen Sather, was starting to believe Muckler's assessment, so they engineered a deal with the Dallas Stars.

On March 12, 2002, the Rangers traded Malhotra and left winger Barrett Heisten to Dallas for wingers Martin Rucinsky and Roman Lyashenko.

Glen "Slats" Sather

NYR Debut: January 27, 1971 (vs. Boston Bruins, 2–2 tie)
Regular Season Games with Rangers: 186
Playoff Games with Rangers: 38

Most people know Glen Sather as the architect of the Edmonton Oilers dynasty of the late 1980s and the current president and former coach and general manager of the Rangers, but the Alberta native was a former player with the Blueshirts as well. Sather was one of six former Rangers who played for the team and also became their general manager. Hall of Famer Frank Boucher, Muzz Patrick, Emile Francis, Fred Shero, and Phil Esposito were the other five.

Sather began his NHL career with the Boston Bruins, where he played with Hall of Fame defenseman Bobby Orr. After a stint in Pittsburgh, Sather was traded to the Rangers in exchange for center Syl Apps Jr. and defenseman Sheldon Kannegiesser. Reportedly, Sather was tagged with the nickname "Slats" for spending time on the bench during his minor league career.

The left winger played parts of four seasons with the Rangers. His best was in 1972–73, when he scored 11 goals with 15 assists in 77 games. Two games into the 1973–74 season, Sather was traded to St. Louis. In 2000, he became the president and general manager of the Rangers. Sather was inducted into the Hockey Hall of Fame as a "builder" in 1997.

Anton Stralman

NYR Debut: November 23, 2011 (at Florida Panthers, lost 2–1)
Regular Season Games with Rangers: 182
Playoff Games with Rangers: 55
Also wore: #32

At the start of the 2012–13 season, the Rangers' defense corps was plagued by injuries. Marc Staal was still dealing with headaches as a result of a concussion that was incurred eight months previous, while a shoulder injury kept young promising defenseman Michael Sauer on the sidelines. Swedish-born defenseman Anton Stralman was added as a stop gap, but he became much more valuable than that during his short tenure with the Rangers.

Averaged over 24 minutes of ice time in 2014 Cup Finals.

Stralman was signed as an unrestricted free agent in early November and, later that month, he made his Ranger debut. The twenty-five-year-old played 53 games and was a respectable plus-9 in his initial season with the Rangers, but spent time in head coach John Tortorella's dog house and missed six games as a healthy scratch. The defenseman emerged in the playoffs with three goals and three assists as the Rangers made it all the way to the Eastern Conference Finals where they lost to the New Jersey Devils in six games. Stralman proved to be a valuable playoff performer.

In the 2014 Stanley Cup Playoffs, Stralman did not score a goal but had five assists in 25 games, and was a solid performer along the blue line. During the series loss to the Los Angeles Kings in the Finals, Stralman averaged over 24 minutes of ice time including 30 minutes in two of the three losses that went to overtime. After the loss, Stralman was a free agent. There was a reported miscommunication between Stralman and the Rangers, and the defenseman ended up signing with the Tampa Bay Lightning.

Gilles Marotte

NYR Debut: December 2, 1973 (at Toronto Maple Leafs, won 6–4)
Regular Season Games with Rangers: 180
Playoff Games with Rangers: 15

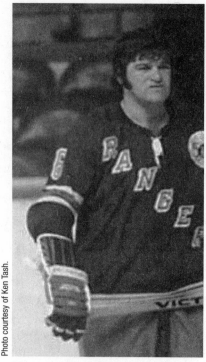

Photo courtesy of Ken Tash.

Hard hits earned him nickname of "Captain Crunch."

Defenseman Gilles Marotte overcame his relatively small size of 5-foot-9 to become one of the hardest hitters in the National Hockey League, earning the nickname "Captain Crunch."

Marotte began his career with the Boston Bruins in the 1965–66 season, but was part of the infamous trade with the Chicago Black Hawks in 1967 that brought Hall of Famer Phil Esposito to Beantown. After his time in Chicago, Marotte was traded to the Los Angeles Kings where he spent parts of five seasons before being dealt to the Rangers in November of 1973.

During his three years with the Rangers, Marotte scored 76 points in 180 games. He also did not hesitate to challenge some of the enforcers around the league, including Philadelphia's Dave Schultz and Boston's Don Awrey. In October of 1976, the Rangers placed Marotte on waivers where he was claimed by the St. Louis Blues.

John Hanna

> **NYR Debut:** October 8, 1958 (vs. Detroit Red Wings, 1–1 tie)
> **Regular Season Games with Rangers:** 177
> **Playoff Games with Rangers:** 0
> **Also wore:** #2 and #4

John Hanna had an unusual start to his Ranger career. The first time that he wore a Ranger jersey, he did not see a second of ice time. On November 16, 1957, the Rangers were in Montreal and needed an emergency replacement for Bill Gadsby. Hanna was called up from Providence and wore Gadsby's #4, but stayed on the bench for the entire game.

Hanna made the team for the 1958–59 season and tied for the league lead as he played in all 70 games. The defenseman played parts of two more seasons with the Rangers before being traded to the Montreal Canadiens in June of 1961 for defenseman Albert Langlois.

Doug Lidster

NYR Debut: October 5, 1993 (vs. Boston Bruins, lost 4–3)

Regular Season Games with Rangers: 177

Playoff Games with Rangers: 31

Defenseman Doug Lidster had two separate stints with the Rangers.

The first one landed him on the 1994 Stanley Cup-winning team. The Rangers acquired Lidster from the Vancouver Canucks in June of 1993 to complete a deal for goaltender John Vanbiesbrouck. Lidster did not crack the regular lineup and was limited to 34 games.

In the Stanley Cup Playoffs, Lidster played in the final nine games—including the Final against his former team from Vancouver. The Rangers lost Game One in overtime but Lidster scored the first goal of Game Two and they went on to even the series. The steady defenseman was in the lineup when the Rangers ended their 54-year drought with a win in Game Seven.

A little over a month after the Cup victory, Lidster and winger Esa Tikkanen were traded to St. Louis for center Petr Nedved. In July of 1995, Lidster was traded back to the Rangers for defenseman Jay Wells. The native of British Columbia had another solid showing in the 1997 Stanley Cup Playoffs with a goal and five assists in 15 games. Lidster played one more season with the Rangers, after which he became a free agent.

Don Johns

NYR Debut: October 5, 1960 (vs. Boston Bruins, won 2–1)

Regular Season Games with Rangers: 148

Playoff Games with Rangers: 0

Also wore: #5

The 6-foot Don Johns was a prototypical "stay-at-home" defenseman. The St. George, Ontario, native had a solid rookie season where he played 63 games in the 1960–61 season. Johns was a good puck handler and made good decisions in his own end, but the Rangers were frustrated by his lack of physical play. In his second season, Johns spent most if it with the Rangers' AHL affiliate in Baltimore. He returned to a regular spot in the lineup for the 1963–64 season.

After playing 22 games in the 1964–65 season, Johns was part of a famous trade in franchise history. The defenseman was traded to the Chicago Black Hawks as part of a seven-player deal that also sent popular Ranger center Camille Henry to the Windy City.

Joe Cirella

NYR Debut: January 25, 1991 (at Edmonton Oilers, won 4–3)
Regular Season Games with Rangers: 141
Playoff Games with Rangers: 19
Also wore: #18

Defenseman Joe Cirella made his NHL debut as an eighteen-year-old with the defunct Colorado Rockies franchise in the 1981–82 season. The franchise relocated to New Jersey and became the Devils, where Cirella played for seven more seasons. After a season and a half with the Quebec Nordiques, Cirella was traded to the Rangers in January of 1991.

In the 1992 Stanley Cup Playoffs, Cirella helped the Rangers beat his former team, the Devils, in a thrilling seven-game division semifinals series. Cirella had an assist in the deciding seventh game.

The 6-foot-3, 210-pound Hamilton, Ontario, native was not known to back down and had a number of fights during his Rangers' tenure. In April of 1993, Cirella made Ranger fans take notice when he took on Washington Capitals tough guy Dale Hunter.

Pat Egan

NYR Debut: October 15, 1949 (at Montreal Canadiens, lost 3–1)
Regular Season Games with Rangers: 140
Playoff Games with Rangers: 12

Pat Egan was a durable defenseman who did not miss a game during his two seasons in New York.

Egan made his bones with the Boston Bruins from 1943–49. Right before the 1949–50 season, the Rangers acquired Egan from the Bruins for veteran defenseman Bill Moe and the rights to left winger Lorne Ferguson (who never played a game for the Rangers).

The feisty Egan made an impact in his very first game as a Ranger when he scored his first goal in Montreal. In his first season, Egan played in all 70 games as the Rangers made the playoffs after missing out in 1949.

The Blackie, Alberta-born Egan scored two goals to help the Rangers eliminate the Canadiens in five games in the Stanley Cup Semifinals. In the Final loss to Detroit, Egan scored the first goal of Game Two to help the Rangers even the series, but they went on to lose in seven games.

In his second and final season of 1950–51 with the Rangers, Egan played all 70 games but the team failed to make the playoffs. He was traded to Providence of the AHL in January of 1952.

Bob Chrystal

NYR Debut: October 8, 1953 (at Detroit Red Wings, lost 4–1)
Regular Season Games with Rangers: 132
Playoff Games with Rangers: 0

Bob Chrystal was a rugged defenseman who found himself as part of a famous incident in Ranger history.

On December 20, 1953, the Rangers hosted the Montreal Canadiens at Madison Square Garden. Late in the second period, Chrystal was engaged along the boards with Hall of Famer Bernie "Boom Boom" Geoffrion. Rangers' left winger Ron Murphy tried to help Chrystal and began to fight the future Ranger. Geoffrion had dropped his stick but he picked it up and, with two hands, chopped down on Murphy. Geoffrion was forbidden to play any more games against the Rangers for the rest of the 1953–54 season.

Chrystal's NHL career consisted of his two seasons with the Rangers, scoring 11 goals with 14 assists. His most memorable moment as a professional came while he was playing with the Cleveland Barons in the 1953 Calder Cup Finals. Chrystal scored the game-winning and Calder Cup-winning goal in overtime in the seventh and deciding game to give Cleveland a 1–0 win over the Pittsburgh Hornets. A little over six minutes into the overtime, Chrystal flipped the puck in the air toward the net from the blue line, but it took a bad hop and went past Pittsburgh goaltender Gil Mayer for the game and series winner. Former Ranger great "Bun" Cook was the Barons' head coach.

Steve Kraftcheck

NYR Debut: October 18, 1951 (at Montreal Canadiens, lost 3–2)
Regular Season Games with Rangers: 127
Playoff Games with Rangers: 0

Steve Kraftcheck was an offensive defenseman who shined in the American Hockey League, but could never translate that to a prosperous NHL career.

The 5-foot-11 Ontario native played two seasons with the Rangers. He began his NHL career with the Boston Bruins in the 1950–51 season, but was sold to the Rangers in May of 1951.

Kraftcheck scored a goal in his first game with the Rangers. He totaled eight goals with nine assists in his first season. Kraftcheck's second and final season with the Rangers was cut short by an ankle injury. His rights were dealt to the Cleveland Barons in 1953 in exchange for defenseman Bob Chrystal (see above).

Pat Hannigan

NYR Debut: November 9, 1960 (vs. Detroit Red Wings, lost 4–3)
Regular Season Games with Rangers: 109
Playoff Games with Rangers: 4

In early November of 1960, the Rangers sent left winger Eddie Shack to the Toronto Maple Leafs for a left winger that had one game of NHL experience. Pat Hannigan was brought up by the Maple Leafs after having a brilliant season with the Rochester Americans of the American Hockey League. During the 1959–60 season, Hannigan scored 62 points (29 goals, 33 assists) in 65 games. The Rangers were hoping to see similar production out of Hannigan who played two seasons and scored 19 goals. In four playoff games, Hannigan did not record a point.

Al Hamilton

NYR Debut: February 2, 1966 (at Chicago Black Hawks, lost 4–3)
Regular Season Games with Rangers: 81
Playoff Games with Rangers: 6
Also wore: #25

In parts of four seasons with the Rangers, defenseman Al Hamilton was a victim of bad timing. Hamilton joined the team at a time when they had such stalwart defensemen as Brad Park, Jim Neilson, and Arnie Brown. Hamilton debuted with the Rangers and the NHL as a nineteen-year-old in the 1965–66 season, but only played in four games. The Edmonton, Alberta, native spent most of his Rangers' tenure with their minor league affiliates.

After his Ranger career, Hamilton went on to the World Hockey Association with the Edmonton Oilers. When the team joined the NHL in 1979, Hamilton played one more season. He wore #3 with the Oilers and it became the first number in franchise history to be retired.

Wilfred "Bucko" McDonald

NYR Debut: November 27, 1943 (at Montreal Canadiens, lost 6–3)
Regular Season Games with Rangers: 81
Playoff Games with Rangers: 0

Wilfred McDonald was reputed to have acquired the nickname "Bucko" as a youngster because he was "athletically inclined." The Ontario-born Irishman was a three-time Stanley Cup winner and also a professional lacrosse player in the Canadian Professional League.

After winning two Stanley Cups with Detroit and one with Toronto, McDonald joined the Rangers in November of 1943. In parts of two seasons, McDonald scored 7 goals with 15 assists. He retired after his second Ranger season of 1944–45.

Miloslav Horava

NYR Debut: March 1, 1989 (vs. Toronto Maple Leafs, won 7–4)
Regular Season Games with Rangers: 80
Playoff Games with Rangers: 2

Czechoslovakian-born Miloslav Horava was already an international star when he made his NHL debut with the Rangers in March of 1989. Horava had already played in two Olympic Games, and over 200 games for the Czech National Team. The defenseman was a ninth-round pick of the Edmonton Oilers in the 1981 NHL Entry Draft. He remained in Europe and was traded to the Rangers in 1986.

Horava played six games in his first season, but it was the 1989–90 campaign where he showed glimpses of the offensive talent that scouts saw during his days in Europe. The twenty-eight-year-old had 14 points in 45 games and helped the Rangers make the playoffs. In Horava's final season, he was plagued by injuries and limited to just 29 games. He returned to play in Europe and would participate in two more Olympics.

Don Awrey

NYR Debut: October 12, 1977 (vs. Vancouver Canucks, won 6–3)

Regular Season Games with Rangers: 78

Playoff Games with Rangers: 3

Photo courtesy of Ken Tash.

Another Bruin import of the late '70s.

The Rangers and Boston Bruins have always been fierce rivals, but never more so than in the 1970s. Both teams were perennial Stanley Cup contenders, and the rivalry reached new heights when Boston beat the Rangers in six games in the 1972 Stanley Cup Finals.

The Rangers knew all about hard hitting defenseman Don Awrey from playing against him in those emotionally charged games. The thirty-four-year-old defenseman signed a free agent contract with the Rangers in October of 1977. Awrey played in just one season with the Rangers, as he became a victim of a numbers game as the team overhauled their roster to add younger players.

Curt Giles

NYR Debut: November 14, 1986 (vs. Philadelphia Flyers, won 2–1)

Regular Season Games with Rangers: 74

Playoff Games with Rangers: 5

In two separate tenures with the Minnesota North Stars, defenseman Curt Giles had a short tenure with the Rangers sandwiched in-between.

Giles played parts of seven seasons in Minnesota before he was traded to the Rangers along with wingers Tony McKegney and Troy Mallette for center Bob Brooke in November of 1986. He played 61 games and scored 19 points. Giles played 13 games and had no points and was a minus-5 in 13 games. A little over a year after he was acquired, Giles was traded back to Minnesota.

Bill Baker

NYR Debut: October 6, 1982 (vs. Washington Capitals, lost 5–4)
Regular Season Games with Rangers: 70
Playoff Games with Rangers: 2

American-born defenseman Bill Baker is best known for being a member of the 1980 Gold Medal-winning US Hockey team that stunned the world with their upset victory in Lake Placid. Baker played his only full season in his final NHL season with the Rangers in the 1982–83 season.

The native of Grand Rapids, Minnesota, was a third-round pick of the Montreal Canadiens in the 1976 NHL Amateur Draft. He was traded to Colorado in March of 1981, and seven months later was dealt to the St. Louis Blues in exchange for defenseman and current Rangers broadcaster Joe Micheletti. Baker had 4 goals and 14 assists in 70 games during his one season with the Rangers. A year later, he played for the Tulsa Oilers of the Central Hockey League and retired after the 1983–84 season.

Tim Bothwell

NYR Debut: January 15, 1979 (vs. Minnesota North Stars, lost 8–1)
Regular Season Games with Rangers: 62
Playoff Games with Rangers: 9
Also wore: #2

Tim Bothwell knew how to use his 6-foot-3 frame to his advantage. Known as a hard-hitting defenseman who had the hands to handle the puck, Bothwell was signed as a free agent out of Brown University in June of 1978.

Bothwell split time between the Rangers and their AHL affiliate in New Haven during his four-year tenure. His best season was 1979–80, when he played in 45 games and scored four goals with six assists. The Rangers placed him on waivers after the 1981–82 season, and he was claimed by the St. Louis Blues in October of 1982.

Jere Gillis

NYR Debut: November 14, 1980 (vs. Pittsburgh Penguins, 3–3 tie)
Regular Season Games with Rangers: 61
Playoff Games with Rangers: 14

NEW YORK RANGERS BY THE NUMBERS

The Rangers acquired defenseman Jere Gillis along with defenseman Jeff Bandura from the Vancouver Canucks for defenseman Mario Marois and left winger Jim Mayer in November of 1980. Gillis was the fourth-overall pick of the Canucks in the 1977 NHL Amateur Draft, and spent parts of four seasons with Vancouver before coming to New York.

Gillis had a very good first year with the Rangers as he scored a goal in his first game and finished the 1980–81 season with 10 goals with 10 assists in 35 games. He had 12 points in 26 games in the 1981–82 season, but was traded to the Quebec Nordiques in December of 1981.

Gillis's post playing career was more exciting than his time on the ice with the Rangers. The Montreal native became a professional stuntman who has appeared in such movies as *Pacific Rim* and *300*.

Mike McMahon

NYR Debut: November 27, 1963 (vs. Detroit Red Wings, won 3–2)
Regular Season Games with Rangers: 61
Playoff Games with Rangers: 0
Also wore: #2 and #4

Defenseman Mike McMahon made his Rangers debut just five days after the assassination of President John F. Kennedy. It was the Rangers' second game since the tragic event.

McMahon had two separate stints in New York. He signed with the Rangers as a free agent in 1959, and was brought up in November of 1963. McMahon, who was the son of former NHLer Mike McMahon Sr., played in 18 games in his first season. After playing just one game in the 1964–65 season, McMahon got his most extensive time the next season when he appeared in 41 games.

The Quebec native was claimed by the Montreal Canadiens in the 1966 NHL Intra-League Draft. He eventually returned to the Rangers in October of 1971, and played one more game with the Blueshirts before he was chosen by the Minnesota franchise in the World Hockey Association in 1972.

Al MacNeil

NYR Debut: October 19, 1966 (vs. Chicago Black Hawks, lost 6–3)
Regular Season Games with Rangers: 58
Playoff Games with Rangers: 4

Al MacNeil came to the Rangers in 1966 and helped them return to the play-offs for the first time in five seasons. The Rangers claimed the defenseman from the Montreal Canadiens in the June 1966 NHL Intra-League Draft. Mac-Neil played 58 games and then four more in the 1967 postseason, but was left unprotected in the June 1967 expansion draft where he was claimed by the Pittsburgh Penguins.

Bob Kirkpatrick

NYR Debut: October 31, 1942 (at Toronto Maple Leafs, lost 7–2)
Regular Season Games with Rangers: 49
Playoff Games with Rangers: 0

Twenty-five-year-old center Bob Kirkpatrick signed with the Rangers as a free agent in 1941. He put up some impressive numbers during the 1941–42 season with the Rangers' affiliate in the Eastern Hockey League, the New York Rovers. Kirkpatrick scored 34 goals with 43 assists for 77 points in 59 games.

The native of Saskatchewan then joined the Rangers for the 1942–43 season. For most of his 49 games, he played on the top line with Hall of Famers Lynn Patrick and Bryan Hextall. Kirkpatrick tallied 24 points (12 goals, 12 assists) in his one and only NHL season.

Dylan McIlrath

NYR Debut: October 18, 1951 (at Montreal Canadiens, lost 3–2)
Regular Season Games with Rangers: 127
Playoff Games with Rangers: 0

A 6-foot-5 defenseman, Dylan McIlrath was the Rangers' 10th overall selection in the 2010 NHL Entry Draft. The Winnipeg native brought size and a blistering slap shot to the rink, but never really developed during parts of four seasons with the Rangers.

McIlrath's signature Ranger moment came in February of 2016, when he fought Philadelphia Flyers winger Wayne Simmonds as payback for a sucker punch on Rangers captain Ryan McDonagh in a Game Eight days previous. McIlrath never really endeared himself to head coach Alain Vigneault, and was traded to the Florida Panthers in November of 2016.

Syl Apps Jr.

NYR Debut: October 10, 1970 (at St. Louis Blues, lost 3–1)

Regular Season Games with Rangers: 31

Playoff Games with Rangers: 0

Syl Apps Jr. drew comparisons to his Hall of Fame father, Syl Apps Sr. The scouting report read: "good skater, good puck handler and play maker, just like his father."

Apps Jr. was a fourth-round pick of the Rangers in the 1964 NHL Amateur Draft. He worked his way through the minors until he was brought up for the 1970–71 season. The Rangers were not thrilled with his play, and he got limited ice time during his 31-game tenure. In January of 1971, Apps Jr. was traded to Pittsburgh in exchange for left winger Glen Sather.

Bruce Cline

NYR Debut: October 31, 1956 (at Toronto Maple Leafs, lost 7–2)

Regular Season Games with Rangers: 30

Playoff Games with Rangers: 0

The Rangers caught wind of right winger Bruce Cline after he won the American Hockey League's top rookie award in 1956. The Quebec native was signed by the Rangers as a free agent in 1950, but his game did not start to develop until he totaled 57 points for the Providence Reds in the 1955–56 season. Cline was named the winner of the Dudley "Red" Garrett Memorial award as the league's top rookie. He joined the Rangers for the 1956–57 season and amassed just five points in 30 games. After his only NHL season, Cline played 11 more years in the AHL.

Bobby Sheehan

NYR Debut: April 18, 1979 (at Philadelphia Flyers, won Game Two Stanley Cup Quarterfinals 7–1)

Regular Season Games with Rangers: 0

Playoff Games with Rangers: 15

Bobby Sheehan is credited with having the most unique Rangers career in franchise history. The American-born, 5-foot-7 center did not appear in any regular season games for the Rangers, yet became a huge factor in the 1979 Stanley Cup Playoffs.

Sheehan had completed his season with the New Haven Nighthawks of the AHL and the Rangers had lost Game One of their quarterfinal series against the Philadelphia Flyers. Rangers head coach Fred Shero felt the team needed more speed in the lineup, so he decided to call up Sheehan to center a line with Ron Duguay and Pat Hickey.

The move worked as Sheehan helped spark the Rangers on a magical run to qualify for the 1979 Stanley Cup Final. The thirty-year-old scored his first Stanley Cup playoff goal in Game Four against the Flyers as the Rangers won the series in five. The diminutive pivot man from Weymouth, Massachusetts, was a huge factor in the upset win over the New York Islanders in the semifinals.

Sheehan had a goal and an assist to key a 4–1 win in Game One. He scored a goal in the Game Two loss and then opened the scoring in Game Three with his fourth goal of the playoffs. The Rangers went on to beat the Islanders in six games. In the Finals, Sheehan had one assist but the Rangers lost in five to the Montreal Canadiens.

Sheehan never played another game for the Rangers. After the season, he was traded to the Colorado Rockies.

The following played less than 30 games with NYR:

Jeff Woywitka - defenseman

NYR Debut: October 15, 2011 (at New York Islanders, lost 4–2)
Regular Season Games with Rangers: 27
Playoff Games with Rangers: 0

Mark Tinordi - defenseman

NYR Debut: November 4, 1987 (at Edmonton Oilers, lost 7–2)
Regular Season Games with Rangers: 24
Playoff Games with Rangers: 0

Bryan Hextall Jr. - center

NYR Debut: February 2, 1963 (at Toronto Maple Leafs, 2–2 tie)
Regular Season Games with Rangers: 21
Playoff Games with Rangers: 0

Photo by Sarah Connors via Wikimedia Commons.

Jeff Woywitka donned the Broadway Hat despite only playing 27 games as a Ranger.

Mike Korney - defenseman

NYR Debut: October 15, 1978 (vs. Colorado Rockies, won 4–1)
Regular Season Games with Rangers: 18
Playoff Games with Rangers: 0

Dean Kennedy - defenseman

NYR Debut: December 14, 1988 (vs. New York Islanders, won 2–1)
Regular Season Games with Rangers: 16
Playoff Games with Rangers: 0

Larry Patey - center

NYR Debut: March 14, 1984 (vs. Philadelphia Flyers, won 6–3)
Regular Season Games with Rangers: 16
Playoff Games with Rangers: 0

Bob Blackburn - defenseman

NYR Debut: February 23, 1969 (vs. Boston Bruins, won 9–0)
Regular Season Games with Rangers: 11
Playoff Games with Rangers: 0

Sandy Fitzpatrick - center

NYR Debut: March 14, 1965 (vs. Montreal Canadiens, lost 6–4)
Regular Season Games with Rangers: 4 (0 points)
Playoff Games with Rangers: 0

Archie Fraser - center

NYR Debut: October 30, 1943 (at Toronto Maple Leafs, lost 5–2)
Regular Season Games with Rangers: 3 (1 assist)
Playoff Games with Rangers: 0

Ken Hammond - defenseman

NYR Debut: November 2, 1988 (at Buffalo Sabres, lost 6–4)

Regular Season Games with Rangers: 3 (0 points)

Playoff Games with Rangers: 0

Ralph Keller - defenseman

NYR Debut: March 9, 1963 (at Montreal Canadiens, won 5–2)

Regular Season Games with Rangers: 3 (1 goal, 0 assists)

Playoff Games with Rangers: 0

Bob Jones - left wing

NYR Debut: January 2, 1969 (vs. Boston Bruins, lost 4–2)

Regular Season Games with Rangers: 2

Playoff Games with Rangers: 0

Dean Turner - defenseman

NYR Debut: February 24, 1979 (at Toronto Maple Leafs, won 4–2)

Regular Season Games with Rangers: 1

Playoff Games with Rangers: 0

#7: ROD

Rod Gilbert

NYR Debut: November 27, 1960 (vs. Chicago Black Hawks, 3–3 tie)

Regular Season Games with Rangers: 1,065

Playoff Games with Rangers: 79

Also wore: #16

In the history of the Rangers' franchise, only five players have worn #7. One of those is arguably the greatest Ranger in the team's storied history.

Rod Gilbert played his entire 18-year career in a Rangers uniform. He is the all-time franchise leader with 1,065 games played, 406 goals, and 1,021 points. Gilbert was a 30-goal scorer five times, scored 20 or more 12 times, and had a career-best 43 goals during the 1971–72 season.

Gilbert played in a team record nine All-Star games and was part of the famous "Goal-A-Game" (GAG) line that was centered by Jean Ratelle and also featured left winger Vic Hadfield.

Mr. Ranger.

Hockey card from the public domain via Wikimedia Commons.

Gilbert's career, however, came close to never getting started. While playing in juniors during the 1959–60 season, he tripped over some debris on the ice and broke his back. Blood clots developed in Gilbert's legs and doctors were concerned that they may have to amputate. The Rangers helped Gilbert recover, and he rewarded their faith in him with 54 goals and 103 points in 47 games while playing with the Guelph Biltmores during the 1960–61 season.

In his first game in November of 1960 at Madison Square Garden, Gilbert had an assist on the game-tying goal against Chicago. He appeared in one game in each of the 1960–61 and 1961–62 seasons. Because of an injury during the postseason, Gilbert was added to the Rangers' roster for the 1962 Stanley Cup Playoffs. The Montreal native had an assist in his first postseason game as the Rangers beat Toronto 5–4 at Madison Square Garden in Game Three of the semifinals. Gilbert delighted the Garden crowd in Game Four with two goals as the Rangers evened the series. The Rangers went on to lose the series in six, but Gilbert had made quite an impression with the team and the diehard fans.

Gilbert's playoff performance convinced the team that he was ready to be a full-time player. Beginning with the 1962–63 season, Gilbert did not miss a game for three straight years while scoring 60 goals over that span. In the 1965–66 season, Gilbert was limited to 34 games because he needed a second spinal fusion surgery.

The twenty-five-year-old right winger came back with a bang in 1966–67, scoring 28 goals and leading the Rangers to the playoffs for the first time in five seasons. The fan favorite had two goals and two assists as the Rangers were swept in the semifinals by the Montreal Canadiens in four games. In the 1970 Stanley Cup Playoffs, the Rangers lost in six but Gilbert was the Rangers' best player. The right winger scored a point in all six games, highlighted by a two-goal game in Game Four that evened the series at two apiece.

The famous "GAG" line had perfect symmetry in that all three members started to come into their own as hockey players around the same time. The 1971–72 season was a remarkable display of offensive production from the hockey trio. Hadfield became the first Ranger to score 50 goals in a season and the entire line may have had 50 goals each were it not for injuries that curtailed Ratelle's (46 goals) and Gilbert's (43 goals) seasons.

The Rangers made it all the way to the 1972 Stanley Cup Finals, but lost to the Boston Bruins in a hard fought, six-game series. Gilbert acquitted himself very well once again as he scored 7 goals with 8 assists in 16 games. In the four-game sweep of the Chicago Black Hawks in the Stanley Cup Semifinals, Gilbert had a goal and three assists in Game Four. In the Finals, Gilbert had a two-goal game to help the Rangers win Game Three.

The line essentially broke up after Hadfield was traded to Pittsburgh in May of 1974. Gilbert, however, proved to be incredibly consistent. From the 1973–74 through the 1975–76 seasons, Gilbert scored 36 goals in each of the three seasons. In the 1974 Stanley Cup Semifinals against the Philadelphia Flyers, Gilbert scored the game-winning goal in overtime of Game Four.

On December 12, 1976, Gilbert had three assists in his 1000th NHL game. He lasted only 19 games into the 1977–78 season before deciding to hang up his skates.

On October, 14, 1979, Gilbert was honored by being the first Ranger to have his number retired and hoisted to the ceiling at Madison Square Garden. He was inducted into the Hockey Hall of Fame in 1982.

Phil Watson

NYR Debut: November 19, 1935 (vs. Detroit Red Wings, 2–2 OT tie)

Regular Season Games with Rangers: 546

Playoff Games with Rangers: 45

Also wore: #15

The Rangers knew they had some competition for the services of twenty-year-old center Phil Watson. The Montreal native was highly touted while leading the Montreal Royals of the Quebec Junior Hockey League to the Allan Cup Finals. The hometown Canadiens were also very interested, but Rangers general manager Lester Patrick won out and lured Watson to New York with a contract worth a reported $4500.

Watson was a fiery player with a temper that never quit. Opponents tried to get under his skin to throw him off of his game, and many times it worked. Watson didn't speak much English when he joined the Rangers in 1935. There was one reported incident where an opposing veteran player kept teasing Watson to the extent that, in his broken English, he called the player a "you lousy been has."

Watson split his first season between the Rangers and their Philadelphia Ramblers affiliate in the Canadian-American League, despite trying to talk Patrick into keeping him with the big club from the start.

Watson played a large role in the Rangers' 1940 Stanley Cup Championship. He scored two goals in the six-game semifinal win over the Boston Bruins, including the game winner in Game One. In the Finals against Toronto, Watson was a one-man show in the series-clinching sixth game that went into overtime.

With the score tied at two in the third period, Watson appeared to score the go-ahead goal off of a scramble in front of the net, but the officials ruled otherwise and the game remained tied. With under a minute remaining, Watson's pass sent teammate Dutch Hiller in on a breakaway, but Maple

Leafs goaltender Turk Broda made a great save to send the game to overtime. In the extra session, Watson's pass set up Bryan Hextall for an historic goal that gave the Rangers their third Stanley Cup victory.

Watson played 12 of his 13 years with the Rangers. The one exception was the 1943–44 season when he was loaned to the Canadiens, an agreement that was completed due to wartime travel restrictions.

Watson's temper got the best of him during his stint in Montreal. In January of 1944, during a game in Toronto, he struck linesman Jim Primeau. NHL president Red Dutton initially suspended Watson indefinitely, but the Montreal center sat out only one game before returning to the lineup. Watson's one year in Montreal paid off with his second Stanley Cup Championship. During the four game Finals sweep of Chicago, Watson scored the game-winning goal in Game Three.

He was returned to the Rangers for the 1944–45 season as part of the original loan agreement. In his final season of 1947–48, Watson scored a career-high 18 goals. The thirty-three-year-old retired after that season, and eventually became the head coach of the Rangers for parts of five seasons in the late 1950s.

Don Raleigh

NYR Debut: October 30, 1943 (at Toronto Maple Leafs, lost 5–2)
Regular Season Games with Rangers: 535
Playoff Games with Rangers: 18
Also wore: #9

When seventeen-year-old center Don Raleigh made his NHL debut in October of 1943, he became the youngest Rangers' regular in franchise history. It's a distinction that still holds to this day. Unfortunately, the young forward suffered a fractured jaw during a game against Toronto as the result of an errant stick and was limited to just 15 games in his rookie campaign.

"Bones" played his entire 10-year career with the Rangers, but it was interrupted for a three-year period when he served in the Canadian Army. Raleigh was nicknamed Bones because of his skinny 5-foot-11, 150-pound frame. He once bragged that "he didn't get hit because he knew how to collapse his body." Raleigh was a slick puck handler and playmaker.

After his first season, Raleigh's military service lasted three years before he returned to the Rangers for the 1947–48 season. His best year was in 1951–52, when he scored 19 goals with 42 assists. Bones's shining moment with the Rangers came during the 1950 Finals against the Detroit Red Wings. With the Rangers trailing in the series three games to one, Raleigh kept the Rangers' hopes alive by scoring game-winning overtime goals in Games Five and Six, before they lost the series in seven.

Raleigh, who served as the Rangers' captain from 1953 until his final game in December of 1955, was feeling the pressure of a league that was beginning to take on bigger and more physical players who could also pass and score goals. That was never more evident than when feisty Phil Watson took over as the head coach in 1955. After 29 games, Raleigh decided to retire at the age of twenty-nine.

Frank Boucher

NYR Debut: November 16, 1926 (vs. Montreal Maroons, won 1–0)
Regular Season Games with Rangers: 533
Playoff Games with Rangers: 54
Also wore: #17

If anyone deserves to be called "Mr. Ranger," it's Hall of Famer Frank Boucher. The Ottawa native spent 34 years of his life in the Ranger organization as a player, coach, and general manager.

Boucher, who was an original Ranger, actually began his NHL career with the Ottawa Senators as a twenty-year-old in the 1921–22 season. After four years with Vancouver in the Western Hockey League, he was traded to the Rangers in September of 1926. Boucher centered "the Bread Line" that featured the Cook brothers, Bill and Bun. The threesome turned into one of the most potent lines in NHL history.

In the first game, Bill Cook scored the winning goal in a 1–0 win but Boucher had a fight with Montreal

Another Mr. Ranger.

Photo from the public domain.

Maroons' center Bill Phillips and was fined $15 by the NHL. The irony of that incident was that Boucher would go on to win seven Lady Byng Trophies (Best Sportsmanship) with the Rangers.

Boucher was a key member of the Rangers' team that won their first Stanley Cup in 1928. He scored 23 goals in the regular season and then led all players in goals (7) and assists (3) during the playoffs. In the Stanley Cup Finals against the Montreal Maroons, Boucher won Game Two with an overtime goal and scored four of the Rangers' five total goals in the series.

The 5-foot-9 center proved to be a clutch player during his 13-year playing career with the Blueshirts. In the 1933 Stanley Cup Quarterfinals against the Montreal Canadiens, he set up the first of two goals in a 27-second span of the first period that stunned the opposition as the Rangers went on to a 5–2 win. Boucher scored the fifth goal of the game, which proved to be a key because the two-game series was decided by total number of goals. He also scored a goal in the semifinals against Detroit and had an assist in the Finals (the series was a best-of-five in 1933) as the Rangers beat the Toronto Maple Leafs three games to one.

Boucher continued his playing career for five more seasons, but retired after playing in only 15 games during the 1937–38 season. The Rangers had already planned for Boucher's post-playing career and had named him the head coach of the New York Rovers, the club's minor league affiliate for the 1938–39 season. The team played their home games at Madison Square Garden, which allowed Boucher the opportunity to get used to being behind the same bench as the big club.

General manager Lester Patrick decided to step away from his added duties as head coach in 1939. After one season with the Rovers, Boucher was hired by Patrick to be his replacement. It couldn't have gone any better for the first-year head coach as the Rangers won their third Stanley Cup Championship. Boucher laid claim to being part of all three Stanley Cup winners.

After the 1941–42 season, when the team finished first in the regular season, the Rangers began a period of their history where they were less than successful. Players got older and some of the younger ones were serving in the military during World War II. Things got so bad during the 1943–44 season that Boucher, at forty-two years old, came out of retirement to play 15 games where he scored 4 goals and had 10 assists. As a player, Boucher went out with a bang. In his final game on February 10, 1944, he scored his final Ranger goal in an 8–3 loss to the Detroit Red Wings at the Garden.

Boucher continued to coach the team, but also became the general manager when Patrick stepped down. Boucher eventually stepped away from coaching but went back behind the bench for the 1953–54 season after which he stepped down from both positions.

George "Red" Sullivan

NYR Debut: October 12, 1956 (at Chicago Black Hawks, won 3–0)
Regular Season Games with Rangers: 322
Playoff Games with Rangers: 6

When the Rangers acquired center "Red" Sullivan from the Chicago Black Hawks in June of 1956, he would have some pretty big shoes to fill. Popular right winger Wally Hergesheimer, who was the Rangers' leading goal scorer in the early 1950s, was dealt to the Black Hawks in part because the Rangers felt he was too injury prone. Sullivan was an aggressive-type forward who wasn't afraid to challenge goaltenders, particularly Montreal Canadiens goalie Jacques Plante. He would be paid back for that harassment.

In late November of his first season in New York, Sullivan was injured when he was speared by Montreal Canadiens defenseman Doug Harvey which ruptured his spleen. The injury was so severe that a priest was summoned to the hospital to administer last rites. Sullivan was able to recover and returned later that season, not missing a game for the remainder of his Rangers career.

Sullivan was a good fit in New York. He enjoyed the night life and admitted that he broke a curfew or two, but was always ready to play. Sullivan served as team captain from 1957–58 through his final season of 1960–61. The Ontario native went on to become the head coach of the Rangers for parts of four seasons from 1962–63 through 1965–66.

#8: EIGHTS BEGIN WITH A GUY NAMED STANLEY

Allan Stanley

> **NYR Debut:** December 11, 1948 (at Detroit Red Wings, lost 5–3)
>
> **Regular Season Games with NYR:** 307
>
> **Playoff Games with NYR:** 12

Defenseman Allan Stanley, who was the first Ranger to wear #8, was a highly touted prospect when he was acquired from Providence of the American Hockey League in December of 1948 for three players and an astonishing sum of $70,000. The Rangers were in a down period and needed a young player to stir interest in the team, so general manager Frank Boucher worked with publicity director Stan Saplin in an effort to hype Stanley as an up-and-coming star.

With the hype came the pressure of performing in front of a very critical fan base. Stanley's career got off to a good start. He finished second in the voting to teammate Pentti Lund for the Calder Trophy. He may have won the award had he not had an ankle injury which slightly derailed his season. In the 1950 Stanley Cup Play-

Scored first goals in Games Six and Seven of 1950 Stanley Cup Final.

offs, Stanley scored the first goal of Games Six and Seven of the Finals, but the Rangers lost to Detroit.

The 6-foot-1, 270-pound defenseman was named captain in 1951, but the Rangers continued to miss the playoffs and Stanley became the scapegoat for the team's misfortunes. Every time he touched the puck, he was being booed unmercifully. During the 1953–54 season, he played 10 games and then was stunningly sent to Vancouver of the Western Hockey League for the remainder of the season. Stanley returned to play 12 games, but was traded to the Chicago Black Hawks in November of 1954. Stanley's career path took him to Toronto where he won four Stanley Cups with the Maple Leafs in the 1960s. He was inducted into the Hockey Hall of Fame in 1981.

Steve "Sarge" Vickers

NYR Debut: October 7, 1972 (at Detroit Red Wings, lost 5–3)

Regular Season Games with NYR: 698

Playoff Games with NYR: 68

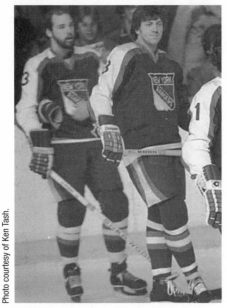

Photo courtesy of Ken Tash.

"Sarge" played his entire career as a Ranger.

The Rangers made left winger Steve Vickers their first-round pick and 10th overall in the 1971 NHL Amateur Draft. A little over a year later, Vickers made his debut and had a spectacular first season that culminated with the Calder Trophy as the NHL's best rookie. He scored his first goal in his first game, and finished with 30 for the season. The highlight of Vickers's first season came on November 12 and 15, when he became the first rookie and first Ranger to score back-to-back hat tricks, which he did against the Los Angeles Kings and Philadelphia Flyers, respectively.

The nickname of "Sarge" was given to Vickers by teammate Pete Stemkowski, because he wore an old army shirt to practice. Vickers's goal total increased in each of his first three years, with a career high of 41 in the 1974–75 season.

Sarge played a big role in the Rangers' run to the 1979 Stanley Cup Final. He scored five goals and added three assists. In the semifinal upset of the New York Islanders, he scored a big goal in the Rangers' 3–1 win in Game Three. Vickers brought the sellout crowd at the Garden to its feet when he stole the puck from Islanders defenseman Stefan Persson, skated past the Islanders' net, and then scored on a wraparound to beat Islanders goaltender Chico Resch. The third period goal gave the Rangers a two-goal cushion and a two games to one lead in the series. In the first round of the 1980 playoffs, Vickers set a Ranger record for the fastest overtime goal, as he scored 33 seconds into the extra session to beat the Atlanta Flames, 2–1, in Game One of a four-game sweep.

The Rangers left winger etched his name into the franchise record books on February 18, 1976, when he scored seven points (three goals, four assists) in an 11–4 victory against the Washington Capitals at Madison Square Garden.

The Ontario native, who played his entire 10-year career with the Rangers, scored double-digit goals in his first nine seasons. Vickers began his final season of 1981–82 with the Rangers' Springfield affiliate in the American Hockey League. First-year head coach Herb Brooks did not feel that Vickers fit what they were doing. He was brought up in mid-season and retired after the season. Vickers finished his career with 246 regular season goals and 24 playoff goals.

Bob Nevin

NYR Debut: February 22, 1964 (at Toronto Maple Leafs, lost 5–2)
Regular Season Games with NYR: 505
Playoff Games with NYR: 33
Also wore: #17

Bob Nevin never got the ice time in Toronto that he did during his seven and a half years with the Rangers. The right winger came to the Rangers as part of a huge seven-player deal with the Maple Leafs in February of 1964. Hall of Fame winger Andy Bathgate went back to Toronto, and it didn't take long for those involved to play against their former teams. On the day the trade was made, the Maple Leafs hosted the Rangers in the first of a home-and-home portion of the schedule. Bathgate had an assist and his new team beat his old team, 5–2, in Toronto and then 4–3 at Madison Square Garden as Nevin scored his first goal in a Rangers uniform.

Nevin played with two Stanley Cup winners in Toronto and was a solid playoff performer, but he struggled during his early playoff appearances with the Rangers. Nevin did not score a playoff goal with the Rangers until his fourth series and Game One of the 1970 Stanley Cup Semifinals against the Boston Bruins. In the 1971 Stanley Cup Quarterfinals against his old team, the Ontario native was a one-man wrecking crew as he led the Rangers past the Maple Leafs in six games. Nevin scored five goals in the series, all of them coming in the four wins, and capped off his fabulous series by scoring two goals in the series clincher, including the game-winning goal in overtime. A little over three weeks after the Rangers were eliminated by the Chicago Black Hawks in a seven-game, semifinal series, Nevin was traded to the Minnesota North Stars for future considerations that resulted in the acquisition of Bobby Rousseau. Nevin averaged over twenty goals per season with the Rangers and finished with a career total of 168.

Lou "Leapin' Louie" Fontinato

NYR Debut: October 27, 1954 (vs. Detroit Red Wings, lost 4–0)
Regular Season Games with NYR: 418
Playoff Games with NYR: 15

Photo from the public domain.

"Leapin' Lou" was known for his devastating hits.

During the 1955–56 season, rugged Ranger defenseman Lou Fontinato became the first player in NHL history to serve more than 200 minutes in the penalty box.

Fontinato joined the Rangers for the 1954–55 season to add some toughness to their defense corps. He was an instant hit with the fans because of his hard hitting and relentless style of play. In his very first game, the fans gave Fontinato a standing ovation and he had them roaring with his devastating hits on opponents. As the story goes, Fontinato got the nickname "Leapin' Louie" because he would leave his feet when he leveled an opponent with a body check.

Fontinato's physical style put him up against the toughest player in the game in a memorable incident that took place at Madison Square Garden on February 1, 1959, when the Rangers were hosting the Detroit Red Wings. Late in the first period, Fontinato came to the defense of his teammate Eddie Shack, who was being roughed up by Hall of Famer Gordie Howe. Fontinato got in some early punches, but once Howe absorbed the initial blows, he responded to the point that he broke the winger's nose.

In June of 1961, Fontinato was traded to the Montreal Canadiens for Hall of Fame defenseman Doug Harvey, who was in the twilight of his career. Unfortunately, Fontinato's career ended nearly two years later when he was involved in a horrific accident on the ice against the Rangers. Fontinato and Rangers' left winger Vic Hadfield crashed into the boards while chasing a loose puck. Fontinato's head slammed into the boards and broke his neck. He was paralyzed for a month and did not regain the feeling in his arms for four months. Nevertheless, his career on the ice was over.

Cecil Dillon

NYR Debut: January 1, 1931 (vs. Boston Bruins, lost 4–3 OT)
Regular Season Games with NYR: 409
Playoff Games with NYR: 38

Cecil Dillon was the Rangers' version of Lou Gehrig, as he did not miss a regular season game in his nine-and-a-half-year Rangers' career, a span of 409 games.

The Toledo, Ohio–born right winger was one of the few American-born players of that time. He joined the Rangers in January of 1931, and paid immediate dividends. In February, Dillon put on a show for the home fans as he scored both goals in a 2–0 whitewashing of the New York Americans, the Rangers' co-tenants at Madison Square Garden. The first goal came late in the first period, as Dillon went to the net and put a second rebound past Americans' goaltender

The Rangers' Lou Gehrig

Photo from the public domain.

Roy Worters. The second goal sent the Garden into a frenzy. After the Americans' stormed the Rangers' net with five skaters, Dillon played the puck in his own end and went end-to-end to beat Worters on a breakaway.

If there was an MVP award given for the 1933 Stanley Cup Playoffs, Dillon would've been a unanimous winner. The right winger led all scorers with 8 goals and 10 points in 8 games. Dillon scored three goals in the quarterfinals, two goals in the semifinals, and three more goals in the Finals against Toronto.

Dillon went on to play every game right through the 1938–39 season. Ironically, he played in the first game of the playoffs against Boston but missed his first game as a Ranger and the rest of the series beginning with Game Two. After that season, Dillon was traded to the Detroit Red Wings.

Darren Turcotte

NYR Debut: October 6, 1988 (at Chicago Blackhawks, 2–2 OT tie)
Regular Season Games with NYR: 325
Playoff Games with NYR: 25

He was born in Boston but he starred on Broadway.

Center Darren Turcotte was a sixth-round pick of the Rangers in the 1986 NHL Entry Draft. In his first game, the twenty-year-old skated on a line that featured Hall of Famers Guy LaFleur and Marcel Dionne. After the game, the young center admitted he was in awe of his linemates.

Turcotte was sent back to the minors after six games and was recalled again in February. In his second game back, he scored his first NHL goal against New Jersey Devils goaltender Sean Burke. He scored his first hat trick against the Toronto Maple Leafs on March 1, 1989, and began to show signs of being the goal scorer that the Rangers thought he would be when they'd drafted him.

In his first four full seasons with the Rangers, Turcotte scored 113 goals, but wasn't a consistent postseason performer. He made the playoffs four times with the Rangers and, in the first three, scored only two goals in 17 games. In the 1992 Patrick Division Semifinals against the Devils, Turcotte scored two goals in the seventh and deciding game, but had only one goal in the semifinal loss to the Pittsburgh Penguins.

Mike Keenan's hiring as head coach in 1993 spelled the end of Turcotte's tenure with the Rangers. Keenan employed Turcotte on the fourth line because he felt he was a soft player who didn't fit the philosophy of the team. After playing 13 games in the 1993–94 season, Turcotte, along with defenseman James Patrick (another player that Keenan did not want) was traded to the Hartford Whalers for right winger Steve Larmer, left winger Nick Kypreos, defenseman Barry Richter, and a draft pick. It turned out to be a case of bad timing for the Massachusetts native, as the Whalers finished out of the playoffs and the Rangers won the Stanley Cup.

Grant Warwick

NYR Debut: November 1, 1941 (at Toronto Maple Leafs, won 4–3)
Regular Season Games with NYR: 293
Playoff Games with NYR: 6

Diminutive right winger Grant Warwick became the second Ranger player, other than left winger Kilby McDonald in 1939–40, to win the Calder Trophy as the NHL's best rookie for the 1941–42 season. The 5-foot-6 native of Saskatchewan avoided military service due to a medical condition that left him nearly deaf, but healthy enough to battle on the ice.

Warwick had a pair of 20-goal years during parts of seven seasons with the Rangers. His best year was 1944–45, when he scored 20 goals with 22 assists. He was limited to 18 games the year before after suffering a skull fracture.

In February of 1948, Warwick was traded to the Boston Bruins. In his Ranger career, Warwick scored 117 goals with 116 assists in 293 games. Warwick was inducted into the Saskatchewan Sports Hall of Fame in 1986. Grant's younger brother, Billy, played 14 games as a Ranger.

Kevin Klein

NYR Debut: January 23, 2014 (vs. St. Louis Blues, lost 2–1)
Regular Season Games with NYR: 224
Playoff Games with NYR: 45

In January 2014, the Rangers sent defenseman Michael Del Zotto to the Nashville Predators for veteran defenseman Kevin Klein. The Rangers needed a right-handed defenseman to balance out their corps of back liners, so the left-handed Del Zotto was used as bait.

With a blistering slap shot, Klein was solid playing the point on the power play. He played in all 25 games in the 2014 Stanley Cup Playoffs, adding a goal and three assists.

In the next two seasons, Klein put up identical numbers with 9 goals and 17 assists for 26 points, but his play began to drop off as injuries began to take their toll. In his final season of 2016–17, Klein missed time with a back issue and played just one game in the postseason. After the season, Klein announced his retirement from the NHL, despite having one season left on his contract.

Dutch Hiller

NYR Debut: February 26, 1938 (vs. Toronto Maple Leafs, won 4–2)

Regular Season Games with NYR: 198

Playoff Games with NYR: 23

Also wore: #14 and #18

The Rangers signed speedy left winger Dutch Hiller as a free agent in February of 1938 after his dominating performance as a member of the New York Rovers of the Eastern League. During the 1937–38 season, Hiller scored 26 goals and had 56 points.

Hiller played parts of five seasons with the Rangers. In his first game, he skated on a line with center Phil Watson and fellow winger and Hall of Famer Bryan Hextall. Later on, he would play on a line with Alf Pike and Clint "Snuffy" Smith that helped lead the Rangers to the 1940 Stanley Cup Championship.

Hiller's speed is what made him stand out. According to Hiller's coach, Frank Boucher, "Nobody could keep up with Dutch. Nobody."

Hiller's rights were sold to Detroit in April of 1941, but he was with Montreal when he was returned to the Rangers in 1943 to put up his best season with the Blueshirts. Hiller scored 18 goals with 22 assists in his final Rangers season of 1943–44. After that season, he was returned to the Canadiens.

Brandon Prust

NYR Debut: February 2, 2010 (at Los Angeles Kings, lost 2–1)

Regular Season Games with NYR: 190

Playoff Games with NYR: 24

Left winger Brandon Prust added some toughness and defensive prowess to the Rangers when he was acquired from the Calgary Flames in February of 2010.

Prust was not expected to add much scoring but, in his first full season with the Rangers in 2010–11, he was one of seven players to score at least ten goals and be involved in at least ten fights. Prust, who was strong on the penalty kill unit, scored seven shorthanded goals with the Rangers including five during the 2010–11 season.

The Ontario native did a lot of the "dirty work" with the Rangers, but was recognized for it. Prust was awarded the Steven McDonald Extra Effort

Award at the end of the 2010–11 season. As voted by the fans, the award goes to the player who "goes above and beyond the call of duty."

After the 2011–12 season, Prust became a free agent and signed with the Montreal Canadiens. While with Montreal, Prust faced his old team in the 2014 Eastern Conference Finals and was suspended for two games for a hit that broke the jaw of Rangers center Derek Stepan.

Hard work earned Prust a Steven McDonald Award.

Marek Malik

NYR Debut: October 5, 2005 (at Philadelphia Flyers, won 5–3)

Regular Season Games with NYR: 185

Playoff Games with NYR: 14

A 6-foot-6 defenseman, Marek Malik was never known for his offense, though his shining moment in a Ranger uniform came in a shootout.

Malik was a nine-year veteran when the Rangers signed the thirty-year-old as a free agent in August of 2005. The National Hockey League returned after missing the entire 2004–05 season due to a labor dispute, and it was the first season that the shootout would be used to decide regular season games. Malik scored six goals with the Rangers but the one that didn't count for him personally, but helped the team win, was an eye opener.

The Rangers and Washington Capitals were engaged in a shootout at Madison Square Garden. On November 26, 2005, the teams were still tied after a record-setting 14 rounds when the Ranger defenseman was called upon to take his shot. Malik skated in on Capitals goaltender Olaf Kolzig and put the puck between his legs before he put it in top shelf for the win in what was a record 15-round shootout. After scoring his memorable goal, Malik implored the crowd with a half gesture of his arm that said "had it all the way."

The Czech Republic native went on to play two more seasons in New York before signing as a free agent with the Tampa Bay Lightning in 2008.

117

Robbie Ftorek

NYR Debut: January 7, 1982 (vs. Vancouver Canucks, won 4–1)
Regular Season Games with NYR: 170
Playoff Games with NYR: 14
Also wore: #38

A 5-foot-10 center, Robbie Ftorek was a star at Needham High School in Needham, Massachusetts, but some pro scouts thought he would be too small to play in the National Hockey League. He began his NHL career with Detroit in 1972, but made his name in the World Hockey Association.

While playing for the Phoenix Roadrunners and the Cincinnati Stingers of the WHA, Ftorek put together a string of four consecutive seasons with 100 or more points. In the 1977–78 season, Ftorek scored 59 goals. When the league disbanded after the 1978–79 season, Ftorek signed with the Quebec Nordiques as a free agent. He was traded to the Rangers in December of 1981.

In the 1982 Stanley Cup Playoffs, Ftorek was the Rangers leading scorer with 7 goals and 4 assists for 11 points in 10 games. He scored three in the Patrick Division Semifinal four-game sweep of the Philadelphia Flyers and four more in the Division Final loss to the New York Islanders. Ftorek retired after the 1984–85 season, his final one in New York.

Walt Poddubny

NYR Debut: October 9, 1986 (vs. New Jersey Devils, lost 5–3)
Regular Season Games with NYR: 152
Playoff Games with NYR: 6

Not many players in Ranger history had as much of an impact on the team in such a short time. Winger Walt Poddubny played two seasons with the Rangers and led the team in scoring both years. In 152 games with the Rangers, Poddubny totaled 175 points.

Poddubny was traded to the Rangers from Toronto in August of 1986, in exchange for left winger Mike Allison. Except for one season, when he scored 28 goals with the Maple Leafs, the Ontario native never really blossomed in Toronto. In his first game with the Rangers, Poddubny got on the score sheet with two assists in a loss to the Devils.

The Rangers were winless through the first four games of the 1986–87 season, when they finally got their first win thanks to Poddubny. The twenty-five-year-old had a goal and two assists as the Rangers beat the New York Islanders 3–2.

Poddubny scored 40 goals in his first season and finished with 87 points in 75 games played. He was voted the team's Most Valuable Player and won the Frank Boucher trophy as the most popular Ranger. Poddubny did not score a point in six postseason games.

In his second and final season of 1987–88, Poddubny scored 38 goals and finished with 88 points in 77 games. It was a remarkable stretch of offensive production for Poddubny, who was plagued by knee injuries throughout his career and was traded to the Quebec Nordiques after the season (with Jari Gronstad, Bruce Bell, and a draft pick) in exchange for Jason Lafrieniere and Normand Rochefort.

Bill Boyd

NYR Debut: November 16, 1926 (vs. Montreal Maroons, won 1–0)
Regular Season Games with NYR: 95
Playoff Games with NYR: 10

Right wing Bill Boyd was an original Ranger who played his entire four-year NHL career in New York. Boyd played the first three years with the Rangers and his final season with the co-tenants of Madison Square Garden, the New York Americans.

Boyd played on a checking line with center Paul Thompson and fellow winger Murray Murdoch, and was a member of the 1928 Stanley Cup-winning team. During the Finals vs. the Montreal Maroons, Boyd's line did a nice job defensively on Montreal's top line of Nels Stewart, Hooley Smith, and Jimmy Ward. Boyd split the 1928–29 season with Springfield of the AHL, and was claimed by the New York Americans in the 1929 NHL Inter-League Draft.

Michal Grosek

NYR Debut: October 7, 2000 (at Atlanta Thrashers, won 2–1)
Regular Season Games with NYR: 80
Playoff Games with NYR: 0
Also wore: #22

Michal Grosek was a seven-year NHL veteran when he was traded to the Rangers from the Chicago Blackhawks in October of 2000. The Czech-born winger played with Winnipeg, Buffalo, and Chicago before joining the Rangers. He went on to finish his NHL career with the Boston Bruins. In his second season with the Rangers, Grosek split time with the Hartford Wolf Pack, the Rangers' top minor league affiliate in the American Hockey League.

Patrick Flatley

NYR Debut: October 5, 1996 (at Boston Bruins, 4–4 OT tie)
Regular Season Games with NYR: 68
Playoff Games with NYR: 11

It was bit of an awkward start for Patrick Flatley when he joined the Rangers in 1996. The Toronto native had tormented the Rangers for 13 years as a member of the hated New York Islanders, so it was an interesting twist when he joined the Blueshirts.

Flatley scored a goal in his first home game with the Rangers. His best effort was in the penultimate game of the 1996–97 season, when he scored two goals to lead the Rangers past the Philadelphia Flyers. Flatley finished with 10 goals and 12 assists in his only season with the team.

Ted Donato

NYR Debut: November 5, 2002 (vs. Edmonton Oilers, won 5–2)
Regular Season Games with NYR: 49
Playoff Games with NYR: 0

In July of 2002, the Rangers signed thirty-three-year-old veteran center Ted Donato. The native of Boston split his lone season in New York with the Rangers and their AHL affiliate in Hartford. Donato was released after one season.

Norm "Dutch" Gainor

NYR Debut: November 12, 1931 (at Montreal Canadiens, won 4–1)
Regular Season Games with NYR: 46
Playoff Games with NYR: 7

Center Norm "Dutch" Gainor made his name as a member of the Boston Bruins "Dynamite Line" that featured Hall of Famers Cooney Weiland and Dit Clapper. Gainor was a proficient passer and outstanding playmaker.

Gainor, who helped Boston win the 1929 Stanley Cup, was traded to the Rangers in August of 1931 for rugged defenseman Joe Jerwa. Reportedly, the Calgary, Alberta, native was dealt from Beantown because of a drinking problem. Gainor, who did have problems with varicose veins that eventually ended his career, played 46 games before he was traded to the Ottawa Senators in December of 1932.

Darroll Powe

NYR Debut: February 5, 2012 (at New Jersey Devils, lost 3–1)
Regular Season Games with NYR: 35
Playoff Games with NYR: 3

Darroll Powe was born in Saskatchewan and earned a sociology degree at Princeton, where he played on the hockey team for four years. Upon graduating, he was signed by the Philadelphia Flyers as an undrafted free agent in May of 2008.

The Ivy League grad was known as a solid defensive forward who was exceptionally good on the penalty kill. Powe was acquired from the Minnesota Wild for winger Mike Rupp in February of 2013. Powe did not score a point in parts of two seasons with the Rangers. After his final NHL season, Powe signed with the Lehigh Valley Phantoms of the American Hockey League, where he played one more season before retiring.

Pierre Jarry

NYR Debut: October 16, 1971 (at Toronto Maple Leafs, won 5–3)
Regular Season Games with NYR: 34
Playoff Games with NYR: 0

Rookie left winger Pierre Jarry scored three goals in his short time with the Rangers, but two of those goals were historic.

On November 21, 1971, Jarry scored the fastest two goals in Rangers' franchise history as he led the way in a 12–1 thrashing of the California Golden Seals at Madison Square Garden. In the second period, Jarry scored his first National Hockey League goal. Eight seconds later, he scored his second to set the mark for the fastest two goals in Rangers' history. On the same night that he was overshadowed by a four-goal game from Jean Ratelle, Jarry put himself into the Rangers' record books. Jarry scored one more goal with the Rangers before he was traded to Toronto after the season.

Howie Glover

NYR Debut: October 12, 1963 (at Montreal Canadiens, lost 6–2)
Regular Season Games with NYR: 25
Playoff Games with NYR: 0

Right winger Howie Glover is best known as a Ranger, and for being suspended by the team for refusing an assignment to the minor leagues during the 1963–64 season. Glover, who was known as a goal scorer, scored only one for the Rangers during his 25-game tenure.

Jan Mertzig

NYR Debut: October 9, 1998 (vs. Philadelphia Flyers, lost 1–0)
Regular Season Games with NYR: 23
Playoff Games with NYR: 0

Swedish-born defenseman Jan Mertzig was a ninth-round pick of the Rangers in the 1998 NHL Entry Draft. Mertzig's tenure with the Rangers in the 1998–99 season lasted a little over three months. After the season, he returned to play in Europe.

Larry Kwong

NYR Debut: March 13, 1948 (at Montreal Canadiens, lost 3–2)
Regular Season Games with NYR: 1
Playoff Games with NYR: 0

Right winger Larry Kwong has the distinction of being the first of Asian heritage to play in the National Hockey League. It was only one game and only one shift, but it was historic nonetheless.

The following played less than 20 games with the Rangers:

Elwin "Moe" Morris - defenseman

NYR Debut: October 14, 1948 (at Montreal Canadiens, 1–1 tie)
Regular Season Games with NYR: 18
Playoff Games with NYR: 0

Jean-Yves Roy - right wing

NYR Debut: January 25, 1995 (vs. Pittsburgh Penguins, lost 3–2)

Regular Season Games with NYR: 3

Playoff Games with NYR: 0

Jim Dorey - defenseman

NYR Debut: February 22, 1972 (at Montreal Canadiens, won 7–3)

Regular Season Games with NYR: 1

Playoff Games with NYR: 1

Henry Dyck - left wing

NYR Debut: December 25, 1943 (at Toronto Maple Leafs, won 5–3)

Regular Season Games with NYR: 1

Playoff Games with NYR: 0

Buck Davies - center

NYR Debut: April 4, 1948 (vs. Detroit Red Wings, Game Six of Stanley Cup Semifinals, lost 4–2)

Regular Season Games with NYR: 0

Playoff Games with NYR: 1

#9: "GRAVY BATH"

Adam "Gravy" Graves

NYR Debut: October 3, 1991 (at Boston Bruins, lost 5–3)

Regular Season Games with NYR: 772

Playoff Games with NYR: 68

Also wore: #11

The #9 sweater in Ranger franchise history is unique in that it is retired for two of the team's all-time greatest players.

The free agent signing of left winger Adam Graves in 1991 proved to be one of the best additions in franchise history. Graves began his NHL career with the Detroit Red Wings in the 1987–88 season. In November of 1989, he was traded to the Edmonton Oilers where he

Topps trading Cards used courtesy of The Topps Company Inc.

Adam was loved for his work on and off the ice.

hooked up with Hall of Famers and future Ranger teammates Wayne Gretzky and Mark Messier to win a Stanley Cup in 1990.

Graves wore #11 in his first Ranger game, but switched to #9 when Messier was acquired a day later. In his first season, Graves scored 26 goals and added 33 assists as the Rangers captured the President's Trophy with 105 points.

On the ice, Graves was known as a fierce competitor. Off the ice, he was known as a caring and giving individual—so what happened in the 1992 Patrick Division Finals against the Pittsburgh Penguins was totally out of character.

In Game Two, Graves was assessed a two-minute penalty for slashing Penguins superstar Mario Lemieux who suffered a fractured hand. Three days later, NHL vice president Brian O'Neill handed down a four-game suspension for Graves. The Rangers had a two-games-to-one lead in the series when Graves was suspended, but they did not win a game the rest of the way and were eliminated in six games. As a result of the incident, Graves was unfairly vilified.

The left winger was not known for his offensive prowess before he came to the Rangers, but in the 1993–94 season everything came together for the twenty-five-year-old when Graves became the second Ranger (Vic Hadfield scored 50 in the 1971–72 season) to score 50 goals in a single season. Graves was at 49 goals with seven games left when he set the Ranger record for most goals in a single season against his old team, the Edmonton Oilers. On March 23, 1994, Graves scored twice to set a new Ranger record with 51 goals in one season. He would add one more to finish at 52, a record that stood until Jaromir Jagr scored 54 in the 2005–06 season.

In the playoffs, Graves scored 10 goals and, were it not for Brian Leetch's Conn Smythe Trophy-winning performance, he may have been voted the MVP. Graves had a pair of two-goal games and added a huge goal in the seventh and deciding game of the Finals against the Vancouver Canucks, as the Rangers snapped their fifty-four-year drought without a Stanley Cup Championship.

"Gravy" was one of the Rangers' most consistent players throughout his 10-year career. After the lockout-shortened season of 1994–95, Graves had two more seasons of 30-plus goals and three more seasons of 20 or more.

Injuries began to take their toll on Graves, who was relegated to the fourth line in his final Ranger season of 2000–01. He played in all 82 games, but scored only 10 goals. After the season, the Rangers traded him to the San Jose Sharks where he finished his career two years later. The popular winger played his final game with the Rangers in April of 2001.

As good as he was on the ice, Graves was one of the most decorated players in franchise history for his charity work and endless contributions to the community. "Gravy" was a five-time winner of the Steven McDonald Extra Effort Award and was named the King Clancy Memorial Trophy winner for community service for the 1993–94 season. In 2001, he was awarded the Masterton Trophy for sportsmanship.

On February 9, 2009, Graves's #9 became the sixth to be retired and hoisted to the rafters at Madison Square Garden. Graves shares the retired number honors with Andy Bathgate.

Andy Bathgate

NYR Debut: October 18, 1952 (at Toronto Maple Leafs, lost 4–3)
Regular Season Games with NYR: 719
Playoff Games with NYR: 22
Also wore: #10, #16, and #14

Andy Bathgate was a great player who wore #9 with the Rangers some three decades before Adam Graves honored it with his play.

Bathgate is considered one of the greatest players in franchise history. In 1958–59, he became one of four Rangers to be named the winner of the Hart Trophy, emblematic of the NHL's Most Valuable Player. Bathgate led the team in scoring eight times, was a first team All-Star two times, and was the Rangers' captain beginning with the 1961–62 season until the end of his tenure in 1964.

In his first season of 1952–53, the right winger played 20 games as he split time between the Rangers and the Vancouver Canucks of the Western Hockey League. It took him until the following season to score his first

Andy's slap shot was the reason Jacque Plante wore the first goalie mask in NHL history.

NHL goal. On February 18, 1953, Bathgate scored his first goal against the Chicago Black Hawks at Madison Square Garden.

Bathgate was a superb offensive player who was incredibly skillful with the puck. He had a blistering slap shot and a unique ability to work his way through the opposition for quality scoring chances.

In his first full season of 1954–55, Bathgate broke out with 20 goals and 20 assists. After netting only 19 in the 1955–56 season, his totals began to rise and culminated with 40 goals during the 1958–59 Hart Trophy–winning season.

In November of 1959, Bathgate's slap shot became a part of history when he hit Montreal Canadiens' goaltender Jacques Plante in the face. There was no backup goalie dressed, so play was halted while Plante got medical attention in the locker room. When Plante returned to the ice, he was wearing a mask for the first time.

In the 1961–62 season, Bathgate tied Chicago's Bobby Hull for the most points in the league with 84, but lost out on the Art Ross Trophy because the Black Hawks winger had more goals, 50–28. During the 1962–63 season, he set a Rangers' record of scoring a goal in ten straight games, a mark that still stands.

Bathgate played 12-plus seasons with the Rangers, but only made the playoffs four times in a six-team league. During the 1961–62 season, the Rangers and Detroit Red Wings were battling for the fourth and final playoff spot. On March 14, 1962, the teams met for the final time. The game was tied at two in the third period when the Rangers were awarded a penalty shot when Red Wings goalie Hank Bassen threw his stick at the puck. Bathgate was chosen to take the penalty shot and converted to key a 3–2 win that helped them hold off Detroit and make the playoffs.

In February of 1964, Bathgate was traded to the Toronto Maple Leafs in one of the biggest trades in team history. Bathgate combined with Hall of Famers Red Kelly and Frank Mahovlich to form Toronto's top line that led them to the 1964 Stanley Cup Championship. In Game Seven of the Finals against Detroit, Bathgate scored the first goal of their 4–0 victory.

Bathgate played for the Red Wings and Pittsburgh Penguins before ending his pro career in the 1974–75 season as a member of the Vancouver Blazers of the World Hockey Association.

Less than two weeks after the Rangers honored Adam Graves by retiring his #9 in February of 2009, they did the same for Bathgate in a separate ceremony that also saw Harry Howell's #3 hoisted to the rafters at the Garden. Bathgate was inducted into the Hockey Hall of Fame in 1978.

Murray Murdoch

NYR Debut: November 16, 1926 (vs. Montreal Maroons, won 1–0)
Regular Season Games with NYR: 508
Playoff Games with NYR: 55

On January 23, 1934, the Rangers beat the Ottawa Senators 5–2 at Madison Square Garden before a reported crowd of 14,000. What was significant about this regular season game was that it was the 400th in franchise history. It also marked the 400th consecutive game for left winger Murray Murdoch.

Murdoch was one of seven original Rangers (Bill and "Bun" Cook, Frank Boucher, "Ching" Johnson, Murdoch, coach Lester Patrick, and trainer Harry Westerby) who were honored between the first and second periods with a diamond ring. When it came time to present Murdoch's ring, New York Yankees' "Iron Man" Lou Gehrig was on hand to make the presentation.

The 5-foot-10, 180-pound left winger anchored the Rangers' checking line for two Stanley Cup winners in 1928 and 1933. Murdoch did not miss a game—regular season or playoffs—in his entire 11-year Ranger career.

In the 1933 Finals against Toronto, Murdoch had a goal and an assist in Game One.

Murdoch followed up the 1933 championship by scoring a career high 17 goals. In the 1934–35 season, he set a career high in points with 29. Murdoch ended his career with 508 consecutive games played. It was a record that stood until Andy Hebenton broke it in 1963.

After his playing career, Murdoch went on to become a successful college hockey coach at Yale University. In 1974, he was named the winner of the Lester Patrick Trophy for service to hockey in the United States.

Murray did not miss a regular season or playoff game in his 11-year Ranger career.

Lynn Patrick

NYR Debut: November 10, 1934 (at St. Louis Eagles, lost 4–2)	
Regular Season Games with NYR: 455	
Playoff Games with NYR: 44	
Also wore: #18	

It wasn't easy for Rangers' left winger/center Lynn Patrick when he debuted in the 1934–35 season. Being the son of the head coach, Lester Patrick, put enormous pressure on him to succeed right away—not to mention the fact that his father was hesitant to sign him because of the relationship. Lynn Patrick got off to a slow start and the fans gave him a hard time because he had replaced a popular player in center Art Somers, who retired after the 1933–34 season.

Patrick played in all 48 games in his first season, but his game came to the forefront in the Stanley Cup Playoffs when he scored two goals and had two assists in four postseason games.

Played with his brother Muzz on 1940 Stanley Cup Championship team.

In 1938, Lynn's younger brother Muzz joined the team and the two played on the 1940 Stanley Cup Championship team that was coached by their father. Lynn Patrick played on a line with Phil Watson and Bryan Hextall and had his best season in 1941–42, when he scored a career high 32 goals with 22 assists.

After the 1942–43 season, Patrick served two years in the military before returning to the Rangers for one more season in 1945–46.

After his playing career ended, Patrick was named the coach of the Rangers affiliate in New Haven of the AHL for the 1946–47 season. Midway through the 1948–49 season, he was named the Rangers' head coach. Patrick guided the team to the 1950 Stanley Cup Finals where they lost to Detroit. Following the loss, the Bruins used a lucrative contract to lure Patrick to Boston to become their head coach. Patrick eventually became Boston's general manager. In 1967, he was named the first head coach of the expansion St. Louis Blues. Patrick was inducted into the Hockey Hall of Fame in 1980.

Paul Ronty

NYR Debut: October 14, 1951 (at Chicago Black Hawks, lost 3–2)
Regular Season Games with NYR: 260
Playoff Games with NYR: 0

He only played parts of four seasons with the Rangers but center Paul Ronty was quite a productive player.

Ronty began his career as a nineteen-year-old with the Boston Bruins in the 1947–48 season. He was acquired by the Rangers in September of 1951 for defenseman Gus Kyle and right winger and former Calder Trophy winner Pentti Lund. Ronty came to the Rangers with a reputation as a proficient playmaker and lived up to the hype.

The Rangers put that rep to good use as Ronty centered a line that featured high-scoring Wally Hergesheimer and Herb Dickenson. Ronty's best season with the Rangers was 1952–53, when he led the team with 38 assists and finished second to Hergesheimer in scoring. In the 1953–54 season, Ronty led the team in scoring with 46 points.

The Rangers did not make the playoffs during Ronty's tenure so he did not play in any postseason games. In February of 1955, the twenty-seven-year-old was placed on waivers and claimed by the Montreal Canadiens.

Reggie Fleming

NYR Debut: January 15, 1966 (at Detroit Red Wings, 4–4 tie)

Regular Season Games with NYR: 241

Playoff Games with NYR: 13

Right winger Reggie Fleming literally fought his way into the National Hockey League. Fleming was as tough as they come and was groomed to be that way. When he was growing up in Montreal, he got into a number of fights. While playing junior hockey, he was encouraged to get into an altercation or two.

Although he was only 5-foot-8, Fleming was a physical specimen who was nicknamed "Mr. Clean" for his resemblance to the iconic figure who represents the famous cleaning product. He was also a versatile player who could play winger or defense.

Fleming was dealt to the Rangers in January of 1966, and led the league with 166 penalty minutes. Fleming spent so much time in the penalty box that he was once quoted as saying, "I got my mail delivered there."

His reputation for being a tough player notwithstanding, Fleming was also a capable offensive player. In fact, he scored a goal in each of his first two games with the Rangers. During parts of four seasons in New York, Fleming scored 50 goals.

After the 1968–69 season, he was traded to the Philadelphia Flyers for wingers Leon Rochefort and Don Blackburn.

Wayne Dillon

NYR Debut: October 8, 1975 (vs. Chicago Black Hawks, 2–2 tie)

Regular Season Games with NYR: 216

Playoff Games with NYR: 3

Also wore: #11

Center Wayne Dillon began his professional career in the World Hockey Association with a 30-goal season for the Toronto Toros in 1973. In the 1975 NHL Amateur Draft, the Rangers made him the 12th overall pick.

Dillon scored 21 goals in his rookie season of 1975–76, but he was plagued by injuries and was never able to take his game to the next level. In July of 1979, Dillon's rights were sold by the Rangers to the Winnipeg Jets, who was entering its first season in the National Hockey League.

Ulf Dahlen

NYR Debut: October 8, 1987 (vs. Pittsburgh Penguins, 4–4 tie)
Regular Season Games with NYR: 189
Playoff Games with NYR: 4
Also wore: #16

Swedish-born winger Ulf Dahlen came to the Rangers with such promise. Dahlen was the Rangers' first-round pick and seventh overall in the 1985 NHL Entry Draft. He was a unique combination of speed and power, something that was unusual, at that time, for a European-born player.

After fulfilling a two-year military commitment and winning a bronze medal with Sweden in the 1987 World Championships, Dahlen came to North America to join the Rangers for the 1987–88 season. In his third game, he scored his first NHL goal against the Chicago Blackhawks, but wasn't done for the night as he added two more for the team's only hat trick of the season. In his first season, Dahlen scored 29 goals, 11 on the power play, and finished fourth among all NHL rookies with 52 points.

The 6-foot-3, 204-pound Dahlen was plagued by injuries throughout his career with the Rangers. In his second season, he suffered a number of shoulder injuries that kept him out of the lineup on three separate occasions.

Dahlen scored 71 goals in 189 games as a Ranger. In March of 1990, Dahlen was traded to the Minnesota North Stars for Hall of Fame winger Mike Gartner.

Pentti Lund

NYR Debut: October 14, 1948 (at Montreal Canadiens, 1–1 tie)
Regular Season Games with NYR: 182
Playoff Games with NYR: 12

Right winger Pentti Lund was the first Finnish-born player to play for the Rangers when he joined the team for the 1948–49 season. Before coming to the Rangers in February of 1948, Lund played three postseason games for the Boston Bruins.

Lund became the fourth Ranger in ten years to win the Calder Trophy when he captured the award in the 1948–49 season. He scored 16 goals and added 16 assists, but his best work came during the 1949–50 season. Lund scored 18 goals during the regular season, but he really shined in the

Rangers' run to the 1950 Stanley Cup Final. The second Finnish-born player and the first to score a goal in the NHL, Lund scored six goals in 12 playoff games. In Game Three of the semifinals against Montreal, Lund scored a hat trick as the Rangers advanced to the Finals. Lund added a goal in the Game Seven loss to Detroit. Lund's play dropped off in the 1950–51 season as he only scored four goals in 59 games. He was traded back to Boston in September of 1951 (see Paul Monty above).

Lund's NHL career ended after the 1952–53 season after he suffered an eye injury early in the season from an errant high stick.

Pentii was the first Fin to play for the Blueshirts.

Photo from the public domain.

Rob McClanahan

NYR Debut: February 18, 1982 (vs. Colorado Rockies, 4–4 tie)

Regular Season Games with NYR: 141

Playoff Games with NYR: 19

Center Rob McClanahan was a star of amateur hockey in his native Minnesota before he joined the United States National Team for the World Championships in 1979.

McClanahan was a member of the United States' Gold Medal–winning hockey team in 1980. After the euphoria of winning calmed down, McClanahan made his NHL debut with the Buffalo Sabres.

He came to the Rangers from the Hartford Whalers in February of 1982, and played parts of three seasons in New York.

McClanahan scored 22 goals during the 1982–83 season, his only full season with the Rangers. He was traded to Detroit following the 1983–84 season.

Gene Carr

NYR Debut: November 21, 1971 (at Minnesota North Stars, lost 4–1)

Regular Season Games with NYR: 138

Playoff Games with NYR: 17

Center Gene Carr was a high draft pick who never panned out in the NHL. The St. Louis Blues made the Nanaimo, British Columbia, native their first pick and the fourth overall in the 1971 NHL Amateur Draft.

Carr came to the Rangers as part of a six-player trade with the Blues after he played only 15 games in St. Louis. The speedy skater scored two goals and had an assist in his second game with the Rangers, and seemed to be on his way to being a productive player in the league. The twenty-year-old would score only six more goals the rest of the season, and would never go over double digits during parts of three seasons with the Rangers. A broken collarbone and a concussion during his time in New York contributed to Carr not reaching his potential as an NHL goal scorer.

In February of 1974, the Rangers traded Carr to the Los Angeles Kings for a 1977 first-round pick that turned into right winger Ron Duguay.

Rick Middleton

NYR Debut: October 9, 1974 (vs. Washington Capitals, won 6–3)

Regular Season Games with NYR: 124

Playoff Games with NYR: 3

Photo courtesy of Ken Tash.

Part of worst trade in Rangers history.

Rick Middleton will be forever known in Ranger lore as being one of the worst trades in franchise history.

Middleton was the 14th overall pick of the Rangers in the 1973 NHL Amateur Draft. The right winger scored 67 goals for the Oshawa Generals of the Ontario Junior Hockey League in 1972–73, and was named the Most Valuable Player as a nineteen-year-old.

His career started off well, as he scored two goals in his first game to key a win over Washington. He had 22 and 24 goals in his first and only two seasons, respectively, with the Rangers, however he was gaining a reputation for being lazy at times and a weak defensive player.

In one of the most one-sided trades in franchise history, the Rangers sent the twenty-two-year-old right winger to the Boston Bruins for soon to be thirty-two-year-old right winger Ken Hodge in May of 1976. Middleton went on to a solid 12-year career with the Bruins. He scored 402 goals and won the Lady Byng Trophy for sportsmanship in 1982. Hodge lasted parts of two seasons with the Rangers and became the target of the fans' frustration over a trade that they did not like from the start.

Bernie Nicholls

> **NYR Debut:** January 23, 1990 (at Edmonton Oilers, won 4–3)
> **Regular Season Games with NYR:** 104
> **Playoff Games with NYR:** 15

Center Bernie Nicholls was one of the most underrated players in franchise history. Nicholls scored more points than games played, including in the postseason, during his two-plus seasons with the Rangers.

Nicholls came to the Rangers in January of 1990 for wingers Tomas Sandstrom and Tony Granato. The twenty-eight-year-old was superb down the stretch of the regular season, as he scored 12 goals with 37 points in 32 games. After such a hot start, Nicholls was even better in the playoffs. He scored a goal in each of the first three games of the Patrick Division Semifinals victory over the New York Islanders. In the Division Final against Washington, Nicholls scored a hat trick in a Game One win, but the Rangers went on to lose the next four.

In 1990–91, his one and only full season with the Rangers, Nicholls scored 25 goals, including 8 on the power play, and added 48 assists. In the playoffs against Washington, Nicholls scored four goals in five games but was injured and missed Game Six as the Rangers were eliminated. In 104 career games, Nicholls scored 110 points. He scored 19 points in 15 career playoff games.

After playing just one game in the 1991–92 season, Nicholls was part of, arguably, the most important trade in Rangers history. On October 4, 1991, the high-scoring center, along with winger Steven Rice and Louis DeBrusk, was sent to the Edmonton Oilers for Hall of Famer Mark Messier and "future considerations," that translated into defenseman Jeff Beukeboom.

Dave Gagner

> **NYR Debut:** October 11, 1984 (vs. Hartford Whalers, 4–4 OT tie)
> **Regular Season Games with NYR:** 80
> **Playoff Games with NYR:** 0

NEW YORK RANGERS BY THE NUMBERS

Center Dave Gagner was the Rangers' first-round pick and 12th overall in the 1983 NHL Entry Draft. Gagner was spectacular for the Brantford Alexanders of the Ontario Hockey League in 1982–83, as he scored 55 goals and had 121 points.

After playing for Canada in the 1984 Winter Olympics, Gagner joined the team for the 1984–85 season. It took him awhile to get started, as he didn't score his first NHL goal until his eighth game.

After spending most of the 1986–87 season with the Rangers' AHL affiliate at New Haven, Gagner played in 10 games with the Rangers. He was traded to the Minnesota North Stars after the season and played fifteen years with four other teams including Toronto, Calgary, Florida, and Vancouver.

Doug Sulliman

NYR Debut: October 10, 1979 (at Toronto Maple Leafs, won 6–3)
Regular Season Games with NYR: 63
Playoff Games with NYR: 3

After scoring 38 goals and 115 points for the Kitchener Rangers as a nineteen-year-old, winger Doug Sulliman was the Rangers' first pick and 12th overall in the 1979 NHL Entry Draft. The Nova Scotia native was being scouted when he was sixteen years old.

In his first season in New York, Sulliman played on a line with Swedes Ulf Nilsson and Anders Hedberg. Unfortunately, Sulliman suffered a knee injury in late March and missed the playoffs and the run to the 1979 Stanley Cup Final.

In October of 1981, Sulliman was traded to the Hartford Whalers as part of a deal that brought center Mike Rogers to New York.

Real Lemieux

NYR Debut: October 12, 1969 (at Boston Bruins, lost 2–1)
Regular Season Games with NYR: 62
Playoff Games with NYR: 0
Also wore: #14

Left winger Real Lemieux went from the Los Angeles Kings to the Rangers to the Kings and then back to the Rangers.

Lemieux was a double-digit goal scorer with Los Angeles, but his offensive skills never materialized with the Rangers. Lemieux played 55 games in his first go-round with the Rangers. He scored four goals, but an incident that took place in a February 1970 game against Boston led to his first departure.

Bruins noted agitator John McKenzie was doing his best against the Rangers, particularly Lemieux. Head coach and general manager Emile Francis was reportedly so incensed by Lemieux's lack of a response that, before the next game, he was traded back to the Kings for noted tough guy Ted Irvine.

Lemieux was re-acquired from the Kings in November of 1973, but he played only seven more games in New York before he was traded to Buffalo in January of 1974.

Pavel Bure

NYR Debut: March 19, 2002 (vs. Vancouver Canucks, lost 3–1)

Regular Season Games with NYR: 51

Playoff Games with NYR: 0

By the time Hall of Fame right wing Pavel Bure joined the Rangers, he was already on the downside of a fabulous career.

Before coming to New York, Bure was best known to Ranger fans as the Vancouver Canucks' player that was stopped by Rangers goaltender Mike Richter on a penalty shot in Game Three of the 1994 Stanley Cup Final (see Chapter Thirty-Five).

The Moscow native had blazing speed and could make an opponent look bad with his puck handling skills. That combination and his heritage earned him the nickname of the "Russian Rocket."

The Rangers acquired Bure from the Florida Panthers for defenseman Igor Ulanov and Filip Novak and a number of draft picks with the hope that he could help the offense to make a run for the playoffs. The Rangers trailed the Montreal Canadiens by two points for the final playoff spot in the Eastern Conference at the time the trade was made.

Bure did all he could. He scored a goal in his first Ranger game and then added a goal and an assist two nights later to key a huge 5–2 win over the Ottawa Senators. Bure, who had 406 career goals when he joined the Rangers, scored 12 goals in 12 games. In the final six regular season games, Bure scored seven goals to go along with four assists, but the Rangers missed the playoffs.

Bure was limited to 39 games in his second season of 2002–03 because of a recurring knee injury that would eventually end his career in September of 2003.

Walt Atanas

NYR Debut: October 28, 1944 (at Toronto Maple Leafs, lost 2–1)
Regular Season Games with NYR: 49
Playoff Games with NYR: 0

Right winger Walt Atanas played his entire 49-game, NHL career with the Rangers. He scored 13 goals during the 1944–45 season, but as some players began to return from serving in World War II, Atanas lost his spot and was demoted to the minor leagues.

Dick Duff

NYR Debut: February 22, 1964 (at Toronto Maple Leafs, lost 5–2)
Regular Season Games with NYR: 43
Playoff Games with NYR: 0

Left winger Dick Duff had a stretch during his career where he won four Stanley Cup Championships in a five-year period while playing for the Toronto Maple Leafs and Montreal Canadiens. In the one season he didn't win, Duff played 43 games with the Rangers.

After Duff won two consecutive Stanley Cups with Toronto, the Leafs traded him to the Rangers on February 22, 1964, a deal which sent popular winger Andy Bathgate to the Maple Leafs. Duff played parts of two seasons with the Rangers before he was traded to Montreal in December of 1964. Duff went on to win two more consecutive Stanley Cups with the Canadiens in the 1964–65 and 1965–66 seasons. Duff went on to win an additional two Cups with Montreal.

Fern Gauthier

NYR Debut: December 19, 1943 (vs. Detroit Red Wings, won 6–2)
Regular Season Games with NYR: 33
Playoff Games with NYR: 0

Right winger Fern Gauthier showed all the signs of being a consistent goal scorer in the National Hockey League. While playing junior hockey for the Shawnigan Cataracts in the late 1930s, he scored 73 goals in a three-year period. The Rangers acquired the twenty-five-year-old on loan from Montreal, who received right winger Phil Watson in the exchange.

Gauthier scored a goal in his very first NHL game on December 19, 1943, to cap off the scoring in a Rangers' 6–2 win over the Detroit Red Wings. It was only the second win of the season for the Rangers, who would win six games all season. He finished his first and only season with the Rangers with 14 goals.

When Gauthier returned to Montreal for the 1944–45 season, he scored a career-high 18 goals. In October of 1945, he was sent to Detroit where he disappointed, as he failed to record double-digit goals. His lack of production was sparking some good-natured ribbing from the local media. They claimed Gauthier could not "put the puck in the ocean."

Local sportswriter Lew Walter, who covered the Red Wings for the *Detroit Times*, convinced Gauthier to go along with a good-natured gag. When the team visited New York for a road game, Walter and Gauthier went to one of New York's docks, along the Hudson River, with sticks and pucks. Walter concocted a fictional story where Gauthier missed the first two shots. The first was picked up by a seagull who swooped down and grabbed the puck before it hit the water. The second landed on a tugboat that was pulling barges.

The following player played less than five regular season games with NYR:

Don Blackburn - left wing

NYR Debut: February 28, 1970 (at Detroit Red Wings, 3–3 tie)
Regular Season Games with NYR: 4
Playoff Games with NYR: 1

#10: FROM DUGUAY TO MILLER

Bill Fairbairn

NYR Debut: February 15, 1969 (at Toronto Maple Leafs, lost 6–2)

Regular Season Games with NYR: 536

Playoff Games with NYR: 52

Also wore: #14

Bill Fairbairn earned his nickname of "Bulldog" for his hard-nosed but clean play when he played junior hockey as a teenager. He was tenacious on the ice, but didn't spend much time in the penalty box.

Fairbairn played one regular-season game during the 1968–69 season, but played in six playoff games. His rookie season was 1969–70, when he scored 23 goals with 33 assists and finished second in the voting for the Calder Trophy. Fairbairn played on a line with Walt Tkaczuk and Dave Balon that was called the "Bulldog Line" for their hard checking and physical style. It was a checking line that also contributed offensively. When Balon was traded in November of 1971, Steve Vickers took his spot (see Chapter Eight).

During the Rangers' run to the 1972 Stanley Cup Final, Fairbairn had 12 points in 16 games. In the six-game quarterfinal win against Montreal, Fairbairn scored five goals. He was also a factor in the four-game semifinal sweep of Chicago and made a contribution in the Finals, although the Rangers lost to Boston in six games.

Fairbairn scored a career-high 30 goals in the 1972–73 season but never reached that plateau again. In the next three seasons, he scored 55 goals but was starting to slow down when he turned thirty years old. Fairbairn finished his Ranger career with 138 goals and 224 assists. He was traded to the Minnesota North Stars in November of 1976.

Ron Duguay

NYR Debut: October 12, 1977 (vs. Vancouver Canucks, won 6–3)

Regular Season Games with NYR: 499

Playoff Games with NYR: 69

Also wore: #44

Rare shot of Ron without his trademark hair.

Ron Duguay had it all when drafted by the Rangers in the 1977 NHL Amateur Draft. The 6-foot-2 right winger had movie star looks, curly hair, and flamboyance on the ice that seemed like a perfect fit for New York.

Duguay was the Rangers' second pick of the first round (Rangers took center Lucien DeBlois with the 8th overall pick) and 13th overall. He did not play junior hockey, and instead went right to the big club for the 1977–78 season.

The Ontario native quickly became a fan favorite. He dazzled the crowds at Madison Square Garden with his overall skill and frantic rushes up the ice. Since players were not required to wear helmets in the late seventies, Duguay's long, brown hair became a trademark when it would violently swirl in the wind that was created by his speed. He finished his first season with 20 goals and 20 assists. In his first taste of the Stanley Cup Playoffs, Duguay had a goal and an assist in three games.

In the 1978–79 season, Duguay tied for fourth on the team with 27 goals and was fifth in scoring with 63 points. Playing on a line with Hall of Famer Phil Esposito, Duguay shined in the 1979 Stanley Cup Playoffs. The first-round pick scored two goals against Philadelphia in the quarterfinals, added a goal against the Islanders in the semifinals, and two against Montreal in a losing effort in the Finals.

Duguay captivated Madison Avenue with his skill and good looks. He was good fodder for the local newspapers, both the sports and gossip columns. Duguay began doing television commercials including a famous one for Sasson Jeans that co-starred teammates Esposito, Dave Maloney, and Anders Hedberg, and featured an often-quoted slogan of "Ooh, La, La, Sasson."

Duguay dominated the first two rounds of the 1981 Stanley Cup Playoffs. In the four-game sweep of the Los Angeles Kings in the preliminary round, Duguay scored in every game and capped it off with two goals in the Game Four clincher. He added three goals to help the Rangers beat the St. Louis Blues in six games.

The 1981–82 season was Duguay's personal best when he scored a career-high 40 goals and 76 points. It was ironic that Duguay's best season coincided with the first year for Rangers' head coach Herb Brooks, who, as it turned out, was not a big fan of the right winger's game.

After he dropped off to 19 goals in the 1982–83 season, the Rangers traded Duguay to Detroit as part of a roster-shifting six-player deal. Duguay made a return engagement with the Rangers when he was picked up in a trade with the Pittsburgh Penguins. During his second stint, Duguay wore #44. He was later traded to the Los Angeles Kings in February of 1988.

Duguay has continued his association with the Rangers as a studio analyst for MSG Network telecasts.

Earl Ingarfield

> **NYR Debut:** October 8, 1958 (at Chicago Black Hawks, 1–1 tie)
> **Regular Season Games with NYR:** 527
> **Playoff Games with NYR:** 10

After playing a total of 55 games in his first two seasons with the Rangers, center Earl Ingarfield finally found his niche. In 1960–61, the Alberta native scored 13 goals and 34 points.

Ingarfield was a proven goal scorer in junior hockey, but it wasn't until he started to center a line with Hall of Famer Andy Bathgate and left winger Dean Prentice that he really came into his own. In the 1961–62 season, Ingarfield scored a career-high 26 goals and 57 points. For the first time in four seasons, the Rangers made the playoffs and Ingarfield carried his outstanding season into the postseason. The Rangers center scored three goals with two assists to help the team score a near upset of the eventual champion Toronto Maple Leafs in the Stanley Cup Semifinals.

Ingarfield had one more season of 20 goals in 1965–66, and played one final season with the Rangers in 1966–67. The thirty-two-year-old was left unprotected and was claimed by the Pittsburgh Penguins in the 1967 NHL Expansion Draft. He played his final three seasons in the NHL with the Oakland Seals/California Golden Seals. In 1972, he became the second head coach of the expansion New York Islanders.

Edgar Laprade

> **NYR Debut:** October 31, 1945 (at Chicago Black Hawks, lost 5–1)
> **Regular Season Games with NYR:** 500
> **Playoff Games with NYR:** 18

A graceful playmaker, who was a gentleman on the ice was center Edgar Laprade. The Port Arthur, Ontario, native was a consistent point producer for six of his ten years with the Rangers.

Laprade's first season was a rousing success, as he won the Calder Trophy with 15 goals and 19 assists. The Hall of Famer rarely spent time in the penalty box. In fact, Laprade did not serve a penalty in three seasons and drew only 42 penalty minutes in 500 games. In the 1949–50 season, Laprade won the Lady Byng Trophy for sportsmanship.

Laprade stood at only 5-foot-8, but he was the biggest member of his line that also featured 5-foot-7 Tony Leswick and 5-foot-5 Knobby Warwick. His career was nearly cut short by a horrific car accident that involved three other teammates. Laprade, Buddy O'Connor, Frank Eddolls, and Bill Moe were all injured when the car they were riding in was hit by a truck that forced them off the road. Laprade missed four games with a broken nose and concussion. Despite the accident, Laprade still scored 18 goals. He also had 12 penalty minutes, which was a single-season high.

The Rangers lost the 1950 Stanley Cup Final to Detroit, but Laprade was a huge factor in the series going seven games. After the Red Wings captured Game One, Laprade scored two goals to key a 3–1 win to even the series. In Game Four, Laprade help the Rangers rally for an overtime win to even the series at two games apiece.

Laprade played five more seasons with the Rangers but never played in another playoff game. He was inducted into the Hockey Hall of Fame in 1993.

Butch Keeling

NYR Debut: November 15, 1928 (at Detroit Cougars, won 2–0)
Regular Season Games with NYR: 452
Playoff Games with NYR: 47
Also wore: #11

On October 17, 1928, left winger Butch Keeling was acquired by the Rangers as part of a blockbuster trade with Toronto. Keeling and goaltender John Ross Roach were sent to New York for goalie Lorne Chabot and right winger Alex Gray.

Roach and Keeling paid immediate dividends for the Rangers. The new goaltender blanked the Detroit Cougars, 2–0, while Keeling scored the only goal that actually went in the net. Frank Boucher was awarded the second goal for the Rangers when Detroit goaltender Clarence "Dolly" Dotson threw his stick at the puck.

Keeling made the playoffs nine times in his 10-year career with the Rangers. In the 1929 Stanley Cup Playoffs, he scored an overtime goal against Montreal in Game Two to win the quarterfinal series that was decided by total goals, 1–0. He was also a member of the 1933 Stanley Cup-winning team. During the playoffs, Keeling only had two assists but one was huge as it came on Bill Cook's series and Cup-clinching overtime goal against Toronto in the fourth of a four-game sweep. In the 1936–37 season, Keeling scored a career high 22 goals.

Keeling retired after the 1937–38 season.

Clint Smith

NYR Debut: March 9, 1937 (at New York Americans, won 7–5 OT)
Regular Season Games with NYR: 281
Playoff Games with NYR: 29
Also wore: #14 and #20

The Rangers signed center Clint Smith as a free agent in 1932, but it took him five years to reach the NHL.

Smith was brought up late in the 1936–37 season and played in two games, scoring his first goal against the Chicago Black Hawks in his second game. The Saskatchewan native played regularly for the next six seasons. In 1938, Smith finished as the runner-up for the Lady Byng Trophy, and then won it the very next season—which just so happened to be his best with the Rangers as he scored 21 goals.

Smith played on the 1940 Stanley Cup-winning team. During the playoffs, he scored a goal with three assists in 11 games. His last assist was the primary helper on the game-tying goal in the third period of Game Six of the Finals. The Rangers went on to win the series and the Cup in overtime.

The Rangers sold Smith to Chicago prior to the 1943–44 season. He went on to win a second Lady Byng Trophy in 1944 while with the Black Hawks, setting a record for a 50-game season with 49 assists.

J.T. Miller

NYR Debut: February 5, 2013 (at New Jersey Devils, lost 3–1)
Regular Season Games with NYR: 278
Playoff Games with NYR: 40
Also wore: #47

Photo by Lisa Gansky from New York, NY, USA, via Wikimedia Commons.

JT has had 22 goals in back-to-back seasons.

American-born center J.T. Miller was the Rangers' first round pick and the 15th overall in the 2011 NHL Entry Draft. After a couple of seasons where he was still developing as a player, Miller had a break-out game in the postseason.

The Rangers trailed the Tampa Bay Lightning three games to two in the 2015 Eastern Conference Final. In Game Six, Miller had a goal and three assists as the Rangers scored a 7–3 win to force a seventh and deciding game, which they eventually lost.

Miller followed that performance with a break out season in 2015–16 with 22 goals and 21 assists for 43 points.

In the 2016–17 season, Miller scored 22 goals for a second consecutive season and added 34 assists for a career high 56 points.

With solid regular-season numbers, Miller struggled in the 2015 and 2016 postseason. In 17 postseason games, Miller has not scored a goal and has scored only one goal in 40 career postseason games.

Jean-Guy Gendron

NYR Debut: October 7, 1955 (at Chicago Black Hawks, won 7–4)

Regular Season Games with NYR: 272

Playoff Games with NYR: 22

Also wore: #7

A player that served two tenures in a Ranger sweater and departed via the same draft to the same team was left winger Jean-Guy Gendron. The Rangers acquired Gendron in May of 1955, and in October of that year he made his debut as a twenty-one-year-old.

In his first three seasons, the Montreal native scored 24 goals but was claimed by the Boston Bruins in the 1958 NHL Intra-League Draft. He found his touch in Boston, as he scored 40 goals in parts of three seasons before being traded to Montreal in 1960.

The Rangers re-acquired the winger in the 1961 Intra-League Draft, and he had his best season in 1961–62 when he scored 14 goals while adding three goals and an assist in the playoffs. In June 1962, Gendron went back to the Bruins as he was again claimed by Boston in the Intra-League Draft.

Sandy McCarthy

NYR Debut: October 7, 2000 (at Atlanta Thrashers, won 2–1)
Regular Season Games with NYR: 258
Playoff Games with NYR: 0

A 6-foot-3 right winger, Sandy McCarthy was a blue-collar player who won the affection of the fans with his hustle and hard-nosed play. McCarthy played with four previous teams before joining the Rangers for the 2000–01 season.

The Rangers brought in the towering winger to add toughness to the roster but, in his first season in New York, McCarthy ended up scoring a career-high 11 goals. McCarthy set personal milestones with the Rangers. In the 2001–02 season he scored a career-high 23 points and then played in his 600th NHL game with the Rangers during the 2002–03 season.

McCarthy was a two-time winner of the Steven McDonald Extra Effort Award. He played three seasons with the Rangers before joining the Boston Bruins in 2003 as a free agent. Late in the 2003–04 season, McCarthy was placed on waivers and was claimed by the Rangers, where he played 13 more games.

Marian Gaborik

NYR Debut: October 2, 2009 (at Pittsburgh Penguins, lost 3–2)
Regular Season Games with NYR: 255
Playoff Games with NYR: 25

Going into the 2009–10 season, the Rangers desperately needed a proven goal scorer. On July 1, 2009, the first day of free agency, the Rangers signed unrestricted free agent Marian Gaborik to a five-year contract.

Gaborik spent the first eight years of his career with the Minnesota Wild, where he scored 219 goals and had a five-goal game against the Rangers in 2007. His Ranger career got off to a fast start as he scored a goal in his first game and had 19 goals after 22 games. The right winger tied a franchise record by scoring in his first 8 games. He became the second player in franchise history, since Dave Creighton in the 1955–56 season, to score

Gaborik scored in his first 8 games as a Ranger.

in his first 8 games to start a season. Gaborik scored his first hat trick as a Ranger on January 31 to beat Colorado. He led the team in all the major scoring categories, including tying a career high with 42 goals and a career-high 44 assists.

Three games into the 2010–11 season, Gaborik suffered a shoulder injury that caused him to miss a month but when he returned in mid-November, it seemed like he hadn't skipped a beat. In his second game back, he scored a hat trick to beat Edmonton. Eighteen days later, Gaborik scored his second hat trick of the season against the New York Islanders.

Despite the fast start, Gaborik had some ups and downs in finding the back of the net. In mid-January, Gaborik had 15 goals but he only scored seven more for the rest of the season. In his first taste of the playoffs with the Rangers, Gaborik scored a goal and an assist in five games.

Gaborik got back to his goal scoring ways in 2011–12, as he led the team with 41 goals and 76 points. In the 2012 Eastern Conference Semifinals against the Washington Capitals, Gaborik scored in triple overtime to win Game Three and end one of the longest games in franchise history. The Rangers went on to win the series in seven games.

The Slovakian-born Gaborik's final Ranger season of 2012–13 was lockout shortened. He scored 9 goals in 35 games before being traded to the Columbus Blue Jackets after the season. In a blockbuster trade, Gaborik and two other players went to Columbus for center Derick Brassard, winger Derek Dorsett, and defenseman John Moore.

Pierre Larouche

NYR Debut: October 5, 1983 (vs. New Jersey Devils, won 6–2)
Regular Season Games with NYR: 253
Playoff Games with NYR: 27
Also wore: #24

There is no doubt that center Pierre Larouche had the greatest first season in a Ranger sweater as any player in franchise history. "Lucky Pierre" scored 48 goals (still a Ranger record for centers) in the 1983–84 season and just missed becoming the first player in NHL history to score 50 or more goals with three teams. Larouche previously scored 53 goals for Pittsburgh in 1975–76, and with Montreal in 1979–80.

Larouche, who was a two-time Stanley Cup-winner with Montreal, was a solid playoff performer for the Rangers. In 27 playoff games with the Blueshirts, Larouche scored 14 goals and 26 points. He scored eight goals in 16 games in the 1986 Stanley Cup Playoffs, including five against the Washington Capitals in the Patrick Division Finals that the Rangers won in six games.

The 5-foot-11 native of Taschereau, Quebec, never recaptured the magic he had in his first season in New York. Larouche scored 72 goals in his next three seasons with the Rangers. His final season of 1987–88 was plagued by back problems and he was limited to 10 games before being forced to retire.

Paul Thompson

NYR Debut: November 26, 1926 (vs. Montreal Maroons, won 1–0)
Regular Season Games with NYR: 217
Playoff Games with NYR: 24
Also wore: #8

Left winger Paul Thompson was an original Ranger who signed with the team less than a month before the first game in franchise history. Thompson played five seasons in New York and only missed three games.

Thompson played for the 1928 Stanley Cup-winning team. His best season was in 1928–29, when he scored a Ranger-high 10 goals.

In October 1931, Thompson was traded to Chicago where he went on to become a prolific goal scorer for six of his eight seasons. He also coached the Black Hawks for parts of seven seasons.

Esa Tikkanen

NYR Debut: March 17, 1993 (vs. Edmonton Oilers, lost 4–3 OT)
Regular Season Games with NYR: 144
Playoff Games with NYR: 38

Left winger Esa Tikkanen was a three-time Ranger.

The native of Helsinki, Finland, was acquired from the Edmonton Oilers for center Doug Weight in March 1993. The Rangers failed to make the playoffs, but the acquisition of Tikkanen helped set the stage for the 1993–94 season.

Tikkanen, who was a four-time Stanley Cup winner with the Edmonton Oilers, was one of a number of ex-Oilers who were brought to the Rangers by general manager Neil Smith to complete the task of ending the club's Stanley Cup drought. The defensive-minded winger was a runner up for the Frank Selke Trophy (for best defensive forward) four times. In the 1993–94 regular season, Tikkanen scored 22 goals but his playoff experience is what played a huge role in the Rangers' run to the Cup.

In the epic seventh game of the 1994 Stanley Cup Eastern Conference Finals against New Jersey, Tikkanen had the lone assist in Stephane Matteau's historic game-winning goal in double overtime. In the Final, the aggressive forechecking forward had only one assist but was a key factor in helping the Rangers beat the Vancouver Canucks in seven games.

One month and ten days after he helped the Rangers win the Cup, Tikkanen was traded to the St. Louis Blues, along with defenseman Doug Lidster, for center Petr Nedved. After a short stint with the Devils and Canucks, Tikkanen was traded back to the Rangers in March of 1997. After the season, Tikkanen became an unrestricted free agent and signed with the Florida Panthers. The Finnish-born Tikkanen was traded to Washington during the 1997–98 season. In October of 1998, Tikkanen signed with the Rangers for a third term and played 32 games. Following the season, he returned to play in Europe.

Larry Jeffrey

> **NYR Debut:** October 11, 1967 (at Chicago Black Hawks, won 6–3)
> **Regular Season Games with NYR:** 122
> **Playoff Games with NYR:** 7

Larry Jeffrey's career was defined by a team picture that was taken on ice with the Toronto Maple Leafs after they won the 1967 Stanley Cup. He was on crutches.

Jeffrey's Ranger career, as was his entire 8-year NHL career, was plagued by a series of knee injuries that began when he was teenager in junior hockey. After the left winger scored a career-high 11 goals for the Maple Leafs in 1966–67 season, he was left unprotected and claimed by the Pittsburgh Penguins in the 1967 Expansion Draft. Before he ever played a game with the Penguins, Jeffrey was traded to the Rangers.

He was limited to 47 games in his first season in New York, but played 75 games in the 1968–69 season. Despite missing only five games, injuries wore Jeffrey down and his skills had deteriorated, even at the young age of twenty-eight. In June of 1969, Jeffrey was traded to Detroit for Hall of Fame goalie Terry Sawchuk, but he never played a game for the Red Wings.

Nigel Dawes

NYR Debut: October 5, 2006 (vs. Washington Capitals, won 5–2)
Regular Season Games with NYR: 121
Playoff Games with NYR: 11

A 5-foot-9 left winger, Nigel Dawes was a fifth-round pick of the Rangers in the 2003 NHL Entry Draft. The Winnipeg native signed with the Rangers in 2004 following back-to-back 47-goal seasons in junior hockey.

Dawes was being touted as an exciting young prospect. After winning the Lars-Erik Sjoberg Award as the top rookie in training camp, Dawes began the 2006–07 season with the Rangers but was sent to Hartford after playing in only eight games. Dawes played 61 games and scored 14 goals in the 2007–08 season, including four against New Jersey Devils goaltender Martin Brodeur. The young winger became a nice option for the shootout as he tied a team record with five shootout goals in one season.

Dawes played 52 games in the 2008–09 before he was traded to the Phoenix Coyotes in March.

Kelly Miller

NYR Debut: March 30, 1985 (at Philadelphia Flyers, lost 3–0)
Regular Season Games with NYR: 117
Playoff Games with NYR: 19
Also wore: #40

American-born Kelly Miller was a ninth-round pick in the 1982 NHL Entry Draft who defied the odds and put together a solid NHL career.

Miller put together an outstanding collegiate career at Michigan State, where he was a Hobey Baker Award (top collegiate player) nominee in 1985. The Lansing, Michigan-born Miller went right from college to the Rangers, where he played five games in March.

In his first full season with the Rangers, Miller got off to a good start as he scored the game-winning goal to beat Vancouver and end an early four-game losing streak. Unfortunately, ankle and knee injuries hampered him all season long. Miller played 74 games and scored 13 goals, but in his final season with the Rangers. Midway through the 1986–87 season, Miller was traded to the Washington Capitals.

Miler grew up as part of a hockey family. His father, Lyle, was a former college player. Kelly's younger brother Kevin was a former Ranger while Kip also played in the NHL.

Guy LaFleur

NYR Debut: October 6, 1988 (at Chicago Blackhawks, 2–2 OT tie)
Regular Season Games with NYR: 67
Playoff Games with NYR: 4

When Guy LaFleur put on a Rangers' sweater for the first time, he was already bound for the Hall of Fame.

One of the all-time great right wingers had been out of hockey for three years, but LaFleur decided to make a comeback and signed with the Rangers in September of 1988. "The Flower" had to earn his contract in training camp and did so by outplaying veterans and some younger competitors.

LaFleur, who constructed his Hall of Fame career over 14 years, scored a goal in his first game against his old team at Madison Square Garden in November of 1988. On February 4, 1989, LaFleur returned to what was an emotional evening at the Montreal Forum in his first game as an opponent. The beloved former Canadien received a thunderous standing ovation and scored two goals, but the Rangers lost 7–5.

The legendary player tallied 18 goals in the regular season and one in the playoffs in his one and only season with the Rangers.

Ville Nieminen

NYR Debut: October 10, 2005 (at Washington Capitals, lost 3–2)
Regular Season Games with NYR: 48
Playoff Games with NYR: 0

The Rangers signed veteran left winger Ville Nieminen as an unrestricted free agent in August of 2005. The twenty-eight-year-old got off to a good start in his Ranger career by scoring goals in his second and third game to help the Rangers beat the New Jersey Devils and Atlanta Thrashers, respectively.

Nieminen scored five goals in 48 games before he was traded to the San Jose Sharks in March of 2006.

Ossie Aubuchon

NYR Debut: November 28, 1943 (vs. Montreal Canadiens, 2–2 tie)

Regular Season Games with NYR: 38

Playoff Games with NYR: 0

Left winger Ossie Aubuchon only played two seasons in the NHL but was very productive during his very short tenure with the Rangers.

The 5-foot-10 Quebec native began his career with the Boston Bruins in the 1942–43 season, but played only twelve games in parts of two seasons before he was sold to the Rangers in November of 1943.

In his debut game, Aubuchon figured in both goals as the Rangers played a 2–2 tie against the unbeaten (8–0–3) Montreal Canadiens. In 38 games with the Rangers, Aubuchon scored 16 goals with 12 assists.

The following players played less than 25 games with NYR:

Garth Murray - left wing

NYR Debut: January 30, 2004 (vs. Buffalo Sabres, lost 3–1)

Regular Season Games with NYR: 20

Playoff Games with NYR: 0

Also wore: #25

Dave Archibald - center

NYR Debut: November 6, 1989 (vs. Detroit Red Wings, won 6–1)

Regular Season Games with NYR: 19

Playoff Games with NYR: 0

Art Stratton - center

NYR Debut: January 24, 1960 (at Detroit Red Wings, 2–2 tie)

Regular Season Games with NYR: 18

Playoff Games with NYR: 0

Steven Rice - right wing

NYR Debut: October 4, 1990 (at Chicago Blackhawks, lost 4–3)
Regular Season Games with NYR: 11
Playoff Games with NYR: 2

Jack Mann - center

NYR Debut: October 30, 1943 (at Toronto Maple Leafs, lost 5–2)
Regular Season Games with NYR: 9
Playoff Games with NYR: 0

Hal Cooper - right wing

NYR Debut: November 1, 1944 (at Chicago Black Hawks, lost 8–3)
Regular Season Games with NYR: 8
Playoff Games with NYR: 0

Art Strobel - left wing

NYR Debut: October 31, 1943 (at Detroit Red Wings, lost 8–3)
Regular Season Games with NYR: 7
Playoff Games with NYR: 0

Aggie Kukulowicz - center

NYR Debut: January 7, 1953 (vs. Chicago Blackhawks, lost 6–4)
Regular Season Games with NYR: 11
Playoff Games with NYR: 2

Bill "Chick" Chalmers - center

NYR Debut: November 21, 1953 (at Toronto Maple Leafs, lost 5–2)
Regular Season Games with NYR: 1
Playoff Games with NYR: 0

#11: THE MESSIAH

Mark Messier

NYR Debut: October 5, 1991 (at Montreal Canadiens, won 2–1 OT)

Regular Season Games with NYR: 698

Playoff Games with NYR: 70

On October 4, 1991, the Rangers brought Hall of Famer Mark Messier to New York for one reason: to help win the team a Stanley Cup for the first time since 1940.

When "Mess" came to the Rangers, he was already a five-time Stanley Cup winner with the Edmonton Oilers. Four of those came while playing with all-time great Wayne Gretzky, but Messier captained a fifth winner in 1990.

The first was in 1984 when the Oilers ended the New York Islanders' four-time Cup reign with a five-game victory in the Final. Messier was named the Conn

Photo courtesy Mark Rosenman.

Backed up his "We Will Win" statement with hat trick.

Smythe winner as he scored 26 points (8 goals, 18 assists) in 19 games.

Rumors were running rampant that a deal for Messier was inevitable. Rangers' general manager Neil Smith constructed a deal that was suitable for the Oilers, who insisted on winger Steven Rice being part of the trade. In the most significant trade in franchise history, the Rangers acquired Messier and future consideration (which turned into defenseman Jeff Beukeboom) in exchange for Rice, center Bernie Nicholls, and left winger Louie DeBrusk.

A day after the trade, Messier debuted with the Rangers in Montreal. Adam Graves, Mess's teammate in Edmonton, graciously gave up the #11 that he wore in the opening game so the man, who he revered, could continue to wear it in New York. In the first game, Messier set up the tying goal in the third period and the Rangers went on to beat Montreal in overtime.

Before the first home game against Boston, the Rangers named Messier the team captain with a lavish ceremony. The Rangers beat the Bruins 2–1 in overtime. Messier assisted on both goals including Mike Gartner's OT game winner.

Except for not winning the Cup, Messier's first year with the Rangers couldn't have gone any better. He scored a team-leading 107 points (35 goals and a single season, team record for centers with 72 assists) and won his second Hart Trophy as the League's MVP and the fourth by a Ranger. In the 1992 playoffs, the Rangers won their first ever seventh game of a series as they knocked off the New Jersey Devils. In Game Two, Messier set an NHL record with two shorthanded goals in one playoff game.

In the 1992–93 season, Messier dropped off to 91 points and the Rangers failed to make the playoffs. The Rangers finished under .500, head coach Roger Neilson was replaced by Ron Smith, and the club wound up in last place just one year after winning the President's Trophy as the NHL's winningest team.

The 1993–94 season would finally be the one. The Rangers finished in first place in the Atlantic Division with 112 points and won the President's Trophy for the second time in three years. The pressure was really on the Rangers this time to finally win that elusive Cup.

The postseason began with the Rangers sweeping the New York Islanders and then taking out the Washington Capitals in five games before they faced rookie goaltender Martin Brodeur and their division rivals, the New Jersey Devils, who finished with the second-best record in the league.

New Jersey won Game Five to take a three-games-to-two lead in the series and put the Rangers' chances of ending the drought in a precarious position. The day before Game Six, Messier made headlines in all of the local newspapers with his proclamation that "We will win." Things looked even bleaker as the Rangers were trailing 2–0 late in the second period, but Messier set up Alexei Kovalev for a huge goal to cut the deficit to 2–1. In the third period, Messier put on one of the most memorable performances in Stanley Cup playoff history as he scored a natural hat trick to stun the Devils and win Game Six, 4–2.

Game Seven was an epic that went to double overtime before Stephane Matteau scored the game winner to send the Rangers to the Stanley Cup Finals. Reportedly, in between the end of the third period and the first overtime, Messier told the team that no matter how long it took, the Rangers were going to win that seventh game.

The Rangers faced the Vancouver Canucks in the Final, and the series went to a seventh and deciding game at Madison Square Garden. Messier was credited with the game-winning goal as the Rangers ended a 54-year drought by winning their first Cup since 1940 with a 3–2 win. The Messiah had delivered and ensured his legacy in New York would be secure. Messier scored a team-record 12 goals in the playoffs, but defenseman Brian Leetch was named the Conn Smythe Trophy winner.

The Rangers would not win again with Messier, although they made the playoffs in the next three seasons. After the 1996–97 season, Messier had a dispute with the Rangers over a new contract and ended up signing with the Vancouver Canucks. He returned as a free agent signee in July of 2000 as a thirty-nine-year-old and finished his NHL and Ranger career after four more seasons.

In January of 2006, the Rangers retired Messier's #11. He was inducted into the Hockey Hall of Fame in 2007.

Vic Hadfield

NYR Debut: October 11, 1961 (at Boston Bruins, won 6–2)
Regular Season Games with NYR: 839
Playoff Games with NYR: 61

Left winger Vic Hadfield was originally a Chicago Black Hawks prospect, but the Rangers claimed him in the 1961 Inter-League Draft. It proved to be a smart selection, as Hadfield compiled a terrific 13-year career with the Rangers.

As a young player in junior hockey, Hadfield established himself as a physical presence who spent more time in the penalty box than he did scoring goals. As he matured, Hadfield started to become more of an offensive threat.

Hadfield scored his first National Hockey League goal on October 31, 1961, in Chicago. The twenty-one-year-old tipped in a shot from the point to tie the game in the third period and the Rangers went on to beat the Black Hawks, 4–2. In his first season, Hadfield scored three goals in 44 games. In the 1962–63 season, Hadfield played with the Rangers' AHL affiliate in Baltimore but played 36 games with the Rangers and scored five goals.

Hadfield made the regular lineup in the 1963–64 season and took full advantage by scoring double-digit (14) goals for the first time in his career.

He also logged a team-leading 151 penalty minutes. In the next three seasons, Hadfield tallied 18, 16, and 13 goals before he began an impressive streak of seven-straight seasons with 20 or more goals.

The left winger combined with center Jean Ratelle and right winger Rod Gilbert to form the famous "Goal-A-Game" or "GAG" line. The moniker was coined by Rangers radio announcer Marv Albert. In the 1971–72 season, the "GAG" line finished third, fourth, and fifth in scoring. The line accounted for 139 goals and 312 points. It was also Hadfield's greatest season.

The native of Oakville, Ontario, was named captain and he acquitted himself very well as he became the first Ranger and the sixth in NHL history to score 50 goals in a season. (Adam Graves would break his record in the 1993–94 season; Jaromir Jagr set the current team record of 54 goals in the 2005–06 season.)

Going into the final day of the regular season, Hadfield had 48 goals. The Rangers hosted the Montreal Canadiens in a meaningless finale as far as the standings were concerned, but the fans at Madison Square Garden were hoping to see history made. The Rangers trailed 4–1 in the second period when Rangers' defenseman Brad Park found Rod Gilbert streaking down the right wing in the offensive zone. Gilbert passed the puck across the net to Hadfield who put it in for his 49th goal. It was also the 300th point for the famous line.

In the third period, the Rangers trailed 6–4 when the fans got their wish. With a little over five minutes remaining, Rangers' defenseman Rod Seiling had the primary assist as he found Hadfield all alone at the Montreal net where he was able to score the landmark goal. The crowd gave Hadfield, what was reported as, a three-minute standing ovation. When he sat down on the bench after the historic goal, the crowd of 17, 250 began a chant of "We Want Hadfield" that did not subside until coach Emile Francis put him back on the ice.

In the playoffs, Hadfield scored two goals in the first game (and four in the series) as the Rangers beat Montreal in six games in the first round. In the semifinal sweep against Chicago, Hadfield scored two more goals. In the Game Six Final loss to Boston, Hadfield had a goal and three assists.

Hadfield scored 55 goals in his final two years with the Rangers. After the 1973–74 season, the thirty-three-year-old was traded to Pittsburgh where he played parts of three seasons. Hadfield finished his Ranger career with 262 goals, which currently ranks fifth all-time.

Nick Mickoski

NYR Debut: April 1, 1948 (at Detroit Red Wings, lost Game Five of Stanley Cup semifinal, 3–1)
Regular Season Games with NYR: 362
Playoff Games with NYR: 14

At 6-foot-1, left winger Nick Mickoski gave Ranger fans quite a Christmas present in 1950.

On Christmas Eve, Mickoski set a Ranger record with four goals and an assist to key a 6–1 victory over the Chicago Black Hawks at Madison Square Garden. Mickoski scored a natural hat trick in the second period and added a fourth goal in the final stanza. The irony of the achievement is that the goals came against Black Hawks goaltender and Hall of Famer Harry Lumley, who, eight months earlier, beat the Rangers in double overtime of the seventh game of the 1950 Final.

The Winnipeg native made his NHL and Ranger debut in the 1948 Stanley Cup Playoffs against Detroit. He was impressive enough to earn a spot in training camp as a twenty-year-old for the 1948–49 season. He scored 13 goals in his first season and became a 20-goal scorer two years later.

Mickoski spent parts of seven seasons with the Rangers. Following the 1954–55 season, he was traded to Chicago in a trade that brought back Hall of Famer Bill Gadsby.

Kelly Kisio

NYR Debut: October 25, 1986 (at Montreal Canadiens, 3–3 tie)
Regular Season Games with NYR: 336
Playoff Games with NYR: 18
Also wore: #16

Kelly Kisio was the last Ranger to wear #11 on a steady basis before Adam Graves (one game) and Mark Messier.

In July 1986, Kisio was acquired from Detroit in a multi-player trade that sent goaltender Glen Hanlon to the Red Wings. Kisio made his Ranger debut in relative anonymity as far as the New York sports scene was concerned. It was the same night that the New York Mets scored their miraculous comeback victory in Game Six of the 1986 World Series at Shea Stadium.

The 5-foot-10 center, who was labeled "too small" when he was a young player trying to break into the league, was a consistent goal scorer for the first four of his five-year Ranger tenure. In the 1990 Stanley Cup Playoffs, Kisio had six assists to lead the Rangers to a five-game win in the Patrick Division Semifinal over the New York Islanders. He added a goal and two assists in the five-game, Division Final loss to the Washington Capitals.

Kisio was named the Rangers 21st captain on Christmas Eve, 1987. He held that title until he was claimed by the Minnesota North Stars in the 1991 NHL Expansion Draft.

Walter "Babe" Pratt

NYR Debut: January 28, 1936 (vs. Montreal Canadiens, won 3–2 OT)
Regular Season Games with NYR: 305
Playoff Games with NYR: 39

Rangers coach Lester Patrick first saw Babe Pratt at his Winnipeg hockey school in 1934. The Rangers signed the big defenseman a year later. Pratt was a physical specimen, measuring 6-foot-3 and 215 pounds.

Pratt's immense size was unusual in the 1930s, which gave him a big advantage over his opponents. He also had some skill, as he was a proficient playmaker.

The Winnipeg native was a key contributor of the 1940 Stanley Cup-winning team. In the six-game, semifinal series win over the Boston Bruins, Pratt scored the only goal of Game Five. In the Final against Toronto, Pratt scored the tying goal in Game Two.

Pratt played four games in the 1942–43 season before being traded to Toronto in November of 1942. The native of Stony Mountain, Manitoba, went on to win the Hart Trophy with the Leafs in the 1943–44 season and another Cup in 1945. Pratt was inducted into the Hockey Hall of Fame in 1966.

Photo from the public domain.

Babe was one of the Rangers first "big" defensemen.

Ulf Nilsson

NYR Debut: October 12, 1978 (vs. Philadelphia Flyers, 3–3 tie)

Regular Season Games with NYR: 170

Playoff Games with NYR: 25

Also wore: #19

Swedish-born center Ulf Nilsson was a dynamic scorer for the Winnipeg Jets of the World Hockey Association. In four straight seasons, Nilsson scored 140 goals and averaged 121 points per season.

The Rangers took notice and were prepared to make a lucrative offer for Nilsson and linemate Anders Hedberg (see Chapter Fifteen) to come to New York. The pair signed for $2.4 million, which made them the highest-paid players in the league at the time.

There was much excitement generated over the signing of the two Swedish players. The Rangers felt the additions greatly enhanced their chances of winning the Stanley Cup.

Nilsson got off to a slow start, as he was scoreless for the first five games of his NHL career. In his sixth game, the twenty-eight-year-old finally scored his first Ranger and NHL goal to help the team to a 5–2 win over Toronto at Madison Square Garden.

Things were going smoothly for the team and their Swedish center. The Rangers were playing well under first year head coach Fred Shero and were optimistic about their chances in the upcoming playoffs, while Nilsson was one of the team's scoring leaders. With 21 games left in the regular season, those chances took a huge hit—as did their productive pivot man.

On February 25, 1979, Nilsson suffered a broken ankle on a hit by New York Islanders' defenseman and Hall of Famer Denis Potvin, and was out for the rest of the regular season and playoffs. On the hit, Nilsson's skate got caught in the Garden ice but he never blamed Potvin, although the Ranger fans thought differently. As a result of the incident, the famous "Potvin Sucks" chant was born and it still exists to this day.

Nilsson was never the same, and a second serious injury severely curtailed his career. While playing for Sweden in the 1981 Canada Cup, Nilsson suffered a serious knee injury that caused him to miss the entire 1981–82 season. He came back to play ten more games before retiring after the 1982–83 season.

Bronco Horvath

NYR Debut: October 7, 1955 (at Chicago Black Hawks, won 7–4)
Regular Season Games with NYR: 114
Playoff Games with NYR: 5
Also wore: #6

When center Bronco Horvath made his NHL debut with the Rangers in 1955, he was coming off a 50-goal season in junior hockey while playing for the Edmonton Flyers of the Western Hockey League. He continued with the hot hand in his very first game of the 1955–56 season, scoring the game-winning goal as the Rangers opened the season with a 7–4 win in Chicago. In the playoffs, Horvath scored a goal with two assists.

After only seven games of the 1956–57 season, Horvath was traded to the Montreal Canadiens. He returned for a second stint with the Rangers when he was claimed in the June 1962 NHL Intra-League Draft. Horvath played 41 games in the 1962–63 season before being placed on waivers and claimed by Toronto.

Horvath is one of a few players who, at one time or another, was the property of one of the "Original Six" teams.

Hank Goldup

NYR Debut: November 28, 1942 (at Toronto Maple Leafs, lost 8–6)
Regular Season Games with NYR: 103
Playoff Games with NYR: 0

Hank Goldup was a left winger who could also function as a defenseman. Goldup began his NHL career in Toronto, where he won a Stanley Cup in 1942. He was traded to the Rangers later that season for Hall of Famer Babe Pratt and scored 11 goals in 36 games.

The Kingston, Ontario, native missed the 1943–44 season due to military service, but returned to the Rangers for the 1945–46 season, where he split time between the big club and their AHL affiliate at New Haven.

Steve Patrick

NYR Debut: December 7, 1984 (vs. Pittsburgh Penguins, lost 4–3 OT)
Regular Season Games with NYR: 71
Playoff Games with NYR: 1

James Patrick's (see Chapter Three) older brother, Steve, played parts of two seasons with the Rangers.

Steve Patrick was a mountain of a man who measured 6-foot-4 and weighed 206 pounds. His immense size made him a first-round pick (20th overall) of the Buffalo Sabres in the 1980 NHL Entry Draft. After parts of five seasons with Buffalo, the right winger was traded to the Rangers in December 1984, along with defenseman Jim Wiemer, for defenseman and former captain Dave Maloney.

In his first game with the Rangers, Steve's younger brother, James, scored two goals. In February 1985, the siblings combined for a goal as Steve scored with the lone assist going to James.

In February of 1986, Steve Patrick was traded to the Quebec Nordiques for winger Wilf Paiement.

Bill Regan

NYR Debut: February 18, 1930 (vs. Toronto Maple Leafs, lost 5–1)
Regular Season Games with NYR: 52
Playoff Games with NYR: 8
Also wore: #15

As a seventeen-year-old, defenseman Bill Regan was already playing junior hockey. There was some question about his age because he was already a six-footer.

The Rangers acquired Regan from the Boston Tigers of the Canadian-American League on February 17, 1930, and he was in the lineup the very next day.

Regan played parts of two seasons with the Rangers. In the 1931–32 season, the Rangers loaned the big defenseman to the Bronx Tigers of the Can-Am League. Regan completed his NHL career by playing for the New York Americans in 1932–33.

Melvile "Sparky" Vail

NYR Debut: January 24, 1929 (at Pittsburgh Pirates, won 3–1)
Regular Season Games with NYR: 50
Playoff Games with NYR: 10

Ontario native Melville "Sparky" Vail was a hybrid: he was listed as a defenseman, but also played left wing.

Vail was a speedy skater who put on quite the display during a game against the rival New York Americans. A raucous crowd of 18,000 were treated to Vail's skating ability, as he was like a dynamo who did everything but score. Vail did not get on the score sheet, but his energy helped the Rangers beat the Americans, 2–1.

After the 1930–31 season, the Rangers traded Vail to Providence of the Canadian-American League.

Vic Desjardins

NYR Debut: November 12, 1931 (at Montreal Canadiens, won 4–1)
Regular Season Games with NYR: 48
Playoff Games with NYR: 7

American-born center Vic Desjardins is a member of the United States Hockey Hall of Fame.

Desjardins was acquired by the Rangers from the Chicago Black Hawks in September of 1931. He played every game of the 1931–32 season, his only one with the Rangers, and scored three goals.

Jack McDonald

NYR Debut: October 30, 1943 (at Toronto Maple Leafs, lost 5–2)
Regular Season Games with NYR: 43
Playoff Games with NYR: 0

Right winger Jack McDonald was a player who got an opportunity during wartime.

McDonald had a respectable single season with the Rangers. The native of Swan River, Manitoba, scored 10 goals with 9 assists in 43 games during the 1943–44 season.

Gord Pettinger

NYR Debut: December 25, 1932 (vs. Montreal Maroons, won 2–0)
Regular Season Games with NYR: 34
Playoff Games with NYR: 8

After beginning the 1932–33 season with the Rangers' Springfield affiliate in the American Hockey League, center Gord Pettinger was brought to Manhattan at the right time.

Pettinger made his Ranger and NHL debut on Christmas Day, 1932, and was a member of the 1933 Stanley Cup-winning team. Pettinger was almost like a "good luck charm." After the Rangers sold his rights to Detroit in 1933, Pettinger went on to win three more Stanley Cups, two with Detroit and one with Boston.

Vic Howe

NYR Debut: January 3, 1951 (vs. Detroit Red Wings, won 5–3)
Regular Season Games with NYR: 33
Playoff Games with NYR: 0
Also wore: #16

Vic Howe carried an added burden during his short stay in the National Hockey League. The right winger was the younger brother of Hall of Famer Gordie Howe. He played parts of three seasons with the Rangers. In his final season of 1954–55, Howe played 29 of his 33 career NHL games.

Rick Chartraw

NYR Debut: January 15, 1983 (at Boston Bruins, lost 2–0)
Regular Season Games with NYR: 30
Playoff Games with NYR: 9

Rick Chartraw has an unusual but proud distinction of being the only Venezuelan-born player to play in the National Hockey League. Chartraw was born in Caracas, but his family relocated to Erie, Pennsylvania, where he learned the sport of hockey.

Chartraw was the 10th overall pick of the Montreal Canadiens in the 1974 NHL Amateur Draft. He won four consecutive Stanley Cup Championships with the Canadiens from 1975–76 through 1978–79, and added a fifth with the Edmonton Oilers in 1984.

The Rangers claimed Chartraw off of waivers from the Los Angeles Kings in January of 1983. The defenseman played 26 games and four more in the 1983–84 season before being traded to Edmonton.

Bobby Carpenter

NYR Debut: January 3, 1987 (at Quebec Nordiques, won 5–2)
Regular Season Games with NYR: 28
Playoff Games with NYR: 0

Bobby Carpenter was the first player to go from an American high school to the NHL. The Massachusetts native was labeled a "can't-miss" prospect when he was selected by the Washington Capitals 3rd overall in the 1981 NHL Entry Draft.

The Caps traded Carpenter to the Rangers on New Year's Day, 1987, as the centerpiece of a four-player deal. The twenty-three-year-old center couldn't seem to cut it in New York and was traded to the Los Angeles Kings two months later in a deal that brought Hall of Fame center Marcel Dionne to New York.

Laurie Scott

NYR Debut: November 15, 1927 (at Toronto Maple Leafs, won 4–2)

Regular Season Games with NYR: 23

Playoff Games with NYR: 0

Left winger Laurie Scott was a victim of unfortunate timing. Scott's entire NHL career consisted of 23 games for the Rangers in the 1927–28 Stanley Cup-winning season, but he was with the Rangers' affiliate at Springfield when the playoffs started. Despite playing for the team during their championship season, Scott did not get his name on the Cup.

Alex Levinsky

NYR Debut: November 10, 1934 (at St. Louis Eagles, lost 4–2)

Regular Season Games with NYR: 20

Playoff Games with NYR: 0

Alex Levinsky was a Stanley Cup winner when he came to the Rangers in a trade with Toronto. Levinsky is one of the earliest Jewish players to play in the NHL. The Toronto native recorded four assists in 20 games as a Ranger. Levinsky was traded to Chicago in January 1935, and won his second Cup with the Black Hawks in 1938.

The following players played less than 20 games with NYR:

Ollie Reinikka - center

NYR Debut: November 16, 1926 (vs. Montreal Maroons, won 1–0)

Regular Season Games with NYR: 16

Playoff Games with NYR: 0

Bill MacKenzie - defenseman

NYR Debut: January 31, 1935 (at Toronto Maple Leafs, won 3–2)

Regular Season Games with NYR: 15

Playoff Games with NYR: 3

Lorne Carr - right wing

NYR Debut: November 11, 1933 (at Toronto Maple Leafs, lost 4–3)

Regular Season Games with NYR: 14

Playoff Games with NYR: 0

Carl Voss - center

NYR Debut: November 10, 1932 (at Montreal Maroons, won 4–2)

Regular Season Games with NYR: 10

Playoff Games with NYR: 0

Ron Hutchinson - center

NYR Debut: December 3, 1960 (at Toronto Maple Leafs, lost 5–2)

Regular Season Games with NYR: 9

Playoff Games with NYR: 0

Wilf Paiement - right wing

NYR Debut: February 8, 1986 (at Boston Bruins, won 3–2)

Regular Season Games with NYR: 8

Playoff Games with NYR: 16

Benoit Gosselin - defenseman

NYR Debut: November 4, 1977 (at Vancouver Canucks, won 5–1)

Regular Season Games with NYR: 7

Playoff Games with NYR: 0

Rare photo of Benoit in one of his seven Ranger appearances.

Dave Barr - right wing

NYR Debut: January 12, 1984 (at Philadelphia Flyers, won 2–1)

Regular Season Games with NYR: 6

Playoff Games with NYR: 0

#12: BRYAN TIME

Bryan Hextall Sr.

NYR Debut: February 23, 1937 (vs. Toronto Maple Leafs, won 2–1)

Regular Season Games with NYR: 449

Playoff Games with NYR: 37

Also wore: #15 and #19

A left-handed shooter who played right wing into a Hall of Fame career, Bryan Hextall Sr. is among the greatest players in franchise history.

The patriarch of one of the most famous hockey families of all time, Hextall (sons Bryan Jr. and Dennis, along with grandson Ron, were all NHL players) led the Rangers in scoring for four consecutive seasons. In 1941–42, Hextall led the NHL in scoring with 56 points, becoming the last Ranger to do so.

The Saskatchewan native will always be known as the player who scored, arguably, the most important goal in the history of the franchise.

The Rangers led the Toronto Maple Leafs three games to two in the 1940 Final, but trailed 2–0 going to the third period of Game Six. Neil Colville and Alf Pike scored third period goals to send the game into overtime.

At the 2:07 mark of the extra session, Hextall took a pass from Rangers center Phil Watson and put it past Maple Leafs goaltender Turk Broda for the Stanley Cup-winning goal. A crowd of nearly 15,000 at Maple Leaf Gardens sat in stunned disbelief as the Rangers celebrated on the ice.

Hextall scored 20 or more goals in six straight seasons before the right winger had to miss the 1944–45 season, as he served time in the Canadian military. In the 1945–46 season, Hextall suffered a stomach disorder and a problem with his liver that limited his season to only three games and threatened to end his career. He was able to return for the 1946–47 season, and scored 20 goals in 60 games.

In his final season of 1947–48, Hextall played 43 games and scored 8 goals. He was inducted into the Hockey Hall of Fame in 1969.

Don Maloney

NYR Debut: February 14, 1979 (vs. Boston Bruins, won 5–1)

Regular Season Games with NYR: 653

Playoff Games with NYR: 85

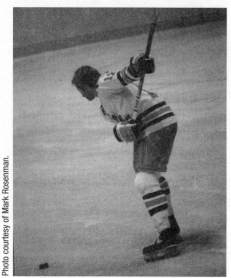

Photo courtesy of Mark Rosenman.

Scored three goals in 2:30. Fastest in franchise history.

Don Maloney wasted no time in making an impression on the Rangers and their loyal fans.

In his first game on Valentine's Day, 1979, Maloney scored a goal in his first NHL shift and assisted on another just 46 seconds later to power the Rangers to a 5–1 win over the Boston Bruins at Madison Square Garden.

After scoring 18 goals and 44 points in 38 games for the New Haven Nighthawks of the American Hockey League, Maloney was recalled by the Rangers. He was placed on a line with Hall of Famer Phil Esposito and Don Murdoch that lovingly became referred to as "The Mafia Line," because of the two players named Don. The left winger was a grinder who did his best work in the corners, which made him a perfect complement for his other two linemates.

Ranger captain Dave Maloney's younger brother played 28 games and totaled 26 points, but was exemplary in the 1979 Stanley Cup Playoffs. The first-year left winger scored 7 goals with 13 assists in 18 games to key the Rangers' run to the Final.

In Game Two of the best-of-three Preliminary Round against the Los Angeles Kings, Maloney assisted on both of Phil Esposito's goals, including the game winner in overtime, as the Rangers swept the short series with a 2–1 win. In the succeeding series against Philadelphia, Maloney scored four goals and added three more in the semifinal win over the New York Islanders. Maloney finished with 20 points which, at the time, was an NHL record (and is still a team record).

In the 1979–80 season, Maloney began a streak of five straight seasons with 20 or more goals. The streak was broken in 1984–85, as Maloney broke his leg and missed three months of the season.

Maloney also holds or shares some impressive team records. In February 1981, he scored three goals in a span of 2:30 minutes to become the fastest Ranger to accomplish the impressive hat trick. In 1987, Maloney scored twice within 8 seconds to share the record with Pierre Jarry (see Chapter Eight) for the fastest two goals in one game.

After playing with and for Esposito, the front office executive for 11 seasons, Maloney was stunned when he was traded to the Hartford Whalers in 1988 on the day after Christmas. Maloney was not one of head coach Michel Bergeron's favorites, so he was sent north to play with the Whalers. Unfortunately for Maloney, he broke his collarbone after only a few games with the Whalers.

Andy Hebenton

NYR Debut: October 7, 1955 (at Chicago Black Hawks, won 7–4)
Regular Season Games with NYR: 560
Playoff Games with NYR: 22

From October 7, 1955, to March 24, 1963, Rangers right winger Andy Hebenton did not miss a game, playing in 560 consecutive contests. If you count his 22 postseason games, Hebenton's streak is extended to 582.

In June 1955, the Rangers purchased Hebenton's rights from the Victoria Cougars of the Western Hockey League. The Winnipeg native made the team out of training camp and never played a minor league game for the Rangers.

Hebenton scored his first NHL goal in his fourth game in Boston, and followed that up with a two-goal game to lead the Rangers to a win over Toronto. He finished with 24 goals and 38 points for the season. The right winger finished second in the 1956 Calder Trophy voting to Detroit Red Wings goaltender Glenn Hall, and was fourth for the Lady Byng Trophy. The very next season, Hebenton won the Lady Byng Trophy and finished top-five in the voting four more times.

Hebenton's best season in New York came in 1958–59, when he set career bests with 33 goals, 29 assists, and 62 points.

After eight years and a corresponding 560 games, Hebenton was claimed by the Boston Bruins in the 1963 Intra-League Draft. He played his ninth full season of 70 games, and finished his career with 630 games played and the distinction of not having missed a game in his NHL career.

Ron Stewart

NYR Debut: November 29, 1967 (vs. Detroit Red Wings, lost 3–1)
Regular Season Games with NYR: 306
Playoff Games with NYR: 37

An off-ice incident that led to the death of a Hall of Fame goaltender tarnished an otherwise solid, 20-year NHL career.

Right winger Ron Stewart was a three-time Stanley Cup winner with Toronto before he came to the Rangers in November 1967. Stewart was claimed by the expansion St. Louis Blues, where he played 19 games before being traded to New York.

Stewart played parts of six seasons with the Rangers, but his life took a fateful turn in the spring of 1970.

The Rangers had been eliminated from the 1970 Stanley Cup Playoffs in early April. Stewart and Ranger goaltender Terry Sawchuk shared a house on Long Island and were drinking at the E and J Pub in Long Beach when an argument ensued. Both were asked to leave and did so, separately.

When the two players arrived at the house they shared, the argument (reportedly over a phone bill) resumed. When the struggle became physical, Sawchuk reportedly fell on Stewart's knee and immediately doubled over in pain. The Hall of Fame goaltender was taken to a local hospital where it was discovered he had suffered damage to his liver and gall bladder.

Sawchuk underwent numerous surgeries during a little over a month in the hospital, but died in his sleep on May 31 as a result of a blood clot. Stewart faced criminal charges, but a grand jury in Mineola, Long Island, found no cause to bring charges and the case was dismissed.

Despite the press that the incident created, the Rangers kept Stewart until November 1971, when he was traded to Vancouver. Stewart returned to the Rangers for a second time in March 1972, and was later traded to the New York Islanders in November.

Stewart was named head coach of the Rangers for the 1975–76 season, but lasted only 39 games before being replaced by John Ferguson in January 1976.

Kris King

NYR Debut: October 8, 1989 (at Chicago Blackhawks, won 5–3)
Regular Season Games with NYR: 249
Playoff Games with NYR: 29
Also wore: #19

Left winger Kris King was a "lunch pail" type of player who did all the dirty work to help his team win.

King was Washington's fourth-round pick in the 1984 NHL Entry Draft, but he was never called up and signed with Detroit as a free agent before being traded to the Rangers in September 1989.

The Ontario native's signature moment with the Rangers came in the 1992 Stanley Cup Playoffs. In Game Three of the Patrick Division Final against Pittsburgh, King scored the game-winning goal in overtime of Game Three. The Rangers lost the series in six games, but King scored three of his four playoff goals in a losing effort.

In December of 1992, the Rangers sent King and winger Tie Domi to Winnipeg for winger Ed Olczyk.

Aldo Guidolin

NYR Debut: January 11, 1953 (at Montreal Canadiens, won 7–0)
Regular Season Games with NYR: 182
Playoff Games with NYR: 0
Also wore: #20

Aldo Guidolin was a versatile player who spent parts of four seasons with the Rangers. Guidolin mostly played right wing with the Rangers, but was also a solid, "stay at home" defenseman.

In his final season of 1955–56, Guidolin began the season with the Rangers but was eventually sent to Providence of the American Hockey League. The native of Credit, Ontario, played 14 seasons in the AHL. After his playing career was over, Guidolin was the head coach of the Colorado Rockies for less than one season in 1978–79.

Leo Bourgeault

NYR Debut: January 27, 1927 (at Montreal Canadiens, won 3–2)
Regular Season Games with NYR: 155
Playoff Games with NYR: 20
Also wore: #2

At 5-foot-6, defenseman Leo Bourgeault was a member of the 1928 Stanley Cup-winning team. Bourgeault played eight seasons in the NHL and parts of five with the Rangers after being acquired from Toronto in January 1927.

Bourgeault was a steady, reliable defenseman who rarely got beat by bigger opponents. During his time with the Rangers, he scored 17 goals and 28 points. In December 1930, he was traded to Ottawa.

Joe Cooper

NYR Debut: November 19, 1935 (vs. Detroit Red Wings, 2–2 tie)
Regular Season Games with NYR: 154
Playoff Games with NYR: 12
Also wore: #11

The Rangers signed defenseman Joe Cooper as a twenty-year-old before the 1935–36 season. He spent one game in New York and played most of that season with Philadelphia of the Canadian-American League.

Cooper played two full seasons before his rights were sold to Chicago in January 1939, though the Rangers brought him back in November of 1946. In his final season, Cooper played 59 games and got into a notable confrontation during a game against Montreal in March 1947.

An all-out brawl developed between the Rangers and Canadiens, and Cooper squared off with Montreal's Erwin "Murph" Chamberlain, who was known as a hard-nosed, tough defenseman with a reputation of having a nasty temper. Chamberlain threw the first punch but missed, and then Cooper answered with a ferocious blow that sent the Canadiens' defenseman flying into the first row of the stands.

Art Somers

NYR Debut: November 12, 1931 (at Montreal Canadiens, won 4–1)
Regular Season Games with NYR: 145
Playoff Games with NYR: 19

In October 1931, the Rangers acquired center Art Somers from Chicago for left winger (see Chapter Ten) Paul Thompson.

Somers had a terrific first season in 1931–32 with the Rangers, as he tied his career high with 11 goals. The Winnipeg native only scored 7 goals in his second season, but was a key member of the 1933 Stanley Cup–winning team. In the playoffs, Somers scored a goal and had 4 assists.

Somers missed almost the entire 1933–34 season with a fractured jaw that became infected and nearly killed him. He returned for one final season in 1934–35, and played in 41 games.

Dunc Fisher

NYR Debut: April 4, 1948 (vs. Detroit Red Wings, playoffs, lost 4–2)
Regular Season Games with NYR: 142
Playoff Games with NYR: 13

Due to an injury, right winger Dunc Fisher was called up to make his NHL debut in the 1948 Stanley Cup Playoffs against the Detroit Red Wings. Fisher recorded an assist in that game, and then joined the Rangers for the 1948–49 season.

Fisher nearly became a hero in the 1950 Stanley Cup Final. The second-year player hit the post in the second overtime of Game Seven, a few moments before the Red Wings scored the Cup-winning goal in one of the greatest finishes in Stanley Cup Final history.

After 16 games in the 1950–51 season, the Rangers traded Fisher to Boston.

Eddie Olczyk

NYR Debut: December 31, 1992 (at Buffalo Sabres, lost 11–6)
Regular Season Games with NYR: 103
Playoff Games with NYR: 1
Also wore: #16

The 1993–94 Rangers had a group of players who were known as the "Black Aces." This group, most of whom were major factors on other teams, provided the depth that was needed for a Stanley Cup Championship team.

Eddie "Eddie-O" Olczyk was a prominent member of the group whose Ranger career can be defined in the one and only playoff game that he was an active player. Game Six of the 1994 Eastern Conference Final against New Jersey is famous for Mark Messier's memorable hat trick, but it was also Olczyk's only playoff appearance for the Rangers. While he didn't get on the score sheet, he gave the Rangers what they needed defensively and in the corners to keep the game within reach.

The Chicago native grew up rooting for his hometown Blackhawks, but the Rangers acquired him from Winnipeg for Kris King and Tie Domi in December 1992. Injuries limited his initial ice time. A broken right thumb in January 1994 kept him out for nearly two months, and he was a healthy scratch throughout the playoffs.

Since Olczyk played in only 37 regular season games and one playoff game, by rule, his name would not be included on the Stanley Cup. The left winger was a popular Ranger, as evidenced by his being named the winner of the "Players' Player" award. His teammates lobbied for his name to be included, and it was etched onto the coveted chalice.

Zellio Toppazzini

NYR Debut: November 18, 1950 (at Toronto Maple Leafs, lost 5–4)
Regular Season Games with NYR: 71
Playoff Games with NYR: 0

Right winger Zellio Toppazzini came to the Rangers from the Bruins for right winger Dunc Fisher (see above) in November 1950. The talented winger had a reputation for being a goal scorer, but it never materialized in Boston.

Toppazzini's career seemed to take a turn upward as he scored a career-high 14 goals in his first season in New York. In 1951–52, the twenty-two-year-old shuffled between the Rangers and the American Hockey League.

After his NHL career ended, Toppazzini went on to become a star in the AHL as he led the league in scoring with 113 points during the 1955–56 season.

Mike Keane

NYR Debut: October 3, 1997 (vs. New York Islanders, 2–2 tie)
Regular Season Games with NYR: 70
Playoff Games with NYR: 0

Mike Keane was a solid NHL winger who signed with the Rangers as an unrestricted free agent in July 1997. Keane was known as a solid defensive forward who always seemed to do his best work in the playoffs, as he was a three-time Stanley Cup winner with Montreal, Colorado, and Dallas.

The 1997–98 season saw the Rangers make a coaching change as Colin Campbell was replaced by John Muckler. Keane, who was a plus-12 in 70 games, was a fit for Campbell's system but not Muckler's. In March 1998, Keane was traded to the Dallas Stars.

Bill Goldsworthy

NYR Debut: November 13, 1976 (vs. Buffalo Sabres, lost 6–2)

Regular Season Games with NYR: 68

Playoff Games with NYR: 0

By the time right winger Bill Goldsworthy joined the Rangers, he was thirty-two years old. Goldsworthy got his chance when the expansion Minnesota North Stars selected him off of the Boston Bruins roster in the 1967 NHL Expansion Draft. In the 1973–74 season, he scored a career high 48 goals.

With the Rangers, Goldsworthy scored 10 goals in parts of two seasons but he was a defensive liability as evidenced by his minus-16. In December 1977, Goldsworthy was traded to Indianapolis of the World Hockey Association.

Photo courtesy of Ken Tash.

Never regained his 48 goal season form as a Ranger.

Alexandre Daigle

NYR Debut: November 20, 1999 (at Toronto Maple Leafs, lost 4–3 OT)

Regular Season Games with NYR: 58

Playoff Games with NYR: 0

The pressure of being a former #1 overall pick was gone by the time Alexandre Daigle came to the Rangers in October 1999.

Daigle was the top pick of the Ottawa Senators in the 1993 NHL Entry Draft. The expectations were enormous, and Daigle was worn down by the time he was traded to the Philadelphia Flyers in January 1998. After a stint with Edmonton and Tampa Bay, Daigle joined the Rangers and appeared to be revitalized as he got off to a quick start with three goals and eight assists in his first nine games. The production began to fall off for the pivot-man, and Daigle retired after the season but came out of retirement in 2002 to play three more seasons in the NHL.

Lee Stempniak

NYR Debut: October 9, 2014 (at St. Louis Blues, won 3–2)
Regular Season Games with NYR: 53
Playoff Games with NYR: 0

Journeyman winger Lee Stempniak made the Rangers his sixth NHL team when he signed on as a free agent in July 2014. The native of West Seneca, New York, was a third- and fourth-line player with the Rangers during the 2014–15 season. In March 2015, he was traded to the Winnipeg Jets for winger Carl Klingberg.

Dick Meissner

NYR Debut: October 9, 1963 (at Chicago Black Hawks, lost 3–1)
Regular Season Games with NYR: 36
Playoff Games with NYR: 0

Right winger Dick Meissner took an unusual route to the Rangers. Meissner was the property of the Boston Bruins and was playing at Providence of the AHL when he was traded to the Rangers in February 1963. There was one stipulation to the deal: that the right winger would finish the season with Providence and would not join the Rangers until the following season. He played parts of two seasons with the Rangers and was traded to Chicago in June 1965.

Tim Kerr

NYR Debut: October 3, 1991 (at Boston Bruins, lost 5–3)
Regular Season Games with NYR: 32
Playoff Games with NYR: 8

Winger Tim Kerr scored 370 goals during his NHL career. However, only seven of those were with the Rangers.

Kerr made his reputation by being a big bodied player who would screen goaltenders and score a number of "garbage goals" from in front of the net. The 6-foot-3, 230-pound native of Windsor, Ontario, was acquired by the Rangers from San Jose in May of 1991 for winger Brian Mullen.

Kerr, who was brought to New York to enhance the power play, was thirty-two years old when he put on a Ranger sweater. Unfortunately, injuries limited him to seven goals in 32 games (as well as one goal in the playoffs). After the season, he was traded to the Hartford Whalers.

Glenn Brydson

NYR Debut: November 10, 1935 (at Detroit Red Wings, 1–1 tie)
Regular Season Games with NYR: 30
Playoff Games with NYR: 0

Glenn Brydson has a unique distinction of playing in more games in one season than the schedule dictates.

The Rangers claimed the right winger in the NHL Dispersal Draft October 1935, but he was traded three months later to the Chicago Black Hawks. Because of the way the schedule was set up, Brydson ended up playing 52 games in a 48-game regular season schedule.

Jim Mikol

NYR Debut: October 12, 1964 (at Boston Bruins, won 6–2)
Regular Season Games with NYR: 30
Playoff Games with NYR: 0

Versatile winger Jim Mikol's place in Ranger lore came at the end of his tenure. Mikol played 30 games with the Rangers and scored one goal. In May 1965, Mikol was traded to Providence of the American Hockey League as part of a five-player deal that brought Hall of Fame goaltender Ed Giacomin to New York.

Matt Puempel

NYR Debut: November 25, 2016 (at Philadelphia Flyers, won 3–2)
Regular Season Games with NYR: 27
Playoff Games with NYR: 0

Olli Jokinen

NYR Debut: February 2, 2010 (at Los Angeles Kings, lost 2–1)
Regular Season Games with NYR: 26
Playoff Games with NYR: 0

Thirty-one-year-old Finnish center Olli Jokinen scored four goals with 11 assists in 26 games with the Rangers. He was acquired from the Calgary Flames, along with Brandon Prust, for Chris Higgins and Ales Kotalik in February 2010. After the season, Jokinen went back to the Flames as a free agent.

Leo Quenneville

NYR Debut: November 14, 1929 (at Montreal Maroons, won 2–1)
Regular Season Games with NYR: 25
Playoff Games with NYR: 3

Winger Leo Quenneville was a good minor league scorer who could never translate those skills to the NHL. Quenneville played his entire 25-game career with the Rangers and did not score a goal. His rights were traded to London, Ontario, of the International Hockey League in May 1930.

Rich Brennan

NYR Debut: February 17, 1999 (vs. Montreal Canadiens, lost 6–3)
Regular Season Games with NYR: 24
Playoff Games with NYR: 0

Rich Brennan was born in Schenectady, New York, and got to play a short time with the Rangers. The 6-foot-2, 212-pound defenseman was acquired from San Jose in March 1998, and began the 1998–99 season with the Rangers' affiliate in Hartford. In Brennan's second game with the Rangers, he scored a goal in a 6–1 win over the Penguins. Brennan became a free agent after the season. In six NHL seasons, Brennan played with six different teams.

Myles Lane

NYR Debut: November 15, 1928 (at Detroit Cougars, won 2–0)
Regular Season Games with NYR: 24
Playoff Games with NYR: 0

Defenseman Myles Lane was a collegiate star who was the first to go directly from college to the National Hockey League. Lane, who played at Dartmouth, signed with the Rangers in October 1928. Lane scored a goal in 24 games and was sold to Boston in January 1929.

Eddie Rodden

NYR Debut: November 30, 1930 (at Philadelphia Quakers, won 3–0)
Regular Season Games with NYR: 24
Playoff Games with NYR: 0

Center Eddie Rodden had a reputation as a playmaker, but he bounced around the NHL for four seasons and never lived up to his potential. Rodden came to the Rangers after an outstanding season with the London Panthers of the International Hockey League, where he scored 43 points in 42 games. After 24 games, the Rangers sold Rodden's rights to Pittsburgh of the IHL.

Bob MacMillan

NYR Debut: November 27, 1974 (vs. Toronto Maple Leafs, won 4–3)
Regular Season Games with NYR: 22
Playoff Games with NYR: 0

Right winger Bob MacMillan was selected by the Rangers as their second of two first-round picks and the 15th overall in the 1972 NHL Entry Draft. MacMillan played two seasons with the Minnesota Fighting Saints of the rival World Hockey Association before joining the Rangers for the 1974–75 season. After 22 games, MacMillan was traded to St. Louis. He eventually won the Lady Byng Trophy while playing for the Atlanta Flames in 1979.

Ralph Taylor

NYR Debut: January 9, 1930 (vs. Montreal Maroons, lost 5–4)
Regular Season Games with NYR: 22
Playoff Games with NYR: 4
Also wore: #15

Despite his smallish 5-foot-9 size, defenseman Ralph Taylor's nickname was "Bouncer" for his hard-nosed play on the ice. The Rangers claimed Taylor on waivers in January 1930 but, after 22 games and 32 penalty minutes, he was sold to Chicago of the American Hockey Association.

Howie Morenz

NYR Debut: January 28, 1936 (vs. Montreal Canadiens, won 3–2)
Regular Season Games with NYR: 19
Playoff Games with NYR: 0

One of the greatest players in the history of the sport, Hall of Fame center Howie Morenz came to the Rangers as a thirty-three-year-old who was in his 13th NHL season. Morenz was traded to the Rangers from the Chicago Black Hawks, his second team after eleven sparkling seasons in Montreal.

Morenz lasted in New York for 19 games, and gave his former fans a remembrance of years past when he scored a goal in his first game with the Rangers to key a 3–2 victory over his old team. The three-time Hart Trophy winner was sent back to Montreal in September 1936. On March 4, 1937, Morenz suffered a horrific injury where he broke his leg. Four days later, Morenz died in the hospital of a heart condition.

The following players played less than 19 games with NYR:

Todd White - center

NYR Debut: October 18, 2010 (vs. Colorado Avalanche, lost 3–1)
Regular Season Games with NYR: 18
Playoff Games with NYR: 0

Bob Errey - left wing

NYR Debut: March 25, 1998 (vs. Ottawa Senators, lost 3–2)
Regular Season Games with NYR: 12
Playoff Games with NYR: 0

Ken Gernander - right wing

NYR Debut: March 9, 1996 (at Washington Capitals, won 6–1)
Regular Season Games with NYR: 12
Playoff Games with NYR: 15

Dixon Ward - right wing

NYR Debut: October 9, 2002 (at Carolina Hurricanes, won 4–1)
Regular Season Games with NYR: 8
Playoff Games with NYR: 0

Jerry Byers - left wing

NYR Debut: December 7, 1977 (vs. Philadelphia Flyers, 3–3 tie)
Regular Season Games with NYR: 7
Playoff Games with NYR: 0
Also wore: #15

Sam McAdam - center

NYR Debut: January 11, 1931 (vs. Chicago Black Hawks, lost 2–0)
Regular Season Games with NYR: 5
Playoff Games with NYR: 0

Gord Haworth - center

NYR Debut: December 31, 1952 (vs. Toronto Maple Leafs, 3–3 tie)
Regular Season Games with NYR: 2
Playoff Games with NYR: 0

Joe Krol - left wing

NYR Debut: January 19, 1937 (vs. Montreal Canadiens, 1–1 OT tie)
Regular Season Games with NYR: 2
Playoff Games with NYR: 0

Patrick Rissmiller - left wing

NYR Debut: October 11, 2008 (at Philadelphia Flyers, won 4–3)
Regular Season Games with NYR: 2
Playoff Games with NYR: 0

#13: SUPERSTITION AIN'T THE RANGER WAY

Sergei Nemchinov

NYR Debut: October 3, 1991 (at Boston Bruins, lost 5–3)

Regular Season Games with NYR: 418

Playoff Games with NYR: 52

A twelfth-round pick who became one of the first Russian-born players to have his name etched onto the Stanley Cup, center Sergei Nemchinov was a solid two-way player for the Rangers during parts of six seasons in New York.

The Rangers took a chance in the 1990 NHL Entry Draft with their selection of Nemchinov. He was playing for the Soviet Union National Team and was a participant in the 1987 Canada Cup. The Rangers were hoping that he could be released from his commitments to come to play in the NHL. Nemchinov became available and was on the roster for the 1991–92 season. The native of Moscow had a fabulous first season in the NHL, as he scored 30 goals and 58 points and helped the Rangers win the President's Trophy.

Nemchinov scored his first NHL goal in a memorable regular season game. It was his second game and Mark Messier's debut with the Rangers. In fact, he scored the game-winning goal in overtime as the Rangers beat the Canadiens in Montreal 2–1. It was the Rangers' first win at the Montreal Forum in nearly eight years.

In the Stanley Cup-winning season of 1993–94, Nemchinov's ability as a two-way player proved to be a key component in the Rangers' snapping their 54-year drought without a championship. Nemchinov played all 23 postseason games, scoring two goals with five assists, but his defensive work and ability to win faceoffs served the Rangers well during the run.

Nemchinov went on to play parts of three more seasons with the Rangers before being traded, with winger Brian Noonan, to Vancouver in March 1997 for Esa Tikkanen and Russ Courtnall. The Russian center eventually wound up on the New Jersey Devils team that won the Stanley Cup in 2000.

Kevin Hayes

NYR Debut: October 12, 2014 (vs. Toronto Maple Leafs, won 6–3)
Regular Season Games with NYR: 234
Playoff Games with NYR: 34

The Chicago Blackhawks made center Kevin Hayes their first-round pick and 24th overall in the 2010 draft. Hayes declined to sign with Chicago and became an unrestricted free agent. The former Boston College star signed a deal with the Rangers and made his debut in October 2014.

Hayes scored 17 goals in his rookie season. In the playoffs, he added two goals and five assists including the game-winning goal in overtime of Game Four of the 2015 Eastern Conference First Round over Pittsburgh. He dropped off to 14 goals in the 2015–16 season, but rebounded to score a career-high 49 points during the 2016–17 season.

Bob Brooke

NYR Debut: March 9, 1984 (at Winnipeg Jets, won 6–5 OT)
Regular Season Games with NYR: 175
Playoff Games with NYR: 32

Melrose, Massachusetts, native Bob Brooke made his NHL debut with the Rangers. Drafted by the Blues in 1980, the center was acquired from St. Louis and immediately joined the Rangers for nine games in his first season. Brooke was a standout at Yale and a Hobey Baker finalist in 1983. He also played for the United States Olympic Hockey Team in the 1984 Winter Games at Sarajevo.

Brooke was a grinder who was a good faceoff man, but he had his best season in 1985–86 when he scored a career-high 24 goals. Brooke's signature moment as a Ranger came in the 1986 Stanley Cup Playoffs.

The Rangers trailed the Washington Capitals two games to one in the Patrick Division Final. Washington had a 5–3 lead in the third period of Game Four at Madison Square Garden, but a goal by Rangers' defenseman Willie Huber narrowed the gap to 5–4.

With a little over two and a half minutes remaining, Brooke tied the game as he took a pass from Brian McClellan from behind the net and beat Caps goalie Pete Peeters in close. In overtime, Brooke stole a pass and put a wrist shot past Peeters from the right faceoff circle for the game winner. The

Rangers went on to beat Washington in six games. Brooke was outstanding in the 1986 playoffs with six goals and 15 points in 16 games.

After 15 games in the 1986–87 season, Brooke was traded to the Minnesota North Stars.

Valeri Kamensky

> **NYR Debut:** October 1, 1999 (at Edmonton Oilers, 1–1 OT tie)
> **Regular Season Games with NYR:** 123
> **Playoff Games with NYR:** 0

Russian-born Valeri Kamensky made his professional debut in the Soviet Union at the age of sixteen. By the time he was twenty years old, he had already played over 100 professional games.

Kamensky starred with the Quebec Nordiques and helped the franchise win a Stanley Cup in 1996 after their move to Denver, Colorado. The Rangers signed the veteran winger to a two-year, free agent contract in July 1999.

Kamensky had 166 career goals when he came to New York, but only scored a total of 27 over two seasons. His best game was late in the 1999–2000 season, when he scored two goals to help the Rangers beat the Philadelphia Flyers, 3–2. Kamensky did not play any postseason games with the Rangers and was not re-signed after the 2000–01 season.

Photo by Keith Allison via Wikimedia Commons.

After 23 goal campaign left to play in Soviet Union.

Nikolai Zherdev

> **NYR Debut:** October 4, 2008 (at Tampa Bay, won 2–1)
> **Regular Season Games with NYR:** 82
> **Playoff Games with NYR:** 0

Right winger Nikolai Zherdev was a highly regarded prospect who was the 4th overall pick of the Columbus Blue Jackets in the

2003 NHL Entry Draft. After scoring 27 goals in the 2005–06 season, Zherdev's production tailed off and his clashes with management increased.

In July 2008, the Rangers acquired Zherdev from Columbus as part of a multi-player trade. The twenty-three-year-old had a solid season in New York with 23 goals and 58 points in 82 games. After the season, the Ukraine-born Zherdev went to play in the Soviet Union, but returned to the NHL for one season in 2010–11.

Jack Stoddard

> **NYR Debut:** January 2, 1952 (vs. Detroit Red Wings, won 1–0)
>
> **Regular Season Games with NYR:** 80
>
> **Playoff Games with NYR:** 0

Jack Stoddard was a big man who was nicknamed "The Octopus" because of the length of his arms. The 6-foot-3, 185-pound right winger scored 20 goals and 48 points in 35 games while playing for Providence of the American Hockey League in 1951–52. The Rangers acquired his rights in January 1952, and he was brought right up to the big club.

Stoddard scored 16 goals in parts of two seasons with the Rangers.

Daniel Carcillo

> **NYR Debut:** January 8, 2014 (at Chicago Blackhawks, won 3–2)
>
> **Regular Season Games with NYR:** 31
>
> **Playoff Games with NYR:** 8

Daniel Carcillo had a reputation as a hard-nosed player who sometimes crossed the line. Carcillo spent many minutes in the penalty box, and was acquired by the Rangers from the Los Angeles Kings in January 2014.

Carcillo was brought in to add toughness to the Rangers' roster, but he provided an added bonus with some surprising offensive

Carcillo had big goal in 2014 Stanley Cup Semifinal.

Photo courtesy of Mark Rosenman.

production. In 31 games, Carcillo scored three goals. In the 2014 Stanley Cup Playoffs, Carcillo scored the first goal in the Rangers' Game Seven victory of the Metropolitan Division Semifinal against the Philadelphia Flyers.

Richard Scott

NYR Debut: October 27, 2001 (at Boston Bruins, won 2–1)
Regular Season Games with NYR: 10
Playoff Games with NYR: 0

Right winger Richard Scott played his entire 10-game, NHL career in parts of two seasons with the Rangers. Scott split time with the Rangers and their AHL affiliate in Hartford. He failed to score a single point in his short tenure.

#14: "FACE OFF AND THE WAITING IS OVER"

Craig MacTavish

NYR Debut: March 22, 1994 (at Calgary Flames, 4–4 OT tie)

Regular Season Games with NYR: 12

Playoff Games with NYR: 23

Veteran center Craig MacTavish was acquired by the Rangers in part because of his faceoff prowess. It proved to be a prophetic move when Mac-Tavish won the final faceoff of Game Seven of the 1994 Stanley Cup Final.

MacTavish, who was the last player allowed to play without a helmet, was an impending free agent when he was acquired by the Rangers from Edmonton in March of 1994. Known as one of the best defensive forwards, MacTavish filled a need for the Rangers who were preparing to make a run for the Cup.

The London, Ontario, native played the final 12 games of the regular season and was a factor in the playoffs. Head coach Mike Keenan made sure to use MacTavish on all the big faceoffs throughout the postseason.

In Game Seven of the Final against Vancouver, the Rangers were leading 3–2 when an icing call with 1.6 seconds left in the game created a faceoff to the right of goaltender Mike Richter. Right before the faceoff took place, Rangers captain Mark Messier, who had been taking faceoffs for most of the third period, said something to MacTavish and took a spot to the right of the faceoff circle. MacTavish directed Messier to move to the other side.

Vancouver was looking to win the faceoff and get it to their sniper, Pavel Bure, for a one-timer. As the puck was dropped, MacTavish timed it perfectly to get his stick on it and his body in the way so that Canucks center Trevor Linden would not get possession. MacTavish ushered the puck toward the end boards, the clock hit zero, and the Rangers had finally won the elusive Stanley Cup.

MacTavish will go down as the answer to two trivia questions:

Who was the last helmetless player in the NHL?

Who was the player who took the final faceoff in the Rangers Stanley Cup-winning Game Seven of the 1994 Final?

Mark Hardy

NYR Debut: February 25, 1988 (vs. Pittsburgh Penguins, won 2–1)
Regular Season Games with NYR: 284
Playoff Games with NYR: 26

Mark Hardy was born in Switzerland, but grew up in Montreal. The Rangers acquired the veteran defenseman from the Los Angeles Kings in February 1988, in exchange for popular winger Ron Duguay.

Hardy played 19 games in his first stint with the Rangers, but was traded after the 1987–88 season to the Minnesota North Stars. After 15 games, he was dealt back to the Rangers where he played parts of the next four seasons. Hardy was a hard-nosed defenseman who led the Rangers in penalty minutes in 1988–89.

Hardy's best season on the score sheet was 1989–90, when he had 15 assists. In March 1993, Hardy was traded back to the Kings.

Mike Allison

NYR Debut: October 9, 1980 (at Boston Bruins, lost 7–2)
Regular Season Games with NYR: 266
Playoff Games with NYR: 63

Numerous injuries curtailed Mike Allison's career. The Ontario native was a second-round pick of the Rangers in the 1980 NHL Entry Draft.

Allison was projected as a goal scorer, and his career started off with a bang when he scored his first NHL goal on the first shot of his first shift in Boston. In his second game, Allison scored his first hat trick to key an 8–3 win in Toronto. In the 1980–81 season, the Rangers' center set a franchise record for assists (38) and points (64) by a rookie, which was broken the very next season by Mark Pavelich.

During the next five seasons, Allison suffered a series of ankle and knee injuries that limited his production and made him change his game. Allison's mobility was such that he could not be as productive offensively as he once was, but he used his instinct to remain in the NHL as a grinder and defensive forward.

In August 1986, Allison was traded to the Toronto Maple Leafs for center Walt Poddubny.

Theo Fleury

NYR Debut: October 1, 1999 (at Edmonton Oilers, 1–1 OT tie)
Regular Season Games with NYR: 224
Playoff Games with NYR: 0

Theo Fleury played bigger than his 5-foot-6 stature would suggest.

The Rangers needed an offensive winger when they signed Fleury as a free agent to a three-year contract in July 1999. The diminutive right winger was a major contributor to a Calgary Flames team that won the 1989 Stanley Cup. In the 1990–91 season, Fleury scored a career-high 51 goals and finished in the top five in the voting for the Hart and Selke trophies.

In Fleury's first season with the Rangers, he scored 64 points. In the 2000–01 season, Fleury scored 30 goals in 62 games. He also had 20 multi-point games and was named an All-Star, but the Rangers failed to make the playoffs.

Fleury finished his Rangers career with 24 goals in the 2001–02 season.

Don Murdoch

NYR Debut: October 6, 1976 (vs. Minnesota North Stars, won 6–5)
Regular Season Games with NYR: 221
Playoff Games with NYR: 21

In the 1976 NHL Amateur Draft, the Rangers used the 6th overall selection to draft promising right winger Don Murdoch.

The nineteen-year-old dominated the Western Hockey League for back-to-back 80-plus goal seasons, which made for high expectations after he was chosen by the Rangers.

The young winger wasted no time in making his presence felt at Madison Square Garden, as he scored two goals in his first NHL game to key a win over Minnesota. Six days later, the Rangers played the North Stars

Photo courtesy of Ken Tash.

Murdoch scored 32 goals in his rookie season.

193

in Minnesota and Murdoch had a night to remember. The Ranger rookie scored a team-record five goals in a 10–4 thrashing. That gave him eight goals on the young season, seven of them against the North Stars.

Murdoch finished his first season of 1976–77 with a Ranger rookie record of 32 goals. He only played 59 games because he tore a tendon in his ankle during a practice on Valentine's Day 1977 and finished second to Atlanta's Willi Plett for the Calder Trophy.

The injury was the beginning of a downturn for Murdoch's career. His ankle required multiple surgeries, and he had legal trouble following his first season. In August 1977, the Ranger winger was arrested at the Toronto airport for possession of cocaine. The case was tied up in the courts so he played the 1977–78 season, scoring 27 goals. After pleading guilty, the NHL suspended Murdoch for the entire 1978–79 season. Following an appeal, the suspension was reduced to 40 games.

Murdoch, who later admitted to also having a drinking problem, played 56 games in the 1979–80 season before he was traded to Edmonton in March 1980 for Cam Connor and their third-round pick in the 1981 Entry Draft.

Bruce MacGregor

NYR Debut: February 4, 1971 (at Detroit Red Wings, won 1–0)
Regular Season Games with NYR: 220
Playoff Games with NYR: 51
Also wore: #12

Veteran center Bruce MacGregor was not sure if he wanted to play for the Rangers after he was acquired in a trade with the Detroit Red Wings in February 1971. MacGregor played ten-plus seasons in Detroit, and the trade caught him completely by surprise.

MacGregor eventually decided to join the Rangers, and his first game came against his former team. He didn't get on the scoresheet that night, and it took a while for the veteran center to blend in. On February 21, MacGregor played against his old team again and had three assists to lead the Rangers to a 4–1 win. Six days later, MacGregor scored his first Ranger goal in a 4–0 win over Pittsburgh.

The Edmonton, Alberta, native capped off a six-game winning streak with a hat trick and two assists to lead the Rangers to an 8–1 rout of the California Golden Seals at Madison Square Garden.

MacGregor played 27 games and had 12 goals and 25 points in his first season. In his second season with New York, MacGregor scored 19 goals but was also outstanding in the run to the 1972 Stanley Cup Final. The center scored two goals with six assists in 16 games. In the 1974 playoffs, MacGregor scored six goals in the Rangers' six-game series win over Montreal. After the season, MacGregor left the Rangers to join the World Hockey Association.

Kilby MacDonald

NYR Debut: November 11, 1939 (at Toronto Maple Leafs, 1–1 OT tie)

Regular Season Games with NYR: 151

Playoff Games with NYR: 15

Also wore: #8 and #2

Left winger Kilby MacDonald is best known as being the first Ranger to win the Calder Trophy.

The Rangers saw MacDonald in the Gold Belt Hockey League during the 1935–36 season, and signed him to play with the New York Rovers for the following season. After two years with the Philadelphia Ramblers of the AHL, MacDonald joined the Rangers for the 1939–40 season.

MacDonald scored 15 goals in his first season and recorded two assists in the playoffs as the Rangers went on to win the 1940 Stanley Cup.

The Ottawa native suffered from a stomach disorder that limited his time in the 1940–41 season and cut short his term in the Canadian Army. MacDonald returned to the Rangers for the second half of the 1943–44 season, playing in an additional 36 games before retiring after the 1944–45 season.

Brendan Shanahan

NYR Debut: October 5, 2006 (vs. Washington Capitals, won 5–2)

Regular Season Games with NYR: 140

Playoff Games with NYR: 20

Brendan Shanahan spent two years of his Hall of Fame career with the Rangers. The thirty-eight-year-old left winger signed a free agent contract with the Rangers in July 2006, feeling that he still had something left.

Photo by Michael Miller via Wikimedia Commons.

Shanahan made the All-Star team his first season as a Ranger.

In his first game with the Rangers, Shanahan scored two goals to key a season-opening win over Washington at Madison Square Garden, 5–2. The second goal was the 600th of his NHL career. The future Hall of Famer got off to a fast start in New York as he scored 12 goals in his first 13 games. Shanahan scored 29 goals in his first season and was named to the All-Star team. He added 23 goals during his second season of 2007–08.

Jason Ward

NYR Debut: October 5, 2005 (at Philadelphia Flyers, won 5–3)

Regular Season Games with NYR: 127

Playoff Games with NYR: 1

Also wore: #16

Right winger Jason Ward was a former first-round pick of the Montreal Canadiens who could never find the goal-scoring touch which he displayed in the American Hockey League.

When Ward signed with the Rangers before the 2005–06 season, he had made himself into a gritty, defensive forward.

Ward scored 14 goals in a little over a season and a half with the Rangers. He was traded to the Los Angeles Kings in February 2007 for winger Sean Avery.

Parker MacDonald

NYR Debut: October 31, 1956 (at Toronto Maple Leafs, lost 7–2)

Regular Season Games with NYR: 119

Playoff Games with NYR: 7

The Rangers drafted left winger Parker MacDonald off of the Toronto roster with the hope that he would develop into the offensive player he was projected to be with the Maple Leafs. MacDonald never really became that offensive threat in New York. He scored 15 goals during parts of three seasons with the Rangers, while also playing 134 games for the team's minor league affiliates.

MacDonald was claimed by Detroit in the 1960 NHL Intra-League Draft.

Brian Cullen

NYR Debut: October 7, 1959 (at Chicago Black Hawks, lost 5–2)
Regular Season Games with NYR: 106
Playoff Games with NYR: 0

Brian Cullen was the first of the Cullen family to play for the Rangers when he joined the team for the 1959–60 season. His younger brother Ray (see Chapter Seventeen) would play for the Rangers six years later.

The Ottawa-born center scored 59 points (19 goals) in parts of two seasons with the Rangers.

Val Fonteyne

NYR Debut: October 9, 1963 (at Chicago Black Hawks, lost 3–1)
Regular Season Games with NYR: 96
Playoff Games with NYR: 0

Val Fonteyne was known as one of the cleanest players in the National Hockey League, yet he never won a Lady Byng Trophy. Fonteyne put together five full seasons with zero penalty minutes. With the Rangers, he had six penalty minutes in parts of two seasons.

In February 1965, Fonteyne was placed on waivers and claimed by Detroit.

Taylor Pyatt

NYR Debut: January 19, 2013 (at Boston Bruins, lost 3–1)
Regular Season Games with NYR: 70
Playoff Games with NYR: 12

Many felt Taylor Pyatt never used his size to his advantage. The left winger, who was the New York Islanders' first round and 8th overall pick in the 1999 NHL Entry Draft, was 6-foot-4 and 230 pounds. He got off to a fast start with the Rangers by scoring three goals in his first four games.

In the 2013 Eastern Conference Quarterfinal, Pyatt scored a big goal in the Rangers' Game Seven victory over the Washington Capitals. The native of Thunder Bay, Ontario, played parts of two seasons with the Rangers.

Bert Wilson

> **NYR Debut:** February 27, 1974 (vs. Vancouver Canucks, won 4–2)
> **Regular Season Games with NYR:** 66
> **Playoff Games with NYR:** 0

Persistence paid off for left winger Bert Wilson. The Rangers' second round pick in the 1969 NHL Entry Draft played five years in the minors with three teams before getting an opportunity in 1974.

After scoring six points in 61 games during the 1974 season, Wilson was traded to the St. Louis Blues in July 1975 in a deal that brought back goaltender John Davidson.

Fred Thurier

> **NYR Debut:** October 28, 1944 (at Toronto Maple Leafs, lost 2–1)
> **Regular Season Games with NYR:** 50
> **Playoff Games with NYR:** 0

After playing two seasons with the New York/Brooklyn Americans from 1940–42, center Fred Thurier served two years in the Canadian Military.

He was given an early release and played his only full season with the Rangers in 1944–45. Thurier scored 16 goals with 19 assists for 35 points. However, with many of the NHL regulars returning from the war, the twenty-nine-year-old was out of a job.

Leroy Goldsworthy

> **NYR Debut:** March 29, 1929 (vs. Boston Bruins, Game Two Stanley Cup Final, lost 2–1)
> **Regular Season Games with NYR:** 44
> **Playoff Games with NYR:** 4

The only Ranger to make his debut in a Stanley Cup Final is right winger Leroy Goldsworthy.

Born in Two Harbors, Minnesota, Goldsworthy was known as a solid two-way forward. After playing in all 44 games in 1929–30, Goldsworthy's rights were traded to London of the International Hockey League in October 1930.

Mattias Norstrom

NYR Debut: October 11, 1993 (vs. Washington Capitals, won 5–2)
Regular Season Games with NYR: 43
Playoff Games with NYR: 3
Also wore: #5

Swedish-born defenseman Mattias Norstrom was a second-round pick of the Rangers in the 1992 NHL Entry Draft. The Rangers liked his size (6-foot-2, 210 pounds) and skating ability.

Norstrom played parts of three seasons in New York before becoming part of a seven-player trade with the Los Angeles Kings in March 1996.

Frank "Patsy" Callighen

NYR Debut: November 20, 1927 (at New York Americans, won 2–1)
Regular Season Games with NYR: 36
Playoff Games with NYR: 9

As a 5-foot-6 defenseman, Frank "Patsy" Callighen had to be tough to play in the NHL. Callighen came aboard at the right time as the Rangers went on to win their first Stanley Cup in 1928.

"Patsy" Callighen played a total of 36 NHL games with the Rangers, though he did not score a point.

Angus "Scotty" Cameron

NYR Debut: October 31, 1942 (at Toronto Maple Leafs, lost 7–2)
Regular Season Games with NYR: 35
Playoff Games with NYR: 0

Back issues curtailed Angus "Scotty" Cameron's career with the Rangers. Cameron, who earned the nickname "Scotty" for his parents who were born in Scotland and his talent for golf, was scheduled to join the Rangers for the 1941–42 season, but a back injury prevented his call up.

He did join the team for the 1942–43 season and scored eight goals. Cameron did a stint in the Canadian Army and eventually finished his pro career in the minors.

John McKenzie

NYR Debut: October 24, 1965 (vs. Montreal Canadiens, lost 4–3)
Regular Season Games with NYR: 35
Playoff Games with NYR: 0

John McKenzie was one who got away and would haunt the Rangers for the next few years.

McKenzie was a smallish, 5-foot-9 winger who would rile the opponent with his physical play. He was traded to the Rangers from the Chicago Black Hawks in June 1965. After playing 35 games in the 1965–66 season, McKenzie was traded to the Boston Bruins for winger Reggie Fleming.

McKenzie's career took an upswing in Boston (comparable to Brad Marchand) and he became an immediate hit with the fans.

The former Ranger came back to burn his old team as a member of the Bruins' Stanley Cup-winning team in 1972. As the Bruins were celebrating their victory on Madison Square Garden ice, McKenzie went to center ice and took a "Statue of Liberty" pose and grabbed his neck in a choking gesture. He then started jumping up and down which didn't sit well with the fans.

Gene Carrigan

NYR Debut: November 11, 1930 (at Philadelphia Quakers, won 3–0)
Regular Season Games with NYR: 33
Playoff Games with NYR: 0

After he led the Canadian-American League with 28 goals in the 1929–30 season, center Gene Carrigan joined the Rangers for 33 games. Carrigan did not get regular ice time and scored two goals.

Ike Hildebrand

NYR Debut: October 8, 1953 (at Detroit Red Wings, lost 4–1)
Regular Season Games with NYR: 31
Playoff Games with NYR: 0

Ike Hildebrand grew up in British Columbia and was an all-around athlete who excelled at lacrosse in Canada.

The right winger scored six goals during his short tenure with the Rangers. He was sold to Vancouver of the Western Hockey League in January 1954, and played seven more NHL games with Chicago.

Hildebrand was inducted into Canada's Lacrosse Hall of Fame in 1972 and the Canadian Sports Hall of Fame in 1985.

Mike Murphy

NYR Debut: March 3, 1973 (at Detroit Red Wings, won 6–3)
Regular Season Games with NYR: 31
Playoff Games with NYR: 10

Mike Murphy was the Rangers' second-round pick in the 1970 NHL Amateur Draft. The Toronto native spent most of the 1970–71 season with the Rangers' Omaha affiliate in the Central Hockey League, where he scored 24 goals and was named Rookie of the Year.

After playing in 15 games, the right winger was traded to the St. Louis Blues in November 1971, and then dealt back to the Rangers in March 1973. He played 16 more games with the Rangers before being traded to the Los Angeles Kings in late November 1973.

Russell Oatman

NYR Debut: January 1, 1929 (at Toronto Maple Leafs, won 3–2)
Regular Season Games with NYR: 27
Playoff Games with NYR: 4

At 5-foot-10, left winger Russell Oatman was a member of the Montreal Maroons when he impressed the Rangers with his play in the 1928 Stanley Cup Final.

Oatman was a solid checking forward who played with an edge. He was acquired from the Maroons in December 1928 and had a goal and an assist in 27 games.

Bud Poile

NYR Debut: October 15, 1949 (at Montreal Canadiens, lost 3–1)
Regular Season Games with NYR: 27
Playoff Games with NYR: 0

By the time winger Bud Poile came to the Rangers in 1950, he was an "old" twenty-five years old. Poile began his NHL career as an eighteen-year-old with the Toronto Maple Leafs in the 1942–43 season. The Fort William, Ontario, native won a Stanley Cup with the Leafs in 1947.

Poile, who is the father of former Washington Capitals general manager David Poile, was acquired from the Detroit Red Wings in August 1949. He played a little under half of the season before being traded to Boston in December.

Poile was inducted into the Hockey Hall of Fame as a "builder" in 1990.

Stan Brown

NYR Debut: December 23, 1926 (at Ottawa Senators, lost 1–0)
Regular Season Games with NYR: 24
Playoff Games with NYR: 2

At 5-foot-10, defenseman Stan Brown was a player who was acquired in the midst of the Rangers' first season in the National Hockey League. Brown was playing with the Detroit Greyhounds of the American Hockey Association when the team folded. The Rangers signed Brown in December 1926.

The left winger scored six goals with two assists in 24 games with the Rangers. He was also part of the first Ranger team to make the playoffs, but was traded to the Detroit Cougars after the 1926–27 season.

Don Luce

NYR Debut: March 11, 1970 (at Montreal Canadiens, lost 5–3)
Regular Season Games with NYR: 21
Playoff Games with NYR: 5

Center Don Luce began his career with the Rangers after being selected in the third round of the 1966 NHL Amateur Draft. After three seasons with the Rangers' CHL affiliate in Omaha, he joined the Rangers late in the 1969–70 season.

Luce played 21 games in parts of two seasons with the Rangers. He was traded to the Detroit Red Wings in November 1970, but went on to a productive career with the Buffalo Sabres.

Doug Bentley

NYR Debut: January 20, 1954 (vs. Boston Bruins, won 8–3)

Regular Season Games with NYR: 20

Playoff Games with NYR: 0

Hall of Famer Doug Bentley amassed a fabulous career for 12 seasons with the Chicago Black Hawks. Bentley played with a pair of Hall of Famers, his brother, Max, and Bill Mosienko, on what is considered one of the best lines of all time. Max was surprisingly traded in 1947, but Doug continued to thrive for the Hawks. Injuries curtailed Bentley's production in the 1949–50 season. After playing only eight games the following season, he left the NHL to assume a player/coaching position with the Saskatoon Quakers of the Western Hockey League.

A year later, he made a comeback with the Rangers who had already added brother Max. In their first game together for the Rangers, Doug scored a goal with three assists while Max had two goals and two assists to key an 8–3 thrashing of the Boston Bruins at Madison Square Garden.

After the 1953–54 season, Bentley went back to Saskatoon to coach the Quakers in the playoffs.

Geoff Smith

NYR Debut: March 18, 1998 (vs. Montreal Canadiens, won 2–1 OT)

Regular Season Games with NYR: 19

Playoff Games with NYR: 0

Defenseman Geoff Smith was a free agent signing before the 1997–98 season. The 6-foot-2 Edmonton native spent most of the season with the Hartford Wolf Pack of the AHL. He was brought up late in the season and lasted 19 games. In February 1999, Smith was traded to the St. Louis Blues.

Gord Walker

NYR Debut: April 4, 1987 (at Hartford Whalers, lost 5–3)

Regular Season Games with NYR: 19

Playoff Games with NYR: 0

Also wore: #36

Right winger Gord Walker was taken by the Rangers in the third round of the 1983 NHL Entry Draft. Walker played 19 games and scored two goals and four assists in parts of two seasons with the Rangers. In January 1988, Walker was traded with Mike Siltala to the Los Angeles Kings in exchange for Joe Paterson.

Lane Lambert

NYR Debut: December 10, 1986 (vs. Los Angeles Kings, won 5–4)
Regular Season Games with NYR: 18
Playoff Games with NYR: 0

The Rangers acquired right winger Lane Lambert as part of a multi-player deal with the Detroit Red Wings in July 1986. Lambert debuted with a 20-goal season for the Red Wings in 1983–84, but his production slipped from that point on. Lambert scored two goals in 18 games for the Rangers. He was traded to the Quebec Nordiques in March 1987.

Hub Macey

NYR Debut: February 22, 1942 (vs. Chicago Black Hawks, won 3–2)
Regular Season Games with NYR: 18
Playoff Games with NYR: 1
Also wore: #17

The Rangers caught wind of left winger Hub Macey in junior hockey when he scored 15 points in ten playoff games to lead the Winnipeg Rangers to the 1941 Allan Cup.

Macey was signed as a free agent and played 18 games in parts of two seasons with the Rangers. In each season, Macey played nine games and scored three goals. After the 1942–43 season, Macey served in the Canadian military. While doing service, Macey was traded to the Montreal Canadiens in August 1946.

Wes Trainor

NYR Debut: February 6, 1949 (at Chicago Black Hawks, won 2–0)
Regular Season Games with NYR: 17
Playoff Games with NYR: 0

Wes Trainor was developing as a solid player in junior hockey when he left it all to join the Canadian military, missing four seasons. He returned to the ice for the 1945–46 season and was signed by the Rangers as a free agent in September 1947. He scored a goal with two assists in 17 games with the Blueshirts.

Chris Ferraro

NYR Debut: April 8, 1996 (vs. Florida Panthers, lost 5–3)
Regular Season Games with NYR: 14
Playoff Games with NYR: 0

Born in Long Island, New York, center Chris Ferraro and his identical twin brother, Peter, became the second set of identical twins to play on the same team. Chris was the Rangers' fourth-round pick in the 1992 NHL Entry Draft. He played two games with brother Peter in the 1995–96 season, and scored a goal in his first game. Chris Ferraro was claimed by the Pittsburgh Penguins off waivers following the 1996–97 season.

Billy Warwick

NYR Debut: February 21, 1943 (vs. Montreal Canadiens, won 6–1)
Regular Season Games with NYR: 14
Playoff Games with NYR: 0

When left winger Billy Warwick joined his older brother, Grant, in the 1942–43 season, they became the fourth brother combination to play for the Rangers. Billy Warwick played in 14 games in parts of two seasons, and scored three goals with the Rangers.

Henry Maracle

NYR Debut: February 12, 1931 (at Detroit Falcons, 1–1 OT tie)
Regular Season Games with NYR: 11
Playoff Games with NYR: 4

The Rangers needed an extra forward down the stretch of the 1930–31 season, so they acquired Henry "Bud" Maracle from Springfield of the Canadian-American Hockey League. The left winger scored a goal in 11 games and played four games in the 1931 Stanley Cup Playoffs. In November 1931, the Rangers sold Maracle's rights to the Bronx Tigers of the Can-Am League.

John McIntyre

NYR Debut: March 26, 1993 (vs. Chicago Blackhawks, lost 3–1)
Regular Season Games with NYR: 11
Playoff Games with NYR: 0

Late in the 1992–93 season, the Rangers sent defenseman Mark Hardy back to the Los Angeles Kings in exchange for center John McIntyre. The Ontario native played out the remainder of the season and then was claimed by Vancouver in the NHL Waiver Draft in October 1993.

Aldo Palazzari

NYR Debut: February 22, 1944 (vs. Chicago Black Hawks, lost 8–4)
Regular Season Games with NYR: 11
Playoff Games with NYR: 0

American-born Aldo Palazzari was just beginning to get his career in order when he became a victim of fate.

The Eveleth, Minnesota-born right winger was acquired from Boston in February 1944. He scored a goal in his first game as a Ranger and played the final 11 games of the 1943–44 season.

During training camp in 1944, Palazzari suffered a career-ending eye injury and was forced to retire.

The following players played ten or less games with the Rangers:

Jean Paul Denis - right wing

NYR Debut: February 16, 1947 (vs. Toronto Maple Leafs, won 6–2)
Regular Season Games with NYR: 10
Playoff Games with NYR: 0

Jeff Jackson - left wing

NYR Debut: March 11, 1987 (vs. Boston Bruins, won 3–2)
Regular Season Games with NYR: 9
Playoff Games with NYR: 6

Joe Levandoski - right wing

NYR Debut: January 2, 1947 (vs. Toronto Maple Leafs, lost 5–4)

Regular Season Games with NYR: 8

Playoff Games with NYR: 0

Bob Cunningham - center

NYR Debut: March 4, 1961 (at Toronto Maple Leafs, lost 5–4)

Regular Season Games with NYR: 4

Playoff Games with NYR: 0

Also wore: #19

Troy Loney - left wing

NYR Debut: April 7, 1995 (vs. New York Islanders, lost 4–3)

Regular Season Games with NYR: 4

Playoff Games with NYR: 1

Ian Mackintosh - right wing

NYR Debut: December 17, 1952 (vs. Boston Bruins, won 5–0)

Regular Season Games with NYR: 4

Playoff Games with NYR: 0

Kelly Burnett - center

NYR Debut: November 26, 1952 (vs. Toronto Maple Leafs, won 4–2)

Regular Season Games with NYR: 3

Playoff Games with NYR: 0

Guy Trottier - right wing

NYR Debut: January 5, 1969 (vs. Minnesota North Stars, won 5–1)

Regular Season Games with NYR: 2

Playoff Games with NYR: 0

Jimmy Jamieson - defenseman

NYR Debut: January 13, 1944 (vs. Chicago Black Hawks, lost 5–2)

Regular Season Games with NYR: 1

Playoff Games with NYR: 0

Bob McDonald - right wing

NYR Debut: January 6, 1944 (vs. Detroit Red Wings, lost 5–0)

Regular Season Games with NYR: 1

Playoff Games with NYR: 0

Doug Wickenheiser - center

NYR Debut: October 8, 1988 (at St. Louis Blues, won 4–2)

Regular Season Games with NYR: 1

Playoff Games with NYR: 0

Bill Wylie - center

NYR Debut: January 20, 1951 (at Montreal Canadiens, 2–2 tie)

Regular Season Games with NYR: 1

Playoff Games with NYR: 0

#15: HAIL TO THE CHIEF

Jim Neilson

NYR Debut: October 11, 1962 (vs. Detroit Red Wings, lost 2–1)

Regular Season Games with NYR: 810

Playoff Games with NYR: 65

Jim Neilson was a big defenseman who was steady as a rock and gave the Rangers twelve solid seasons of play from the back line.

Neilson's mother was a Cree Indian, thus he was tagged with the nickname of "Chief." The Rangers signed the free agent as an eighteen-year-old in 1958. He debuted with the Rangers in 1962–63, appearing in 69 games. He finished fifth in the voting for the Calder Trophy as the top rookie, and never went back to the minors.

Neilson was paired with Hall of Famer Doug Harvey early in his career, but would play alongside Rod Seiling and, later on, helped groom rookie defenseman Brad Park (see Chapter Two).

Jim Neilson, "The Chief."

Neilson used his 6-foot-2 frame very well. He was adept at playing positional defense, excellent with the poke check because of his long arms, and also displayed offensive skills that allowed him to play a forward spot on occasion.

His best season was in 1968–69, when he scored 10 goals with 34 assists for 44 points. Neilson was a two-time All-Star with the Rangers and was a second team All-Star in the 1967–68 season.

In February 1970, Neilson suffered a serious knee injury in a game against the Oakland Seals. Luckily, Neilson was a fast healer and was skating a month later.

The native of Big River, Saskatchewan, was a solid playoff performer. In the 1972 run to the Final, Neilson had two assists in Game Four of the Quarterfinal win over Montreal. He added an assist against the Boston Bruins in the Final.

Neilson went on to play two more seasons with the Rangers. His final game was the Game Seven loss to the Philadelphia Flyers in the 1974 playoffs. The Rangers left the thirty-three-year-old Neilson unprotected in the 1974 NHL Intra-League Draft, and he was claimed by the California Golden Seals. Neilson went on to play over a thousand games in the NHL. He finished his Rangers career as one of the most reliable defenseman in franchise history.

Andres Hedberg

> **NYR Debut:** October 12, 1978 (vs. Philadelphia Flyers, 3–3 tie)
> **Regular Season Games with NYR:** 465
> **Playoff Games with NYR:** 58

Right winger Anders Hedberg joined the Rangers in June 1978, along with fellow Swede Ulf Nilsson (see Chapter Eleven), as part of a much-heralded signing of two dynamic European players that would help the Rangers move closer to the goal of winning a Stanley Cup.

Hedberg and Nilsson starred on the same line (with Hall of Famer Bobby Hull) for the Winnipeg Jets of the World Hockey Association in the mid-1970s. The Rangers needed star power, so the duo was promoted as the beginning of a new era for the team.

While Nilsson's career was partly curtailed by the infamous hit by New York Islanders' defenseman Denis Potvin, Hedberg thrived in New York. In his first season, Hedberg played all 80 games, scored 33 goals, and was named team MVP. In the playoffs, he played all 18 games and scored four goals with five assists in the Rangers' run to the Final. In Game Five of the 1979 Semifinal against the Islanders, Hedberg scored the winning goal with less than three minutes left to give the Rangers a 4–3 win and a 3–2 lead in the series, which they would win in six games.

Hedberg went on to three consecutive seasons where he scored 30 or more goals. He played only four games due to a knee injury in the 1981–82 season, but returned the following year and scored 25 goals in 78 games.

The Swedish-born winger scored 32 goals in the 1983–84 season and 20 more in his final season of 1984–85. Hedberg scored 397 points in parts of seven seasons with the Rangers, making him the highest scorer among European-born players in franchise history.

Blair Betts

NYR Debut: October 5, 2005 (vs. Philadelphia Flyers, won 5–3)
Regular Season Games with NYR: 304
Playoff Games with NYR: 28

Blair Betts was the ultimate defensive forward who was strong on faceoffs. He was acquired from the Calgary Flames in March 2004.

Unfortunately, Betts is best known for being involved in a nasty incident that occurred during the 2009 Stanley Cup Playoffs Eastern Conference Quarterfinal against the Washington Capitals.

In Game Six, the 6-foot-3 center took a hard hit to the head from Capitals winger (and future Ranger) Donald Brashear. Betts had just sent the puck into the Capitals' zone from center ice when Brashear slammed him with a high elbow that many deemed to be dirty. Brashear was not penalized on the play but Rangers' defenseman and teammate Paul Mara went after Brashear, in defense of Betts, and both were assessed two-minute penalties.

Brashear received a six-game suspension after the game, but the Rangers missed Betts's faceoff prowess and defensive skills in Game Seven and lost to Washington, 2–1.

Betts played a total of four seasons and 304 games with the Rangers. He signed with the Philadelphia Flyers as a free agent in October 2009.

Darren Langdon

NYR Debut: February 18, 1995 (at Montreal Canadiens, lost 5–2)
Regular Season Games with NYR: 277
Playoff Games with NYR: 12
Also wore: #19

During the 1994–95 season, the Rangers were lacking toughness, so 6-foot-1, 205-pound left winger Darren Langdon was promoted from Binghamton of the AHL to provide some muscle.

Langdon provided a spark in his first game with his first NHL goal. In 18 games, Langdon accumulated 62 penalty minutes, but that number grew to 175, 195, and 197 in the next three seasons.

Langdon was popular with his teammates, as evidenced by his being named a two-time winner of the "Players' Player" award.

In August 2000, Langdon was traded to the Carolina Hurricanes.

Ron Murphy

NYR Debut: October 19, 1952 (at Boston Bruins, 2–2 tie)
Regular Season Games with NYR: 207
Playoff Games with NYR: 10
Also wore: #17 and #10

Ron Murphy was so impressive in leading Guelph Biltmore to the 1952 Memorial Cup that the Rangers signed him as a free agent. The left winger played 15 games in his first season, but maintained his rookie status for the 1953–54 season.

On December 20, 1953, Murphy suffered a concussion and a broken jaw when he was hit in the head by the stick of Montreal Canadiens' winger Bernie "Boom Boom" Geoffrion. Both players' sticks were up when Murphy confronted Geoffrion. A few other players were involved in minor skirmishes (see Chapter Six), but Murphy and Geoffrion were both given match penalties.

As Geoffrion left the ice through the 50th Street runway at Madison Square Garden, the Canadiens' winger was attacked by a fan standing in the aisle above. The Canadiens' bench stood up with the intent of going after the fan, but Garden security intervened to prevent an ugly scene. The Canadiens blamed Murphy, who did not receive much support from the Rangers concerning the incident.

In June 1957, the Rangers traded Murphy to the Chicago Black Hawks.

Ab DeMarco Sr.

NYR Debut: December 4, 1943 (at Toronto Maple Leafs, lost 11–4)
Regular Season Games with NYR: 180
Playoff Games with NYR: 0

Ab DeMarco Sr.'s career took an upswing when he came to the Rangers from the Boston Bruins in November 1943. The native of North Bay, Ontario, played parts of three seasons with the Chicago Black Hawks, Toronto Maple Leafs, and Boston, but never really got a chance to stick with any of those teams.

DeMarco Sr. scored a goal in his first game with the Rangers. He played 36 games and scored 33 points that first year. He had his best year as a

Ranger in 1944–45, when he was named the team's Most Valuable Player after scoring 24 goals with 30 assists in 50 games.

After scoring 9 goals in the 1946–47 season, the center was traded to Cleveland of the American Hockey League. DeMarco's son, Ab Jr., played with the Rangers from 1969–73.

Murray "Muzz" Patrick

NYR Debut: March 17, 1938 (vs. New York Americans, won 5–3)

Regular Season Games with NYR: 166

Playoff Games with NYR: 25

Also wore: #2

Being part of the Patrick family was pressure enough for a young hockey player, but "Muzz" Patrick was the son of the Rangers' original head coach, Lester Patrick. He was also the younger brother of Lynn Patrick, who was already with the team when he joined the Rangers late in the 1937–38 season.

Patrick, who was nicknamed "Muzz" for his childhood haircut, was a 6-foot-2, 205-pound defenseman best known for being a physical, hard-nosed player. Patrick was a key member of the 1940 Stanley Cup-winning Ranger team.

In the 1939–40 season, Patrick scored two goals, but added three in 12 playoff games. Patrick scored the only goal of the Rangers' Game Four win over the Boston Bruins in the Stanley Cup Semifinal. That win evened the series at two games apiece, and the Rangers went on to eliminate the Bruins in six.

In the Stanley Cup Final against the Toronto Maple Leafs, Patrick scored the game-winning goal in overtime of Game Five, and the Rangers went on to win the Cup in six games.

Following the 1940–41 season, Patrick served in the United States military during the next four years. His stint included combat duty in southern France and Sicily. After World War II ended, he returned to the Rangers for one more season in 1945–46. In his post-playing career, Patrick became a head coach for the Rangers' minor league affiliate at St. Paul, as well as the head coach and general manager for Tacoma. Midway through the 1953–54 season, Patrick was named the Rangers' head coach. After the 1954–55 season, he moved up to the general manager position but returned as head coach for two games in the 1959–60 season and 34 games in the 1962–63 season.

John MacLean

> **NYR Debut:** October 9, 1998 (vs. Philadelphia Flyers, lost 1–0)
> **Regular Season Games with NYR:** 161
> **Playoff Games with NYR:** 0

Right winger John MacLean was an outstanding player for the New Jersey Devils for 14 years. That also made him a "villain" to the Ranger fans, who had to warm up to him when he signed on with the Rangers in July 1998.

MacLean scored 28 goals and 55 points in his first season with the Rangers in 1998–99, but was already thirty-four years old. He played a full season in 1999–2000, but only two more games in 2000–01 after which he was traded to the Dallas Stars in February 2001.

Mark Janssens

> **NYR Debut:** January 19, 1988 (at Los Angeles Kings, lost 6–3)
> **Regular Season Games with NYR:** 157
> **Playoff Games with NYR:** 15
> **Also wore:** #27 and #47

At 6-foot-3, center Mark Janssens was a fourth-round pick of the Rangers in the 1986 NHL Entry Draft. The British Columbia native was a physical presence on the ice, but was not fast on skates.

After a few "cups of coffee" with the Rangers in the 1987–88 and 1988–89 seasons, Janssens played his first full season in 1989–90. He scored nine goals, but had 162 penalty minutes and a minus-26. After that, his goal totals and his penalty minutes increased.

Janssens played four games in the 1991–92 season, as he spent most of his time with the Rangers' minor league affiliate at Binghamton. In March 1992, Janssens was traded to the Minnesota North Stars.

Tanner Glass

> **NYR Debut:** October 9, 2014 (won 3–2)
> **Regular Season Games with NYR:** 134
> **Playoff Games with NYR:** 30

The Rangers signed left winger Tanner Glass as a free agent before the 2014–15 season to add a physical presence to the roster.

Glass's finest Ranger moment came in the 2017 postseason. Glass, who was not known as a goal scorer, scored the first goal of the game as the Rangers went on to a 2–0 win over the Montreal Canadiens in Game One of the opening round of the playoffs. The Rangers won the series and advanced to the next round, where they lost in six games to the Ottawa Senators.

Glass played well in a losing effort, as he recorded three assists in games three and four, the only two games that the Rangers won.

Glass played out his contract following the 2016–17 season.

Gus Kyle

NYR Debut: October 15, 1949 (at Montreal Canadiens, lost 3–1)
Regular Season Games with NYR: 134
Playoff Games with NYR: 12
Also wore: #6

Gus Kyle went from being a member of the Royal Canadian Mounted Police to a defenseman in the NHL with the Rangers. The Saskatchewan native, who served five years in the RCMP, was a 6-foot-1 plodding type who was tough to play against.

Kyle played a full season in 1949–50 and compiled 143 penalty minutes. He played 12 games in the playoffs and was part of the team that lost the double overtime Game Seven of the 1950 Stanley Cup Final to the Detroit Red Wings. In September 1951, Kyle was traded to the Boston Bruins where he played his final NHL season.

Irv Spencer

NYR Debut: October 7, 1959 (at Chicago Black Hawks, lost 5–2)
Regular Season Games with NYR: 131
Playoff Games with NYR: 1
Also wore: #16

Defenseman Irv Spencer toiled in the minor leagues for five seasons for the Montreal Canadiens before being claimed by the Rangers in the 1959 Intra-League Draft. When referring to his stint in the minors without a call up, Spencer was quoted as saying, "You had to wait until somebody died to get a position."

Spencer got an opportunity with the Rangers in the 1959–60 season and played in 32 games. The native of Sudbury, Ontario, played two more seasons with the Rangers before he was claimed by Boston in the 1962 Intra-League Draft.

Hank Ciesla

NYR Debut: October 10, 1957 (at Detroit Red Wings, won 3–2)
Regular Season Games with NYR: 129
Playoff Games with NYR: 6

At 6-foot-2, center Hank Ciesla was one of those players who was not interested in taking advantage of his superior size. Ciesla was a consistent goal scorer in the minors, which, unfortunately, did not translate to the NHL.

Ciesla's head coach during his Rangers' tenure was Phil Watson, who didn't appreciate his center's approach to the game. Ciesla was traded to Toronto before the 1959–60 season. Watson began that season as the Rangers coach, but was replaced by general manager Alf Pike after 15 games.

Doug Brennan

NYR Debut: November 12, 1931 (at Montreal Canadiens, won 4–1)
Regular Season Games with NYR: 123
Playoff Games with NYR: 16

The Rangers acquired twenty-six-year-old defenseman Doug Brennan from Vancouver of the Pacific Coast Hockey League in October 1931. A month later, Brennan made his Ranger debut.

Brennan was a member of the Rangers' 1933 Stanley Cup-winning team. He was released following the 1933–34 season.

Bert Connelly

NYR Debut: November 10, 1934 (vs. St. Louis Eagles, lost 4–2)
Regular Seasons Games with NYR: 72
Playoff Games with NYR: 4

After leading the Moncton Hawks to back-to-back Allan Cup Championships in 1933 and 1934, left winger Bert Connelly was signed by the Rangers in October 1934. Connelly scored ten goals in his first season, but only two the following year. In the 1936–37 season, the native of Montreal played for the Rangers' AHL affiliate in Philadelphia. He was released after the season.

Jim Ross

NYR Debut: October 14, 1951 (at Chicago Black Hawks, lost 3–2)

Regular Seasons Games with NYR: 62

Playoff Games with NYR: 0

Also wore: #2

Scottish-born defenseman Jim Ross was signed by the Rangers as a free agent following a solid 1950–51 season with the Quebec Aces of the Quebec Hockey League. Ross scored six goals with 21 assists in 50 games.

Ross, who was born in Edinburgh, played 62 games in parts of two seasons with the Rangers.

Clint Albright

NYR Debut: October 14, 1948 (at Montreal Canadiens, tie 1–1)

Regular Seasons Games with NYR: 59

Playoff Games with NYR: 0

A 6-foot-2, center Clint Albright was one of the few players who wore his eyeglasses on the ice.

During his one and only season with the Rangers, Albright scored 19 points (14 goals and 5 assists) in 59 games. Albright, who was known as "The Professor," walked away from the Rangers and the NHL after one season to return to school to complete an engineering degree.

Chris Jensen

NYR Debut: March 6, 1986 (at Calgary Flames, won 5–2)

Regular Seasons Games with NYR: 53

Playoff Games with NYR: 0

Also wore: #39

The Rangers used their fourth-round pick in the 1982 NHL Entry Draft to select right winger Chris Jensen.

The nineteen-year-old elected to go to South Dakota, where he played until joining the Rangers late in the 1985–86 season. Jensen was a goal scorer in juniors, but developed into more of a role player in the NHL.

Jensen played parts of three seasons with the Rangers. He was traded to the Philadelphia Flyers in September 1988.

Derek Dorsett

NYR Debut: May 4, 2013 (Game Two Eastern Conference Quarterfinals at Washington Capitals, lost 1–0 OT)

Regular Seasons Games with NYR: 51

Playoff Games with NYR: 34

Right winger Derek Dorsett will be forever known as being part of a significant trade that the Rangers completed with the Columbus Blue Jackets. On April 3, 2013, the Rangers acquired center Derick Brassard, defenseman John Moore, Dorsett, and a draft choice for three players including left winger Marian Gaborik.

Dorsett did not make his Ranger debut until the 2013 Stanley Cup Playoffs, as he had suffered a broken clavicle late in the regular season while with Columbus. The Saskatchewan native played only one season with the Rangers, and was traded to Vancouver in June 2014.

Bill Collins

NYR Debut: October 8, 1975 (vs. Chicago Black Hawks, 2–2 tie)

Regular Seasons Games with NYR: 50

Playoff Games with NYR: 0

Center Bill Collins was originally signed by the Rangers in 1963, but he did not get to play with the team until 1975.

Collins was Ranger property until he was claimed by the Minnesota North Stars in the 1967 NHL Expansion Draft. Before coming to the Rangers, the Ottawa native also played with the Montreal Canadiens, Detroit Red Wings, and St. Louis Blues.

In June 1975, the Rangers acquired Collins and goaltender John Davidson from the Blues in exchange for three players, including left winger Ted

Irvine. After one season, Collins elected to become a free agent and signed with the Philadelphia Flyers.

Mike Hudson

NYR Debut: October 7, 1993 (vs. Tampa Bay Lightning, won 5–4)
Regular Season Games with NYR: 48
Playoff Games with NYR: 0

He was on the 1993–94 Stanley Cup-winning team and his name is etched onto the coveted chalice, but center Mike Hudson did not play in one playoff game during the magical run.

Just before the season began, Hudson was claimed by the Edmonton Oilers in the NHL Waiver Draft. He played 48 games and became part of the "Black Aces" (see Chapter Twelve), a group of players that didn't see much ice time and, for the most part, were healthy scratches.

In January 1995, Hudson was claimed by the Pittsburgh Penguins in the NHL Waiver Draft.

Bob Kabel

NYR Debut: December 3, 1959 (at Montreal Canadiens, won 7–4)
Regular Season Games with NYR: 48
Playoff Games with NYR: 0
Also wore: #11

After six years in minor-league hockey, center Bob Kabel finally got his shot with the Rangers in 1959.

The twenty-five-year-old, who was solid on faceoffs and an efficient playmaker, scored 16 points in 44 games during the 1959–60 season.

Kabel played 542 minor league games for the Rangers' affiliates through the 1965–66 season.

Jason Lafreniere

NYR Debut: November 15, 1988 (at Philadelphia Flyers, 3–3 OT tie)
Regular Season Games with NYR: 38
Playoff Games with NYR: 3

In August 1988, the Rangers acquired center Jason Lafreniere as part of a five-player trade with the Quebec Nordiques.

The St. Catherines, Ontario, native was fairly productive during his limited time in a Ranger uniform. Lafreniere scored 24 points in 38 games, including a four-point game (goal and three assists) against the New Jersey Devils in February 1989. After playing the 1989–90 season in the minors, Lafreniere left the Rangers to join Team Canada.

Jimmy Conacher

NYR Debut: October 28, 1951 (at Montreal Canadiens, won 2–1)

Regular Season Games with NYR: 33

Playoff Games with NYR: 0

Also wore: #5

Center Jimmy Conacher completed his NHL career with parts of two seasons with the Rangers.

Conacher finished second in the voting for the Calder Trophy in 1946–47 as a member of the Detroit Red Wings. He came to the Rangers as a thirty-year-old in 1951, and retired after the 1952–53 season.

Red Garrett

NYR Debut: November 29, 1942 (vs. Boston Bruins, won 3–2)

Regular Season Games with NYR: 33

Playoff Games with NYR: 0

World War II gave defenseman Red Garrett a chance to play with the Rangers, but it also cost him his life.

The Toronto native made his debut with the Rangers as an eighteen-year-old in the 1942–43 season. Garrett got a chance because of the number of players that were serving in the war left the NHL rosters a little short.

Garrett was called to military duty before the season ended. On November 25, 1944, Garrett was killed when the destroyer escort that he was working on was struck by a German U-boat. In 1947, the American Hockey League initiated the "Red Garrett Award" for the top rookie in the league. Past winners include Brett Hull in 1987 and Daniel Briere in 1998.

Jeff Halpern

NYR Debut: January 19, 2013 (at Boston Bruins, lost 3–1)
Regular Season Games with NYR: 30
Playoff Games with NYR: 0

In July 2012, the Rangers signed thirty-six-year-old center Jeff Halpern to add some experience down the middle.

Halpern was a goal scorer early in his career but, as his skills declined, he became more of a defensive forward who was solid on faceoffs. He didn't score a goal for the Rangers, and was placed on waivers in March 2013.

Pete Babando

NYR Debut: January 11, 1953 (vs. Montreal Canadiens, won 7–0)
Regular Season Games with NYR: 29
Playoff Games with NYR: 0

Left winger Pete Babando made his mark in Ranger history before he joined the team midway through the 1952–53 season. The Pennsylvania-born winger scored the game-winning goal in double overtime for the Detroit Red Wings against the Rangers in Game Seven of the Stanley Cup Final.

In 29 games with the Rangers, Babando scored four goals with four assists. He was traded to Montreal in August 1953.

Dallas Smith

NYR Debut: December 23, 1977 (vs. Cleveland Barons, won 5–4)
Regular Season Games with NYR: 29
Playoff Games with NYR: 1

Defenseman Dallas Smith won two Stanley Cups with the Boston Bruins in the 1970s. It didn't hurt that he was paired with Hall of Famer Bobby Orr.

Smith retired after the 1976–77 season, but the Rangers lured him out of retirement on December 19, 1977. The thirty-six-year old played 29 regular season games and one playoff game. After the season, Smith retired once again.

Orville Heximer

NYR Debut: December 14, 1929 (at Toronto Maple Leafs, lost 7–6 OT)

Regular Season Games with NYR: 19

Playoff Games with NYR: 0

Left winger Orville "Obs" Heximer came to the Rangers with the reputation of being a goal scorer, but was unable to have success at the NHL level. Heximer played 19 games with the Rangers and spent most of his time—and better results—with the Springfield Indians of the Can-Am League.

Heximer infuriated Ranger management in 1931, when he held out over a contract dispute. The Rangers were reportedly trying to force the Ontario native to take a pay cut. In August 1932, Heximer's rights were sold to the Boston Bruins.

The following players played less than 20 games with NYR:

Brad Isbister - left wing

NYR Debut: December 21, 2006 (at Florida Panthers, lost 3–2)

Regular Season Games with NYR: 19

Playoff Games with NYR: 4

Frank Waite - center

NYR Debut: November 11, 1930 (at Philadelphia Quakers, won 3–0)

Regular Season Games with NYR: 17

Playoff Games with NYR: 0

Gerry Carson - defenseman

NYR Debut: February 14, 1929 (at Toronto Maple Leafs, lost 3–1)

Regular Seasons Games with NYR: 14

Playoff Games with NYR: 5

Norm Burns - center

NYR Debut: November 1, 1941 (at Toronto Maple Leafs, won 4–3)

Regular Seasons Games with NYR: 11

Playoff Games with NYR: 0

Lin Bend - center

NYR Debut: October 31, 1942 (at Toronto Maple Leafs, lost 7–2)

Regular Seasons Games with NYR: 8

Playoff Games with NYR: 0

Noel Price - defenseman

NYR Debut: November 1, 1959 (vs. Montreal Canadiens, lost 3–1)

Regular Seasons Games with NYR: 7

Playoff Games with NYR: 0

Hartland Monahan - right wing

NYR Debut: December 19, 1974 (at Boston Bruins, lost 11–3)

Regular Seasons Games with NYR: 6

Playoff Games with NYR: 0

Ron Rowe - left wing

NYR Debut: March 13, 1948 (at Montreal Canadiens, lost 3-2)

Regular Seasons Games with NYR: 5

Playoff Games with NYR: 0

Chad Wiseman - left wing

NYR Debut: January 8, 2004 (at Carolina Hurricanes, lost 3–2)

Regular Seasons Games with NYR: 5

Playoff Games with NYR: 1

Also wore: #21

Mike Labadie - right wing

NYR Debut: January 25, 1953 (at Boston Bruins, won 2–1)

Regular Seasons Games with NYR: 3

Playoff Games with NYR: 0

Hub Anslow - left wing

NYR Debut: March 7, 1948 (vs. Detroit Red Wings, 2-2 tie)

Regular Seasons Games with NYR: 2

Playoff Games with NYR: 0

Also wore: #20

Jeff Taffe - center

NYR Debut: October 27, 2005 (vs. New York Islanders, won 3-1)

Regular Seasons Games with NYR: 2

Playoff Games with NYR: 0

Billy Taylor Sr. - center

NYR Debut: February 7, 1948 (at Toronto Maple Leafs, lost 3–0)

Regular Seasons Games with NYR: 2

Playoff Games with NYR: 0

Vic Lynn - left wing

NYR Debut: 1942–1943 season

Regular Seasons Games with NYR: 1

Playoff Games with NYR: 0

#16: A SEILING OF 16

Rod Seiling

NYR Debut: March 4, 1964 (vs. Chicago Black Hawks, won 4-3)
Regular Season Games with NYR: 644
Playoff Games with NYR: 54

On February 22, 1964, Rangers general manager Muzz Patrick completed a controversial, seven-player trade with the Toronto Maple Leafs.

Thirty-two-year-old, former Hart Trophy winner, Andy Bathgate was sent to Toronto as the marquee name in the trade but, as part of the return package, the Rangers acquired a nineteen-year-old defenseman who would become a staple in the defensive zone for 12 seasons.

Rod Seiling made his NHL debut as an eighteen-year-old with the Maple Leafs, and played one game in the 1962–63 season. In junior hockey, Seiling showed some offensive prowess as a winger but transitioned to a solid "stay-at-home" defenseman. In his first game with the Rangers, Seiling was credited with the lone assist on the game-tying goal in the second period by Hall of Famer Harry Howell.

After four seasons, Seiling was left unprotected and was claimed by St. Louis in the June 6, 1967, NHL Expansion Draft, but the Rangers wasted no time in re-acquiring him as they swung a deal with the Blues on the same day.

Seiling played a large role in the Rangers' run to the 1972 Stanley Cup Final with a goal and four assists to go along with stout defensive play. The Kitchener, Ontario, native's best season on the score sheet was his tenth year with the Rangers. He scored 42 points (9 goals and 33 assists) in 1972–73 season.

When the 1974–75 season began, the Rangers had a young defenseman named Ron Greschner who replaced the thirty-year-old Seiling in the line-up. The veteran defenseman was later placed on waivers, where he was claimed by the Washington Capitals in October 1974.

Pat Hickey

NYR Debut: October 8, 1975 (vs. Chicago Black Hawks, 2–2 tie)
Regular Season Games with NYR: 370
Playoff Games with NYR: 21
Also wore: #14 and #24

Left winger Pat Hickey was a popular player in the early 1970s. He was selected by the Rangers in the second round of the 1973 NHL Amateur Draft, but was also chosen by the Toronto Toros of the World Hockey Association. Hickey decided to join Toronto, but after two seasons joined the Rangers for the 1975–76 season.

Pat lit the lamp 40 times in 1977–78 season.

Photo courtesy of Ken Tash.

Hickey brought a lot of speed with a fairly good scoring touch. According to the Rangers' website, Hickey wore #14 but switched to #16 when Derek Sanderson left the team in late October 1975. In his first season with the Rangers, Hickey scored 14 goals with 22 assists.

In 1977–78, Hickey helped the Rangers make the playoffs for the first time in three seasons as he scored a career-high 40 goals. In the postseason, Hickey scored two goals in three games.

In November 1979, the Rangers traded Hickey to the Colorado Rockies as part of a multi-player deal that brought back defenseman Barry Beck. Hickey was re-acquired from Toronto in October 1981, and played one more season with the Rangers. He scored 15 goals in 53 games in the 1981–82 season before being traded to the Quebec Nordiques in March 1982. Hickey finished his Ranger career with 128 goals and 129 assists.

Mark Pavelich

NYR Debut: October 6, 1981 (vs. Detroit Red Wings, lost 5–2)
Regular Season Games with NYR: 341
Playoff Games with NYR: 23
Also wore: #40

In the summer of 1981, Rangers head coach Herb Brooks, who was in his first season with the team, convinced the front office to sign center Mark Pavelich, a player that he coached as a member of the famed United States Hockey team that won the gold medal in the 1980 Winter Olympics. After the Olympics, Pavelich played a year in Switzerland before joining the Rangers.

The Eveleth, Minnesota, native scored his first NHL goal in his second career game. His first season was a smashing success, as he tied Bill Cook's rookie record with 33 goals. He also had 76 points, which is still a Rangers' rookie record.

Pavelich set a career high with 37 goals in his second season. It included a memorable game where he tied a franchise record.

On February 23, 1983, Pavelich tied Don Murdoch's single-game record by scoring five goals against the Hartford Whalers at Madison Square Garden. Since Murdoch accomplished his feat on the road, Pavelich is the only player to ever score five goals on Garden ice. He is also the first American-born player to score five goals in a game.

Pavelich had his best postseason with the Rangers in the 1983 Stanley Cup Playoffs, scoring four goals in nine games. All four goals came in winning games, although the Rangers lost to the New York Islanders in the Patrick Division Final.

In the 1983–84 season, Pavelich led the team in scoring with a career-high 82 points, but his numbers began to tail off over the next two seasons.

When Ted Sator replaced Brooks in 1985, Pavelich's style of play conflicted with the new head man's philosophy. In October of 1986, Pavelich was traded to his hometown Minnesota North Stars.

Sean Avery

NYR Debut: February 6, 2007 (at New Jersey Devils, lost 3–2 SO)
Regular Season Games with NYR: 264
Playoff Games with NYR: 28

The Rangers were looking for a spark to help them make a run at the play-offs in the 2006–07 season. On February 5, 2007, the Rangers acquired Sean Avery from the Los Angeles Kings, and the left winger was just what the doctor ordered.

Avery scored 20 points in 29 games to help the Rangers qualify for the playoffs. In Game Two of the 2007 Eastern Conference Quarterfinal against the Atlanta Thrashers, Avery scored a goal and an assist in a 2–1 win.

The Ontario native was often embroiled in controversy, but his most notable moment came in the 2008 playoffs. The Rangers were playing the New

Sean Avery was the spark the Rangers needed in 2006–07.

Photo by Michael Miller via Wikimedia Commons.

Jersey Devils and their Hall of Fame goalie Martin Brodeur in a first round match-up. Avery and Brodeur were the main combatants in a heated confrontation that lasted throughout the five-game series.

The Rangers took a 2–0 lead in the series thanks to Avery, who scored a goal in the Game One win and added the game-winning goal in Game Two. Avery added a third goal in Game Three, but made his mark in that game by his interaction with Brodeur.

Avery was screening Brodeur in front of the net, a common practice in hockey. However, instead of having his back to the goaltender, the left winger faced the Devils goalie. It wasn't a penalty at the time, but it became one the very next day. The NHL expanded the interpretation of the unsportsmanlike conduct penalty to include facing the goaltender.

After the 2008 playoffs, Avery was a free agent and signed with the Dallas Stars, but was claimed by the Rangers on waivers in March 2009. Avery went on to play three more seasons, from 2009–12, before retiring.

Alf Pike

NYR Debut: November 5, 1939 (at Detroit Red Wings, 1–1 OT tie)

Regular Season Games with Rangers: 234

Playoff Games with Rangers: 21

Also wore: #2 and #14

Alf Pike was a third-line center who played for the 1940 Stanley Cup Championship team. The nineteen-year-old was another in a long line of players who were part of Lester Patrick's hockey school in Winnipeg, where he grew up.

Pike was nicknamed "The Embalmer" because he was a licensed mortician, which he did during the offseason.

Pike's strength was his versatility, as he could also play defense. In his first season of 1939–40, he scored eight goals in the regular season while adding three in the 1940 Stanley Cup Playoffs, including two huge goals in the Final.

In Game One against the Toronto Maple Leafs, Pike scored the game-winning goal in overtime. In the Game Six clincher, Pike tied the game midway through the third period as the Rangers rallied from a 2–0 deficit. The goal also set up Bryan Hextall's historic game- and Cup-winning goal in overtime. According to the obit in the *New York Times* of March 10, 2009, former Public Relations Executive John Halligan told a story about something Pike said to Hextall between the second and third periods. According to Halligan, Pike told his teammate that he would "get the tying goal and you get the winner."

Pike's career was interrupted by World War II, but he returned to the Rangers for two more seasons from 1945–47. He went on to play two seasons in the minors before transitioning into coaching the Rangers' minor league affiliates. Pike, who was a taskmaster behind the bench, was hired to be the head coach of the Rangers for the 1959–60 season. He stayed on the job through 18 games of the next season and compiled a 36-66-21 record.

Dave Creighton

NYR Debut: October 7, 1955 (at Chicago Black Hawks, won 7–4)

Regular Season Games with Rangers: 210

Playoff Games with Rangers: 16

Center Dave Creighton made his NHL debut with the Boston Bruins in the 1948–49 season as an eighteen-year-old. By the time he joined the Rangers in 1955, he had already played seven years in the league—six with Boston and one with Chicago.

Creighton was traded to Detroit after the 1954–55 season, but never played a game with the Red Wings. Instead, he was dealt to the Rangers before the 1955–56 season began.

Creighton's first game with the Rangers was a smashing success, as he had three assists in a 7–4 season-opening win in Chicago. The native of Port Arthur, Ontario, had at least one point in each of his first eight games with the Rangers, finishing his first season in New York with 51 points (20 goals and 31 assists). He also finished fifth in the voting for the Lady Byng Trophy for sportsmanship.

Creighton scored 35 goals in two more full seasons for the Rangers before he was claimed by Montreal in the June 1958 Intra-League Draft.

Bobby Holik

NYR Debut: October 9, 2002 (at Carolina Hurricanes, won 4–1)
Regular Season Games with Rangers: 146
Playoff Games with Rangers: 0

Known to Rangers fans as a "villain" with the rival New Jersey Devils, center Bobby Holik was signed by the Rangers as a free agent in July 2002. The Rangers paid a high price ($45 million over five years) for the 6-foot-4, 230-pound center out of the Czech Republic.

Holik never really fit in with the Rangers. In his two seasons with the team, he scored 16 goals in 2002–03 and 25 goals in 2003–04, but the team missed the playoffs both times.

After his second season, the Rangers bought out Holik's contract.

Dave Silk

NYR Debut: March 5, 1980 (vs. Buffalo Sabres, won 4–2)
Regular Season Games with Rangers: 141
Playoff Games with Rangers: 9

Right winger Dave Silk was the Rangers' fourth-round pick in the 1978 NHL Amateur Draft, but he experienced glory before ever putting on a

Photo courtesy of Mark Rosenman.

Dave Silk was first 1980 USA Olympic Gold Medal winner to play for Rangers.

Blueshirts' sweater. Silk was a member of the 1980 Gold Medal-winning United States Hockey Team, and the first from that historic team to play for the Rangers.

Less than two weeks after the Olympics ended, the Massachusetts-born Silk made his NHL debut with the Rangers and played two games. In the 1980–81 season, Silk scored 14 goals in 59 games. He had his best season with the Rangers in 1981–82, when he set career highs with 15 goals and 35 points.

After playing in 16 games, Silk was traded to the Boston Bruins in October 1983.

Marcel Dionne

NYR Debut: March 11, 1987 (vs. Boston Bruins, won 3–2)

Regular Season Games with Rangers: 118

Playoff Games with Rangers: 6

The final three years of Marcel Dionne's Hall of Fame career were spent with the Rangers.

231

After 12 years with the Los Angeles Kings, Dionne requested a trade and was granted his wish. Right before the trade deadline, the Rangers acquired the thirty-five-year-old center in exchange for defenseman Tom Laidlaw and center Bobby Carpenter.

It didn't take long for Dionne to dent the score sheet, as he scored his first goal in a Rangers' sweater in his second game. In his only full season with the Rangers, in 1987–88, Dionne tallied 65 points (31 goals and 34 assists).

Dionne was a healthy scratch for much of the 1988–89 season and played nine games for the Rangers' minor league affiliate at Denver of the International Hockey League. After the season, he announced his retirement.

Brian Noonan

NYR Debut: March 22, 1994 (at Calgary Flames, 4–4 OT tie)

Regular Season Games with Rangers: 101

Playoff Games with Rangers: 27

Also wore: #28

On March 21, 1994, the Rangers completed a trade with the Chicago Blackhawks that became historic because the two players who came to New York played large roles in winning the 1994 Stanley Cup. Right winger Brian Noonan was one of those players.

The native of Boston, Massachusetts, along with Stephane Matteau, joined the team at the trade deadline. Despite having the best record in the league, head coach Mike Keenan felt they weren't gritty or physical enough to fulfill the goal of winning the cup. Keenan had both players when he was the head coach in Chicago, so he convinced Rangers' GM Neil Smith to make a deal. It was one of five separate deals made by the Rangers at the time.

Noonan was acquired for his size (6-foot-1, 200 pounds) and experience, and the move paid off in dividends. He scored four goals in 12 regular season games, but his presence was really felt in the playoffs.

In Game One of the 1994 Eastern Conference Semifinal, Noonan scored two goals to lead the Rangers to a 6–3 win over the Washington Capitals. In Game Seven of the Stanley Cup Final against Vancouver, Noonan assisted on what became the game-winning goal by Mark Messier in the second period. Many observers felt Noonan touched the puck last and should've been credited with the goal, but it went down in the books as Messier's goal.

After the 1994–95 season, Noonan became a free agent and signed with the St. Louis Blues. He was traded back to the Rangers in November 1996, and was later traded to Vancouver in March of 1997.

Johnny Wilson

> **NYR Debut:** November 9, 1960 (vs. Detroit Red Wings, lost 4–3)
>
> **Regular Season Games with NYR:** 96
>
> **Playoff Games with NYR:** 6

Johnny Wilson was not cut out to play in New York.

The left winger was acquired from Toronto in November of 1960, but he had already logged 10-plus years in the NHL with the Leafs, Detroit (where he won four Stanley Cups), and Chicago.

Wilson wasn't comfortable with having to practice at a rink other than Madison Square Garden. Players had to pay for parking for games at the Garden, travel costs, and other domestic charges like finding baby sitters, which became a burden.

The Ontario native played parts of two seasons with the Rangers. In the 1962 Stanley Cup Playoffs, Wilson scored two goals in Game Three of the semifinals against Toronto. Wilson retired after the 1961–62 season and went on to become a head coach in the NHL with Los Angeles, Detroit, and Pittsburgh.

Oscar "Ossie" Asmundson

> **NYR Debut:** November 10, 1932 (at Montreal Maroons, won 4–2)
>
> **Regular Season Games with NYR:** 94
>
> **Playoff Games with NYR:** 9

Known as a defensive forward, center Oscar Asmundson impressed the Rangers with his play for the Bronx Tigers in the Can-Am League.

He joined the team for the 1932–33 season and was a member of the 1933 Stanley Cup-winning team. In the Final against Toronto, the native of Red Deer, Alberta, had an assist in Game One.

Pete Conacher

NYR Debut: November 24, 1954 (vs. Boston Bruins, won 3–1)
Regular Season Games with NYR: 93
Playoff Games with NYR: 5
Also wore: #6

Left winger Pete Conacher grew up in the sport of hockey. Pete's father, Charlie, along with his uncles, Lionel and Roy, are all Hall of Famers.

The Rangers acquired Conacher from Chicago in November 1954. In parts of two seasons with the Rangers, Conacher scored 21 goals.

Church Russell

NYR Debut: January 16, 1946 (at Boston Bruins, lost 3–2)
Regular Season Games with NYR: 90
Playoff Games with NYR: 0

Left winger Church Russell had a reputation for being a goal scorer. He played parts of three seasons with the Rangers, but only had one outstanding year while playing in New York.

In the 1946–47 season, the Winnipeg native scored 20 goals. After playing 19 games without scoring a goal in the 1947–48 season, Russell was traded to Cleveland of the American Hockey League in December 1947.

Pat Verbeek

NYR Debut: March 23, 1995 (at New York Islanders, lost 1–0)
Regular Season Games with NYR: 88
Playoff Games with NYR: 21
Also wore: #17

During seven years with the New Jersey Devils and parts of six with the Hartford Whalers, Ranger fans knew all about left winger Pat Verbeek.

On March 23, 1995, Ranger fans saw Verbeek make his debut in a Ranger uniform. Earlier that day, the Rangers completed a deal with Hartford to bring Verbeek to New York. Verbeek would eventually finish his NHL career with 522 goals. By the time he got to the Rangers, he had already scored 362 goals.

Verbeek played bigger than his 5-foot-9 size, and combined that physicality with a nose for the net. He scored 10 goals in 19 games to close out the 1994–95 regular season. Verbeek was terrific in the playoffs as he tallied 10 points (4 goals, 6 assists) in 10 games, but the Rangers came up short in their attempt to win back-to-back Cups.

Verbeek had one of the great seasons in franchise history in 1995–96, scoring 41 goals with 41 assists, and was solid again in the playoffs with nine points (3 goals, 6 assists) in nine games. After the season, he became an unrestricted free agent and signed with the Dallas Stars.

Gaye Stewart

NYR Debut: October 14, 1951 (at Chicago Black Hawks, lost 3–2)
Regular Season Games with NYR: 87
Playoff Games with NYR: 0

Former Calder Trophy winner Gaye Stewart was a goal scorer in his early years in the NHL, but transitioned to be more a playmaker when he joined the Rangers in June 1951. Stewart debuted as a nineteen-year-old left winger with the Toronto Maple Leafs in the 1942–43 season, scoring 24 goals.

Stewart scored 15 goals with 25 assists for 40 points in the 1951–52 season. The Ontario native's numbers dropped severely in the next season. He scored one goal in 19 games and was placed on waivers in December 1952, being claimed by the Montreal Canadiens.

Derek Sanderson

NYR Debut: October 9, 1974 (vs. Philadelphia Flyers, won 6–3)
Regular Season Games with NYR: 83
Playoff Games with NYR: 3
Also wore: #4

Center Derek Sanderson was one of the most controversial players of his era. He began his career with the Boston Bruins as a nineteen-year-old in the 1965–66 season. He was known as "The Turk" for his style of play, and

235

became beloved by the fans, but dealt with "demons" throughout his career that would eventually spell his downfall.

Sanderson was part of two Stanley Cup-winning teams in Boston. He also had the primary assist on what is arguably the most famous goal in NHL history. Sanderson made the pass that set up Bobby Orr's game-winning overtime goal in Game Four of the Final against St. Louis that clinched the Stanley Cup.

After nine seasons in Boston (interrupted by one with the Philadelphia Blazers of the WHA), Sanderson was traded to the Rangers in June 1974. In his first season with the team, Turk scored 25 goals with 25 assists in 75 games.

Sanderson had battled alcohol problems, and playing in New York did not help that situation. After eight games in the 1975–76 season, Sanderson was traded to St. Louis in October 1975.

Charlie Mason

NYR Debut: November 15, 1934 (at Detroit Red Wings, lost 8–2)
Regular Season Games with NYR: 74
Playoff Games with NYR: 4

Right winger Charlie Mason played 95 games in the National Hockey League, with 74 of those being spent with the Rangers.

Mason was a smallish 5-foot-10 winger who was an amateur star in Saskatchewan. He played parts of two seasons with the Rangers and did a stint in the minors before being sent to Detroit in October 1938.

Randy Gilhen

NYR Debut: December 29, 1991 (vs. Pittsburgh Penguins, lost 6–3)
Regular Season Games with NYR: 73
Playoff Games with NYR: 13

Randy Gilhen was born in Germany but grew up in Winnipeg.

Gilhen was a scorer in junior hockey but, when he came to the NHL, became more of a defensive forward and faceoff specialist. Before coming to the Rangers, Gilhen played for Hartford, Winnipeg, Pittsburgh, and the Los Angeles Kings. The twenty-eight-year-old center was traded from the Kings to the Rangers in December 1991.

In Gilhen's second game with the Rangers, he scored his first goal against his old Winnipeg teammates. He played parts of two seasons with the Rangers before being traded to Tampa Bay in March 1993.

Les Colwill

> **NYR Debut:** October 8, 1958 (at Chicago Black Hawks, 1–1 tie)
> **Regular Season Games with NYR:** 69
> **Playoff Games with NYR:** 0

Right winger Les Colwill played over 400 minor league games in the Ranger organization. He was signed in 1951, but didn't make it to the big club until 1958.

In his only NHL season, Colwill scored seven goals in 69 games.

Pat LaFontaine

> **NYR Debut:** October 3, 1997 (vs. New York Islanders, 2–2 tie)
> **Regular Season Games with NYR:** 67
> **Playoff Games with NYR:** 0

American-born Pat LaFontaine came to the NHL with high expectations and lived up to the billing by sculpting a Hall of Fame career that featured a stop with the Rangers.

The St. Louis-born LaFontaine was the 3rd overall pick of the New York Islanders in the 1983 NHL Entry Draft. He starred with the Islanders and, later on, the Buffalo Sabres. He had two seasons of 50-plus goals and scored 40 or more five times.

LaFontaine was traded to the Rangers from Buffalo in September 1997. In his first game for the Rangers, he scored a goal against his old team, the Islanders. In his one and only season with the Rangers, LaFontaine scored 23 goals.

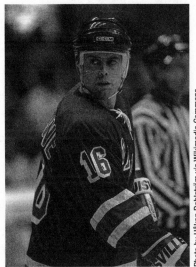

Photo by Håkan Dahlström via Wikimedia Commons.

Lafontaine scored 23 goals in his only season as a Ranger.

In March 1998, LaFontaine suffered a concussion after a collision with teammate Mike Keane in practice. It was the culmination of a series of debilitating concussions which led to his announcement in August that he was retiring from hockey.

Jack Lancien

NYR Debut: March 23, 1947 (vs. Chicago Black Hawks, won 4–3)
Regular Season Games with NYR: 63
Playoff Games with NYR: 6

Jack Lancien was a model of persistence. The 6-foot, 188-pound defenseman played nearly 900 minor league games in a 16-year career, but in only 63 NHL games (all of which with the Rangers).

The Saskatchewan native was promoted for the final regular season game of the 1946–47 season. Lancien got another chance when regular defenseman Wally Stanowski was injured during the 1949–50 season. He was impressive enough to remain on the roster for the remainder of the season. He played 19 more games in the 1950–51 season, but was returned to the minors where he finished his pro career.

Daniel Goneau

NYR Debut: October 5, 1996 (at Boston Bruins, 4–4 tie)
Regular Season Games with NYR: 53
Playoff Games with NYR: 0
Also wore: #36 and #39

Left winger Daniel Goneau was a second-round pick of the Rangers in the 1996 NHL Entry Draft. Goneau scored ten goals in his rookie season, highlighted by a two-goal game against the New Jersey Devils in late October 1996. The Montreal native played parts of three seasons with the Rangers, but never lived up to expectations.

Billy Gooden

NYR Debut: October 31, 1942 (at Toronto Maple Leafs, lost 7–2)
Regular Season Games with NYR: 53
Playoff Games with NYR: 0

Billy Gooden had a reputation as a sniper, but it never translated to the NHL. Gooden was signed by the Rangers in 1942 as a nineteen-year-old, as rosters were short due to World War II. He played 12 games in the 1942–43 season. In the 1943–44 season, he scored nine goals in 41 games. The left winger was released following the 1945–46 season.

Jean Paul Lamirande

> **NYR Debut:** October 17, 1946 (at Montreal Canadiens, lost 3–0)
> **Regular Season Games with NYR:** 48
> **Playoff Games with NYR:** 8
> **Also wore:** #3, #21, and #22

Jean Paul Lamirande was projected to be a star when he was playing junior hockey, and joined the Rangers for the beginning of the 1946–47 season. In parts of three seasons with the Rangers, the defenseman played in 48 games and scored five goals.

Larry Molyneaux

> **NYR Debut:** March 8, 1938 (vs. Toronto Maple Leafs, won 4–3)
> **Regular Season Games with NYR:** 45
> **Playoff Games with NYR:** 10

In the fall of 1938, the Rangers were hoping defenseman Larry Molyneaux and Muzz Patrick would fill a need on the back lines. Patrick, the son of head coach Lester Patrick, went on to have a solid NHL career, while Molyneaux lasted a total of 45 games in parts of two seasons.

Bobby Kirk

> **NYR Debut:** November 7, 1937 (at Detroit Red Wings, won 3–0)
> **Regular Season Games with NYR:** 39
> **Playoff Games with NYR:** 0

Bobby Kirk was never the "Captain" of the Rangers. In fact, he didn't even play an entire season. The Rangers selected the right winger off the roster of the Vancouver Lions of the PCHL in the 1935 Inter-League Draft. Kirk tallied 12 points (4 goals, 8 assists) in 39 NHL games. After the season, the

Rangers demoted Kirk to their Philadelphia affiliate of the AHL, where he completed his career in the minors.

Jack Gordon

NYR Debut: December 31, 1948 (vs. Boston Bruins, 2–2 tie)
Regular Season Games with NYR: 36
Playoff Games with NYR: 0
Also wore: #19

Left winger Jack Gordon had quite a New Year's Eve in 1948, as he made his NHL debut with the Rangers at Madison Square Garden. As an eighteen-year-old with the New York Rovers of the Eastern Amateur Hockey League in 1946–47, Gordon scored 37 goals in 54 games, and was named an All-Star.

In parts of three seasons, Gordon played 36 NHL games. In the 1950 Stanley Cup Playoffs, Gordon had a goal and an assist in nine games in the Rangers' run to the Final.

Mel Pearson

NYR Debut: January 30, 1960 (at Toronto Maple Leafs, lost 3–2)
Regular Season Games with NYR: 36
Playoff Games with NYR: 0
Also wore: #18

As an eighteen-year-old, playing junior hockey for the Flin Flon Bombers of the SJHL, left winger Mel Pearson put up some amazing numbers in the 1956–57 season. Pearson scored 59 goals with 49 assists for 108 points in 56 games. That prompted the Rangers to sign him as a free agent in 1958.

He made it to the big club in the second half of the 1959–60 season. Pearson played parts of four seasons before he was traded to Chicago in June 1965.

Glen Sonmor

NYR Debut: December 29, 1953 (vs. Boston Bruins, lost 6–2)
Regular Season Games with NYR: 28
Playoff Games with NYR: 0

Left winger Glen Sonmor is best known in Rangers history as the player that was loaned to the team from Cleveland of the AHL in exchange for Andy

Bathgate, and then was returned in a succeeding deal for the future Hall of Famer.

Sonmor played parts of two seasons with the Rangers before being returned to Cleveland in November 1954. Sonmor went on to coach the Minnesota North Stars to the Stanley Cup Final in 1981.

Leon Rochefort

NYR Debut: October 5, 1960 (vs. Boston Bruins, won 2–1)
Regular Season Games with NYR: 24
Playoff Games with NYR: 0

Right winger Leon Rochefort began his NHL career with the Rangers in the 1960–61 season. The Cap-de-la-Madeleine, Quebec, native would go on to play with seven teams during his NHL career.

In parts of two seasons in New York, Rochefort played in 24 games and scored five goals. He was dealt to Montreal as part of a famous seven-player trade in June 1963. The Rangers got back wingers Phil Goyette and Don Marshall, and Hall of Fame goaltender Jacques Plante.

The following players played less than 20 games with NYR:

Bing Juckes - left wing

NYR Debut: December 25, 1947 (vs. Detroit Red Wings, won 2–0)
Regular Season Games with NYR: 16
Playoff Games with NYR: 0
Also wore: #15

Billy Dea - left wing

NYR Debut: October 8, 1953 (at Detroit Red Wings, lost 4–1)
Regular Season Games with NYR: 14
Playoff Games with NYR: 0

Hal Brown - right wing

NYR Debut: November 3, 1945 (at Toronto Maple Leafs, won 4–1)
Regular Season Games with NYR: 13
Playoff Games with NYR: 0

George Senick - left wing

NYR Debut: January 22, 1953 (at Detroit Red Wings, won 8–2)
Regular Season Games with NYR: 13
Playoff Games with NYR: 0

Rob DiMaio - right wing

NYR Debut: March 11, 2000 (at Pittsburgh Penguins, lost 3–1)
Regular Season Games with NYR: 12
Playoff Games with NYR: 0

Marc Dufour - right wing

NYR Debut: November 27, 1963 (vs. Detroit Red Wings, won 3–2)
Regular Season Games with NYR: 12
Playoff Games with NYR: 0
Also wore: #6

Ernest Kenny - defenseman

NYR Debut: January 11, 1931 (vs. Chicago Black Hawks, lost 2–0)
Regular Season Games with NYR: 6
Playoff Games with NYR: 0

Frank Bathgate - center

NYR Debut: February 22, 1953 (vs. Detroit Red Wings, lost 2–1)
Regular Season Games with NYR: 2
Playoff Games with NYR: 0

Jim Drummond - defenseman

NYR Debut: January 9, 1945 (at Toronto Maple Leafs, won 5–4)
Regular Season Games with NYR: 2
Playoff Games with NYR: 0

Jim Hiller - right wing

NYR Debut: October 30, 1993 (at Hartford Whalers, won 4–1)

Regular Season Games with NYR: 2

Playoff Games with NYR: 0

Val Delory - left wing

NYR Debut: March 13, 1949 (vs. Montreal Canadiens, 1–1 tie)

Regular Season Games with NYR: 1

Playoff Games with NYR: 0

Dick Kotanen - defenseman

NYR Debut: March 25, 1951 (vs. Chicago Black Hawks, 5–2)

Regular Season Games with NYR: 1

Playoff Games with NYR: 0

Brian McReynolds - center

NYR Debut: February 22, 1991 (at Washington Capitals, lost 3–2)

Regular Season Games with NYR: 1

Playoff Games with NYR: 0

Al "Red" Staley - center

NYR Debut: November 14, 1948 (vs. Toronto Maple Leafs, 4–4 tie)

Regular Season Games with NYR: 1

Playoff Games with NYR: 0

Lester Patrick - goaltender

NYR Debut: March 20, 1927 (vs. New York Americans, won 2–1)

Regular Season Games with NYR: 0

Playoff Games with NYR: 1

#17: A PRENTICE AND A FORBES

Dean Prentice

> **NYR Debut:** October 22, 1952 (vs. Boston Bruins, 3–3 tie)
> **Regular Season Games with NYR:** 666
> **Playoff Games with NYR:** 19

Dean Prentice was a left winger who played second-fiddle to Hall of Famer Andy Bathgate. Prentice debuted in 1952, and played the bulk of his career on a line with Bathgate and center Larry Popein.

The Rangers signed the Ontario native in 1950. After two seasons of junior hockey with the Guelph Biltmores of OHA, Prentice was promoted to begin the 1952–53 season with the Rangers.

Prentice became an excellent two-way player, and was matched up against some of the great forwards including Hall of Famer Gordie Howe. Prentice would try and get Howe off of his game, but he didn't do it with physicality. Instead, Prentice would engage in needling the all-time great. On one occasion, Howe reportedly told Prentice, "You keep bothering me and I'll knock every tooth out of your mouth." Prentice flashed a wide smile and said, "I'm afraid somebody's already beat you to it."

His best season was 1959–60, when he was named an NHL second team All-Star after scoring a career-high 32 goals. He was also named the team's Most Valuable Player. Prentice would go on to score 20 and 22 goals in his next two seasons, but would drop off to 13 in the 1962–63 season. After 11 seasons with the Rangers, Prentice was traded to Boston in February 1963.

Brandon Dubinsky

> **NYR Debut:** March 8, 2007 (at New York Islanders, won 2–1)
> **Regular Season Games with NYR:** 393
> **Playoff Games with NYR:** 31
> **Also wore:** #54

In the 2004 NHL Entry Draft, the Rangers used their second-round pick to select eighteen-year-old Brandon Dubinsky. The 6-foot-2 Dubinsky was being groomed as a first- or second-line center. He was big and could put the puck in the net.

After being named the co-winner (along with Nigel Dawes) of the 2006 Lars-Erik Sjoberg Award as the best rookie in camp, Dubinsky played the entire season with the Rangers' AHL affiliate in Hartford. The Anchorage, Alaska-born Dubinsky was promoted to play six games with the big club at the end of the 2006–07 season. In his first full season, Dubinsky got off to a slow start with only one assist in his first 15 games. He finally scored his first NHL goal in November, and finished tenth in the voting for the Calder Trophy after scoring 14 goals with 26 assists for 40 points in his rookie season.

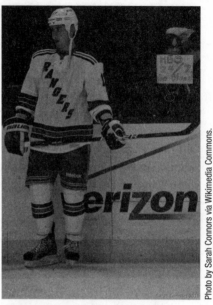

Was part of multi-player deal that brought Rick Nash to the Rangers.

Photo by Sarah Connors via Wikimedia Commons.

Dubinsky took his game up a notch in his first taste of postseason play. In ten games, Dubinsky scored four goals with four assists. In the first round, he had a goal and an assist in the series-clinching Game Five against the New Jersey Devils. In the next round, Dubinsky added a goal and an assist as the Rangers won Game Four against Pittsburgh to avoid being swept.

Over the next couple of seasons, Dubinsky became a staple of the Rangers' lineup. In 2009–10, he scored 20 goals and bettered that the next season with 24. After scoring ten goals in the 2011–12 season, Dubinsky was traded to Columbus in July 2012 as part of a multi-player deal that brought left winger Rick Nash to New York.

Eddie Johnstone

NYR Debut: December 10, 1975 (vs. Buffalo Sabres, tie 2–2)

Regular Season Games with NYR: 371

Playoff Games with NYR: 53

Also wore: #14

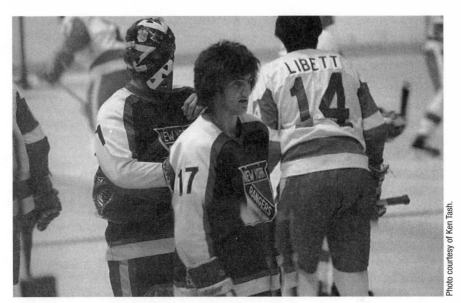

Eddie Johnstone's style of play made him a fan favorite.

Eddie Johnstone only stood 5-foot-9, but he was a feisty winger who became a fan favorite with his gritty, hard-working style of play.

Johnstone was a sixth-round pick of the Rangers in the 1974 NHL Amateur Draft, but decided to sign with the Michigan Stags of the World Hockey Association. After one season in the WHA, Johnstone joined the Rangers and spent most of the 1975–76 season with the team's AHL affiliate in Providence.

The native of Brandon, Manitoba, broke out with 13 goals and 26 points in the 1977–78 season. He toiled through an injury-plagued regular season in 1978–79, but was healthy enough to help the Rangers make a run to the Final. In the 1979 Stanley Cup Quarterfinal against Philadelphia, Johnstone scored four goals and added one more against the New York Islanders in the semifinal.

In the 1980–81 season, Johnstone was named the team's Most Valuable Player with a career high in goals (30) and points (68). He recorded a second consecutive 30-goal season in 1981–82.

Johnstone spent one more season in New York. In the 1983 Stanley Cup Playoffs, he scored four goals with one assist in nine games. After the season, Johnstone was traded to Detroit as part of a multi-player deal.

Kevin Stevens

NYR Debut: October 3, 1997 (vs. New York Islanders, 2–2 OT tie)

Regular Season Games with NYR: 199

Playoff Games with NYR: 0

By the time Kevin Stevens came to the Rangers in 1997, he was a shell of his former self.

In 1991–92, Stevens, who was born in Brockton, Massachusetts, and playing for the Pittsburgh Penguins, scored 123 points (54 goals, 69 assists) to set a record for an American-born player and a left winger. The next season, Stevens tied the record for an American-born player by scoring 55 goals and helping lead the Penguins to their second consecutive Stanley Cup title.

At 6-foot-3, Stevens brought a physical aspect to his game—but that all changed after one hit in the 1993 Stanley Cup Playoffs. While being checked, New York Islanders' defenseman Rich Pilon's visor struck Stevens in the face. The blow knocked him out and, when Stevens fell to the ice, he suffered numerous facial injuries. He was never the same after that hit.

The Rangers acquired Stevens from the Los Angeles Kings in August 1997. In 1997–98, Stevens scored 14 goals and added 23 in the next season, but things started to go downhill after that.

After playing 38 games in the 1999–2000 season, Stevens entered the NHL/NHLPA Substance Abuse Program and never played another game for the Rangers.

Alex Kaleta

NYR Debut: October 14, 1948 (at Montreal Canadiens, 1–1 tie)

Regular Season Games with NYR: 181

Playoff Games with NYR: 10

Alex Kaleta was a speedy left winger who was best known for the creation of one of hockey's most coveted and iconic monikers. Scoring three goals in a game is a "hat trick," but the term came to light as a result of an offer made to Kaleta. A Toronto haberdasher named Sammy Taft offered Kaleta a hat if he scored three goals in the game that night. Toronto Maple Leafs and visiting players would shop for hats in Taft's shop, and Kaleta had his eye on one particular fedora. Kaleta ended up scoring three goals that night, and the rest is history.

The Rangers acquired Kaleta, along with goaltender Emile Francis, from the Chicago Black Hawks for goaltender Jim Henry (see Chapter One) in October 1948. In parts of three seasons, Kaleta scored 32 goals.

Dave Balon

NYR Debut: January 30, 1960 (at Toronto Maple Leafs, lost 3–2)
Regular Season Games with NYR: 161
Playoff Games with NYR: 29
Also wore: #8, #11, and #22

Left winger Dave Balon was a player who proved "you can go home again." The Saskatchewan native had two tenures with the Rangers, but it was the second one in which he shined.

Balon signed with the Rangers in 1958, and joined the team in the 1959–60 season. After he played 70 games in the 1962–63 season, Balon was part of a huge multi-player trade that included Hall of Fame goaltender Gump Worsley (see Chapter One) going to Montreal for a package that included another Hall of Fame goalie, Jacques Plante, coming to the Rangers.

After winning two Stanley Cups with the Canadiens, Balon was selected by Minnesota in the 1967 NHL Expansion Draft and then dealt back to the Rangers in June 1968.

From 1968–71, Balon, who was playing on a line with center Walt Tkaczuk (see Chapter Eighteen) and right winger Billy Fairbairn (see Chapter Ten), a.k.a. the "Bulldog Line," was an All-Star and twice led the team in goals.

After 16 games in the 1971–72 season, Balon was traded to the Vancouver Canucks.

Bill Hicke

NYR Debut: December 23, 1964 (at Montreal Canadiens, lost 2–0)
Regular Season Games with NYR: 137
Playoff Games with NYR: 0
Also wore: #12 and #18

Right winger Bill Hicke played parts of three seasons with the Rangers. Hicke was acquired in a trade with Montreal in December 1964.

Before the start of the 1965–66 season, Hicke contracted pneumonia and missed the start of the season. Hicke's last season with the Rangers was 1966–67, as he was claimed by Oakland in the 1967 NHL Expansion Draft.

Cal Gardner

NYR Debut: December 31, 1945 (vs. Montreal Canadiens, 0–0 tie)
Regular Season Games with NYR: 126
Playoff Games with NYR: 5
Also wore: #12

After serving in World War II, 6-foot-1 center Cal Gardner returned to junior hockey and scored 41 goals for the New York Rovers of the EAHL in the 1945–46 season. The Rangers took notice, and he joined the team later that season.

Gardner lasted parts of three seasons with the team before being traded to Toronto in June 1948.

John Moore

NYR Debut: April 3, 2013 (vs. Pittsburgh Penguins, won 6–1)
Regular Season Games with NYR: 125
Playoff Games with NYR: 33

In April 2013, defenseman John Moore was acquired by the Rangers in a multi-player trade with the Columbus Blue Jackets that also netted center Derick Brassard. Hours after the trade was made, Moore scored his first Ranger goal in a 6–1 win over Pittsburgh.

At 6-foot-2 and 210 pounds, Moore provided a physical presence for the Rangers on the back line, but there were times that he went "over the line." In the 2014 Eastern Conference Finals against Montreal, Moore received a two-game suspension for a hit to the head of Canadiens winger Dale Weise. In October 2014, Moore received a five-game suspension for a hit to the head of Minnesota Wild center Erik Haula.

In March 2015, Moore was traded to the Arizona Coyotes in a deal that brought defenseman Keith Yandle to the Rangers.

Jerry Butler

NYR Debut: December 21, 1972 (vs. Atlanta Flames, lost 5–2)

Regular Season Games with NYR: 112

Playoff Games with NYR: 15

Also wore: #20

Right winger Jerry Butler was drafted by the Rangers in the fourth round of the 1971 NHL Amateur Draft, but will go down in franchise history as the player who was traded to the St. Louis Blues for goaltender John Davidson (see Chapter One).

Butler alternated between the Rangers' minor league affiliates and the NHL club in the 1972–73 and 1973–74 seasons. He finally got a full-time chance and scored 17 goals with 16 assists in the 1974–75 season. Butler scored one goal in 15 playoff games, and was dealt to the Blues in June 1975.

Lou Angotti

NYR Debut: October 12, 1964 (at Boston Bruins, won 6–2)

Regular Season Games with NYR: 91

Playoff Games with NYR: 0

At twenty-six years old, center Lou Angotti had finally made his NHL debut—and he made it count. Angotti scored a goal to cap off a 6–2 win in Boston in his first NHL game with the Rangers. The Toronto native had toiled in the minors since the 1955–56 season, when he was an eighteen-year-old with the St. Micheal's Majors of the OHA.

Angotti scored 11 goals in parts of two seasons with the Rangers. He was traded to Chicago in January 1966, and later became the first captain of the expansion Philadelphia Flyers in 1967.

Carey Wilson

NYR Debut: December 26, 1988 (vs. New Jersey Devils, won 5–1)

Regular Season Games with NYR: 82

Playoff Games with NYR: 14

Carey Wilson was born in Manitoba, but graduated from Dartmouth and played for Canada in the 1984 Olympics before making his NHL debut with the Calgary Flames late in the 1983–84 season.

Wilson was a consistent goal scorer who was acquired by the Rangers from the Hartford Whalers in December 1988 to enhance the team's offense.

Wilson's Ranger debut featured three assists in a win against New Jersey. His first season in New York was a success, as he scored 21 goals in 41 games. In the 1989–90 season, he scored 9 goals in 41 games and was traded back to Hartford in July 1990.

Greg Gilbert

NYR Debut: October 5, 1993 (vs. Boston Bruins, lost 4–3)
Regular Season Games with NYR: 76
Playoff Games with NYR: 23

Left winger Greg Gilbert was already a 12-year NHL veteran and a two-time Stanley Cup champ when he joined the Rangers, but was able to etch his name onto the coveted chalice one more time. Gilbert had previously won two Cups with the New York Islanders in the early 1980s.

Gilbert signed with the Rangers as a free agent for the 1993–94 season. He played in 76 games and was a steady presence as a third- and fourth-line player. In the playoffs, he appeared in all 23 games and scored a goal with three assists.

Don McKenney

NYR Debut: February 6, 1963 (vs. Montreal Canadiens, won 6–3)
Regular Season Games with NYR: 76
Playoff Games with NYR: 0

Center Don McKenney was a former Calder Trophy and Lady Byng Memorial Trophy winner when he was traded to the Rangers from the Boston Bruins in February 1963, in exchange for left winger Dean Prentice.

In his first game since the trade from Boston, McKenney scored a goal as part of a 6–3 win over Montreal. McKenney played parts of two seasons with the Rangers, from 1962–64, and scored 17 goals. In 1964, he was named an NHL All-Star. In February 1964, McKenney was part of the multi-player trade that sent Hall of Famer Andy Bathgate to Toronto.

Mike Rupp

NYR Debut: October 7, 2011 (at Los Angeles Kings, lost 3–2 OT)

Regular Season Games with NYR: 68

Playoff Games with NYR: 20

Also wore: #71

Going into the 2011–12 season, the Rangers needed to add more size and toughness to the roster, so they signed the 6-foot-5, free agent center Mike Rupp.

Rupp was the 9th overall selection of the New York Islanders in the 1998 NHL Entry Draft. He played 60 games in his first season with the Rangers, but his ice time lessened in the 2012–13 season and he was traded to the Minnesota Wild in February 2013.

Chris Simon

NYR Debut: October 10, 2003 (at Minnesota Wild, lost 5–3)

Regular Season Games with NYR: 65

Playoff Games with NYR: 0

Chris Simon's most impressive stat during his short stint with the Rangers was accumulating 225 penalty minutes.

The 6-foot-3 left winger signed with the Rangers as a free agent for the 2003–04 season. Despite a reputation for his toughness, Simon had some skill as evidenced by his 108 goals scored before he joined the Blueshirts. In his one season, he scored 14 goals with 9 assists for 23 points.

After his season in New York, Simon was traded to the Calgary Flames. Three years later, while playing for the New York Islanders, Simon was suspended 25 games after he swung his stick and hit Rangers' forward Ryan Hollweg in the face. Hollweg had previously checked Simon, who fell face first into the boards. That was just one of a number of on-ice incidents for Simon, who was suspended a total of eight times in his career.

Herb Dickenson

NYR Debut: November 21, 1951 (vs. Boston Bruins, 3–3 tie)

Regular Season Games with NYR: 48

Playoff Games with NYR: 0

Also wore: #14

Off of his first season with the Rangers, it appeared left winger Herb Dickenson was on his way to a productive career. Dickenson began his career with the Guelph Biltmores as an eighteen-year-old in 1949. After two impressive seasons, the Rangers promoted the Hamilton, Ontario, native.

In the 1951–52 season, Dickenson scored 14 goals with 13 assists in 37 games, but tragedy struck during his second season.

Dickenson was off to a fast start in the 1952–53 season with four goals and four assists in eight games. On November 5, 1952, the Rangers were in Toronto to play the Maple Leafs. During the pre-game warm ups, Dickenson suffered a career-ending injury when he was struck in the eye by a puck.

Rem Murray

> **NYR Debut:** March 21, 2002 (at Ottawa Senators, won 5–2)
> **Regular Season Games with NYR:** 43
> **Playoff Games with NYR:** 0

After being acquired from Edmonton in March 2002, left winger Rem Murray played parts of two seasons with the Rangers from 2001–03. Murray had an assist in his first game with the Rangers. He scored his first goal with the Rangers during a 6–4 win against Tampa Bay in early April 2002.

During his second season, Murray scored two goals, including the game winner, against San Jose. After playing 32 games, Murray was traded to the Nashville Predators.

Petr Sykora

> **NYR Debut:** January 10, 2006 (vs. Calgary Flames, won 4–2)
> **Regular Season Games with NYR:** 40
> **Playoff Games with NYR:** 4

Right wing Petr Sykora was acquired from Anaheim as a "rental" toward the latter part of the 2005–06 season. Sykora was an impending free agent.

Sykora scored the game-winning goal in his first game with the Rangers, and finished with 16 goals with 15 assists in 40 games. Sykora was not re-signed, and left the team to join Edmonton as a free agent after the season.

Rob Whistle

NYR Debut: December 8, 1985 (vs. Philadelphia Flyers, won 3–1)
Regular Season Games with NYR: 32
Playoff Games with NYR: 3
Also wore: #39

In August 1985, defenseman Rob Whistle signed with the Rangers as an un-drafted free agent. Whistle played in 32 games and scored four goals. He was with the Rangers' minor-league affiliate at New Haven when he was traded to St. Louis in May 1987.

Jeff Brubaker

NYR Debut: November 4, 1987 (at Edmonton Oilers, lost 7–2)
Regular Season Games with NYR: 31
Playoff Games with NYR: 0
Also wore: #24

Left winger Jeff Brubaker was twenty-nine years old when he joined the Rangers in 1987. Brubaker began his pro career in the WHA, and then played with five NHL clubs before he got to New York. After 31 games in the 1987–88 season, Brubaker was sent to the Rangers' minor-league affiliate at Colorado of the IHL. After the season, he left the team as an unrestricted free agent, joining the Red Wings.

Brian Lawton

NYR Debut: October 12, 1988 (vs. Hartford Whalers, lost 4–3)
Regular Season Games with NYR: 31
Playoff Games with NYR: 0

Center Brian Lawton came to the NHL with a lot of hype, but never lived up to the expectations. In the 1983 NHL Entry Draft, the Minnesota North Stars made the eighteen-year-old the 1st overall pick. Lawton had trouble adjusting to the NHL style of play and, after parts of four seasons in Minnesota, was traded to the Rangers.

Lawton scored seven goals with ten assists in 30 games with the Rangers, but was traded in December 1988 to the Hartford Whalers.

Chuck Scherza

NYR Debut: November 28, 1943 (vs. Montreal Canadiens, 2–2 tie)

Regular Season Games with NYR: 27

Playoff Games with NYR: 0

A short time after he was traded to the Rangers from the Boston Bruins in November 1943, center Chuck Scherza faced his old team for the first time. Scherza scored two goals, but on the second tally, he slammed into the old, immovable goal posts and suffered a collapsed lung and played only five games in his first season with the Rangers.

Scherza returned to play 22 games in the 1944–45 season, but was sent to Hershey of the AHL and was released after the season.

Tom Williams

NYR Debut: February 17, 1972 (at Los Angeles Kings, won 6–4)

Regular Season Games with NYR: 25

Playoff Games with NYR: 0

Left winger Tom Williams was a second-round choice of the Rangers in the 1971 NHL Amateur Draft. Williams was a consistent scorer in junior hockey but it never translated to NHL success. He was traded to the Los Angeles Kings in November 1973.

George Allen

NYR Debut: December 20, 1938 (vs. Detroit Red Wings, won 6–2)

Regular Season Games with NYR: 19

Playoff Games with NYR: 8

As a result of some injuries during the 1938–39 season, left winger George Allen was promoted from Philadelphia of the AHL, and things could not have gone any better in his first game. Allen scored two goals and added an assist to lead the Rangers to a 6–2 win over Detroit in a December 1938 game at Madison Square Garden. Unfortunately, his goal total in his first game was a third of what would be his entire season's output.

Allen went scoreless in seven Stanley Cup playoff games and was dealt to Chicago after the season.

The following players played less than 20 games with NYR:

Colin Forbes - left wing

NYR Debut: March 2, 2001 (vs. Pittsburgh Penguins, lost 7–5)
Regular Season Games with NYR: 19
Playoff Games with NYR: 0

Jean Pusie - defenseman

NYR Debut: November 11, 1933 (at Toronto Maple Leafs, lost 4–3)
Regular Season Games with NYR: 19
Playoff Games with NYR: 0

Norm Tustin - left wing

NYR Debut: November 1, 1941 (at Toronto Maple Leafs, won 4–3)
Regular Season Games with NYR: 18
Playoff Games with NYR: 0

Rick Bennett - left wing

NYR Debut: March 21, 1990 (vs. Toronto Maple Leafs, 5–5 OT tie)
Regular Season Games with NYR: 15
Playoff Games with NYR: 0
Also wore: #27

Jari Kurri - right wing

NYR Debut: March 16, 1996 (at Montreal Canadiens, lost 4–2)
Regular Season Games with NYR: 14
Playoff Games with NYR: 11

Clare Martin - defenseman

NYR Debut: December 30, 1951 (vs. Toronto Maple Leafs, 2–2 tie)

Regular Season Games with NYR: 14

Playoff Games with NYR: 0

Greg Holst - center

NYR Debut: November 26, 1975 (vs. Boston Bruins, lost 6–4)

Regular Season Games with NYR: 11

Playoff Games with NYR: 0

The Rangers took a chance with Greg Holst when they drafted the smallish center in the eighth round of the 1974 NHL Amateur Draft. At 5-foot-11 and 170 pounds, Holst was not the kind of forward that the scouts were looking for. He played a total of 11 games in parts of three seasons with the Rangers. After the 1977–78 season, Holst left the United States to play in Austria, where he starred for 15 seasons.

Stan Smith - center

NYR Debut: February 8, 1940 (vs. Toronto Maple Leafs, won 2–1)

Regular Season Games with NYR: 9

Playoff Games with NYR: 1

After scoring 23 goals and 50 points for the New York Rovers of the EHL in 1938–39, center Stan Smith was signed by the Rangers. The native of Coal Creek, British Columbia, played nine games and scored two goals in parts of two seasons with the Rangers. Despite playing in the 1940 Stanley Cup Final, Smith's name was mistakenly left off the Cup.

Ray Cullen - center

NYR Debut: January 15, 1966 (at Detroit Red Wings, 4–4 tie)

Regular Season Games with NYR: 8

Playoff Games with NYR: 0

Herb Foster - left wing

NYR Debut: November 30, 1940 (vs. Montreal Canadiens, won 6–1)

Regular Season Games with NYR: 6

Playoff Games with NYR: 0

Max Labovitch - center

NYR Debut: October 31, 1943 (at Detroit Red Wings, lost 8–3)

Regular Season Games with NYR: 5

Playoff Games with NYR: 0

Ed Harrison - left wing

NYR Debut: November 18, 1950 (at Toronto Maple Leafs, lost 5–4)

Regular Season Games with NYR: 4

Playoff Games with NYR: 0

Lloyd Ailsby - defenseman

NYR Debut: December 15, 1951 (at Toronto Maple Leafs, lost 4–1)

Regular Season Games with NYR: 3

Playoff Games with NYR: 0

Cliff Barton - left wing

NYR Debut: November 16, 1939 (vs. Chicago Black Hawks, lost 3–2)

Regular Season Games with NYR: 3

Playoff Games with NYR: 0

Fedor Fedorov - left wing

NYR Debut: October 27, 2005 (vs. New York Islanders, won 3–1)

Regular Season Games with NYR: 3

Playoff Games with NYR: 0

Bill Allum - defenseman

NYR Debut: November 26, 1940 (vs. Toronto Maple Leafs, lost 4–2)

Regular Season Games with NYR: 1

Playoff Games with NYR: 0

Spence Tatchell - defenseman

NYR Debut: February 20, 1943 (at Montreal Canadiens, lost 6–1)

Regular Season Games with NYR: 1

Playoff Games with NYR: 0

#18: TKACZUK—PRONOUNCING A GREAT RANGER CAREER

Walt Tkaczuk

NYR Debut: January 24, 1968 (vs. Boston Bruins, won 2–1)

Regular Season Games with NYR: 945

Playoff Games with NYR: 93

One of the steadiest players to ever put on a Ranger uniform, Walt Tkaczuk amassed an impressive 14-year career.

After signing as a free agent and polishing his game in the minors, Tkaczuk was brought up for two games in the 1967–68 season. The German-born center made the team for the 1968–69 season and never went back to the minors. He scored 12 goals and 24 assists in his first full season, but broke out in 1969–70 with 27 goals and 50 assists for a career-high 77 points.

Tkaczuk played second fiddle to the famous "GAG" line of Jean Ratelle, Rod Gilbert, and Vic Hadfield, but the 6-foot pivot man who grew up in Kitchener, Ontario, anchored the "Bulldog Line" with wingers Dave Balon (see Chapter Seventeen) and Billy Fairbairn (see Chapter Ten).

Tkaczuk played a huge role in helping the Rangers get to the Final in 1972. He scored

Photo courtesy of Ken Tash.

Anchor of the Rangers Bulldog Line.

the winning goal in the Game Six clincher of the Stanley Cup Quarterfinal against Montreal, and the game-winner in Game One of the four-game, semifinal sweep of Chicago.

The Rangers' center drew the assignment of checking Boston center and Hall of Famer Phil Esposito in the Game Six Final loss to the Bruins. Tkaczuk did an admirable job and earned the respect of his opponent. After the series, Esposito said about Tkaczuk, "I've never run into anyone tougher." In the 1973 Stanley Cup Playoffs, Tkaczuk scored a playoff career high of seven goals.

Tkaczuk was thirty years old in the 1977–78 season, when he put up his last big season with the Rangers as he scored 26 goals and 40 assists for 66 points.

In his final three seasons, Tkaczuk scored a total of 33 goals. In his final season of 1980–81, he scored six goals in 43 games and retired after the season. He finished his Rangers' career with 227 goals and 451 assists for 678 points (which is currently sixth all-time).

Marc Staal

NYR Debut: October 4, 2007 (vs. Florida Panthers, won 5–2)
Regular Season Games with NYR: 689
Playoff Games with NYR: 104

Defenseman Marc Staal has been a stalwart of the Rangers' defense corps since 2007. The Rangers made Staal the 12th overall pick in the 2005 NHL Entry Draft. What was attractive about Staal was his 6-foot-4 frame and his long reach, which allowed him to be an excellent stick checker.

After winning the Lars Erik-Sjoberg Award as the best rookie in the 2007 training camp, Staal played in 80 games for the team that season. He scored his first goal, fittingly in his eighteenth game, against the New Jersey Devils and future Hall of Fame goaltender Martin Brodeur. In his first taste of the Stanley Cup Playoffs, the young defenseman acquitted himself well with the

Photo by Keith Allison from Hanover, MD, USA, via Wikimedia Commons.

Staal scored the game-winning goal in overtime of Game Five of the 2012 Eastern Conference Semifinal.

game-winning goal in Game Four of the 2008 Eastern Conference Quarterfinal series victory against Brodeur and the Devils.

Staal became a reliable defenseman, as he missed only five games over his next three seasons. Staal put together a streak of 247 consecutive games played that ended in 2011 due to a knee injury.

In February 2011, Staal took a hard hit from his brother, Eric, in a game against Carolina and suffered post-concussion symptoms. The hit caused him to miss the start of the 2011–12 season. He made his debut in the Winter Classic on January 2 against Philadelphia, and was outstanding in the 2012 Stanley Cup Playoffs. Staal played 20 games and scored three goals with three assists as the Rangers got all the way to the Eastern Conference Final. During the run, Staal scored the game-winning goal in overtime of Game Five of the Eastern Conference Semifinal series win against the Washington Capitals.

In March 2013, Staal was struck in the eye by a puck and missed the final 27 games of the regular season. He was not wearing a visor and when he returned to play one game in the Stanley Cup Playoffs, he began wearing the protective gear.

In the 2014–15 season, Staal played 80 games and scored five goals and 20 points, but his numbers began to trail off in the next two seasons as he turned thirty years old in 2017.

Tony Leswick

NYR Debut: October 31, 1945 (at Chicago Black Hawks, lost 5–1)
Regular Season Games with NYR: 368
Playoff Games with NYR: 18

Tony Leswick came out of the Canadian Navy to join the Rangers for the 1945–46 season.

The 5-foot-7 left winger was nicknamed "Mighty Mouse" because he was a hard-nosed checker who earned a reputation for challenging the league's top players, including Hall of Famer Maurice "Rocket" Richard.

Leswick knew he could get under Richard's skin and used every opportunity to do so. He would sometimes get into a brawl with the all-time great. That took Richard off the ice for a period of time, something the Rangers did not mind at all.

In the 1946–47 season, Leswick led the Rangers with 27 goals and a berth in the All-Star Game.

The Saskatchewan native was a durable player who missed only two games in six seasons with the Rangers. In two postseason appearances, Leswick scored 11 points in 18 games.

In June 1951, Leswick was traded to the Detroit Red Wings where he went on to win three Stanley Cups.

Wally Hergesheimer

NYR Debut: October 14, 1951 (at Chicago Black Hawks, lost 3–2)
Regular Season Games with NYR: 310
Playoff Games with NYR: 5

Right winger Wally Hergesheimer was the Rangers' leading goal scorer in the early 1950s, which made him a fan favorite.

After scoring 26 goals in his first season of 1951–52, Hergesheimer did even better in his second year. The Winnipeg native finished fourth in the league in scoring and led the team with 30 goals in 1952–53.

Hergesheimer was only 5-foot-8 and was missing two fingers on his right hand from an industrial accident during his teen years, but was able to become a consistent goal scorer for the Rangers.

In June 1956, the Rangers traded Hergesheimer to Chicago for center Red Sullivan, but he was reacquired before the 1958–59 season and played 22 more games with the Rangers to finish his career.

Wally Hergesheimer Right Wing

NEW YORK RANGERS

Hockey card from the public domain.

Despite missing two fingers, Wally was a leading goal scorer for the Rangers.

Ken Schinkel

NYR Debut: October 7, 1959 (at Chicago Black Hawks, lost 5–2)
Regular Season Games with NYR: 265
Playoff Games with NYR: 6
Also wore: #21

Ken Schinkel was just hoping to get an opportunity. The right winger toiled in the minors for six years before being promoted to join the Rangers in 1959 at the age of twenty-seven.

Schinkel developed as a goal scorer in the minors. In the 1958–59 season, he scored 43 goals while playing for Springfield of the AHL. The Rangers used the 5-foot-10 winger as a defensive forward. He mostly played with checking lines and on penalty kills, so his goal-scoring totals never really materialized in the NHL.

Schinkel was claimed by the Pittsburgh Penguins in the 1967 NHL Expansion Draft, and eventually became their head coach in 1972.

Mike York

> **NYR Debut:** October 1, 1999 (at Edmonton Oilers, 1–1 OT tie)
> **Regular Season Games with NYR:** 230
> **Playoff Games with NYR:** 0

While playing four years at Michigan State, American-born center Mike York was a two-time finalist for the Hobey Baker Award as the top collegiate hockey player.

The Rangers selected York in the sixth round of the 1997 NHL Entry Draft. Late in the 1998–99 season, York played three games and the playoffs for the Hartford Wolf Pack of the AHL. He made the big club out of training camp and had a successful first season.

York led the team with 26 goals and 50 points in the 1999–2000 season, and finished third in the voting for the Calder Trophy for the top rookie in the league. York played on a line with left winger Theo Fleury and center Eric Lindros that became known as the "FLY Line." In January 2002, York scored a career-high five points (2 goals, 3 assists) to key an 8–4 win over Boston.

After three seasons with the Rangers, York was traded to the Edmonton Oilers for defenseman Tom Poti in March 2002.

Bill Berg

> **NYR Debut:** March 4, 1996 (vs. New Jersey Devils, 2–2 OT tie)
> **Regular Season Games with NYR:** 152
> **Playoff Games with NYR:** 13

In March 1996, the Rangers needed to add some size and toughness to their lineup, so they acquired left wingers Bill Berg and Sergio Momesso for left winger Nick Kypreos.

Berg, who began his career with the New York Islanders, made his reputation as a physical, in-your-face type player.

He joined the Rangers for the stretch drive of the 1995–96 season and played the next two years in New York before being traded to Ottawa in November 1998.

Gerry Foley

> **NYR Debut:** October 12, 1956 (at Chicago Black Hawks, won 3–0)
> **Regular Season Games with NYR:** 137
> **Playoff Games with NYR:** 9

Massachusetts-born Gerry Foley was a solid role player who spent parts of two seasons with the Rangers.

Foley was born in Ware, Massachusetts, but grew up in Ontario where he fell in love with the sport of hockey. The Rangers claimed Foley from Toronto in the 1956 NHL Intra-League Draft. He scored 16 points in 69 games during his first season of 1956–57.

After the 1957–58 season, the Rangers sent Foley to the minors where he played three more seasons before being released. Foley's career was not over, however. Nearly ten years after playing his final game for the Rangers, Foley returned to the NHL as a member of the Los Angeles Kings.

Mike Ridley

> **NYR Debut:** October 10, 1985 (vs. Washington Capitals, won 4–2)
> **Regular Season Games with NYR:** 118
> **Playoff Games with NYR:** 16

Center Mike Ridley went from being an undrafted free agent to becoming a prominent member of the 1985–86 team.

Ridley got a shot during the 1985 training camp and impressed team brass enough to earn a spot on the roster. Ridley scored a goal in his first game, and it became an omen for his freshman season. Ridley led the team in points and assists while scoring 22 goals and finishing fourth in the voting for the Calder Trophy as the top rookie. In the 1986 Stanley Cup Playoffs, Ridley scored six goals with eight assists for 14 points in 16 games.

The Winnipeg native was off to a solid start in his second Ranger season with 16 goals and 20 assists in 38 games, but just when it seemed like he was ready to become the next big star on Broadway, Ridley was involved in a major trade. On New Year's Day, 1987, Ridley was sent to the Washington Capitals in a multi-player deal for the first American-born player to score 50 goals in one season, center Bob Carpenter.

Tony Granato

NYR Debut: October 6, 1988 (at Chicago Blackhawks, 2–2 OT tie)
Regular Season Games with NYR: 115
Playoff Games with NYR: 4
Also wore: #39

Right winger Tony Granato had what is arguably the greatest rookie season in Rangers franchise history. In the 1988–89 season, the Illinois native set a Ranger rookie record with 36 goals while adding 27 assists for 63 points. His initial season included a four-goal game against Pittsburgh in late October at Madison Square Garden, and two additional hat tricks.

Midway through the 1989–90 season, Granato (and right winger Tomas Sandstrom) was traded to the Los Angeles Kings for center Bernie Nicholls.

Joe Shack

NYR Debut: January 21, 1943 (vs. Toronto Maple Leafs, lost 7–4)
Regular Season Games with NYR: 70
Playoff Games with NYR: 0
Also wore: #16

Left winger Joe Shack played parts of two seasons with the Rangers during war time in the early 1940s. He joined the Rangers for the 1942–43 season, but missed the next season due to military service.

Shack returned to the Rangers to play 50 games in the 1944–45 season, but was sent to the St. Paul Saints. He spent the next three seasons at St. Paul and left the organization in 1948 to play in Europe.

Wayne Presley

NYR Debut: October 7, 1995 (at Hartford Whalers, lost 2–0)
Regular Season Games with NYR: 61
Playoff Games with NYR: 0

Wayne Presley proved himself as a goal scorer with the Rangers, but it wasn't in New York. In the 1983–84 season, Presley scored 63 goals for the Kitchener Rangers of the OHL. He began his NHL career with Chicago in 1984 and after stints with San Jose and Buffalo, he signed with the Rangers as a free agent in 1995.

Presley scored four goals in 61 games before being traded to Toronto in February 1996.

Adam Hall

NYR Debut: October 5, 2006 (at Washington Capitals, won 5–2)
Regular Season Games with NYR: 49
Playoff Games with NYR: 0

At 6-foot-2, right wing Adam Hall had a nomadic NHL career, where he played with seven different teams over eleven seasons—including the Rangers in 2006–07. Hall was brought in to add some toughness to the Ranger lineup. After scoring four goals in 49 games, he was traded to the Minnesota Wild for left winger Pascal Dupuis in February 2007.

Mike Blaisdell

NYR Debut: October 13, 1983 (vs. Washington Capitals, won 4–3)
Regular Season Games with NYR: 48
Playoff Games with NYR: 0

Mike Blaisdell will forever be known in Ranger lore as being a piece of a multi-player trade with Detroit in June 1983 that sent popular right winger Ron Duguay (see Chapter Ten) to Motown.

Blaisdell began his Ranger career in the minors and played parts of two seasons before he was claimed on waivers by Pittsburgh in October 1985.

Vic Myles

NYR Debut: November 14, 1942 (at Boston Bruins, lost 5–3)

Regular Season Games with NYR: 45

Playoff Games with NYR: 0

Vic Myles was a huge defenseman who played one season with the Rangers. At 6-foot-1 and 220 pounds, Myles was an imposing figure.

He joined the Rangers for the 1942–43 season and scored six goals with nine assists in 45 games. Following the season, Myles returned to his native Saskatchewan.

Dave Richardson

NYR Debut: January 4, 1964 (vs. Detroit Red Wings, won 5–2)

Regular Season Games with NYR: 41

Playoff Games with NYR: 0

Left winger Dave Richardson spent most of his Rangers' tenure in the minor leagues, but got a shot with the big club during the 1963–64 season.

Richardson played parts of two seasons in New York before he was sent to Chicago as part of a multi-player trade in June 1965.

Mike Hartman

NYR Debut: April 12, 1993 (at Philadelphia Flyers, lost 1–0)

Regular Season Games with NYR: 39

Playoff Games with NYR: 0

Mike Hartman was a player who combined toughness and speed with an ability to defend.

Hartman finished his NHL career by playing parts of three seasons with the Rangers. He was on the team that won the 1994 Stanley Cup, but didn't play enough games to qualify to have his name etched onto the coveted chalice.

John Brenneman

NYR Debut: February 6, 1965 (at Boston Bruins, lost 3–2)

Regular Season Games with NYR: 33

Playoff Games with NYR: 0

John Brenneman was a hard-working left winger who could skate as well as being a capable offensive player. In February 1965, he was traded from Chicago to the Rangers.

The left winger played the second half of the 1964–65 season and 11 games in the 1965–66 season with the Rangers. He was claimed by Toronto in the 1966 NHL Intra-League Draft.

Wladisaw "Duke" Dukowski

NYR Debut: January 4, 1934 (at Detroit Red Wings, lost 3–1)
Regular Season Games with NYR: 29
Playoff Games with NYR: 2

Defenseman "Duke" Dukowski was a back liner who possessed solid offensive skills. Dukowski had six assists during his 29-game tenure with the Rangers during the 1933–34 season. He retired after the season.

Zdeno Ciger

NYR Debut: October 5, 2001 (at Carolina Hurricanes, lost 3–1)
Regular Season Games with NYR: 29
Playoff Games with NYR: 0

Left winger Zdeno Ciger began his NHL career with the New Jersey Devils in 1990, so the Rangers knew what kind of player they were getting when they signed the native of Slovakia as a free agent in July 2001. Ciger was a proven offensive threat who had played the previous five years in Europe.

In 29 games, Ciger scored six goals with seven assists.

Cory Cross

NYR Debut: December 23, 2002 (vs. New Jersey Devils, 2–2 OT tie)
Regular Season Games with NYR: 26
Playoff Games with NYR: 0

Defenseman Cory Cross was signed by the Rangers as a free agent in December 2002. After playing 26 games in the 2002–03 season, Cross was traded to Edmonton.

The following players played less than 20 games with NYR:

Larry Mickey - right wing

NYR Debut: October 24, 1965 (vs. Montreal Canadiens, lost 4–3)
Regular Season Games with NYR: 19
Playoff Games with NYR: 0
Also wore: #9, #12, #16, and #24

Jim Pavese - defenseman

NYR Debut: October 26, 1987 (vs. Philadelphia Flyers, 2–2 OT tie)
Regular Season Games with NYR: 14
Playoff Games with NYR: 0

Jim Pavese was a local kid who made it to the Rangers. Born and bred in New York City, the 6-foot-2 defenseman joined the team for 14 games during the 1987–88 season, after seven years with the St. Louis Blues. In March 1988, Pavese was traded to Detroit.

Danny Cox - left wing

NYR Debut: February 3, 1934 (at Montreal Maroons, won 4–2)
Regular Season Games with NYR: 13
Playoff Games with NYR: 2

Albert Leduc - defenseman

NYR Debut: February 18, 1934 (vs. Chicago Black Hawks, lost 2–1)
Regular Season Games with NYR: 10
Playoff Games with NYR: 0

Ted Taylor - left wing

NYR Debut: January 6, 1965 (vs. Boston Bruins, won 5–2)
Regular Season Games with NYR: 8
Playoff Games with NYR: 0
Also wore: #6

Derek Armstrong - center

NYR Debut: January 15, 1999 (vs. Chicago Blackhawks, lost 3–1)
Regular Season Games with NYR: 7
Playoff Games with NYR: 0
Also wore: #17, #21, and #37

Cory Larose - center

NYR Debut: February 16, 2004 (vs. Ottawa Senators, lost 4–1)
Regular Season Games with NYR: 7
Playoff Games with NYR: 0

Al LeBrun - defenseman

NYR Debut: March 4, 1961 (at Toronto Maple Leafs, lost 5–4)
Regular Season Games with NYR: 6
Playoff Games with NYR: 0

Paul Andrea - right wing

NYR Debut: February 16, 1966 (vs. Chicago Black Hawks, lost 5–2)
Regular Season Games with NYR: 4
Playoff Games with NYR: 0

Phil Latreille - right wing

NYR Debut: March 12, 1961 (vs. Detroit Red Wings, won 7–3)
Regular Season Games with NYR: 4
Playoff Games with NYR: 0

Stu Kulak - right wing

NYR Debut: March 14, 1987 (at Pittsburgh Penguins, won 3–2 OT)
Regular Season Games with NYR: 3
Playoff Games with NYR: 3

Ales Pisa - defenseman

NYR Debut: April 1, 2003 (at New York Islanders, 2–2 OT tie)

Regular Season Games with NYR: 3

Playoff Games with NYR: 0

Sandy McGregor - right wing

NYR Debut: December 29, 1963 (vs. Montreal Canadiens, lost 6–2)

Regular Season Games with NYR: 2

Playoff Games with NYR: 0

Bill Carse - center

NYR Debut: December 31, 1938 (vs. Boston Bruins, won 2–1 OT)

Regular Season Games with NYR: 1

Playoff Games with NYR: 6

Center Bill Carse had an unusual career with the Rangers. He played only one regular season game, but appeared in six playoff games in 1939 and scored a goal.

Mike Siklenka - right wing

NYR Debut: October 30, 2003 (vs. Carolina Hurricanes, won 4–1)

Regular Season Games with NYR: 1

Playoff Games with NYR: 0

#19 BETTER LATE THAN NEVER

Jean Ratelle

> **NYR Debut:** March 4, 1961 (at Toronto Maple Leafs, lost 5–4)
> **Regular Season Games with NYR:** 862
> **Playoff Games with NYR:** 65
> **Also wore:** #5 and #14

Hall of Famer Jean Ratelle is one of the greatest players in Rangers' franchise history.

Ratelle was a four-time All Star who led the team in points four times and goals three times. For six straight seasons, from 1967–73, Ratelle scored 70 or more points.

Ratelle's career, however, did not get off to a fast start. After he signed in 1958, the Quebec native shuttled between the Rangers and the minors. Ratelle got his chance when he was promoted late in the 1960–61 season. The 6-foot-1 center scored a goal in each of his first two career games.

Despite showing glimpses of being a consistent NHL player, Ratelle continued to log time in the minors until the 1964–65 season, when an injury to an established player opened the door to a Hall of Fame career.

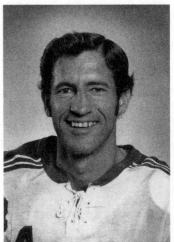

Member of famed GAG Line and first Ranger to score 100 points.

Center Phil Goyette was hurt, which created an opening for Ratelle to center a third line with his boyhood friend and future Hall of Famer, Rod Gilbert (see Chapter Seven). Ratelle scored 14 goals in the 1964–65 season, and then broke out the following year with 21 goals and 30 assists for 51 points.

After an injury-plagued season in 1966–67 that limited him to 41 games, Ratelle started his streak of six consecutive seasons with 70 or more points in 1967–68 with 32 goals and 46 assists for 78 points. The Rangers made the playoffs for the first time in five seasons, and Ratelle got his first taste of the Stanley Cup Playoffs, though went scoreless in four games.

Incredibly, Ratelle duplicated his exact stats of the previous season and, in the 1968 Stanley Cup Playoffs, had four assists in six games.

Ratelle centered one of the most famous lines in Rangers' history. The "Gag Line" was so named for scoring a "goal-a-game." Ratelle centered a line with left winger Vic Hadfield and Gilbert that accounted for the third-, fourth-, and fifth-leading scorers in the league in the 1971–72 season when the famous trio really came into vogue.

Ratelle became the first Ranger to score 100 points when he set career highs with 46 goals and 63 assists for 109 points in 1971–72. Hadfield became the first Ranger to score 50 goals in one season and had 106 points, while Gilbert added 43 goals and 54 assists for 97 points.

With the success of the Gag Line, there was much optimism that this would be the season when the Rangers would snap their Stanley Cup drought, which stood at 32 seasons. On March 1, 1972, Ratelle was trailing Boston's Phil Esposito by one point for the league lead in scoring when disaster struck. In a game against the California Golden Seals at Madison Square Garden, Ratelle suffered a broken right ankle when he was struck by a shot from teammate Dale Rolfe in the second period. Ratelle missed the remainder of the regular season and returned for the Stanley Cup Final against Boston, but was far from the same player and the Rangers lost in six games.

Ratelle rebounded from the injury to score 41 goals in the 1972–73 season. In 1974–75, he had his last big season for the Rangers as he scored 36 goals and 91 points, but was now thirty-five years old.

On November 7, 1975, Ratelle became part of one of the most significant trades in franchise history. The gentlemanly pivot man was traded to Boston with defenseman Brad Park for center Phil Esposito and defenseman Carol Vadnais. Ratelle finished his Ranger career with 336 goals, 481 assists, and a total of 817 points. He was named team MVP twice and won the "Player's Player" award four times. Ratelle was a two-time Lady Byng Trophy winner and won the Bill Masterton Trophy for sportsmanship in 1971. In 1985, he was inducted into the Hockey Hall of Fame.

On February 25, 2018, Ratelle's #19 will be retired to hang in the rafters at Madison Square Garden.

Larry Popein

NYR Debut: October 9, 1954 (at Detroit Red Wings, lost 4–0)
Regular Season Games with NYR: 402
Playoff Games with NYR: 16

Center Larry Popein was known as a "lunch pail" type of player. The Yorkton, Saskatchewan, native played three years with the Vancouver Canucks of the Western Hockey League before being called up to the Rangers for the 1954–55 season.

Popein skated on a line with Hall of Famer Andy Bathgate and Dean Prentice. Popein deferred to the two wingers, as they did most of the scoring. He often referred to himself as the "scoreless pivot."

Popein played parts of seven seasons with the Rangers and stayed in the organization for 17 years. In December 1967, Popein was

Photo from the public domain.

Spent some time as Rangers head coach after his playing days.

traded to the expansion Oakland Seals, but was dealt back to the Rangers in May 1968.

After his playing career was over, Popein was tabbed by general manager Emile Francis to become the head coach of the Rangers for the 1973–74 season. The Rangers' second round playoff exit in the previous season had prompted Francis to name a head coach and devote more time to his GM duties.

Popein was tough on the players and an incident with Rod Gilbert may have cost him his job. The Rangers star winger did not see eye-to-eye with Popein, and it led to Gilbert going above the coach's head to the general manager. It also caused the coach to eventually lose the locker room.

The team got off to a decent start but, right around the midway point, they started to stumble and Francis felt it was time for a change. After 41 games, Francis replaced Popein behind the bench.

Eddie Kullman

NYR Debut: November 12, 1947 (vs. Boston Bruins, lost 8–2)
Regular Season Games with NYR: 343
Playoff Games with NYR: 6
Also wore: #14

After scoring 56 goals for Portland of the PCHL during the 1946–47 season, right winger Eddie Kullman signed to play with the Rangers.

Kullman was known as a stout defensive forward who was matched up against some of the best players of all time, including Hall of Famers Gordie

Howe and Maurice "Rocket" Richard. During one game against Montreal, Richard was so frustrated by Kullman that he wound up and clubbed him in the head with his stick. Kullman left the ice, but later returned wearing a helmet.

The Rangers signed Kullman as a free agent in 1946, and he made his Ranger debut in the 1947–48 season. Despite being renowned for his defense, he scored 15 goals in 51 games. After the season, the Rangers dealt Kullman's rights to Providence of the AHL, but re-acquired him after one season in August 1950.

Kullman played the next four seasons with the Rangers and missed only four games. He was released after the 1953–54 season.

Brian Mullen

NYR Debut: October 8, 1987 (vs. Pittsburgh Penguins, 4–4 OT tie)

Regular Season Games with NYR: 307

Playoff Games with NYR: 19

Born and bred in New York City's "Hell's Kitchen," right winger Brian Mullen was living a dream when he joined the Rangers for the 1987–88 season. As a teenager, Mullen had already experienced hockey games at Madison Square Garden. He got the job thanks to his father, who worked in the building operations department at MSG. Mullen became the second native New Yorker, after Nick Fotiu, to play for the Rangers.

Mullen began his NHL career with the Winnipeg Jets in 1982, and played five seasons before he was dealt to the Rangers in June 1987. He scored 25 goals in his first full season with the Rangers, and added 29 and 27 goals in the following two seasons.

In 1988–89, Mullen was named an All-Star and joined his brother, Hall of Famer Joey, as the first American-born brother combination to play in the same All-Star Game.

Mullen became part of a trivia answer when he was traded to San Jose for right winger Tim Kerr in May 1991. That was the first trade ever made by the Sharks in their franchise history.

Mark Osborne

NYR Debut: October 5, 1983 (vs. New Jersey Devils, won 6–2)

Regular Season Games with NYR: 293

Playoff Games with NYR: 30

Also wore: #20

The Rangers acquired left winger Mark Osborne from Detroit in June 1983 in a controversial multi-player trade that sent popular right winger Ron Duguay to the Red Wings.

The 6-foot-2, 200-pound winger was brought in to add some size to the Ranger lineup, but ended up having a productive first year offensively with 23 goals and 28 assists for 51 points. Osborne was strong in the 1986 Stanley Cup Playoffs as a solid two-way player. He also scored the game-winning goal in the clinching fifth game of the Patrick Division Semifinal to help the Rangers beat Philadelphia.

In March 1987, the Rangers traded Osborne to Toronto, but he came back to the team as a free agent in January 1995 and played 37 games.

Jesper Fast

NYR Debut: October 3, 2013 (at Phoenix Coyotes, lost 4–1)
Regular Season Games with NYR: 216
Playoff Games with NYR: 39
Also wore: #12

Right winger Jesper Fast proved himself to be a player who "flew under the radar," but contributed in so many ways other than scoring goals.

Fast was a strong, defensive forward who was stout on the penalty killing unit. The Swedish-born Fast broke out in the 2015 Stanley Cup Playoffs, as he scored three goals with three assists in 19 games.

In the 2015–16 season, Fast played 79 games and scored 10 goals with 20 assists for 30 points.

Fast was a sixth-round choice of the Rangers in the 2010 NHL Entry Draft who worked his way through the minor-league system to become a valuable third- and fourth-line player.

Fast will have to give up #19 next season, as it is scheduled to be retired for Rangers all-time great Jean Ratelle.

Brad Richards

NYR Debut: October 7, 2011 (at Los Angeles Kings, lost 3–2 OT)
Regular Season Games with NYR: 210
Playoff Games with NYR: 55

Brad Richards never was the captain of the Rangers but, in the 2013–14 season, he was the unofficial leader of a team that made it all the way to the Final.

When Richards signed with the Rangers as an unrestricted free agent in July 2011, he brought with him an impressive resume. In 2004, he won the Conn Smythe Trophy in leading the Tampa Bay Lightning to a Stanley Cup title. Richards also won the Lady Byng Trophy in 2004.

In his first season with the Rangers, Richards scored 25 goals and then toiled through an injury-plagued 2012–13 season, appearing in just 46 games.

During the 2013–14 season, captain Ryan Callahan was traded to Tampa Bay. The Rangers never named another captain for the

Never a Ranger captain, but always a team leader.

remainder of the season, but it was Richards who essentially assumed the role.

In the opening game of the first round of the 2014 playoffs, Richards scored a goal and had two assists to lead the Rangers to a 4–1 win over the Philadelphia Flyers—but his best was yet to come.

The Rangers trailed the Pittsburgh Penguins three-games-to-one, but they rallied to force a seventh and deciding game in the Steel City. Richards scored the game-winning goal as the Rangers advanced to the Eastern Conference Final against Montreal with a 2–1 win.

Richards reportedly injured his knee during the six-game series win against the Canadiens, and it showed in the Final. He was not the same player against the eventual champion Los Angeles Kings. He didn't dent the score sheet until the fifth and final game, and was even "demoted" to the fourth line.

After the season, the Rangers bought out the remainder of his contract.

Dean Talafous

NYR Debut: October 12, 1978 (vs. Philadelphia Flyers, 3–3 tie)
Regular Season Games with NYR: 202
Playoff Games with NYR: 19

A familiar theme throughout Rangers' franchise history was the need for size on their roster. In July 1978, the Rangers signed 6-foot-4, 180-pound right winger Dean Talafous as an unrestricted free agent.

Talafous played a season with the Atlanta Flames and parts of four seasons with the Minnesota North Stars. The Duluth, Minnesota, native used his size to win the one-on-one battles along the boards.

His first season in New York was going well until he suffered a pinched nerve in his neck and missed the run to the 1979 Stanley Cup Final. Midway through the 1981–82 season, Talafous announced his retirement.

Bill Juzda

> **NYR Debut:** December 5, 1940 (at Montreal Canadiens, won 3–2)
> **Regular Season Games with NYR:** 187
> **Playoff Games with NYR:** 12
> **Also wore:** #18

Defenseman Bill Juzda was only 5-foot-9, but he prided himself on playing bigger than that.

Juzda signed with the Rangers as a free agent and made his debut in the 1940–41 season, appearing in five games. In the 1941–42 season, Juzda missed only three games but he missed the next three seasons. Juzda served as a pilot in the Royal Canadian Air Force in World War II and did not return to the Rangers until the 1945–46 season.

He went on to play three more seasons with the Rangers before being traded to Toronto in a multi-player deal in April 1948.

Scott Gomez

> **NYR Debut:** October 4, 2007 (at Florida Panthers, won 5–2)
> **Regular Season Games with NYR:** 158
> **Playoff Games with NYR:** 17

In July 2007, center Scott Gomez inked a seven-year, $51.5 million contract with the Rangers.

Gomez was a two-time Stanley Cup winner with the rival New Jersey Devils, and was "jumping ship" to the other side. And if the pressure of living up to a big contract wasn't enough, Gomez was also trying to win over the Garden fans who had booed him during the past eight years while a member of the Devils.

In his first season with the Rangers, Gomez scored 16 goals with 54 assists for 70 points and was an All-Star. During his second season of 2008–09, Gomez scored 16 goals again but dropped off with only 42 assists. The Rangers' hierarchy were beginning to feel like they weren't getting enough bang for their buck, and that Gomez was aging.

After Gomez's second season, Rangers general manager Glen Sather traded him

Traded for future captain Ryan McDonagh.

Photo by Keith Allison from Owings Mills, USA, via Wikimedia Commons.

to Montreal as a part of a multi-player deal that landed defenseman and future captain Ryan McDonagh.

Nick Kypreos

NYR Debut: November 8, 1993 (vs. Tampa Bay Lightning, won 6–3)

Regular Season Games with NYR: 128

Playoff Games with NYR: 13

Left winger Nick Kypreos was a fourth-line player who forged a seven-year NHL career thanks to his strength and determination for success.

The Rangers acquired Kypreos as part of a multi-player trade with the Hartford Whalers in November 1993. The Toronto native came to the Rangers at the right time.

During the 1993–94 season, Kypreos played in 46 games. In the playoffs, he played in only three games but was in the lineup for the Seventh Game of the Stanley Cup Final vs. Vancouver. Left winger Joe Kocur was scratched, so Kypreos got an opportunity to play in one of the most significant games in franchise history.

After the Stanley Cup win, Kypreos played two more seasons with the Rangers. He was traded to Toronto in February 1996.

Mark Heaslip

NYR Debut: October 6, 1976 (vs. Minnesota North Stars, won 6–5)
Regular Season Games with NYR: 48
Playoff Games with NYR: 3

In May 1976, the Rangers acquired Duluth, Minnesota, native Mark Heaslip from the Los Angeles Kings. Heaslip wasn't the biggest winger but he silenced his doubters by being an undrafted player who earned his way into the NHL through his hard work.

Heaslip played parts of two seasons with the Rangers before becoming a free agent after the 1977–78 season ended.

Tom Younghans

NYR Debut: November 18, 1981 (vs. Philadelphia Flyers, won 5–2)
Regular Season Games with NYR: 47
Playoff Games with NYR: 2
Also wore: #39

Right winger Tom Younghans completed his modest NHL career with the Rangers in the 1981–82 season. He scored a goal in his first game as a Ranger, but would only score two more in 47 games. After the season, Younghans retired as a pro.

Alan Kuntz

NYR Debut: November 20, 1941 (vs. Brooklyn Americans, lost 4–1)
Regular Season Games with NYR: 45
Playoff Games with NYR: 6
Also wore: #17

Left winger Alan Kuntz got off to a good start in his Rangers career. In his first season of 1941–42, he scored 10 goals with 11 assists for 21 points in 31 games, but World War II interrupted his career for the next three seasons.

Kuntz returned in the 1945–46 season, but spent most of his time with the Rangers' USHL affiliate in St. Paul, Minnesota. He was released after the 1946–47 season.

Christian Dube

NYR Debut: October 8, 1996 (at Florida Panthers, 1–1 OT tie)
Regular Season Games with NYR: 33
Playoff Games with NYR: 3
Also wore: #14

The Rangers chose center Christian Dube with their second-round pick in the 1995 NHL Entry Draft. Dube played parts of two seasons before he went to play in Europe after the 1998–99 season.

Floyd Smith

NYR Debut: January 18, 1961 (at Toronto Maple Leafs, 4–4 tie)
Regular Season Games with NYR: 29
Playoff Games with NYR: 0

During his one season with the Rangers, right winger Floyd Smith scored five goals and nine assists for 14 points in 29 games. Smith came to the Rangers in a trade with Boston in September 1957. After playing in the minors for a few seasons, Smith was claimed in the NHL Intra-League Draft by Detroit in June 1962.

Gord Labossiere

NYR Debut: October 9, 1963 (at Chicago Black Hawks, lost 3–1)
Regular Season Games with NYR: 16
Playoff Games with NYR: 0
Also wore: #6

In June 1963, the Rangers claimed center Gord Labossiere off waivers from Detroit. The 6-foot-1 center was projected to be a goal-scorer in the NHL, but he did not record a point in 16 games over parts of two seasons in New York.

Len Ronson

> **NYR Debut:** October 5, 1960 (vs. Boston Bruins, won 2–1)
> **Regular Season Games with NYR:** 13
> **Playoff Games with NYR:** 0
> **Also wore:** #17

Signed as a free agent in 1960, left winger Len Ronson lasted a day over a month with the Rangers. In his very first game in October 1960, Ronson scored the game-winning goal as the Rangers opened the season at home for the first time since 1926.

In June 1963, Ronson was traded to Montreal as a part of a multi-player deal that brought center Phil Goyette and Hall of Fame goaltender Jacques Plante to New York.

The following players played less than ten games with the Rangers:

Pete Goegan - defenseman

> **NYR Debut:** February 15, 1962 (at Detroit Red Wings, lost 4–3)
> **Regular Season Games with NYR:** 7
> **Playoff Games with NYR:** 0

Doug Adam - left wing

> **NYR Debut:** February 2, 1950 (at Montreal Canadiens, lost 4–1)
> **Regular Season Games with NYR:** 4
> **Playoff Games with NYR:** 0

Danny Belisle - right wing

> **NYR Debut:** December 21, 1960 (vs. Chicago Black Hawks, 2–2 tie)
> **Regular Season Games with NYR:** 4
> **Playoff Games with NYR:** 0

Wayne Hall - left wing

> **NYR Debut:** December 14, 1960 (at Chicago Black Hawks, lost 4–0)
> **Regular Season Games with NYR:** 4
> **Playoff Games with NYR:** 0

Norm Odie Lowe - center

NYR Debut: March 13, 1949 (vs. Montreal Canadiens, 1–1 tie)
Regular Season Games with NYR: 4
Playoff Games with NYR: 0

Bill McDonagh - left wing

NYR Debut: October 15, 1949 (at Montreal Canadiens, lost 3–1)
Regular Season Games with NYR: 4
Playoff Games with NYR: 0

Sherman White - center

NYR Debut: December 18, 1946 (at Boston Bruins, lost 3–2)
Regular Season Games with NYR: 4
Playoff Games with NYR: 0

Craig Duncanson - left wing

NYR Debut: February 13, 1993 (at New York Islanders, lost 5–2)
Regular Season Games with NYR: 3
Playoff Games with NYR: 0

Bill Kyle - defenseman

NYR Debut: January 7, 1950 (at Montreal Canadiens, won 3–1)
Regular Season Games with NYR: 3
Playoff Games with NYR: 0

Johnny Polich - right wing

NYR Debut: March 12, 1940 (at Boston Bruins, lost 2–1)
Regular Season Games with NYR: 3
Playoff Games with NYR: 0

Bucky Buchanan - center

NYR Debut: February 12, 1949 (at Boston Bruins, lost 4–2)

Regular Season Games with NYR: 2

Playoff Games with NYR: 0

Duane Rupp - defenseman

NYR Debut: March 20, 1963 (vs. Boston Bruins, 3–3 tie)

Regular Season Games with NYR: 2

Playoff Games with NYR: 0

Billy Taylor Jr. - center

NYR Debut: October 18, 1964 (vs. Toronto Maple Leafs, 3–3 tie)

Regular Season Games with NYR: 2

Playoff Games with NYR: 0

Son of Billy Taylor Sr. who played two games for the Rangers (see Chapter Fifteen).

Eddie Wares - right wing

NYR Debut: February 23, 1937 (vs. Toronto Maple Leafs, won 2–1)

Regular Season Games with NYR: 2

Playoff Games with NYR: 0

Norm Larson - right wing

NYR Debut: October 20, 1946 (at Detroit Red Wings, won 3–1)

Regular Season Games with NYR: 1

Playoff Games with NYR: 0

Ray Manson - left wing

NYR Debut: March 20, 1949 (vs. Chicago Black Hawks, won 3–1)

Regular Season Games with NYR: 1

Playoff Games with NYR: 0

Alex Ritson - left wing

NYR Debut: January 14, 1945 (vs. Montreal Canadiens, lost 6–2)

Regular Season Games with NYR: 1

Playoff Games with NYR: 0

Len Wharton - defenseman

NYR Debut: March 4, 1945 (vs. Toronto Maple Leafs, lost 6–3)

Regular Season Games with NYR: 1

Playoff Games with NYR: 0

Also wore: #12

#20: DROP THE PUCK AND GIVE ME TWENTY

Chris Kreider

NYR Debut: April 16, 2012 (Game Three Eastern Conference Quarterfinal at Ottawa, won 3–2)

Regular Season Games with NYR: 323

Playoff Games with NYR: 77

The Rangers drafted promising left winger Chris Kreider with the 19th overall pick in the 2009 NHL Entry Draft with the hope that he would develop into a physical forward who had blazing speed and an ability to put the puck in the net.

The 6-foot-3, 228-pound winger made his Ranger and NHL debut in the 2012 Stanley Cup Playoffs after he completed his final collegiate season with Boston College. Kreider signed a professional contract on April 10, and was on the ice six days later for Game Three of the Eastern Conference Quarterfinal vs. Ottawa.

Made his debut in 2012 NHL Playoffs.

Photo by Lisa Gansky from New York, NY, USA, via Wikimedia Commons.

Kreider's first professional goal proved to be a big one, as he scored the game-winning goal in Game Six of a series that the Rangers went on to win in seven games.

But the Boxford, Massachusetts, native wasn't done yet. In Game One of the Eastern Conference Semifinal against the Washington Capitals, Kreider again scored the game-winning goal. He then went on to score three goals against the New Jersey Devils in the Eastern Conference Final, but it wasn't enough to stave off elimination in six games.

The Rangers were hoping for big things from Kreider off his terrific play-off performance, but he struggled and scored two goals in 23 games during the lockout-shortened 2012–13 season. Head coach John Tortorella, who was tough on Kreider, sent him back to the AHL multiple times but he partially salvaged his season by scoring the game-winning goal in overtime of Game Four of the Eastern Conference Semifinal vs. Boston.

In 2013–14, he got off to a fast start (under new head coach Alain Vigneault, who replaced Tortorella) that was capped off by his first career hat trick in late November vs. Vancouver at Madison Square Garden. Kreider had 6 goals and 10 assists through 20 games, but scored only 11 goals the rest of the way. In the playoffs, Kreider again showed a knack for producing in the postseason as he scored five goals and eight assists in 15 games as the Rangers won the Eastern Conference and advanced to the 2014 Stanley Cup Final.

Along the way, Kreider found himself embroiled in a controversy that erupted during the Eastern Conference Final against Montreal. In the second period of Game One in Montreal, Kreider beat two Canadiens' defenders and missed a shot as he drove toward Canadiens' goaltender Carey Price. After missing the shot, Kreider, who was tripped by Montreal defenseman Alexei Emelin's stick, collided with the Montreal goaltender. Price suffered a right knee injury and was ruled out of the playoffs. Kreider was accused in some circles of making a dirty play, while others said it was accidental contact. The Rangers went on to win the series in six games, but Kreider became "public enemy number one" in Montreal.

In the 2015 Stanley Cup Playoffs, Kreider scored a playoff career-high seven goals in 15 games, but the Rangers lost Game Seven of the Eastern Conference Final to Tampa Bay.

Kreider had a career year in 2016–17 when he set a career high in goals (28), assists (25), and points (53). In the playoffs, Kreider failed to score a goal against Montreal in the Rangers' first-round victory. He did contribute in their second-round match-up against Ottawa, scoring three goals, but the Rangers would go on to lose the series.

Jan Erixon

NYR Debut: October 5, 1983 (vs. New Jersey Devils, won 6–2)
Regular Season Games with NYR: 556
Playoff Games with NYR: 58

If ever there was a player in Rangers franchise history that deserved to win the Frank Selke Trophy as the best defensive forward, it was Swedish-born Jan Erixon.

The Rangers drafted Erixon in the second round of the 1981 NHL Entry Draft. He continued to play in Sweden until he joined the team for the 1983–84 season. Erixon was not known as an offensive player, but he tallied a career high 25 assists in his first season.

Erixon was a physical player who was respected around the league because of his clean, yet aggressive playing style. He always played against the top forwards in the league, and was known as someone who constantly outworked his opponents.

In the 1987–88 season, Erixon played 70 games and finished third in the voting for the Selke Trophy.

Erixon played ten seasons with the Rangers and never played a minor league game. He retired after the 1992–93 season as a thirty-year-old, and returned to Sweden. Jan's son, Tim, who was born while his father was active, played in the NHL and was with the Rangers for one season in 2011–12.

Phil Goyette

NYR Debut: October 9, 1963 (at Chicago Black Hawks, lost 3–1)
Regular Season Games with NYR: 397
Playoff Games with NYR: 26
Also wore: #9

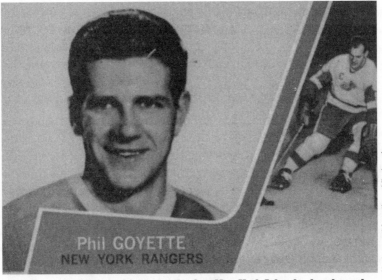

Hockey card from the public domain.

The former Ranger would go on to be first New York Islander head coach.

Center Phil Goyette was a victim of the numbers game in Montreal. The Canadiens already boasted a number of outstanding centers, including Hall of Famers Jean Beliveau, Henri Richard, and Ralph Backstrom, so Goyette was eventually traded and the Rangers were the ones who benefitted.

In June 1963, the Rangers completed a multi-player trade with the Canadiens. Hall of Fame goalie Gump Worsley and three others went to Montreal for Hall of Fame goaltender Jacques Plante, Don Marshall, and Goyette.

The Quebec native was a four-time Stanley Cup winner in Montreal in his first four seasons in the league and was a former 20-goal scorer, so the Rangers felt they were getting a quality player. Goyette's strengths were his skating and passing skills, and he had a unique ability to see the ice which made him an effective player at both ends of the ice.

Goyette scored 24 goals with 41 assists in the 1963–64 season, but the Rangers failed to make the playoffs. During his six-season tenure, Goyette had three 60-point seasons and the Rangers made the playoffs twice in those years. He was not as effective in the postseason, however. In 26 playoff games, Goyette scored only two goals.

In June 1969, the Rangers traded Goyette to the St. Louis Blues, but he was re-acquired from Buffalo in March of 1972 to join the team for the stretch drive and the playoffs. In the series-clinching Game Four of the 1972 Stanley Cup Semifinals against Chicago, Goyette had a goal and an assist. The 5-foot-11 center did not score in three games in the Final against Boston, and retired after the season.

In 1972, Goyette became the first head coach in New York Islanders' history.

Ed Slowinski

> **NYR Debut:** October 16, 1947 (at Montreal Canadiens, won 2–1)
> **Regular Season Games with NYR:** 291
> **Playoff Games with NYR:** 16
> **Also wore:** #11

World War II delayed Ed Slowinski's NHL career, but the Rangers saw a 5-foot-11, 195-pound right winger who could be a physical offensive player.

Slowinski played junior hockey with the Winnipeg Monarchs, as well as playing during his stint in the military. The Rangers signed Slowinski in 1947. The year prior, the Rangers thought they had the winger's name on a contract, but Slowinski went to the Ottawa Senators of the Quebec Hockey League. The Rangers tried to trade Slowinski to Detroit, but the deal fell through.

Slowinski began the 1947–48 season with the big club, but spent part of the season at New Haven of the AHL. In the 1948–49 season, Slowinski only played 20 games as he dealt with a knee injury. His best season was 1951–52, when he scored 21 goals with 22 assists for 43 points.

In the 1950 Stanley Cup Playoffs, Slowinski led the team and the NHL in assists, as the Rangers went all the way to the Final.

In August 1953, Slowinski was traded to Montreal but he never played for the Canadiens or any other NHL team.

Greg Polis

NYR Debut: October 9, 1974 (vs. Washington Capitals, won 6–3)

Regular Season Games with NYR: 275

Playoff Games with NYR: 3

Also wore: #4

When the Rangers acquired left winger Greg Polis from St. Louis in August 1974, they were hoping to find a replacement for Vic Hadfield, who had been traded to Pittsburgh just three months earlier.

Photo courtesy of Ken Tash.

Replaced Vic Hadfield on the Gag Line.

Polis got off to a great start as he scored two goals in his Ranger debut to key a 6–3 win, spoiling the Washington Capitals' first game in franchise history.

Polis skated on a line with Jean Ratelle and Rod Gilbert and scored 26 goals in his first season, but the Alberta native never clicked with two-thirds of the "Gag Line." Polis had blinding speed, but the other two were more disciplined and less flashy with their games. Polis was criticized for not passing the puck and playing "out of control" during a rush up the ice.

Polis began to develop knee problems during his five seasons with the Rangers, and was placed on waivers and claimed by Washington in January 1979.

Radek Dvorak

NYR Debut: January 2, 2000 (at Montreal Canadiens, 2–2 OT tie)
Regular Season Games with NYR: 256
Playoff Games with NYR: 0

As a fifteen-year-old, right winger Radek Dvorak caught the attention of hockey scouts when he scored 46 goals with 44 assists for 90 points in Czech junior hockey. His showing as a youngster prompted the Florida Panthers to select the eighteen-year-old with the 10th overall pick in the 1995 NHL Entry Draft.

Dvorak joined the Rangers as part of a three-team trade that featured the Panthers sending the 6-foot-2 winger to San Jose, before he was dealt to New York. Dvorak finished the 1999–2000 season with the Rangers, scoring 11 goals including a hat trick against Nashville in late January 2000.

Dvorak had a career year in 2000–01, setting career highs with 31 goals, 36 assists, and 67 points. The highlight of his season came on March 29, 2001, when he blitzed the New York Islanders with a career-high four goals to lead a 6–4 win at Nassau Coliseum.

Dvorak played two more seasons with the Rangers before being traded to Edmonton in March 2003.

Luc Robitaille

NYR Debut: October 7, 1995 (at Hartford Whalers, lost 2–0)
Regular Season Games with NYR: 146
Playoff Games with NYR: 26

To many Ranger fans, Luc Robitaille was another one of those Hall of Fame players who did not play like it when they came to New York.

Robitaille was acquired, along with defenseman Ulf Samuelsson (see Chapter Five), for center Petr Nedved and defenseman Sergei Zubov, who led the team in scoring during the Stanley Cup season of 1993–94.

A lot was expected of the twenty-nine-year-old. Robitaille scored 63 goals and added two more 50-goal seasons for the Los Angeles Kings after being chosen as a ninth-round pick in 1984. Robitaille finished his career with 668 goals, but only 47 of those with the Rangers.

Topps trading Cards used courtesy of The Topps Company Inc.

Hall of Famer scored 47 goals as a Ranger.

In his first season in New York, Robitaille scored a modest 23 goals in 77 games in 1995–96, and scored only one goal in 11 playoff games. In his second and final Ranger season, the Hall of Famer scored 24 goals in the regular season and four in the playoffs, including three in the first-round win against Florida. Robitaille scored only one more goal the rest of the way as the Rangers were eliminated by the Philadelphia Flyers in the 1997 Eastern Conference Final.

After the season, the Rangers traded Robitaille back to the Kings for left winger Kevin Stevens.

Jack Egers

> **NYR Debut:** December 21, 1969 (vs. Oakland Seals, won 3–1)
> **Regular Season Games with NYR:** 111
> **Playoff Games with NYR:** 16

Despite a blistering slap shot and a nose for the net, left winger Jack Egers never lived up to his potential as an NHL goal scorer.

Egers was a fourth-round pick of the Rangers in the 1966 NHL Amateur Draft. The Sudbury, Ontario, native spent most of the 1969–70 season in the minors, but appeared in six NHL games while scoring three goals.

In his second season of 1970–71, Egers hit his head on the ice during a game at Madison Square Garden against Minnesota in late November. The left winger had just fired a slap shot from the North Stars blue line when he was checked by rookie defenseman Fred Barrett. Egers was knocked unconscious and had swallowed his tongue. Ranger trainer Frank Paice saved Egers's life when he ran out on the ice and used forceps to free his tongue.

From then on, injuries continued to plague Egers's career. After scoring two goals in 17 games in the 1971–72 season, Egers was traded to the St. Louis Blues in November 1971. The Rangers re-acquired Egers from the Blues in exchange for defenseman Glen Sather and Rene Villemure in October 1973.

After scoring one goal in 28 games in the 1973–74 season, Egers was left unprotected and claimed by the expansion Washington Capitals in the 1974 Expansion Draft.

Vinny Prospal

NYR Debut: October 2, 2009 (at Pittsburgh Penguins, lost 3–2)
Regular Season Games with NYR: 104
Playoff Games with NYR: 5

Center Vinny Prospal was on the "back nine" of his NHL career when he joined the Rangers for the 2009–10 season.

The Czech Republic native scored 20 goals for the fifth time in his career in his first season with the Rangers. A knee injury limited Prospal to 29 games in the 2010–11 season, his final one with the Rangers.

Fredrik Sjostrom

NYR Debut: February 28, 2008 (at Carolina Hurricanes, won 4–2)
Regular Season Games with NYR: 97
Playoff Games with NYR: 17

Fredrik Sjostrom was a former first-round pick of the Phoenix Coyotes in the 2001 NHL Entry Draft. The Swedish-born defenseman came to the Rangers in a multi-player trade with the Coyotes in February 2008. He played a full season in 2008–09, and played out his contract to become a free agent.

Steve Rucchin

NYR Debut: October 5, 2005 (at Philadelphia Flyers, won 5–3)
Regular Season Games with NYR: 72
Playoff Games with NYR: 4

During his one season with the Rangers, center Steve Rucchin scored 13 goals with 23 assists for 36 points. He became a free agent following the 2005–06 season.

Todd Harvey

NYR Debut: October 9, 1998 (vs. Philadelphia Flyers, lost 1–0)
Regular Season Games with NYR: 68
Playoff Games with NYR: 0
Also wore: #10

Todd Harvey was a first-round pick who never lived up to the offensive hype. Harvey was the 9th overall pick of the Dallas Stars in the 1993 NHL Entry Draft. The right winger was a physical player who was projected to provide an offensive presence but, as his career progressed, Harvey became more of a third- and fourth-line player.

Harvey played parts of two seasons with the Rangers. In December 1999, he was traded to the San Jose Sharks.

Joe Bell

NYR Debut: October 31, 1942 (at Toronto Maple Leafs, lost 7–2)
Regular Season Games with NYR: 62
Playoff Games with NYR: 0
Also wore: #5

Due to World War II, many NHL players were called for military service. That opened the door for some to get a chance to play at the NHL level at a young age. One of those players was left winger Joe Bell.

At the age of nineteen, Bell made his Ranger and NHL debut in 1942. He played 15 games, but was called for military service for the next three years. He returned to play with the Rangers in the 1946–47 season and was released after the season.

Brian Skrudlund

NYR Debut: October 3, 1997 (at New York Islanders, 2–2 OT tie)
Regular Season Games with NYR: 59
Playoff Games with NYR: 0

The Rangers signed veteran center Brian Skrudlund as an unrestricted free agent in July 1997. Skrudlund was the Florida Panthers' first ever captain but, after four seasons in South Beach, he decided to head to New York.

Skrudlund played one season with the Rangers and was traded in March 1998 to the Dallas Stars.

Juha Widing

NYR Debut: October 12, 1969 (at Boston Bruins, lost 2–1)
Regular Season Games with NYR: 44
Playoff Games with NYR: 0

After signing as a free agent in 1964, Juha Widing played five seasons in the minors before getting his chance with the Rangers.

The Finnish-born center played 44 games in the 1969–70 season, scoring seven goals with seven assists. In February 1970, the Rangers traded Widing to the Los Angeles Kings.

Cam Connor

NYR Debut: March 12, 1980 (vs. Colorado Rockies, won 6–0)
Regular Season Games with NYR: 28
Playoff Games with NYR: 12

Cam Connor is best known in Ranger lore for the trade that brought him to New York. In March 1980, the Rangers acquired Connor from the Edmonton Oilers in exchange for enigmatic winger Don Murdoch.

Connor played a total of 28 games in three seasons with the Rangers. After the 1982–83 season, Connor played with the Rangers' AHL affiliate in Tulsa for a year before retiring from pro hockey.

Guy Labrie

NYR Debut: November 26, 1944 (at Boston Bruins, lost 8–4)
Regular Season Games with NYR: 27
Playoff Games with NYR: 0

In November 1944, the Rangers acquired defenseman Guy Labrie from Boston in exchange for $12,000. He scored two goals with two assists during his short tenure with the team.

Claude Larose

NYR Debut: November 21, 1979 (vs. Winnipeg Jets, lost 6–4)
Regular Season Games with NYR: 25
Playoff Games with NYR: 2

Left winger Claude Larose was selected by the Rangers in the seventh round of the 1975 NHL Amateur Draft, but he was the #1 overall pick of the Cincinnati Stingers of the World Hockey Association.

Larose played in the WHA for four seasons before he joined the Rangers. The following players played less than 20 games with NYR:

Pascal Rheaume - center

NYR Debut: October 25, 2003 (vs. Detroit Red Wings, won 3–1)
Regular Season Games with NYR: 17
Playoff Games with NYR: 0

Curt Bennett - center

NYR Debut: October 7, 1972 (at Detroit Red Wings, lost 5–3)
Regular Season Games with NYR: 16
Playoff Games with NYR: 0

Jozef Balej - right wing

NYR Debut: March 9, 2004 (at Atlanta Thrashers, won 2–0)
Regular Season Games with NYR: 13
Playoff Games with NYR: 0

Jason Krog - center

NYR Debut: January 13, 2007 (vs. Boston Bruins, won 3–1)

Regular Season Games with NYR: 9

Playoff Games with NYR: 0

Dunc McCallum - center

NYR Debut: January 1, 1966 (at Montreal Canadiens, lost 5–1)

Regular Season Games with NYR: 2

Playoff Games with NYR: 0

#21: OH' HENRY

Camille Henry

NYR Debut: October 11, 1953 (at Chicago Black Hawks, won 5–3)

Regular Season Games with NYR: 637

Playoff Games with NYR: 22

Camille Henry played bigger than his 5-foot-7 frame would indicate.

In the 1953–54 season, Henry burst upon the NHL to score 24 goals in 66 games and capture the Calder Trophy as the top rookie in the league.

The native of Quebec City, Quebec, was known as "The Eel" for his elusiveness and ability to maneuver through traffic on the ice.

Despite that early success, Henry's career took a step back when he was demoted to the minors during his second season. The Rangers were reportedly concerned about his size and ability to function in the league, so they put him on a weight training program after his rookie season. It didn't help, as he played 29 games and spent most of his second season in the minors.

Photo from the public domain.

Camille "The Eel" scored 32 goals and won Lady Byng in 1957–58 season.

After a year in Providence with the Rangers' AHL affiliate, Henry came back to New York and played 36 games. He became a regular in the lineup beginning with the 1956–57 season.

In 1957–58, Henry scored 32 goals and was named the winner of the Lady Byng Trophy. He scored a career high in goals (37) and points (60) in 1962–63.

In February 1965, Henry was traded to Chicago but was re-acquired from the Black Hawks in August 1967. He was with the Rangers when they opened the current Madison Square Garden in February 1968, something he referred to as one of the thrills of his career.

In June 1968, Henry was traded to the St. Louis Blues. In 12 seasons with the Rangers, he scored 256 goals.

Derek Stepan

NYR Debut: October 9, 2010 (at Buffalo Sabres, won 6–3)
Regular Season Games with NYR: 515
Playoff Games with NYR: 97

Center Derek Stepan was taken by the Rangers in the second round of the 2008 NHL Entry Draft, but he elected to play collegiately with the Wisconsin Badgers for two years before signing with the Rangers in July 2010 following his sophomore year.

Stepan's Ranger and NHL career could not have begun any better, as he became the first player in franchise history to score a hat trick in his first game when he keyed a 6–3 win in Buffalo. Stepan finished his first season with 21 goals and 24 assists for 45 points.

Stepan's best season was 2015–16, when he scored a career-high 22 goals, but he saved his best moments for the Stanley Cup Playoffs.

In the Rangers' run to the 2014 Stanley Cup Final, Stepan played 24 games and set personal milestones with five goals and 10 assists for 15 points. In 2015, he scored the game-winning, overtime goal to beat the Washington Capitals in Game Seven at Madison Square Garden and help the Rangers advance to the Eastern Conference Final.

Unfortunately, Stepan took some memorable hits as well during his seven years with the Rangers. In the 2014 Playoffs, former teammate and Montreal Canadiens winger Brandon Prust broke Stepan's jaw with a late hit in Game Three of the Eastern Final. Prust was suspended and Stepan underwent surgery, but he returned four days later to play in Game Five with a protective shield.

Photo by Sarah Connors via Wikimedia Commons.

First player in franchise history to score hat trick in debut.

On June 22, 2017, the Rangers traded Stepan and goaltender Antii Raanta to the Arizona Coyotes in exchange for defenseman Anthony DeAngelo and the #7 overall pick in the Draft. Stepan finished his Ranger career with 128 goals and 232 assists for 360 points.

Pete Stemkowski

NYR Debut: November 4, 1970 (at California Golden Seals, lost 3–1)

Regular Season Games with NYR: 496

Playoff Games with NYR: 55

Center Pete Stemkowski played seven seasons with the Rangers but will always be remembered in franchise lore for one of the most significant goals in team history.

The Rangers acquired the Winnipeg native from the Detroit Red Wings in July 1970. He was not really known as a goal scorer in his early years in the league, but broke out for a pair of 20-goal seasons with the Red Wings.

With the Rangers, Stemkowski had a string of three consecutive seasons, from 1972–75 where he scored twenty or more goals.

With Stemkowski, the Rangers went to the semifinals four straight years, but his shining moment came in the 1971 Playoffs.

The Rangers trailed the Chicago Black Hawks three games to two as they hosted Game Six of the series at Madison Square Garden. After three regulation periods and two overtimes, the teams remained tied at two as they headed to a third overtime.

At 1:29 of the third overtime, Stemkowski put a rebound off the shot by Ted Irvine, past Black Hawks HOF goaltender Tony Esposito to tie the series and send the Garden into a frenzy. It was Stemkowski's second overtime winner of the series (he also won Game One), which the Rangers lost in seven games.

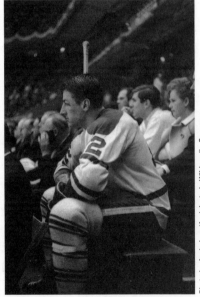

Before Matteau, his was biggest Rangers OT goal.

Photo by Arnie Lee (Arnielee) via Wikimedia Commons.

After the 1976–77 season, the thirty-three-year-old Stemkowski became a free agent and played one more season with the Los Angeles Kings.

Bill Moe

NYR Debut: November 26, 1944 (at Boston Bruins, lost 8–4)
Regular Season Games with NYR: 261
Playoff Games with NYR: 1

During his time with the Rangers, Bill Moe was one of only three American-born players in the National Hockey League.

The Massachusetts-born defenseman was the American Hockey League's Most Valuable Player in 1944, and joined the Rangers for the 1944–45 season. Moe was not the same player that he proved to be in the minors, but was a solid defenseman for five seasons. Before the start of the 1949–50 season, the Rangers traded Moe to Detroit, but he never played an NHL game with the Red Wings.

David Shaw

NYR Debut: October 8, 1987 (vs. Pittsburgh Penguins, 4–4 OT tie)
Regular Season Games with NYR: 240
Playoff Games with NYR: 10
Also wore: #27

Not only did David Shaw have size, but he had the instincts to become a steady defenseman with the Rangers. The 6-foot-2 Ontario native was acquired in a deal with the Quebec Nordiques in September 1987.

Shaw will be forever known for an infamous incident that took place in October 1988. During the third period of a game against the Penguins, the Ranger defenseman was cross-checked by Pittsburgh's Mario Lemieux. Shaw's retaliation came in the form of his stick being used to injure Lemieux in the area of his neck and chest.

Lemieux suffered a badly bruised sternum, while Shaw was hit with a 12-game suspension which was, at the time, the third longest in NHL history.

After parts of five seasons with the Rangers, Shaw was traded to the Edmonton Oilers in November 1991.

Sergei Zubov

NYR Debut: December 6, 1992 (vs. Toronto Maple Leafs, won 6–0)
Regular Season Games with NYR: 165
Playoff Games with NYR: 32

The Rangers used a fifth-round pick in the 1990 NHL Entry Draft to select a Russian-born defenseman named Sergei Zubov. It would prove to be one of the shrewdest draft picks in team history.

Zubov played parts of three seasons with the Rangers, but made an impact with the team that finally ended their Stanley Cup drought in 1994. In the 1993–94 season, Zubov was the team's leading scorer in the regular season (12 goals, 77 assists, 89 points), and is only the second defenseman in NHL history (Bobby Orr in 1969-70) to lead a first-place team in scoring.

One of Zubov's strengths was his shot from the point on the power play. By having HOF Brian Leetch as his partner with the man advantage, it created a lethal combination for the Rangers.

In the opening game of the first round of the 1994 Stanley Cup Playoffs against the New York Islanders, Zubov had a goal and two assists to key a 6–0 win. In Game Seven of the Final against Vancouver, Zubov assisted on the first two goals as the Rangers went on to capture the Stanley Cup. Were it not for Leetch, Zubov could've been named the Conn Smythe Winner. He had 5 goals and 14 assists for 19 points in 22 games.

Zubov played one more season before the Rangers used him in a multiplayer trade with Pittsburgh. The Rangers acquired Hall of Fame left winger Luc Robitaille and defenseman Ulf Samuelsson for Zubov and center Petr Nedved.

Mathieu Schneider

NYR Debut: October 16, 1998 (vs. New Jersey Devils, lost 2–1)
Regular Season Games with NYR: 155
Playoff Games with NYR: 0
Also wore: #25

New York-born Mathieu Schneider was a promising young defenseman who was taken in the third round of the 1987 NHL Entry Draft.

Schneider emerged as a solid back liner with Montreal in 1990, and was part of the 1993 Stanley Cup-winning team. He was traded to the Rangers from Toronto for defenseman Alexander Karpovtsev in October 1998.

Schneider was good on the power play as evidenced during his two-year tenure in New York. He scored 20 goals, and eight of those were with the man advantage. In June 2000, Schneider was left unprotected and was taken by Columbus in the NHL Expansion Draft.

Reg Sinclair

NYR Debut: October 11, 1950 (at Detroit Red Wings, lost 3–2)
Regular Season Games with NYR: 139
Playoff Games with NYR: 0

From his collegiate days with the McGill University Redmen of the Senior Intercollegiate Hockey League in the mid-1940s, right winger Reg Sinclair proved he could score. Sinclair holds a collegiate record (that still stands) when he scored three goals and seven assists in one game. The Rangers took notice, and signed the Quebec native in October 1950.

Sinclair made the team out of training camp and led all rookies in scoring with 18 goals and 21 assists, but lost out on the Calder Trophy as the top rookie to Detroit Red Wing and Hall of Fame goaltender Terry Sawchuk.

Sinclair played in the NHL All-Star Game during his rookie season, and duplicated the achievement in his second and final season with the Rangers. He went on to score 20 goals and 10 assists for 30 points in 1951–52. After the season, Sinclair was traded to Detroit where he played one more year in the NHL.

Jamie Lundmark

NYR Debut: October 9, 2002 (at Carolina Hurricanes, won 4–1)
Regular Season Games with NYR: 114
Playoff Games with NYR: 0
Also wore: #26 and #17

The Rangers thought they had something when they drafted center Jamie Lundmark with their second, first-round pick and 9th overall of the 1999 NHL Entry Draft. (Rangers drafted right winger Pavel Brendl with the fourth overall selection).

While playing with the Hartford Wolf Pack in 2001–02, Lundmark was tied for first among AHL rookies with 32 assists and second with 27 goals and 59 points. Unfortunately, the production never showed up at the NHL level.

After scoring eight goals in 55 games in his first season, Lundmark scored two goals in 56 games in 2003–04. He played for Hartford during the 2004–05 season and, after playing just three games in the 2005–06 season, was traded to Phoenix in October 2005.

Ray Ferraro

NYR Debut: October 7, 1995 (at Hartford Whalers, lost 2–0)
Regular Season Games with NYR: 65
Playoff Games with NYR: 0

Center Ray Ferraro was one of the few players who joined the Rangers after playing the previous season with the rival New York Islanders.

Ferraro signed as an unrestricted free agent before the 1995–96 season. He was the second-line center behind Mark Messier, and put up decent numbers. In 65 games, Ferraro scored 25 goals with 29 assists for 54 points. His best game was on January 1, 1996, when he scored the hat trick to key a 7–4 win over Montreal at Madison Square Garden.

Ferraro became expendable before his first season with the club was over and was traded to the Los Angeles Kings as part of a seven-player trade in March 1996.

Garry Peters

NYR Debut: October 24, 1965 (vs. Montreal Canadiens, lost 4–3)
Regular Season Games with NYR: 63
Playoff Games with NYR: 0

After a cup of coffee with the Montreal Canadiens, center Garry Peters was traded to the Rangers in June 1965.

Peters, who played 13 games for Montreal during the 1964–65 season, was known as a playmaker in junior hockey. In 63 games with the Rangers, Peters scored seven goals with three assists for ten points and finished fifth in the voting for the Calder Trophy as the top rookie. In June 1966, he was traded back to Montreal for center Red Berenson.

Steve McKenna

> **NYR Debut:** November 6, 2001 (vs. Minnesota North Stars, won 3–1)
> **Regular Season Games with NYR:** 54
> **Playoff Games with NYR:** 0

At 6-foot-8, left winger Steve McKenna is one of the tallest players to ever play in the NHL.

McKenna signed a one-year deal with the Rangers as an unrestricted free agent in August 2001. McKenna scored two goals during his Ranger tenure, but one came in his first game which proved to be the game winner. After the season, McKenna elected free agency.

Neil Strain

> **NYR Debut:** November 19, 1952 (vs. Detroit Red Wings, 2–2 tie)
> **Regular Season Games with NYR:** 52
> **Playoff Games with NYR:** 0

Left winger Neil Strain came to the Rangers in a September 1950 trade with the Cleveland Barons of the AHL as the return for right winger Wally Hergesheimer, who would eventually go on to become a 30-goal scorer for the Rangers.

In his one season, Strain scored 11 goals and 13 assists for 24 points in 52 games. After the season, Strain was released.

Jody Hull

> **NYR Debut:** October 6, 1990 (at Hartford Whalers, lost 5–4)
> **Regular Season Games with NYR:** 50
> **Playoff Games with NYR:** 0

Right winger Jody Hull played parts of two seasons with the Rangers after being acquired from Hartford in July 1990.

His tenure lasted a little more than a calendar year, and he scored five goals with eight assists for 13 points during that time. He spent most of the 1991–92 season with Binghamton of the AHL while playing just three games for the NHL club.

Hull was traded to Ottawa in July 1992.

Johan Lindbom

NYR Debut: November 12, 1997 (vs. New Jersey Devils, lost 3–2)
Regular Season Games with NYR: 38
Playoff Games with NYR: 0

Swedish-born right winger Johan Lindbom was selected by the Rangers in the fifth round of the 1997 NHL Entry Draft.

In the 1997–98 season, Lindbom played seven games for Hartford and 38 games with the Rangers. He scored one NHL goal and, after the season, returned to Europe to play in Sweden.

Lance Nethery

NYR Debut: November 5, 1980 (at Chicago Black Hawks, 3–3 tie)
Regular Season Games with NYR: 38
Playoff Games with NYR: 14

For such a short career with the Rangers, center Lance Nethery was relatively productive.

The Rangers drafted Nethery in the eighth round of the 1977 NHL Amateur Draft. The Toronto native completed four collegiate seasons with Cornell before joining the New Haven Nighthawks of the AHL for the 1978–79 season.

Nethery was promoted to the Rangers during the 1980–81 season and scored his first NHL goal in his first game. He finished with 11 goals with 12 assists for 33 points in 33 games. In the 1981 Stanley Cup Playoffs, Nethery scored five goals with three assists in 14 games.

Nethery played only five more games for the Rangers in the 1981–82 season before being sent back to the minors. In December 1981, he was traded to the Edmonton Oilers for veteran goaltender Eddie Mio.

Scott Fraser

NYR Debut: October 12, 1998 (vs. St. Louis Blues, lost 4–2)
Regular Season Games with NYR: 28
Playoff Games with NYR: 0

Scott Fraser was a rare ninth-round pick that stuck in the NHL, even though it was for only a short time. Montreal selected Fraser with their ninth-round pick in the 1991 NHL Entry Draft. After playing the 1995–96 season with Montreal and one season in Edmonton in 1997–98, the twenty-six-year-old right winger signed a free agent contract with the Rangers.

Fraser played 28 games and scored two goals and four assists for six points, then retired after the season.

Frank Beaton

NYR Debut: February 24, 1979 (at Toronto Maple Leafs, won 4–2)
Regular Season Games with NYR: 25
Playoff Games with NYR: 0

At 5-foot-11 and 200 pounds, Frank Beaton fit right in with the physical play of the 1970s NHL. Beaton was considered one of the league's "goons" during his short time in the league. Appropriately enough, his nickname was Frank "Seldom" Beaton.

Beaton began his career in the World Hockey Association but, after three seasons, he signed with the Rangers as a free agent in 1978. He was added for his toughness and began the 1978–79 season with the Rangers' AHL affiliate in New Haven, later being promoted for two games.

In the 1979–80 season, Beaton played 23 games and scored the only goal of his NHL career. It happened on November 4, 1979, in a game won by the Rangers, 4–2, in Vancouver. In November 1980, Beaton was traded to the Calgary Flames.

The following players played less than 20 games with NYR:

Mike Backman - right wing

NYR Debut: March 4, 1982 (at Philadelphia Flyers, 4–4 tie)
Regular Season Games with NYR: 18
Playoff Games with NYR: 10

Jayson More - defenseman

NYR Debut: November 6, 1988 (at New Jersey Devils, lost 6–5)
Regular Season Games with NYR: 15
Playoff Games with NYR: 0
Also wore: #40

Blaine Stoughton - right wing

NYR Debut: February 29, 1984 (at Toronto Maple Leafs, lost 3–1)
Regular Season Games with NYR: 14
Playoff Games with NYR: 0

John "Chick" Webster - left wing

NYR Debut: December 17, 1949 (at Boston Bruins, won 3–1)
Regular Season Games with NYR: 14
Playoff Games with NYR: 0

Russ Courtnall - center

NYR Debut: March 12, 1997 (vs. Washington Capitals, won 3–2)
Regular Season Games with NYR: 14
Playoff Games with NYR: 15

Dennis Hextall - center

NYR Debut: April 14, 1968 (vs. Chicago Black Hawks, Game Five Stanley Cup Playoff Quarterfinals, lost 2–1)
Regular Season Games with NYR: 13
Playoff Games with NYR: 2

Don Smith - center

NYR Debut: February 26, 1950 (vs. Boston Bruins, won 4–3)
Regular Season Games with NYR: 11
Playoff Games with NYR: 1

Richard Lintner - defenseman

NYR Debut: October 12, 2002 (at Pittsburgh Penguins, lost 6–0)
Regular Season Games with NYR: 10
Playoff Games with NYR: 0

Bill McCreary - left wing

NYR Debut: November 21, 1953 (at Toronto Maple Leafs, lost 1–0)

Regular Season Games with NYR: 10

Playoff Games with NYR: 0

Mark Morrison - center

NYR Debut: January 7, 1982 (vs. Vancouver Canucks, won 4–1)

Regular Season Games with NYR: 10

Playoff Games with NYR: 0

Also wore: #11

Peter Ferraro - right wing

NYR Debut: October 17, 1995 (at New York Islanders, won 5–1)

Regular Season Games with NYR: 8

Playoff Games with NYR: 2

Also wore: #17 and #14

Simo Saarinen - defenseman

NYR Debut: October 13, 1984 (at Minnesota North Stars, lost 3–1)

Regular Season Games with NYR: 8

Playoff Games with NYR: 0

Wayne Rivers - right wing

NYR Debut: December 8, 1968 (vs. Detroit Red Wings, lost 5–2)

Regular Season Games with NYR: 4

Playoff Games with NYR: 0

Bert Robertsson - defenseman

NYR Debut: November 22, 2000 (at New York Islanders, win 4–3 OT)

Regular Season Games with NYR: 2

Playoff Games with NYR: 0

Dick Bouchard - right wing

NYR Debut: January 2, 1955 (vs. Boston Bruins, 3–3 tie)
Regular Season Games with NYR: 1
Playoff Games with NYR: 0

Mike Keating - left wing

NYR Debut: January 29, 1978 (vs. Los Angeles Kings, lost 4–1)
Regular Season Games with NYR: 1
Playoff Games with NYR: 0

Bud Stefanski - center

NYR Debut: April 9, 1978 (vs. Chicago Black Hawks, won 3–2)
Regular Season Games with NYR: 1
Playoff Games with NYR: 0

#22: STATEN ISLAND'S OWN

Nick Fotiu

NYR Debut: October 6, 1976 (vs. Minnesota North Stars, won 6–5)

Regular Season Games with NYR: 455

Playoff Games with NYR: 24

While he wasn't the most talented player that ever wore the Ranger sweater, he was certainly one of the most popular.

Staten Island-born Nick Fotiu was one of the few players that had the honor of playing for their hometown team. Fotiu was a blue-collar, hard-nosed player who endeared himself to the fans with his thunderous hits and all-out hustle.

Hometown hero.

Photo courtesy of Mark Rosenman.

The 6-foot-2, 210-pound left winger played two seasons with the WHA's New England Whalers from 1974–76, before signing with the Rangers in July 1976.

Fotiu played 70 games in his first season with the Rangers and, to no one's surprise, compiled a team-leading 174 penalty minutes. He also scored four goals with eight assists for 12 points. In 1978–79, Fotiu was assessed 190 minutes in penalties.

Fotiu was beloved by fans, not only for his energetic, all-out style of play, but also because he was a native New Yorker. Fotiu returned the love with a pre-game ritual before the home games at Madison Square Garden. When the team finished its pre-game warmups, Fotiu would take a number of pucks and toss them into the stands. He would not only toss them into the lower sections but would throw many into the famous "blue seats" section that occupied the top tier of the Arena.

Donnie Marshall

NYR Debut: October 9, 1963 (at Chicago Black Hawks, lost 3–1)

Regular Season Games with NYR: 479

Playoff Games with NYR: 15

Left winger Donnie Marshall came to the Rangers from the Montreal Canadiens as part of a blockbuster, multi-player deal in June 1963. Marshall won five consecutive Stanley Cups in Montreal from 1956–60, but they wanted to go in another direction and so traded the thirty-one-year-old, along with center Phil Goyette (see Chapter Twenty) and Hall of Fame goaltender Jacques Plante, for four players including Hall of Fame goalie Gump Worsley and winger Dave Balon.

Marshall, who was known as a top penalty killer, got off to a slow start but was able to develop his offensive game during his Ranger tenure.

Marshall scored 11 goals in his first season of 1953–64, but his totals steadily increased as he scored career highs in goals (26), assists (28), and points (54) during the 1965–66 season.

Marshall went on to have one more 20-goal season in 1968–69, including seven on the power play.

After the 1969–70 season, the Rangers left Marshall unprotected and he was claimed by the Buffalo Sabres in the 1970 NHL Expansion Draft.

Brian Boyle

NYR Debut: October 2, 2009 (at Pittsburgh Penguins, lost 3–2)

Regular Season Games with NYR: 355

Playoff Games with NYR: 58

Brian Boyle added much-needed size to the Ranger lineup and proved to be a valuable performer come playoff time.

The Rangers acquired the 6-foot-6 center from the Los Angeles Kings before the 2009–10 season. In his first season with New York, Boyle scored four goals and had only two assists, but broke out in the 2010–11 season to score a career-high 21 goals with 14 assists for 35 points.

Boyle was the Rangers' best player during their 2012 first-round series against Ottawa. He became the fourth player in franchise history to score a goal in the first three games of a postseason. Unfortunately for Boyle and the Rangers, in Game Five, he was concussed after an open-ice hit from

Senators tough guy Chris Neil. Boyle returned to play in the next series, but was not the same for the remainder of the playoffs.

Even though he did not score much during the 2014 playoffs, Boyle's presence made a huge difference in helping lead the Rangers to the Stanley Cup Final against his old team, the Kings. Boyle, along with Brad Richards, helped fill the leadership void that was created when the Rangers traded captain Ryan Callahan to Tampa Bay during the season.

Boyle became an unrestricted free agent after the season and signed with Tampa Bay.

Mike Gartner

NYR Debut: March 8, 1990 (at Philadelphia Flyers, won 7–5)

Regular Season Games with NYR: 322

Playoff Games with NYR: 29

Hall of Fame right winger Mike Gartner was one of the greatest goal scorers in the history of the National Hockey League. Taking into account his relatively short tenure with the Rangers, Gartner was one of the greatest goal scorers in franchise history.

The Rangers acquired Gartner from the Minnesota North Stars in March 1990, and he was an instant hit. In his very first game as a Ranger, Gartner scored two goals in a win in Philadelphia against the hated rival Flyers. Gartner finished the 1989–90 season with the Rangers by scoring 11 goals in 12 games. He was just as good in the playoffs, with five goals and three assists in 10 games.

Photo from the public domain.

Gartner became the first player in franchise history to have three consecutive 40-goal seasons, from 1990–93. In the 1990–91 season, Gartner nearly became the second Ranger to score 50 goals in a season (Vic Hadfield in 1972), but came up short with 49. During the season, Gartner scored two or more goals in a game eleven times.

Mike was first Ranger to put together three consecutive 40-goal seasons.

By the time the 1993–94 season came around, Gartner was playing in his 16th NHL season but had yet to experience the sweet taste of winning a Stanley Cup. The Rangers were primed to end their 54-year drought and win the Cup, and Gartner was hoping this would be his opportunity.

His hopes were crushed on March 21, 1994 when, with only 13 games left in the regular season, he was traded to the Toronto Maple Leafs for two players, including former Stanley Cup winner Glenn Anderson. Rangers' head coach Mike Keenan felt the team needed a little more toughness, something he wasn't getting from Gartner (who was not that type of player).

Gartner finished with 173 goals as a Ranger, the second most that he scored for any of the five NHL teams that he played for. Gartner was inducted into the Hockey Hall of Fame in 2001.

Danny Lewicki

NYR Debut: October 9, 1954 (at Detroit Red Wings, lost 4–0)
Regular Season Games with NYR: 280
Playoff Games with NYR: 16

Danny Lewicki was a goal scorer who overcame his smallish 5-foot-8 frame to play nine NHL seasons. That stint included four productive years with the Rangers.

The Rangers purchased Lewicki's rights from Toronto in July 1954. He was a highly-regarded prospect when he joined the Leafs for the 1950–51 season. After scoring 16 goals in his first season, Lewicki struggled and spent a lot of time in the minors. The left winger had a successful first season in New York when he set a career high in goals (29) and points (53), go to along with 24 assists.

Lewicki scored 47 goals from 1954–57 but, in 16 postseason games with the Rangers, did not score a playoff goal.

Following the 1957–58 season, Lewicki was claimed by the Chicago Black Hawks in NHL Intra-League Draft.

Bobby Rousseau

NYR Debut: October 9, 1971 (at Montreal Canadiens, tie 4–4)
Regular Season Games with NYR: 236
Playoff Games with NYR: 38

After a fabulous 10-year career with the Montreal Canadiens, where he won four Stanley Cups, right winger Bobby Rousseau made his mark with the Rangers during their run to the 1972 Stanley Cup Final.

The Rangers acquired Rousseau before the 1971–72 season from Minnesota after he played one season with the North Stars. He scored 21 goals with 36 assists for 57 points during the regular season, and then turned it up a notch in the postseason.

In the six-game series win over Montreal in the quarterfinals, Rousseau had two goals and four assists. He then added five assists and two goals in the four-game semifinal sweep of Chicago, as the Rangers advanced to the Final against Boston.

With the Bruins leading the series three games to one and dreams of hoisting the Stanley Cup on home ice, the Rangers trailed Game Five, 2–1, going to the third period. Rousseau spoiled the celebration by scoring a pair of third-period goals to give the Rangers a 3–2 win and force Game Six at Madison Square Garden, where Boston would end up winning the series.

Rousseau went on to play parts of three more seasons with the Rangers and ended his career in November 1974, after playing eight games in the 1974–75 season.

Ted Hampson

NYR Debut: October 5, 1960 (vs. Boston Bruins, won 2–1)
Regular Season Games with NYR: 183
Playoff Games with NYR: 6

In 1959, the Rangers placed twenty-three-year-old center Ted Hampson on waivers, where he was claimed by the Toronto Maple Leafs. After playing the 1959–60 season with the Leafs, Hampson went back to the Rangers who claimed him in the NHL Intra-League Draft.

The 5-foot-8 center was a third-line player for parts of three seasons with the Rangers. Following the 1962–63 season, Hampson was claimed by Detroit in the Intra-League Draft.

Mike Knuble

NYR Debut: October 9, 1998 (vs. Philadelphia Flyers, lost 1–0)
Regular Season Games with NYR: 141
Playoff Games with NYR: 0

Mike Knuble was a prolific scorer in the minors who transitioned into a defensive forward in the NHL.

Knuble, who was acquired from Detroit in October 1998, was steady with the puck and excellent on the penalty kill. In his first season with the Rangers, Knuble scored 15 goals with 20 assists for 35 points.

His second season lasted 59 games before he was traded to Boston for right winger Rob Di-Maio in March 2000.

Future Hall of Famer was brought in to help on the power play.

Photo courtesy of Mark Rosenman.

Dan Boyle

> **NYR Debut:** October 9, 2014 (at St. Louis Blues, won 3–2)
> **Regular Season Games with NYR:** 139
> **Playoff Games with NYR:** 23

Defenseman Dan Boyle was a 16-year NHL veteran by the time he got to the Rangers for the 2014–15 season. The Rangers needed help on the power play, and Boyle's strength was on the point with the man advantage, but the veteran defenseman had a tough time in New York.

Boyle didn't live up to expectations, and the fans at Madison Square Garden were letting him know about it with a steady stream of boos. Boyle's contract ran out after the 2015–16 season.

Jimmy Bartlett

> **NYR Debut:** December 18, 1955 (vs. Toronto Maple Leafs, won 4–1)
> **Regular Season Games with NYR:** 126
> **Playoff Games with NYR:** 0
> **Also wore:** #14

Left winger Jimmy Bartlett was not known as a New York sports icon, but he did have a hand in two sports.

Bartlett was a 5-foot-9, 165-pound bundle of dynamite who was always willing to drop the gloves. In parts of three seasons with the Rangers, he scored 19 goals with 14 assists for 33 points.

Bartlett was indirectly linked to the New York Yankees after his hockey career, when he became owner George Steinbrenner's personal driver.

Tomas Kloucek

NYR Debut: November 12, 2000 (vs. Phoenix Coyotes, lost 2–0)
Regular Season Games with NYR: 95
Playoff Games with NYR: 0

Tomas Kloucek was a fifth-round draft pick of the Rangers in the 1998 NHL Entry Draft. The Czech-born Kloucek attracted scouts with his size, being 6-foot-3 and weighing 235 pounds.

In parts of two seasons, Kloucek spent a lot of time in the penalty box. He was traded to Nashville in December 2002.

Nick Holden

NYR Debut: October 13, 2016 (vs. New York Islanders, won 5–3)
Regular Season Games with NYR: 80
Playoff Games with NYR: 11

Nick Holden had an up and down first season with the Rangers. He was acquired from Colorado in June 2016 to add to the depth on the back line, as well as the power play.

The 6-foot-4 defenseman scored three of his 11 goals on the power play. In the 2017 Stanley Cup Playoffs, Holden scored two goals and four points but struggled defensively and was a minus-3 in 11 games.

Thomas Pock

NYR Debut: March 23, 2004 (vs. Pittsburgh Penguins, lost 5–2)
Regular Season Games with NYR: 59
Playoff Games with NYR: 4

Austrian-born defenseman Thomas Pock came to North America in 2000 and enrolled at U Mass-Amherst, where he played collegiately. In 2004, he was a Hobey Baker finalist as the top collegiate player in the country, and signed a free agent contract with the Rangers in March.

Pock played six games in his first season and scored two goals (including one in his first game) with two assists. He had a breakout season in 2006–07, as he played in 44 games though was a minus-4 on the season.

In September 2008, the Rangers placed Pock on waivers where he was claimed by the New York Islanders.

Max Bentley

NYR Debut: October 8, 1953 (at Detroit Red Wings, lost 4–1)
Regular Season Games with NYR: 57
Playoff Games with NYR: 0
Also wore: #10

Hall of Fame center Max Bentley finished off a fabulous 14-year NHL career by playing one season in New York. His ability to skate and maneuver past defenders with eye-opening moves earned him the nickname "The Dipsy Doodle Dandy." Some observers considered the former Hart Trophy winner the "Wayne Gretzky" of his time.

Bentley played on a successful line with his brother Doug (see Chapter Fourteen) when both were with Chicago, but the combination was broken up when Max was sent to Toronto in a controversial trade that backfired on the Black Hawks (Bentley went on to play on three Stanley Cup winners with the Maple Leafs).

Rangers' general manager Frank Boucher thought he could recapture some of the brothers' magic in New York, so he convinced Doug to leave his minor league coaching job to come back and play with Max.

Their first game together was January 20, 1954, when the Rangers hosted the Boston Bruins. A reported crowd of 13,463 was on hand at Madison Square Garden to see the brothers put on a show in an 8–3 victory. Max scored two goals (Doug assisted on one) and assisted on two others while Doug scored a goal with three assists for a four-point night.

Max Bentley scored 14 goals with 18 assists for 32 points during his lone season in New York.

Shane Churla

NYR Debut: March 16, 1996 (at Montreal Canadiens, lost 4–2)
Regular Season Games with NYR: 55
Playoff Games with NYR: 26

Shane Churla needed to embrace the "enforcer" role if he was to make it in the NHL . . . and he did just that, enough so to forge an 11-year NHL career that concluded with a two-year stint in New York.

The Rangers acquired Churla as part of a huge, seven-player trade with the Los Angeles Kings.

The right winger appeared in 45 games, but tore his knee during the 1996–97 season. Churla underwent surgery and was eventually forced to retire.

Anson Carter

NYR Debut: March 13, 2003 (at Ottawa Senators, lost 3–2 OT)
Regular Season Games with NYR: 54
Playoff Games with NYR: 0

Right winger Anson Carter played parts of two seasons with the Rangers. He was acquired in a trade with the Edmonton Oilers in March 2003. Carter played with eight NHL teams during his playing career.

During the 2003–04 season, Carter scored 10 goals in 43 games. In January 2004, he was traded to the Washington Capitals in exchange for left winger Jaromir Jagr.

Paul Cyr

NYR Debut: December 31, 1987 (vs. Quebec Nordiques, won 6–1)
Regular Season Games with NYR: 41
Playoff Games with NYR: 0

Left winger Paul Cyr's Ranger career never really got a chance to take off. Cyr was acquired by the Rangers from Buffalo in December 1987, but his time in New York was mostly spent dealing with knee injuries that limited him to 41 games in parts of three seasons.

Jerry Holland

NYR Debut: December 19, 1974 (at Boston Bruins, lost 11–3)
Regular Season Games with NYR: 37
Playoff Games with NYR: 0

Jerry Holland was a third-round pick of the Rangers in the 1974 NHL Amateur Draft. The left winger was a two-time, 50-goal scorer in junior hockey.

After playing parts of two seasons with the Rangers, Holland left to join the Edmonton Oilers of the World Hockey Association.

Ian Laperriere

NYR Debut: December 30, 1995 (at Edmonton Oilers, won 8–3)
Regular Season Games with NYR: 28
Playoff Games with NYR: 0

Ian Laperriere was a feisty, hard-working center who was acquired from St. Louis in December 1995 in exchange for 1994 hero, Stephane Matteau. The Montreal native played 28 games in the 1995–96 season. After the season, he was traded to the Kings as part of a seven-player deal.

Jim Krulicki

NYR Debut: November 25, 1970 (at Philadelphia Flyers, lost 3–1)
Regular Season Games with NYR: 27
Playoff Games with NYR: 0
Also wore: #25

Left winger Jim Krulicki was a victim of the numbers game when he was promoted to the Rangers in November 1970, after a number of successful years in the minors.

Krulicki had trouble getting ice time because the Rangers were stacked at left wing with Vic Hadfield, Steve Vickers, and Ted Irvine (among others). In March 1971, Krulicki was traded to the Detroit Red Wings for defenseman Dale Rolfe.

The following players played less than 25 games with NYR:

Mike Donnelly - left wing

NYR Debut: November 16, 1986 (vs. Edmonton Oilers, lost 8–6)
Regular Season Games with NYR: 22
Playoff Games with NYR: 0

Nathan Lafayette - center

NYR Debut: April 9, 1995 (at New Jersey Devils, lost 2–0)

Regular Season Games with NYR: 17

Playoff Games with NYR: 8

Jason Dawe - right wing

NYR Debut: March 21, 2000 (vs. Florida Panthers, lost 4–3)

Regular Season Games with NYR: 4

Playoff Games with NYR: 0

Also wore: #27

Benoit Dusablon - center

NYR Debut: March 4, 2004 (at Boston Bruins, lost 3–1)

Regular Season Games with NYR: 3

Playoff Games with NYR: 0

Mike McDougal - right wing

NYR Debut: December 20, 1978 (vs. Buffalo Sabres, won 6–3)

Regular Season Games with NYR: 3

Playoff Games with NYR: 0

Also wore: #9

Mike Wilson - defenseman

NYR Debut: February 12, 2003 (at Florida Panthers, won 3–1)

Regular Season Games with NYR: 1

Playoff Games with NYR: 0

#23: "BEEEUUKE"

Jeff Beukeboom

NYR Debut: November 13, 1991 (vs. Washington Capitals, lost 5–3)
Regular Season Games with NYR: 520
Playoffs Games with NYR: 70

Jeff Beukeboom was just what the doctor ordered for a Ranger team that was lacking in size and toughness.

The 6-foot-5, 230-pound native of Lindsay, Ontario, was a welcome addition to the Ranger back line in November of 1991. Beukeboom was actually the "future considerations" portion of the trade with the Edmonton Oilers that brought Mark Messier to the Rangers a month earlier.

Beukeboom was the blueprint for a "stay-at-home" defenseman, and was the perfect partner for Brian Leetch, an offensive defenseman, on the Rangers' top defensive pair.

Beukeboom was always a solid playoff performer and he showed that in his first postseason with the Rangers. In Game Two of the 1992 Patrick Division Final against Pittsburgh, Beukeboom scored the tying goal and added an empty netter in a 4–2 win.

Things clicked for Beukeboom and the Rangers in 1993–94. The big defenseman scored a career-high eight goals as the Rangers won the President's Trophy and put themselves in position for a lengthy run in the postseason. While Beukeboom did not score a goal in the playoffs, he had six assists in 22 games and was a rock defensively as the Rangers ended their 54-year drought with a Stanley Cup.

Beukeboom was a steady presence for the Rangers over eight seasons, but his career was cut short by some unfortunate circumstances. In November 1998, Beukeboom suffered a concussion when he was sucker punched from behind by Los Angeles Kings' tough guy Matt Johnson, who received a 12-game suspension for the hit. Following a second concussion in December, Beukeboom suffered a third head injury on February 12, 1999, in what became his final NHL game. Beukeboom officially announced his retirement after the season.

Lucien DeBlois

NYR Debut: October 12, 1977 (vs. Vancouver Canucks, won 6–3)

Regular Season Games with NYR: 326

Playoffs Games with NYR: 18

Also wore: #35 and #32

Right winger Lucien DeBlois was a major star in Canadian junior hockey during the 1970s. The Rangers thought enough of the twenty-year-old that they made him the 8th overall pick of the 1977 NHL Amateur Draft. DeBlois was also the 9th overall selection of the Quebec Nordiques in the 1977 WHA Draft, but his dream was to play in the NHL so he signed with the Rangers— though not without some actual recruiting.

Rangers' general manager John Ferguson knew DeBlois was coveted by WHA teams. The NHL Draft was two days before the WHA's, so Ferguson worked hard in negotiations with DeBlois's representatives. The night before the WHA Draft, Ferguson flew to Montreal and came to an oral agreement with the young right winger. So as not to violate any anti-trust laws, the WHA draft was at 9:30 a.m. A half hour after Quebec drafted him, DeBlois officially signed with the Rangers.

DeBlois has a solid first season in 1977–78 with 22 goals, but he disappointed in his second season when his total dropped down to 11. In the Rangers' 1979 run to the Stanley Cup Final, DeBlois scored two goals in nine games.

After playing six games, DeBlois was used as a chip in a major trade with the Colorado Rockies in November 1979, which brought defenseman Barry Beck (see Chapter Five) to New York.

The Rangers re-acquired DeBlois when they signed him as an unrestricted free agent to a three-year deal in September 1986. In the previous season, despite not scoring a single point in 11 games, DeBlois won a Stanley Cup as a member of the Montreal Canadiens.

Photo courtesy of Ken Tash.

Was picked seven spots ahead of Mike Bossy in '77 Draft.

Unfortunately for DeBlois, his second stint with the Rangers didn't go well. In three years, he scored 21 goals in 187 games and was a -16 during that time period. He played in two more playoff series with the Rangers, but did not score a point.

DeBlois goes down as one of the most disappointing top picks in Ranger history. Not to mention the fact that seven picks after DeBlois was selected by the Rangers, the New York Islanders selected Hall of Fame right winger Mike Bossy.

Chris Drury

> **NYR Debut:** October 4, 2007 (vs. Florida Panthers, won 5–2)
> **Regular Season Games with NYR:** 264
> **Playoffs Games with NYR:** 21

When the Rangers signed Trumbull, Connecticut-born Chris Drury, they felt they were getting a proven winner. Drury came to the Rangers with a reputation for being a clutch player, but injuries caught up to him during his tenure in New York.

Drury, who won a Stanley Cup with Colorado in 2001, joined the Rangers for the 2007–08 season. He played all 82 games and scored 25 goals (12 on the power play) with 33 assists for 58 points. In the playoffs, he scored three goals with three assists for six points in ten games.

Going into his second season with the Rangers, Drury was named the team's 25th captain. Drury scored 22 goals and played 81 games in 2008–09, but injuries caught up to him in the postseason. He scored only one goal in the playoffs and was unable to play in the Game Seven loss to Washington in the Eastern Conference Quarterfinal.

In the 2009–10 season, Drury took on more of a defensive role as he led all NHL forwards in blocked shots. He scored 14 goals

Photo by Hunting38 via Wikimedia Commons.

Was 25th captain in team history.

(Rangers were 11–2–1 when Drury scored a goal that season) with 18 assists for 32 points, but the Rangers failed to make the playoffs.

Drury played 24 games in his final season of 2010–11, and five games in the playoffs before retiring in August 2011. Drury is now the general manager of the Rangers' AHL Affiliate, the Hartford Wolf Pack.

Vladimir Malakhov

NYR Debut: October 7, 2000 (at Atlanta Thrashers, won 2–1)
Regular Season Games with NYR: 211
Playoff Games with NYR: 0

Vladimir Malakhov's Ranger career couldn't have started any worse. In the season opener of 2000–01, Malakhov, who signed as a free agent during the offseason and had an assist in the game, tore the ACL in his left knee. He would play two more games a month later before needing season-ending surgery.

The big defenseman (6-foot-4, 230 pounds) was once projected as a future Norris Trophy winner, but he was unable to live up to his potential. The Russian-born back liner had a solid first season with the New York Islanders and finished fifth in the voting for the Calder Trophy as the top rookie. His play tailed off after that, and he developed a reputation for "coasting" and showing little desire to succeed.

After a trade to Montreal, Malakhov matured as a player and eventually won a Stanley Cup with the New Jersey Devils in 2000.

The Rangers signed Malakhov after the season but, because of the knee injury, his impact would not be felt until his second season. In 2001–02, Malakhov scored six goals with 22 assists for 28 points.

After parts of four seasons with the Rangers, Malakhov was traded to the Philadelphia Flyers in March 2004.

Ed Hospodar

NYR Debut: November 21, 1979 (vs. Winnipeg Jets, lost 6–4)
Regular Season Games with NYR: 122
Playoff Games with NYR: 19

Ed Hospodar spent so much time in the penalty box, he should've been paying rent.

The American-born defense-man, who grew up in Ontario, was selected by the Rangers with a second-round pick in the 1979 NHL Entry Draft. Hospodar was brought to the Rangers to provide some toughness and a physical presence. He played 20 games in his first season of 1979–80, accumulating 76 penalty minutes.

Hospodar, who was nick-named "Boxcar" for his aggressive checks while playing junior hockey, spent 214 minutes in the penalty box during the 1980–81 season. In the 1981 Stanley Cup Playoffs, he set an NHL record for the most penalties and penalty minutes in one period. In Game Two of the first round against the

Photo courtesy of Mark Rosenman.

"Boxcar" provided a physical presence for Rangers.

Los Angeles Kings, Hospodar accumulated a record six penalties and 39 penalty minutes in the first period.

During the 1981–82 season, Hospodar saw ice time where there was a need to have more of a physical presence in the lineup.

One of Hospodar's targets was New York Islanders' tough guy, Clark Gillies. The 6-foot-2 Hospodar would try and get under the skin of Gillies to take him out of his game. The Islander winger had warned Hospodar to "cut the shit," and on December 30, 1981, Gillies backed up his warning.

The two players stood toe-to-toe and were ready to fight during the third period of a game at Madison Square Garden, but it ended up being a one-sided affair. In a couple of moments, Gillies landed several right hands and then a vicious uppercut that landed squarely on Hospodar's face, sending him to the ice where he laid there for a few minutes. Hospodar was bloodied and suffered a broken jaw from the punch.

In October 1982, the Rangers traded Hospodar to the Hartford Whalers.

John Bednarski

NYR Debut: November 24, 1974 (vs. Pittsburgh Penguins, won 7–5)

Regular Season Games with NYR: 99

Playoff Games with NYR: 1

Defenseman John Bednarski spent seven years in the Rangers' organization, but played most of his games with their minor-league affiliates.

Bednarski, who played 316 minor league games and 99 in the NHL, showed some offensive prowess in the minors but was a defensive liability. After playing with the Rangers' AHL affiliate at New Haven in the 1978–79 season, Bednarski signed a free agent contract with the Edmonton Oilers.

Raimo Helminen

NYR Debut: October 12, 1985 (at Hartford Whalers, lost 8–2)

Regular Season Games with NYR: 87

Playoff Games with NYR: 2

Center Raimo Helminen was a second-round pick of the Rangers in the 1984 NHL Entry Draft. Scouts had Helminen rated as the best European forward heading into the draft, and he played like it in his first season of 1985–86 when he scored 10 goals with 30 assists for 40 points.

After parts of two seasons, Helminen was traded to the Minnesota North Stars in March 1987.

Chris Kontos

NYR Debut: December 26, 1982 (at Pittsburgh Penguins, lost 4–3)

Regular Season Games with NYR: 78

Playoff Games with NYR: 0

Chris Kontos was one of the Rangers' first-round picks that just didn't worked out. Kontos was chosen by the club with the 15th overall pick of the 1982 NHL Entry Draft, after he scored 42 goals and 104 points while playing junior hockey in the 1979–80 season.

Kontos scored eight goals in 44 games in his first season of 1982–83. Unfortunately he never really developed and spent much of the 1983–84 season in the minors. The next season was Kontos' last as a Ranger, as he was traded to the Pittsburgh Penguins in January 1987 in exchange for a reunion with Ron Duguay.

Karel Rachunek

> **NYR Debut:** March 12, 2004 (at Tampa Bay Lightning, lost 5–2)
> **Regular Season Games with NYR:** 78
> **Playoff Games with NYR:** 6

Czech-born Karel Rachunek came to the Rangers in a trade with the Ottawa Senators in March 2004.

Rachunek was a ninth-round pick of the Senators in the 1997 NHL Entry Draft who burst on the scene during the 2000–01 season with three goals and 33 assists for 36 points.

The Rangers acquired the twenty-seven-year-old with the idea of strengthening their power play. In 78 games, Rachunek scored five power play goals, and played out his contract after the 2006–07 season.

Rachunek returned to Russia and was named captain of his KHL team for the 2011–12 season. In September 2011, Rachunek and his teammates tragically perished in a plane crash, as they were taking off for their season opener in Minsk.

Ray Sheppard

> **NYR Debut:** October 4, 1990 (at Chicago Blackhawks, lost 4–3)
> **Regular Season Games with NYR:** 59
> **Playoff Games with NYR:** 0

Right winger Ray Sheppard was never the fastest skater on the ice, but he overcame his lack of speed with a nose for the net.

After three seasons with Buffalo, where he scored 64 goals, Sheppard was traded to the Rangers in July 1990. The Rangers were looking to enhance their offense, and Sheppard paid immediate dividends with a goal in his first game.

In his last year with the Sabres, Sheppard had suffered a serious ankle injury that carried over into the 1990–91 season with the Rangers, limiting him to 59 games. Despite dealing with the injury, Shepard scored 24 goals with 23 assists for 47 points. After the season, Shepard became an unrestricted free agent.

The following players played less than ten games with NYR:

Jayson Megna - center

NYR Debut: January 5, 2016 (vs. Dallas Stars, won 6–2)

Regular Season Games with NYR: 6

Playoff Games with NYR: 0

Bill Heindl - left wing

NYR Debut: November 19, 1972 (vs. Pittsburgh Penguins, lost 5–3)

Regular Season Games with NYR: 4

Playoff Games with NYR: 0

Norm Gratton - left wing

NYR Debut: February 27, 1972 (vs. St. Louis Blues, won 2–0)

Regular Season Games with NYR: 3

Playoff Games with NYR: 0

#24: RYAN'S NUMBER

Ryan Callahan

NYR Debut: December 1, 2006 (at Buffalo Sabres, lost 4–3 SO)

Regular Season Games with NYR: 450

Playoff Games with NYR: 59

Also wore: #43

Ryan Callahan was the type of Ranger that would do whatever it took to help his team win—and that is no exaggeration. Callahan was a hard-working forward who exemplified "blue collar," and endeared himself to the Ranger fans.

Was 26th captain in team history.

Photo by Sarah Connors via Wikimedia Commons.

Callahan was the Rangers' fourth-round pick in the 2004 NHL Entry Draft. The Rochester, New York, native put up some impressive numbers during a four-year stint with Guelph Storm of the Ontario Hockey League from 2002–06. In the 2005–06 season with the Storm, Callahan scored 52 goals with 32 assists for 84 points.

The twenty-one-year-old right winger was promoted to make his debut in December 2006, but spent much of the season with Hartford of the AHL. Callahan was called for a third time in March 2007, and made an impact in the 2007 Stanley Cup Playoffs. In Game Three of the Eastern Conference Quarterfinal against the Atlanta Thrashers, Callahan scored his first two NHL playoff goals in a 7–0 rout.

Throughout his Ranger tenure, Callahan, due in part to his all-out play, suffered numerous injuries. In the 2007–08 season, a knee injury cost him a month and his production waned. Callahan was sent to Hartford for 11 games before returning to score two goals and two assists in the 2008 playoffs.

In the 2008–09 season, Callahan broke out with 22 goals and 18 assists for 40 points in 81 games.

Seeing that Callahan's leadership skills had emerged, the Rangers named him an alternate captain for the 2009–10 season. He played in 77 games, but his production dipped to 19 goals and 18 assists.

In December 2010, Callahan suffered a broken hand blocking a shot and missed 19 games, but returned to have a career game in March 2011 when he scored four goals against the Philadelphia Flyers in a 7–0 win. Late in the season, Callahan was hit by the injury bug once again when he sustained a broken leg after blocking a shot from Boston Bruins 6-foot-8 defenseman Zdeno Chara, forcing him to miss the rest of the season.

Callahan's willingness to put it all on the line for the good of the team led to some memorable shifts. There were times that he would lose his stick, yet would still go down to block a shot or try and get the puck out of his own zone by using his skate or hands. All these traits convinced the team that the time was right. In September 2011, Callahan was named the 26th captain in team history.

Callahan had a talent for embracing the big moment. In February 2012, he scored his 100th career goal in overtime to beat the Buffalo Sabres at Madison Square Garden. In the penultimate game of the 2012–13 season, he scored an overtime goal to beat the Carolina Hurricanes and clinch a playoff spot for the Rangers.

Callahan's Ranger career came to an end due to financial reasons. After the Rangers and the right winger failed to reach an agreement on a new contract, he was traded to the Tampa Bay Lightning for their captain, right winger Martin St. Louis.

Niklas Sundstrom

> **NYR Debut:** October 7, 1995 (at Hartford Whalers, lost 2–0)
>
> **Regular Season Games with NYR:** 315
>
> **Playoff Games with NYR:** 20

The Rangers made right winger Niklas Sundstrom their first-round pick and the 8th overall selection in the 1993 NHL Entry Draft. Sundstrom played for Sweden in the World Junior Championships and was named the top forward three times.

Sundstrom earned a spot on the roster after winning the Lars-Erik Sjoberg Award as the best rookie in training camp in 1995, and played in all 82 games in his first season. Sundstrom scored only nine goals in 1995–96 as he played a mostly defensive role but he broke out for four goals in 11 playoff games.

The Swedish-born winger's game really took off in the 1996–97 season, when he skated on a line with Hall of Famer Wayne Gretzky. Being linked with "The Great One" enabled Sundstrom to score a career-high 24 goals.

Sundstrom played two more seasons with the Rangers before he was part of an NHL draft day trade with Tampa Bay that yielded the team a first-round pick. The team used that pick to select Czech-born right winger Pavel Brendl.

Sylvain Lefevbre

> **NYR Debut:** October 1, 1999 (at Edmonton Oilers, 1–1 OT tie)
>
> **Regular Season Games with NYR:** 229
>
> **Playoff Games with NYR:** 0

Free agent defenseman Sylvain Lefevbre signed a four-year deal with the Rangers in July 1999. Lefevbre was a veteran who had won a Stanley Cup with the Colorado Avalanche in 1996.

Lefevbre's first two seasons were solid, but he dropped off in his last two as injuries began to take their toll.

At the end of the 2000–01 season, Lefevbre missed the final seven games due to a shoulder injury that lingered into the following season. He missed the first 16 games of the 2001–02 season, and played in only 41 games.

In the 2002–03 season, the Quebec native suffered a serious injury to his index finger after blocking a shot. The finger was so badly injured that a doctor compared it to him hitting his hand with a hammer until the bone was shattered into pieces. After he returned, Lefevbre sprained his MCL, thus ending his season and his Ranger career.

Jay Wells

NYR Debut: March 11, 1992 (vs. Chicago Blackhawks, won 7–1)
Regular Season Games with NYR: 186
Playoff Games with NYR: 46

Toward the end of the 1991–92 season, the Rangers were on pace to win the President's Trophy as the best team in the regular season while focusing on a chance to win the Stanley Cup for the first time in 52 years.

The team needed to enhance their defense corps, so they acquired long-time veteran defenseman Jay Wells from the Buffalo Sabres in exchange for defenseman Randy Moeller (see below). The 6-foot-1, 210-pound native of Paris, Ontario, had played in 13 NHL seasons by the time he joined the Rangers.

Despite not getting on the score sheet in the 1994 Stanley Cup Playoffs, Wells was a major contributor on the back line to help the Rangers end their 54-year drought and earn his first Stanley Cup Championship.

After the Rangers clinched the Cup with their win in Game Seven, there stands an indelible image of Wells hoisting the revered chalice above his head with a huge toothless smile.

Following the shortened 1994–95 season, the Rangers traded Wells to the St. Louis Blues to get back defenseman Doug Lidster.

Randy Moller

NYR Debut: October 8, 1989 (at Chicago Blackhawks, won 5–3)
Regular Season Games with NYR: 164
Playoff Games with NYR: 16

Randy Moller was a 6-foot-2 defenseman who used his size to clear the zone. The Rangers acquired Moller from the Quebec Nordiques in October 1989, in exchange for defenseman Michel Petit.

Moller's aggressive play was curtailed as the result of a shoulder injury that he incurred in his first season with the Rangers. After three seasons, Moller was traded to Buffalo for defenseman Jay Wells.

Kent-Erik Andersson

NYR Debut: October 8, 1982 (at New Jersey Devils, lost 3–2)
Regular Season Games with NYR: 134
Playoff Games with NYR: 14

Right winger Kent-Erik Andersson was a star in Sweden, but that star didn't shine as bright in the NHL.

Andersson joined the Rangers via a trade with the Hartford Whalers for defenseman Ed Hospodar in October 1982. He scored 13 goals in his two seasons with the Rangers, but failed to score a goal in 14 playoff games with the club.

Following the 1983–84 season, Andersson returned to play in Sweden.

Oscar Lindberg

NYR Debut: February 24, 2015 (vs. Calgary Flames, won 1–0)
Regular Season Games with NYR: 134
Playoff Games with NYR: 14
Also wore: #48

Swedish-born center Oscar Lindberg was acquired by the Rangers from the Phoenix Coyotes in May 2011. Lindberg continued to play in Sweden until the 2013–14 season, when he joined the Rangers' AHL affiliate in Hartford.

Lindberg was a talented skater and playmaker who was showing signs of becoming a solid NHL player with his performance in the 2017 Stanley Cup Playoffs. In the second-round loss to the Ottawa Senators, Lindberg scored a goal in Game Three and two more in Game Four as the Rangers rallied from a 2–0 series deficit to tie the best-of-seven series at two games apiece.

Lindberg was claimed by the expansion Las Vegas Golden Knights in the 2017 NHL Expansion Draft.

His 2017 playoff performance made him attractive target of the Las Vegas Golden Knights.

Michel Petit

NYR Debut: November 7, 1987 (at Los Angeles Kings, lost 5–4)
Regular Season Games with NYR: 133
Playoff Games with NYR: 4

You could say defenseman Michel Petit knew his way around the NHL. Petit played for ten teams (tying an NHL record) during his 16-year career, including a two-season stint with the Rangers, his second team, from 1987–89.

Petit was the 11th overall pick of the Vancouver Canucks in the 1982 NHL Entry Draft. He came to the Rangers via a trade with the Canucks in November 1987.

While playing in Vancouver, Petit received a reputation as being a player who was soft and often lost focus. With the help of Rangers head coach Michel Bergeron, Petit turned into a more productive player, scoring 17 goals with 49 assists for 66 points in 133 games. He also spent a lot more minutes in the penalty box.

In October 1989, Petit was reunited with Bergeron, who was now the general manager of the Quebec Nordiques, when the Rangers traded him to Quebec for defenseman Randy Moller.

Ab Demarco Jr.

NYR Debut: February 28, 1970 (at Detroit Red Wings, 3–3 tie)
Regular Season Games with NYR: 104
Playoff Games with NYR: 9

Being the son of a former Ranger was not easy for Ad Demarco Jr. when he signed a free agent contract in 1967.

Demarco only got small doses of NHL life, as he played in just a total of five games in parts of his first two seasons. The Cleveland, Ohio-born defenseman, who grew up in Ontario, played parts of four seasons with the Rangers.

Late in the 1972–73 season, Demarco was traded to St. Louis.

Dan Newman

NYR Debut: October 6, 1976 (vs. Minnesota North Stars, won 6–5)
Regular Season Games with NYR: 100
Playoff Games with NYR: 3

At 6-foot-1, left winger Dan Newman was an enforcer during his two seasons with the Rangers, finding himself in a number of fights. But, interestingly, he scored a goal in his Ranger debut.

Photo courtesy of Ken Tash.

Scored goal in Ranger debut, but remembered more for his role as enforcer.

The Windsor, Ontario, native scored 14 goals with 21 assists for 35 points in 100 games. In October 1978, Newman was claimed off waivers by Montreal.

Pierre Plante

NYR Debut: October 15, 1978 (vs. Colorado Rockies, won 4–1)

Regular Season Games with NYR: 70

Playoff Games with NYR: 18

Pierre Plante was another first-round pick who just didn't pan out. The Philadelphia Flyers made Plante the 9th overall pick of the 1971 NHL Amateur Draft.

After two years with the Flyers, Plante played with the St. Louis Blues and Chicago Black Hawks before joining the Rangers as a waiver claim in October 1978.

The right winger appeared in only one season in New York, playing a contributing role in helping the Rangers reach the 1979 Stanley Cup Final. After the season, Plante was claimed by the Quebec Nordiques in the 1979 NHL Expansion Draft.

Warren Miller

NYR Debut: October 18, 1979 (vs. Vancouver Canucks, won 6–3)

Regular Season Games with NYR: 55

Playoff Games with NYR: 6

Right winger Warren Miller was a "lunch pail" type player who was taken by the Rangers in the 21st round of the 1974 NHL Amateur Draft.

Miller played four seasons in the World Hockey Association before joining the Rangers for the 1979–80 season.

Chris Kotsopoulos

NYR Debut: October 30, 1980 (at Philadelphia Flyers, 3–3 tie)
Regular Season Games with NYR: 54
Playoff Games with NYR: 14

Ranger fans loved Chris Kotsopoulos because he was a rugged, hard-working defenseman who wouldn't hesitate to drop the gloves. The Ontario native signed as an undrafted free agent in October 1979.

After a season with the Rangers' AHL affiliate in New Haven, Kotsopoulos joined the Rangers for the 1980–81 season.

According to hockeyfights. com, Kotsopoulos had seven

Kotsy took on all comers in his one season as a Ranger.

Photo courtesy of Mark Rosenman.

fights during his one season with the Rangers. Some of the big names that he went toe-to-toe with included tough guys like Bob Kelly of the Washington Capitals and noted enforcer Tiger Williams of the Toronto Maple Leafs. Kotsopoulos also took on Hall of Famer Mark Messier.

Red Berenson

NYR Debut: October 19, 1966 (vs. Chicago Black Hawks, lost 6–3)
Regular Season Games with NYR: 49
Playoff Games with NYR: 4

Injuries robbed Red Berenson of a chance to shine in the Ranger sweater. Berenson played five seasons in the Montreal Canadiens system but they gave up on him and he was dealt to the Rangers before the 1966–67 season.

Berenson scored two goals in parts of two seasons with the Rangers. He was traded to the St. Louis Blues in November 1967, and went on to have a successful career with the expansion team.

In November 1968, Berenson became the first player in the "modern era" to score six goals in a game when he accomplished the feat against the Philadelphia Flyers.

Sandis Ozolinsh

> **NYR Debut:** March 11, 2006 (at Montreal Canadiens, lost 1–0)
> **Regular Season Games with NYR:** 40
> **Playoff Games with NYR:** 3

Sandis Ozolinsh was the protocol offensive defenseman. He was big (6-foot-3, 215 pounds) and he could skate and set up plays with his stick handling ability.

Unfortunately, Ozolinsh was deficient in his own zone, which caused him to be moved around as he played with five teams previous before joining the Rangers in March 2006 in a trade with the Mighty Ducks of Anaheim.

Ozolinsh finished the 2005–06 season with the Rangers and scored three goals with 11 assists for 14 points in 19 games.

Maxim Kondratiev

> **NYR Debut:** October 8, 2005 (at New Jersey Devils, lost 3–2 OT)
> **Regular Season Games with NYR:** 29
> **Playoff Games with NYR:** 0

Defenseman Maxim Kondratiev is best known for coming over from Toronto in the infamous trade that sent Hall of Fame defenseman Brian Leetch to the Maple Leafs.

Kondratiev played 29 of his 40 career NHL games with the Rangers. He scored a goal and two assists with the Rangers for his only NHL points.

In January 2006, the Rangers traded Kondratiev to the Anaheim Ducks.

Jim Wiemer

> **NYR Debut:** December 7, 1984 (vs. Pittsburgh Penguins, lost 4–3 OT)
> **Regular Season Games with NYR:** 29
> **Playoff Games with NYR:** 9
> **Also wore:** #6

When the Buffalo Sabres drafted 6-foot-4 Jim Wiemer in the 1980 NHL Entry Draft, it was initially as a left winger, but he was eventually converted into a defenseman.

Wiemer played two seasons in Buffalo before being traded to the Rangers in December 1984 for defenseman Dave Maloney.

After playing parts of two seasons with the Rangers, Wiemer was traded to the Edmonton Oilers in October 1986.

The following players played less than 15 games with NYR:

Chris McAllister - defenseman

> **NYR Debut:** March 9, 2004 (at Atlanta Thrashers, 2–0 won)
>
> **Regular Season Games with NYR:** 12
>
> **Playoff Games with NYR:** 0

Jim Johnson - center

> **NYR Debut:** March 23, 1965 (at Chicago Black Hawks, won 3–2)
>
> **Regular Season Games with NYR:** 8
>
> **Playoff Games with NYR:** 0
>
> **Also wore:** #6 and #18

Joe Zanussi - defenseman

> **NYR Debut:** November 24, 1974 (vs. Pittsburgh Penguins, won 7–5)
>
> **Regular Season Games with NYR:** 8
>
> **Playoff Games with NYR:** 0

Jamie Pushor - defenseman

> **NYR Debut:** January 24, 2004 (at Ottawa Senators, lost 9–1)
>
> **Regular Season Games with NYR:** 7
>
> **Playoff Games with NYR:** 0

Ryan Malone - left wing

> **NYR Debut:** October 14, 2014 (vs. New York Islanders, lost 6–3)
>
> **Regular Season Games with NYR:** 6
>
> **Playoff Games with NYR:** 0

Ron Attwell - right wing

NYR Debut: December 2, 1967 (at Pittsburgh Penguins, won 4–1)

Regular Season Games with NYR: 4

Playoff Games with NYR: 0

Jim Leavins - defenseman

NYR Debut: October 22, 1986 (vs. Los Angeles Kings, won 5–4 OT)

Regular Season Games with NYR: 4

Playoff Games with NYR: 0

Trevor Fahey - left wing

NYR Debut: January 10, 1965 (vs. Toronto Maple Leafs, lost 6–0)

Regular Season Games with NYR: 1

Playoff Games with NYR: 0

#25: JOHNNY-O

John Ogrodnick

NYR Debut: October 8, 1987 (vs. Pittsburgh Penguins, 4–4 OT tie)

Regular Season Games with NYR: 338

Playoff Games with NYR: 20

Left winger John Ogrodnick was an offensively gifted player who was brought in by the Rangers to score goals.

Ogrodnick began his career with the Detroit Red Wings in 1979. In the middle of his eighth season in Motown, the Edmonton native was traded to Quebec, where he completed the 1986–87 season. Just before the next season began, Ogrodnick (and defenseman David Shaw) was traded to the Rangers for left winger Jeff Jackson and defenseman Terry Carkner.

The Rangers had a new head coach in Michel Bergeron, who just so happened to be Ogrodnick's coach in Quebec the year before. Ogrodnick scored 22 goals in 60 games during his first season with the

Johnny O had a 43-goal season for the Rangers.

Rangers, but had his ups and downs with the team beginning with his second season in New York.

Ogrodnick got off to a slow start. He had no goals in his first five games and looked lackadaisical on the ice. The Rangers were so frustrated with Ogrodnick's overall play that he was demoted to Denver of the IHL in November for a short, three-game stint. The Rangers tried to trade him but, after no takers and a couple of injuries, he came back to New York later that month.

Ogrodnick finished the 1988–89 season with 13 goals. In 1989–90, he clicked on a line with center Kelly Kisio and right winger Brian Mullen. Ogrodnick finally was able to break out of his slump, and led the team with 43 goals and 31 assists for a team-leading 74 points. He continued his success in the 1990 Stanley Cup Playoffs when he scored six goals and three assists for nine points in ten games.

In the next season, Ogrodnick scored 31 goals, but dropped off to 17 in 55 games during the 1991–92 season, his final one with the Rangers. After the season, he became an unrestricted free agent.

Alexander Karpovtsev

NYR Debut: October 9, 1993 (at Pittsburgh Penguins, lost 3–2)
Regular Season Games with NYR: 280
Playoff Games with NYR: 44

Defenseman Alexander Karpovtsev became one of the first three Russian players (along with Alexei Kovalev and Sergei Nemchinov) to have his name engraved on the Stanley Cup.

Karpovtsev was a steady defenseman who was part of the Stanley Cup-winning team, but did not dress for the seventh and deciding game of the Final.

The 6-foot-3 blue liner was acquired from the Quebec Nordiques in September 1993, after being chosen in the eighth round of the 1990 NHL Entry Draft. Karpovtsev ran into a numbers problem with the Rangers, who were loaded with talented defensemen.

In 1996–97, Karpovtsev scored a career-best nine goals with 29 assists for 38 points, but injuries held him back and the Rangers became frustrated with his lack of physical play. In October 1998, Karpovtsev was traded to the Toronto Maple Leafs for defenseman Mathieu Schneider.

Petr Prucha

NYR Debut: October 8, 2005 (at New Jersey Devils, lost 3–2 OT)
Regular Season Games with NYR: 237
Playoff Games with NYR: 17

As an eighth-round pick in the 2002 NHL Entry Draft, Petr Prucha did alright for himself.

The Czech-born right winger broke out in his first season of 2005–06. While playing on a line with Jaromir Jagr, Prucha scored 30 goals and set a Ranger rookie record with 16 power play goals. In December 2005, Prucha had a streak of six consecutive games with a goal and a total of 12 goals in an eleven-game stretch.

Prucha scored 22 goals during the 2006–07 season, but only seven in 62 games in 2007–08 as the Rangers lost faith in the young player.

Prucha played in only 28 games during the 2008–09 season, and was mostly a healthy scratch. In March 1989, he was traded to the Phoenix Coyotes.

Peter Sundstrom

NYR Debut: October 5, 1983 (vs. New Jersey Devils, won 6–2)
Regular Season Games with NYR: 206
Playoff Games with NYR: 9

In 1981, Peter Sundstrom and his twin brother, Patrik, helped Sweden capture the gold medal in the World Junior Championships. The Rangers selected the Swedish star with their third-round pick in the 1981 NHL Entry Draft.

Sundstrom got on the score sheet in his very first game, as he scored his first NHL goal in a win over the New Jersey Devils. The 6-foot, 180-pound left winger finished his first season of 1983–84 with 22 goals and 22 assists.

He fell off to 18 goals in the 1984–85 season, and was a defensive bust as he posted a minus-26 on the season. In 1985–86, Sundstrom spent some time with the New Haven Nighthawks of the AHL. In 53 games with the Rangers, he put up some modest numbers with eight goals in 53 games.

After his third season with the Rangers, Sundstrom returned to Sweden to play the 1986–87 season. The Rangers traded his rights to the Washington Capitals for a draft pick in August 1987.

Orland Kurtenbach

NYR Debut: March 1, 1961 (vs. Boston Bruins, won 3–1)
Regular Season Games with NYR: 198
Playoff Games with NYR: 15
Also wore: #11

Center Orland Kurtenbach was a player that the Rangers let get away, but were able to get back.

The Saskatchewan native signed with the Rangers as a free agent in 1953 as a seventeen-year-old. After working his way through the minors, he was promoted to make his NHL debut in March 1961—and it was an impressive one. Kurtenbach went on to tally six assists in the last ten games of the season.

After the season, the Rangers lost Kurtenbach in the NHL Intra-League Draft, as he was claimed by the Boston Bruins. After three seasons in Boston and one in Toronto, the Rangers re-acquired Kurtenbach by claiming him in the 1966 Intra-League Draft.

From there, Kurtenbach's career began to take off. From 1966–68, the talented center scored 26 goals with 45 assists for 71 points, but an incident at the beginning of the following season's training camp proved to be disastrous.

Shortly after camp opened, Kurtenbach suffered a severe back injury that required a spinal fusion. Unfortunately, his career was never the same. Kurtenbach came back to play two games during the 1968–69 season, but he was still dealing with the injury in the 1969–70 season.

Kurtenbach was left unprotected in the 1970 NHL Expansion Draft and was claimed by the Vancouver Canucks, where he scored 62 goals over four seasons.

Mario Marois

NYR Debut: November 16, 1977 (vs. Chicago Black Hawks, won 5–2)

Regular Season Games with NYR: 166

Playoff Games with NYR: 28

At 5-foot-11, Mario Marois could be an offensive defenseman, but he also spent a lot of time in the penalty box.

The Rangers signed the Quebec native as a fourth-round pick in the 1977 NHL Amateur Draft. He spent most of the 1977–78 season with New Haven of the AHL but played in eight games with the big club.

Marois broke out for 31 points in the 1978–79 season and helped the team reach the Stanley Cup Final. He again scored 31 points the following season, but the Rangers felt his defensive play had fallen off.

After playing eight games, Marois was traded to the Vancouver Canucks in November 1980.

Nick Beverley

NYR Debut: October 16, 1974 (vs. California Golden Seals, 5–5 tie)

Regular Season Games with NYR: 139

Playoff Games with NYR: 3

In May 1974, the Rangers traded former 50-goal scorer Vic Hadfield to the Pittsburgh Penguins for veteran defenseman Nick Beverley.

The native of Toronto played parts of three seasons with the Rangers before being traded to the Minnesota North Stars in November 1976, along with right winger Bill Fairbairn, for right winger Bill Goldsworthy.

Viktor Stalberg

> **NYR Debut:** October 7, 2015 (at Chicago Blackhawks, won 3–2)
>
> **Regular Season Games with NYR:** 75
>
> **Playoff Games with NYR:** 5

Left winger Viktor Stalberg signed with the Rangers as a free agent in July 2015. Stalberg was brought in to help the offense, but his one season in New York was disappointing.

The Swedish-born forward scored nine goals in 75 games in 2015–16, and was scoreless in five postseason games.

Tony McKegney

> **NYR Debut:** November 14, 1986 (vs. Philadelphia Flyers, won 2–1)
>
> **Regular Season Games with NYR:** 64
>
> **Playoff Games with NYR:** 6

Left winger Tony McKegney made his reputation on the power play, which is what inspired Rangers general manager Phil Esposito to acquire the Ontario native in a trade with Minnesota in November 1986.

McKegney had a terrific regular season. In 64 games, he scored 29 goals—including seven with the man advantage. Unfortunately, McKegney went scoreless in the 1987 Stanley Cup Playoffs. He was traded to the St. Louis Blues in May 1987.

Peter Wallin

> **NYR Debut:** March 10, 1981 (vs. Quebec Nordiques, lost 6–4)
>
> **Regular Season Games with NYR:** 52
>
> **Playoff Games with NYR:** 14

At 5-foot-9, right winger Peter Wallin was small by NHL standards. He signed with the Rangers as an unrestricted free agent on March 8, 1981, and made his debut just two days later.

The Rangers were hoping the Swedish-born Wallin would click with fellow Swedes Ulf Nilsson and Anders Hedberg, but it never panned out. After the 1981–82 season, Wallin returned to play in Sweden.

Bob Plager

> **NYR Debut:** December 5, 1964 (at Boston Bruins, 3–3 tie)
> **Regular Season Games with NYR:** 29
> **Playoff Games with NYR:** 0
> **Also wore:** #6 and #2

Bob Plager put together a solid career with the St. Louis Blues, but that was after he started his NHL career with the Rangers. Plager, one of three brothers to play in the NHL, was signed in 1959.

After playing five seasons in the minors, Plager debuted in December 1964. He played parts of three seasons with the Rangers before being part of a multi-player trade with the Blues that sent defenseman Rod Seiling (see Chapter Sixteen) to New York.

Alexei Gusarov

> **NYR Debut:** December 31, 2000 (at Dallas Stars, lost 6–1)
> **Regular Season Games with NYR:** 26
> **Playoff Games with NYR:** 0

Defenseman Alexei Gusarov was acquired from the Colorado Avalanche in December 2000 to provide some experience on the back line.

Gusarov played 26 games before he was traded to the St. Louis Blues for defenseman Peter Smrek in March 2001.

Steven King

> **NYR Debut:** December 6, 1992 (vs. Toronto Maple Leafs, won 6–0)
> **Regular Season Games with NYR:** 24
> **Playoff Games with NYR:** 0

Steven King was not a "horror show" but a supplemental draft pick of college players in 1991. King played with the Rangers' AHL affiliate in Binghamton before joining the team in the 1992–93 season. King scored a power play goal in his first game and finished with seven in 24 games.

Following his one season in New York, King was selected by the Anaheim Mighty Ducks in the 1993 NHL Expansion Draft.

Peter Smrek

> **NYR Debut:** March 9, 2001 (at Washington Capitals, lost 5–3)
> **Regular Season Games with NYR:** 22
> **Playoff Games with NYR:** 0

When the Rangers execute a trade, they sometimes give the number of the traded player to the new arrival. That was the case with defenseman Peter Smrek when he was acquired from the St. Louis Blues for defenseman Alexei Gusarov.

Smrek spent parts of two seasons with the Rangers. In March 2002, he was traded to the Nashville Predators for defenseman Richard Lintner.

The following players played less than 20 games with NYR:

Mike Robitaille - defenseman

> **NYR Debut:** February 21, 1970 (at Chicago Black Hawks, lost 4–2)
> **Regular Season Games with NYR:** 15
> **Playoff Games with NYR:** 0
> **Also wore:** #24

Jason Doig - defenseman

> **NYR Debut:** November 7, 1999 (at Chicago Blackhawks, won 3–1)
> **Regular Season Games with NYR:** 10
> **Playoff Games with NYR:** 0
> **Also wore:** #21

Graeme Nicolson - defenseman

> **NYR Debut:** January 5, 1983 (vs. Buffalo Sabres, 3–3 tie)
> **Regular Season Games with NYR:** 10
> **Playoff Games with NYR:** 0

Anders Eriksson - defenseman

NYR Debut: March 27, 2010 (at Toronto Maple Leafs, lost 3–2 OT)

Regular Season Games with NYR: 8

Playoff Games with NYR: 0

Andre Dupont - defenseman

NYR Debut: February 28, 1971 (vs. Vancouver Canucks, won 4–2)

Regular Season Games with NYR: 7

Playoff Games with NYR: 0

Jim Lorentz - center

NYR Debut: November 20, 1971 (at Minnesota North Stars, lost 4–1)

Regular Season Games with NYR: 7

Playoff Games with NYR: 0

Paul Healey - left wing

NYR Debut: November 4, 2003 (vs. Dallas Stars, won 3–0)

Regular Season Games with NYR: 4

Playoff Games with NYR: 0

Chad Kolarik - center

NYR Debut: January 20, 2011 (at Carolina Hurricanes, lost 4–1)

Regular Season Games with NYR: 4

Playoff Games with NYR: 0

Jeff Bandura - defenseman

NYR Debut: December 31, 1980 (vs. Colorado Rockies, lost 6–4)

Regular Season Games with NYR: 2

Playoff Games with NYR: 0

Larry Huras - defenseman

NYR Debut: February 26, 1977 (at Chicago Black Hawks, lost 2–1)

Regular Season Games with NYR: 2

Playoff Games with NYR: 0

Dave Tataryn - goaltender

NYR Debut: March 9, 1977 (vs. Minnesota North Stars, won 6–4)

Regular Season Games with NYR: 2

Playoff Games with NYR: 0

Ryan Bourque - center

NYR Debut: April 9, 2015 (vs. Ottawa Senators, lost 3–0)

Regular Season Games with NYR: 1

Playoff Games with NYR: 0

Steve Andrascik - right wing

NYR Debut: April 20, 1972 (vs. Chicago Black Hawks, Game Two Stanley Cup Semifinals, won 3–2)

Regular Season Games with NYR: 0

Playoff Games with NYR: 1

#26: CAPTAIN MALONEY

Dave Maloney

NYR Debut: December 18, 1974 (vs. Minnesota North Stars, won 7–0)
Regular Season Games with NYR: 605
Playoff Games with NYR: 48

Defenseman Dave Maloney was one of the more underrated players in franchise history. He was the youngest captain in Rangers' history and a solid back liner during his 11-year career in New York.

The Rangers made the native of Ontario their first-round pick and the 14th overall selection in the 1974 NHL Amateur Draft. When the eighteen-year-old made his debut in December 1974, he became the youngest player to ever wear a Ranger sweater.

The early portion of Maloney's career was hampered by injuries. A broken leg limited him to 21 games in the 1975–76 season. Maloney missed parts of the next two seasons after suffering an arm injury and torn knee ligaments.

Despite the erratic start to his career, Maloney became the youngest captain in franchise history when he was awarded the "C" in October 1978. Maloney became the seventeenth captain in team history and was the youngest in the league at the time.

In his first year with the C, Maloney (playing with his brother and teammate Don Maloney) led the team to the 1979 Stanley Cup Final. He was particularly good in the postseason when he scored three goals and four assists for seven points in 17 games.

The offensive side of Maloney's game really developed in the 1980s when he became a factor on the power play. His best offensive season was 1982–83, when he set personal marks with 42 assists and 50 points. Maloney's last big season with the Rangers was 1983–84, when he played 68 games and scored seven goals with 26 assists for 33 points.

Photo courtesy of Mark Rosenman.

Was youngest captain in Rangers history.

The Rangers were in transition in the 1984–85 season. After 16 games, Maloney was traded to the Buffalo Sabres in a four-player deal.

In 2005, Maloney began his career as a broadcaster and has been a staple of Rangers' radio broadcasts as a color commentator ever since.

Martin St. Louis

NYR Debut: March 5, 2014 (vs. Toronto Maple Leafs, lost 3–2 OT)

Regular Season Games with NYR: 93

Playoff Games with NYR: 44

In March 2014, the Rangers and Tampa Bay Lightning completed a historic trade of team captains.

Ranger captain Ryan Callahan was an impending free agent and could not come to terms with the team on a new contract. St. Louis had requested a trade from Tampa Bay, so the teams completed the transaction to just beat the 2014 NHL trade deadline.

St. Louis was brought to the Rangers to provide a spark, and that's exactly what he did. The diminutive winger, who played bigger than his 5-foot-8 size would indicate, helped lead the Rangers to the 2014 Stanley Cup Final that featured a number of memorable moments along the way.

In the second round against the Pittsburgh Penguins, the Rangers lost Game Four to fall behind three games to one in the series. After the game, the team flew back to New York when St. Louis was told his mother, France, had passed away. The Rangers seemed to feed off that emotion as they rallied from the 3–1 deficit to defeat the Penguins and advance to the Eastern Conference Final against Montreal. In Game Six at Madison Square Garden, on Mother's Day, St. Louis scored the first goal of the game as the Rangers went on to a 3–1 win to force the deciding Game Seven.

Despite his short time with the team, St. Louis was already a part of the Ranger family and it showed during his time of grief.

Photo courtesy of Mark Rosenman.

His Mothers Day goal is one of the most memorable in Ranger history.

During an off day between games one and two of the East Final, the entire team, players and coaches, all attended the funeral for St. Louis's mother in Laval, Canada.

The Rangers led the series two games to one, and were in overtime of Game Four at Madison Square Garden. A little over six minutes into the extra session, St. Louis made a spectacular play to score the winning goal for a three games to one lead.

The former Art Ross and Lady Byng trophy winner played one more season with the Rangers, and it would be his last in the NHL. In his final season, St. Louis scored 21 goals with 31 assists for 52 points in 74 games. He added a goal in the playoffs and retired after the season.

Joey Kocur

NYR Debut: March 7, 1991 (at Quebec Nordiques, lost 4–2)
Regular Season Games with NYR: 278
Playoff Games with NYR: 48

Right winger Joey Kocur was a physical, defensive player whose offensive skills flew under the radar.

In March 1991, the Rangers acquired Kocur from Detroit in a five-player deal to add some toughness to the roster for the playoffs. The Saskatchewan native joined the team late in the 1990–91 season and was a presence in the playoffs, but the Rangers lost to the Washington Capitals in six games.

In the 1991–92 season, Kocur played 51 games as the Rangers won the President's Trophy with the best record in the NHL.

During their Stanley Cup-winning season of 1993–94, Kocur played 71 games and compiled 129 penalty minutes. In the playoffs, Kocur scored the tying goal in Game Two of the Eastern Conference Semifinal against Washington and provided a much-needed physical presence for the grind of the postseason.

Kocur did not dress for Game Seven of the Final against Vancouver, but his name is etched onto the Stanley Cup.

Kocur went on to play parts of two more seasons with the Rangers before being traded to Vancouver in March 1996. The rugged winger eventually returned to the Red Wings and won two more Stanley Cups in Detroit.

Troy Mallette

NYR Debut: October 6, 1989 (at Winnipeg Jets, won 4–1)
Regular Season Games with NYR: 150
Playoff Games with NYR: 15
Also wore: #16

The Rangers chose 6-foot-3 left winger Troy Mallette with their first pick in the second round of the 1988 NHL Entry Draft. Mallette won the Lars-Erik Sjoberg Award as the top rookie during the 1989 training camp.

In his first game, Mallette recorded his first NHL assist on the game-winning goal. He went on to score 13 goals in his first season while setting a franchise record for the most penalty minutes in one season with 305.

Mallette played two seasons with the Rangers. In September 1991, he was awarded to the Edmonton Oilers as compensation for signing left winger Adam Graves (see Chapter Nine).

Ruslan Fedotenko

NYR Debut: October 9, 2010 (at Buffalo Sabres, won 6–3)
Regular Season Games with NYR: 139
Playoff Games with NYR: 25

Left winger Ruslan Fedotenko was a consistent goal scorer throughout the first nine years of his NHL career. With the idea of enhancing their offense, the Rangers signed the Russian-born skater as an unrestricted free agent in October 2010.

Fedotenko played 66 games in the 2010–11 season and scored 10 goals. In his second season with the Rangers, he appeared to be on his way to a solid season following a two-goal game in late November in a win against Washington, but scored only six more goals in 54 games.

Fedotenko played out his contract after two seasons with the Rangers.

Martin Rucinsky

NYR Debut: March 13, 2002 (vs. Boston Bruins, lost 3–1)
Regular Season Games with NYR: 136
Playoff Games with NYR: 2
Also wore: #19

Czech Republic–born Martin Rucinsky spent three different tenures with the Rangers.

Rucinsky was acquired in a trade with the Dallas Stars in March 2002. He scored three goals with 10 assists for 13 points in 15 games.

The thirty-year-old played out his contract and signed with the St. Louis Blues for the 2002–03 season. Rucinsky then signed with the Rangers as a free agent for the 2003–04 season, scoring 13 goals with 29 assists for 42 points in 69 games. In March 2004, he was traded to Vancouver.

In August 2005, Rucinsky once again signed with the Rangers as a free agent. He scored 16 goals with 39 assists for 55 points in 52 games during the 2005–06 season, his last with the Rangers.

Tim Taylor

NYR Debut: October 1, 1999 (at Edmonton Oilers, 1–1 OT tie)
Regular Season Games with NYR: 114
Playoff Games with NYR: 0

Tim Taylor made his Ranger debut count.

Taylor signed with the Rangers as an unrestricted free agent in July 1999. The Rangers opened the 1999–2000 season in Edmonton, and Taylor scored the Rangers' only goal in a 1–1 overtime tie.

Taylor showed his offensive skills in junior hockey, but developed into a solid defensive forward during his NHL career.

The Stratford, Ontario, native played parts of two seasons with the Rangers. He was traded to the Tampa Bay Lightning in June 2001.

Jimmy Vesey

NYR Debut: October 13, 2016 (vs. New York Islanders, won 5–3)
Regular Season Games with NYR: 80
Playoff Games with NYR: 12

The Rangers won a bidding war for the right to sign highly coveted free agent left winger Jimmy Vesey in August 2016.

The Boston-born Vesey was the third-round pick of the Nashville Predators in the 2012 NHL Entry Draft, but he decided against turning pro and played for Harvard University for four years.

In 2016, Vesey was named the winner of the Hobey Baker Award as the top collegiate player. A few months after his collegiate career ended, Vesey signed with the Rangers.

The twenty-three-year-old scored his first NHL goal in his third game as part of a 7–4 win over San Jose at Madison Square Garden. Vesey had his ups and downs during his first season, but still finished with a respectable 16 goals and 11 assists for 27 points in 80 games.

Rangers head coach Alain Vigneault was tough on the youngster, to the point where he was benched, but Vesey began to become more consistent as the season wore on.

Vesey took his game to another level in the playoffs. Against Ottawa in the second round, Vesey scored the go-ahead goal in the third period of Game Five, but the Rangers couldn't hold the lead and eventually lost the series in six games.

Andreas Johansson

NYR Debut: October 5, 2001 (at Carolina Hurricanes, lost 3–1)
Regular Season Games with NYR: 70
Playoff Games with NYR: 0

Left winger Andreas Johansson came to the Rangers in the 2000 NHL Waiver Draft. Johansson was a veteran who had played with five different teams before spending one season of his 8-year NHL career in New York.

In 70 games, Johansson scored 14 goals with 10 assists for 24 points. After the season, he became a free agent.

Jeff Finley

NYR Debut: October 3, 1997 (vs. New York Islanders, 2–2 OT tie)
Regular Season Games with NYR: 65
Playoff Games with NYR: 0

Defenseman Jeff Finley played parts of two seasons with the Rangers during a 15-year NHL career.

In February 1999, Finley was traded to St. Louis.

Brian MacLellan

NYR Debut: December 14, 1985 (at Boston Bruins, lost 4–2)
Regular Season Games with NYR: 51
Playoff Games with NYR: 16

Brian MacLellan was a big left winger who did not play up to his 6-foot-3 frame. MacLellan joined the Rangers via an in-season trade with the Los Angeles Kings in 1985.

Rangers' head coach Ted Sator wanted MacLellan to play a more physical style, but the winger could never adapt his game to satisfy the coaching staff. MacLellan lasted one season in New York and was traded to Minnesota in September 1986.

Kjell Samuelsson

NYR Debut: October 10, 1985 (vs. Washington Capitals, won 4–2)
Regular Season Games with NYR: 39
Playoff Games with NYR: 9
Also wore: #8

At 6-foot-6, defenseman Kjell Samuelsson was a sixth-round pick of the Rangers in the 1984 NHL Entry Draft.

The Swedish-born Samuelsson spent parts of two seasons with the Rangers. He was traded to the Philadelphia Flyers in exchange for goaltender Bob Froese in December 1986.

The following players played less than 20 games with NYR:

Sheldon Kannegiesser - defenseman

NYR Debut: March 7, 1973 (vs. Philadelphia Flyers, 2–2 tie)
Regular Season Games with NYR: 15
Playoff Games with NYR: 1

David Oliver - right wing

NYR Debut: February 23, 1997 (at Philadelphia Flyers, lost 2–1)
Regular Season Games with NYR: 14
Playoff Games with NYR: 3

Jay Caufield - right wing

NYR Debut: February 24, 1987 (at Buffalo Sabres, won 6–3)
Regular Season Games with NYR: 13
Playoff Games with NYR: 3

Randy Heath - left wing

NYR Debut: December 5, 1984 (vs. Calgary Flames, 4–4 OT tie)
Regular Season Games with NYR: 13
Playoff Games with NYR: 0
Also wore: #40

Igor Liba - left wing

NYR Debut: November 6, 1988 (at New Jersey Devils, lost 6–5)
Regular Season Games with NYR: 10
Playoff Games with NYR: 0

Brad Maxwell - defenseman

NYR Debut: January 26, 1987 (vs. New Jersey Devils, won 6–3)
Regular Season Games with NYR: 9
Playoff Games with NYR: 0

Ron Talakoski - right wing

NYR Debut: February 25, 1987 (at Toronto Maple Leafs, won 4–2)
Regular Season Games with NYR: 9
Playoff Games with NYR: 0
Also wore: #35

Mike Maneluk - left wing

NYR Debut: March 12, 1999 (vs. Boston Bruins, lost 5–4)
Regular Season Games with NYR: 4
Playoff Games with NYR: 0

#27: THE REIGNING CAPTAIN

Ryan McDonagh

> **NYR Debut:** January 7, 2011 (at Dallas Stars, lost 3–2)
>
> **Regular Season Games with NYR:** 467
>
> **Playoff Games with NYR:** 96

Defenseman Ryan McDonagh came to the Rangers as part of one of the most one-sided trades in franchise history.

In June 2009, Rangers general manager Glen Sather sent center Scott Gomez (who was in the midst of a long-term contract) and two players to Montreal in exchange for left winger and Long Island, New York, native Christopher Higgins and McDonagh, who was the Canadiens' first-round pick in the 2007 NHL Entry Draft.

The eighteen-year-old, American-born defenseman was essentially a "throw in," but he turned into a top NHL back liner who would become the Rangers' captain.

As a high school player in Minnesota, McDonagh was named "Mr. Hockey" as the state's top player in 2007. After three outstanding collegiate seasons with the University of Wisconsin, McDonagh decided to skip his senior season and join the Rangers' affiliate in the AHL, the Connecticut Whale, for the 2010–11 season.

McDonagh played 38 games with Connecticut and was called up to make his Rangers' debut in January 2011. The young defenseman finished the season with the Rangers and scored only one goal, but made it a timely one. In the final game of the regular season, McDonagh's first NHL goal was a game winner to beat the New Jersey Devils. In the playoffs, McDonagh did not get on the score sheet but received steady ice time as a portent of things to come.

In the 2011–12 season, McDonagh played in all 82 games while scoring seven goals with 25 assists for 32 points.

Minnesota's Mr. Hockey.

McDonagh broke out in the 2013–14 season with career highs in goals (14), assists (29), and points (43). He carried that success into the 2014 Stanley Cup Playoffs, when he led the Rangers to the Final.

In 25 postseason games, McDonagh scored four goals with 13 assists for 17 points. In the Eastern Conference Final against Montreal, McDonagh became the first defenseman in franchise history to have eight assists in one playoff series. That total included assisting on the only goal of the 1–0 win in the Game Six, series clincher.

McDonagh was named team captain right before the 2014–15 season began, but he began to experience some setbacks due to a number of injuries.

McDonagh played the Final with a shoulder injury and that carried over into next season when he re-injured it in November 2014.

In February 2016, McDonagh was punched in the head by Philadelphia Flyers tough guy Wayne Simmonds and suffered a concussion. McDonagh missed four games and returned to the lineup, but he wasn't the same player and it showed on the ice.

In the 2016–17 season, McDonagh returned to form with six goals and 36 assists for 42 points. In the 2017 playoffs, McDonagh was, arguably, the club's best player but the Rangers lost a second-round series to the Ottawa Senators in six games.

McDonagh will be twenty-eight years old in the 2017–18 season. He's already established himself as a top NHL defenseman, and there's still more to come.

Alexei Kovalev

NYR Debut: October 12, 1992 (vs. Hartford Whalers, won 6–2)
Regular Season Games with NYR: 492
Playoff Games with NYR: 44

The Rangers felt they had a dynamic talent when they made Alexei Kovalev their #1 pick and the 15th overall in the 1991 NHL Entry Draft.

The 6-foot-2, 222-pound Kovalev was a combination of strength and skill who could dazzle the opposition while frustrating his own team with his inconsistency. Kovalev's ability to improvise with the puck would sometimes make him hold on to it too much, a constant criticism that followed him throughout his career. As an eighteen-year-old in 1989, Kovalev was such a talent that he played with a top-ranked Soviet club, the Moscow Dynamo.

Kovalev was a 20-goal scorer in his first season with the Rangers. The Russian-born star excited the home crowd at Madison Square Garden when he scored a goal in his first game. He scored his first career hat trick in December 1992, so you could say it was a fairly successful first season for Kovalev, though the Rangers failed to make the playoffs.

Mike Keenan was hired as the head coach for the 1993–94 season, and the two didn't exactly hit it off right away. The twenty-year-old was frustrating the head coach by not getting off the ice on some shifts and holding onto the puck too long while futilely trying to make a play. The frustrations with Kovalev's game reached a breaking point in February 1994.

A day before Kovalev's birthday, the Rangers hosted the Boston Bruins at the Garden. In the second period, Rangers' head coach Mike Keenan "punished" Kovalev for his penchant for staying on the ice too long. After not coming back to the bench on time, Keenan ordered Kovalev to stay on the ice for what amounted to a seven-minute shift to finish out the period. Instead of succumbing to the fatigue, Kovalev drew a pair of penalties and even scored a power play goal in the final minute.

Kovalev was a pivotal player in the Rangers' run to the 1994 Stanley Cup.

With the Rangers facing elimination and trailing 2–0 in the second period of Game Six of the Eastern Conference Final against the New Jersey Devils, Keenan put Kovalev back on a line with Adam Graves and Hall of Fame center Mark Messier.

With less than two minutes left in the second period, Kovalev scored his fifth goal of the playoffs to narrow the lead and give the Rangers some momentum as they approached the third period. Messier (see Chapter Eleven) went on to score his historic hat trick, and the Rangers turned the series around en route to ending their 54-year drought without a Stanley Cup. Were it not for Brian Leetch's outstanding performance, Kovalev could've been the Conn Smythe Trophy winner.

Kovalev played parts of five more seasons with the Rangers before being traded to Pittsburgh as part of a multi-player trade for center Petr Nedved in November 1998. In February 2003, Kovalev was re-acquired from the Penguins as part of an eight-player trade. In March 2004, Kovalev's Rangers' tenure ended when he was dealt to Montreal.

Ted Irvine

NYR Debut: February 28, 1970 (at Detroit Red Wings, 3–3 tie)

Regular Season Games with NYR: 378

Playoff Games with NYR: 60

Ted Irvine played one NHL game with the Boston Bruins before he was claimed by the Los Angeles Kings in the 1967 NHL Expansion Draft. Irvine was a physical player who could provide some offense, and spent parts of three seasons with the Kings before being traded to the Rangers in February 1970.

The 6-foot-2 left winger played on a solid two-way line with right winger Pete Stemkowski and center Bruce MacGregor during the 1970–71 season. Irvine scored 20 goals and accumulated 137 minutes in the penalty box.

Irvine was a big factor during the 1971–72 season when the Rangers qualified for the Final. Bobby Rousseau was brought in to center Irvine's line with Stemkowski, and the trio clicked as one of the top lines that season. During the postseason, Irvine scored four goals and five assists for nine points in 16 games.

Photo from the public domain.

Chris Jericho's dad was a physical player for the Rangers.

In the 1973–74 season, Irvine scored 26 goals and 46 points, both career highs. After the 1974–75 season, he was traded to the St. Louis Blues.

Mike Rogers

NYR Debut: October 6, 1981 (vs. Detroit Red Wings, lost 5–2)
Regular Season Games with NYR: 316
Playoff Games with NYR: 14
Also wore: #17

Mike Rogers has a place in Ranger history as the third player (joining Jean Ratelle and Vic Hadfield) to record 100 points in a season.

The 5-foot-9 center began his pro career in the World Hockey Association. The Philadelphia Flyers (aka "Broad Street Bullies") made physical hockey the "going thing" in the NHL in the 1970s, so big players were getting more attention.

After five seasons in the WHA, Rogers joined the Hartford Whalers in 1979 for two seasons before being traded to the Rangers four days before the 1981–82 season opener.

Rogers, who had two previous 100-point seasons with Hartford, did not disappoint. In his first season, the Calgary, Alberta, native had 103 points (38 goals, 65 assists) and was named a co-winner (along with defenseman Barry Beck) of the team's MVP award.

When Rogers came to the Rangers, he thrived under head coach Herb Brooks. Unfortunately, declining numbers and a coaching change in 1985 led to the end of his tenure in New York.

Going into the 1985–86 season, Ted Sator replaced Brooks. The new head coach put his imprint on the team and made numerous changes, including having Rogers, the veteran center, start the year in the minors.

Rogers was promoted in December after playing 20 games with New Haven of the AHL. He played 9 games with the Rangers before being traded to Edmonton later in the month.

Mike McEwen

NYR Debut: October 6, 1976 (vs. Minnesota North Stars, won 6–5)
Regular Season Games with NYR: 242
Playoff Games with NYR: 18
Also wore: #6

Mike McEwen was a standout defenseman with the Toronto Marlboros of the OHL, so the Rangers made him a third-round pick in the 1976 NHL Amateur Draft.

McEwen made the team out of training camp and had an outstanding first season. He set a then rookie franchise record (Brian Leetch set a Ranger and NHL record with 23 goals in the 1988–89 season) with 14 goals and 29 assists for 43 points.

Two years later, McEwen would play a key role in the Rangers' run to the 1979 Stanley Cup Final. McEwen scored 20 goals in

Part of Barry Beck blockbuster trade.

Photo courtesy of Ken Tash.

the regular season and then set a franchise record with 13 points and 11 assists in the playoffs.

Four of those assists came during the Rangers' six-game series win over the New York Islanders in the Stanley Cup Semifinal. The ironic twist is that McEwen would eventually join the Islanders, where he would win three Stanley Cups.

After nine games in the 1979–80 season, McEwen was traded to the Colorado Rockies as part of a blockbuster, multi-player deal for defenseman Barry Beck.

The Rangers re-acquired McEwen from the Detroit Red Wings in December 1985, but he was traded to the Hartford Whalers in March 1986.

Willie Huber

NYR Debut: October 5, 1983 (vs. New Jersey Devils, won 6–2)
Regular Season Games with NYR: 238
Playoff Games with NYR: 28

Willie Huber was a big, hulking defenseman who was the 9th overall pick of the Red Wings in the 1978 NHL Amateur Draft.

Huber was an offensive defenseman who scored 14 or more goals in four straight seasons in Detroit.

Following the 1982–83 season, Huber had a reported contract dispute with Detroit management and was sent to the Rangers in June 1983 as part of a blockbuster trade that moved popular center Ron Duguay to Motown.

Huber never reached double-digit totals in goals scored as a Ranger. His best season in New York was 1986–87, when he scored eight goals with 22 assists for 30 points, but the fans became disenchanted with his defensive game.

After playing 11 games, Huber was traded to Vancouver in November 1987 for defenseman Michel Petit.

Jan Hlavac

NYR Debut: October 2, 1999 (at Vancouver Canucks, lost 2–1)
Regular Season Games with NYR: 218
Playoff Games with NYR: 0
Also wore: #37

Left winger Jan Hlavac made a reputation in the Czech Republic for being a big-time goal scorer. That made him attractive to the New York Islanders, who made Hlavac their second-round pick in the 1995 NHL Entry Draft.

After his rights were dealt to Calgary, the Flames traded Hlavac to the Rangers in June 1999 as part of a deal for center Mark Savard.

In his first season of 1999–2000, Hlavac scored 19 goals but did better in his second season thanks to the acquisition of fellow countryman Radek Dvorak.

Head coach Ron Low put together Hlavac with right winger Dvorek and center Petr Nedved to form the productive "Czech Line." Hlavac went on to score 28 goals and 36 assists for 64 points, but the Rangers missed the play-offs which led to personnel changes.

As a result of a change in philosophy, Hlavac was traded to the Philadelphia Flyers in August 2001 as part of a blockbuster deal that brought Eric Lindros to the Rangers. Hlavac came back to sign with the Rangers as an unrestricted free agent in 2003, but he scored only five goals in 72 games and was not re-signed after the season.

Paul Mara

NYR Debut: March 1, 2007 (vs. Pittsburgh Pirates, lost 4–3 SO)

Regular Season Games with NYR: 156

Playoff Games with NYR: 27

Veteran defenseman Paul Mara was acquired by the Rangers from the Boston Bruins for defenseman Aaron Ward at the 2007 NHL trade deadline.

Mara played parts of two seasons with the Rangers and was re-signed for a third in 2008. After the 2008–09 season, Mara played out his contract and signed a free agent deal with Montreal in 2009.

Rico Fata

NYR Debut: October 15, 2001 (at Montreal Canadiens, won 2–1)

Regular Season Games with NYR: 46

Playoff Games with NYR: 0

Also wore: #38

Right winger Rico Fata split parts of two seasons with the Rangers and their AHL affiliate in Hartford.

Fata was the 6th overall pick of the Calgary Flames in the 1988 NHL Entry Draft, and made the team out of training camp. He played in 20 games with the team, but showed that he was not ready for the NHL game and was sent down to the AHL.

After three seasons, Calgary finally gave up on Fata. The Rangers claimed him off the waiver wire in October 2001 but, after five games, he was sent to Hartford.

In the 2002–03 season, Fata played 36 games before being traded to Pittsburgh in February 2003 when the Rangers re-acquired Alexei Kovalev.

Joe Paterson

NYR Debut: January 22, 1988 (at Vancouver Canucks, won 6–3)
Regular Season Games with NYR: 41
Playoff Games with NYR: 0

Joe Paterson was a physical winger who compiled 147 penalty minutes during parts of two seasons with the Rangers. Paterson spent most of his tenure with the Rangers' AHL and IHL affiliates.

Paterson scored a goal in his first game (he would also add two assists), but it would be the only one he would score in his Rangers' career.

The following players played less than 20 games with NYR:

Gary Burns - left wing

NYR Debut: December 20, 1980 (at Minnesota North Stars, 3–3 tie)
Regular Season Games with NYR: 11
Playoff Games with NYR: 5
Also wore: #24

Dale Lewis - left wing

NYR Debut: November 1, 1975 (at Montreal Canadiens, lost 4–0)
Regular Season Games with NYR: 8
Playoff Games with NYR: 0

Paul Boutilier - defenseman

NYR Debut: November 10, 1987 (vs. New Jersey Devils, lost 3–2)
Regular Season Games with NYR: 4
Playoff Games with NYR: 0

#28: THE FINAL CHECK

Steve Larmer

NYR Debut: November 3, 1993 (vs. Vancouver Canucks, won 6–3)

Regular Season Games with NYR: 115

Playoff Games with NYR: 33

Steve Larmer was a veteran right winger who starred with the Chicago Blackhawks for 13 seasons before joining the Rangers in November 1993. The Rangers acquired Larmer from the Hartford Whalers for defenseman James Patrick and center Darren Turcotte, a three-way trade that also included the Blackhawks. Head coach Mike Keenan had Larmer the year before when he coached in Chicago, so he knew what he was getting in the solid, two-way winger who was a former Calder Trophy winner.

Larmer was one of the missing pieces that the Rangers needed to make a run for the Stanley Cup. The team was coming off a disappointing season where they missed the playoffs, so changes were in order.

Larmer had a solid season in New York. He scored a goal in his first game with the Rangers, and finished with 21 goals with 39 assists for 60 points. He also was a key performer on special teams, both the power play and penalty kill.

There was one memorable moment during the regular season. On January 16, 1994, the Rangers were in Chicago for their final game at Chicago Stadium, which was being torn down after the season. Against his old team, Larmer was awarded a penalty shot in the third period. The Rangers were already leading 4–1 when Larmer took the puck at center ice and skated in toward Chicago goaltender Ed Belfour. Instead of trying to finesse the puck past Belfour, Larmer wound up for a slap shot from about 20 feet out to beat his former teammate and score a goal in his final game at the longtime home of the Blackhawks.

Larmer's durability was well renowned. While playing with Chicago between 1982 and 1993, he set a Chicago franchise record by playing in 884 consecutive games.

Larmer's impact was felt during the 1994 Stanley Cup Playoffs. The veteran right winger scored two goals in the opening round sweep of the New

York Islanders, a goal in each of the next two rounds, and four goals against Vancouver in the Final.

In the Cup-clinching Game Seven against the Canucks, Larmer is part of an iconic picture of the final faceoff in the Rangers' zone. Even after the scoreboard strikes zero, Larmer is still checking his man into the boards to make sure he can't get to the front of the net to score the potential tying goal.

Larmer played one more season with the Rangers, but chronic back pain forced him to retire after the lockout-shortened 1995 season.

Tomas Sandstrom

NYR Debut: October 11, 1984 (vs. Hartford Whalers, 4–4 OT tie)
Regular Season Games with NYR: 407
Playoff Games with NYR: 29

Tomas Sandstrom was a Swedish star who was the Rangers' second-round pick in the 1982 NHL Entry Draft. Sandstrom was a 6-foot-2, 205-pound right winger who possessed superior offensive skills.

Sandstrom's NHL career got off to a fast start, as he scored the tying goal late in the third period of his first game in 1984. In his first season, Sandstrom scored 29 goals with 29 assists for 58 points, as well as a top-ten finish in the Calder Trophy voting. He also became the first Ranger to be named to the NHL's All-Rookie team, and was named the team's MVP.

Sandstrom was plagued by injuries in his second season, but got healthy in time for an impressive run in the postseason. During the 1986 Stanley Cup Playoffs, Sandstrom scored four goals with six assists for 10 points in 16 games.

In the 1986–87 season, Sandstrom scored 40 goals with 34 assists for 74 points, but that was not his best season in New York. Two seasons later, in 1988–89, Sandstrom found the net for 32 goals and a career-high 56 assists for 88 points.

Midway through his sixth season in New York, Sandstrom was traded to the Los Angeles Kings, along with left winger Tony Granato, for center Bernie Nicholls.

Colton Orr

NYR Debut: December 3, 2005 (at Washington Capitals, lost 5–1)
Regular Season Games with NYR: 224
Playoff Games with NYR: 12

Photo by Hunting]38 via Wikimedia Commons.

Spent 522 minutes in penalty box as Ranger.

The Rangers claimed right winger Colton Orr on waivers from the Boston Bruins.

The 6-foot-3, 222-pound winger was your classic NHL enforcer. He played parts of four seasons with the Rangers, where he accumulated 522 penalty minutes.

Orr played out his contract after the 2008–09 season and became an unrestricted free agent.

Mikko Leinonen

NYR Debut: October 9, 1981 (at Winnipeg Jets, lost 8–3)	
Regular Season Games with NYR: 159	
Playoff Games with NYR: 19	

Finnish-born center Mikko Leinonen has the distinction of sharing an NHL record with Hall of Famer Wayne Gretzky.

In Game Two of the 1982 Patrick Division Semifinal against the Philadelphia Flyers, Leinonen set a Ranger and NHL playoff mark with six assists in a 7–3 win (Gretzky would tie the record five years later).

Leinonen was a highly skilled center who will go down in Ranger history, unfortunately, for what he didn't do.

In 1984, the Rangers and four-time defending champion New York Islanders were in overtime of a fifth and deciding game of the Patrick Division Semifinal. This was a golden opportunity for the Rangers to be the ones to end the Islander dynasty.

In overtime, Leinonen took a pass from behind the Islander net and was wide open in front, but he fanned on the shot. The Rangers eventually lost in overtime and were denied once again by their hated cross-town rivals.

That excruciating loss would be Leinonen's final game. The twenty-eight-year-old signed with the Washington Capitals for the 1984–85 season, but played only three games before returning to play in Finland.

Eric Lacroix

NYR Debut: February 14, 1999 (vs. Detroit Red Wings, lost 4–2)
Regular Season Games with NYR: 146
Playoff Games with NYR: 0

Left winger Eric Lacroix played parts of three seasons with the Rangers. Lacroix was a big winger who played a defensive role.

Late in the 2000–01 season, Lacroix was traded to the Ottawa Senators.

Tie Domi

NYR Debut: October 13, 1990 (at Washington Capitals, won 5–2)
Regular Season Games with NYR: 82
Playoff Games with NYR: 6

Tie Domi was one of the most popular Rangers of his time. The 5-foot-10, 213-pound right winger was a feisty, in-your-face type of player that went over well with the diehards at Madison Square Garden.

The Rangers acquired Domi from the Toronto Maple Leafs in June 1990. Throughout his Rangers' tenure, Domi found himself in some memorable scraps. Domi did not discriminate, as he took on all comers including a couple of memorable hockey fights with a noted NHL tough guy, Detroit Red Wings' 6-foot-3 left winger Bob Probert.

Domi played parts of three seasons in New York before he was traded, along with left winger Kris King, to the Winnipeg Jets for center Ed Olczyk in December 1992.

Doug Jarrett

NYR Debut: October 29, 1975 (vs. St. Louis Blues, won 3–1)

Regular Season Games with NYR: 54

Playoff Games with NYR: 0

The Rangers acquired hulking defenseman Doug Jarrett from the Chicago Black Hawks for goaltender Gilles Villemure in October 1975.

Injuries limited Jarrett to 45 games with the Rangers in his first season of 1975–76, and his second season was split between the Rangers and their AHL affiliate at New Haven.

Photo courtesy of Ken Tash.

Came to Rangers in trade for Gilles Villemure in October 1975.

Following the 1976–77 season, Jarrett retired from the NHL.

P.J. Stock

NYR Debut: November 21, 1997 (at Carolina Hurricanes, won 4–3)

Regular Season Games with NYR: 54

Playoff Games with NYR: 0

Also wore: #20 and #32

Center P.J. Stock was a scrappy player signed by the Rangers as an undrafted free agent in 1997.

Stock spent parts of three seasons splitting time with the Rangers and their AHL affiliate in Hartford. He played out his contract after the 1999–2000 season, becoming a free agent.

Kris Newbury

NYR Debut: January 15, 2011 (at Montreal Canadiens, lost 3–2)

Regular Season Games with NYR: 24

Playoff Games with NYR: 3

In parts of three seasons with the Rangers, center Kris Newbury played a total of 24 games.

The Ontario native was a solid faceoff man winning 53 percent of the draws while as a Ranger.

Pat Conacher

NYR Debut: January 4, 1980 (vs. Philadelphia Flyers, lost 5–3)
Regular Season Games with NYR: 22
Playoff Games with NYR: 3
Also wore: #11

The Rangers used a fourth-round pick in the 1979 NHL Entry Draft on center Pat Conacher.

The Calgary native split the 1979–80 season between the Rangers and their New Haven AHL affiliate.

Conacher played parts of two seasons with the Rangers and played out his contract after the 1982–83 season.

The following players played less than 20 games with NYR:

Bryan McCabe - defenseman

NYR Debut: February 27, 2011 (vs. Tampa Bay Lightning, lost 2–1)
Regular Season Games with NYR: 19
Playoff Games with NYR: 5

Lawrence Nycholat - defenseman

NYR Debut: January 20, 2004 (vs. Boston Bruins, lost 4–1)
Regular Season Games with NYR: 9
Playoff Games with NYR: 0

Bill Lochead - left wing

NYR Debut: October 10, 1979 (at Toronto Maple Leafs, won 6–3)
Regular Season Games with NYR: 7
Playoff Games with NYR: 0

John Scott - left wing

NYR Debut: March 1, 2012 (at Carolina Hurricanes, won 3–2)

Regular Season Games with NYR: 6

Playoff Games with NYR: 0

Dan McCarthy - left wing

NYR Debut: November 1, 1980 (at Montreal Canadiens, lost 7–4)

Regular Season Games with NYR: 5

Playoff Games with NYR: 0

Dallas Eakins - defenseman

NYR Debut: March 24, 1997 (vs. Pittsburgh Penguins, won 3–0)

Regular Season Games with NYR: 3

Playoff Games with NYR: 4

Greg Hickey - left wing

NYR Debut: April 8, 1978 (at New York Islanders, lost 7–2)

Regular Season Games with NYR: 1

Playoff Games with NYR: 0

John Hughes - defenseman

NYR Debut: April 11, 1981 (vs. Los Angeles Kings, Playoffs Game Three Preliminary Round, won 10–3)

Regular Season Games with NYR: 0

Playoff Games with NYR: 3

#29: TAKING A FLYER ON A SIXTH-ROUND PICK

Reijo Ruotsalainen

> **NYR Debut:** October 6, 1981 (vs. Detroit Red Wings, lost 5–2)
> **Regular Season Games with NYR:** 389
> **Playoff Games with NYR:** 43

At 5-foot-8, defenseman Reijo Ruotsalainen was the Rangers sixth-round pick in the 1980 NHL Entry draft.

Scouts were skeptical that he could make it as an NHL player, but Ruotsalainen was an outstanding skater who maximized that talent to put up some pretty impressive numbers during his Rangers' career.

The Rangers made the playoffs in every one of Ruotsalainen's five seasons. In his first NHL season of 1981–82, Ruotsalainen scored 18 goals and 38 assists for 56 points. To get some help for his lack of size, he was paired with hulking defenseman Barry Beck.

Ruotsalainen acquitted himself very well in the 1982 Stanley Cup Playoffs. In ten games, he scored four goals with five assists for nine points. In Game One of the 1982 Patrick Division Final against the New York Islanders, Ruotsalainen scored the game-winning goal late in the third period to give the Rangers a 5–4 win. The Finnish-born defenseman scored two more goals in the series, but the Rangers lost in six games.

His best season was 1984–85, when he played all 80 games and led the Rangers in scoring with career highs of 28 goals, 45 assists, and 73 points. During that season, Ruotsalainen skated in some games as a right winger on a line with center Mark Pavelich, and with left winger Anders Hedberg.

Just before the 1986–87 season began, the Rangers included Ruotsalainen in a multi-player deal with the Edmonton Oilers. Ruotsalainen went on to win two Stanley Cups with the Oilers.

In 389 career games with the Rangers, Ruotsalainen scored 316 points.

Boris Mironov

> **NYR Debut:** January 8, 2003 (vs. Carolina Hurricanes, won 5–1)
> **Regular Season Games with NYR:** 111
> **Playoff Games with NYR:** 0

Russian-born defenseman Boris Mironov came to the Rangers via a trade with the Chicago Blackhawks in January 2003.

Mironov was a solid back liner who provided some offensive skill. He picked a good time to score his first goal as a Ranger when he found the net in a 5–0 win over the rival New York Islanders in late January.

Mironov retired after the 2003–04 season.

Eric Cairns

NYR Debut: October 8, 1996 (at Florida Panthers, 1–1 OT tie)
Regular Season Games with NYR: 79
Playoff Games with NYR: 3

At 6-foot-6, defenseman Eric Cairns was chosen by the Rangers with their third-round pick in the 1992 NHL Entry Draft.

Cairns was drafted for his obvious size, thus he spent much of his two-year Ranger tenure in the penalty box.

Cairns was placed on waivers in December 1998, where he was claimed by the New York Islanders.

Phil Bourque

NYR Debut: October 9, 1992 (at Washington Capitals, won 4–2)
Regular Season Games with NYR: 71
Playoff Games with NYR: 0

Left winger Phil Bourque was coming off back-to-back Stanley Cup Championships with the Pittsburgh Penguins when he signed with the Rangers as an unrestricted free agent for the 1992–93 season.

Bourque was a versatile player who could play defense, as well as left wing. The native of Chelmsford, Massachusetts, scored a goal in his first game but finished with only six for the season as he was plagued by injuries that limited him to 55 games.

Bourque was with the Rangers for parts of two seasons, including the Stanley Cup-winning season of 1993–94, but he became a part of the overhaul that was made at the deadline in March 1994 when he was traded to Ottawa.

Lauri Korpikoski

NYR Debut: May 4, 2008 (at Pittsburgh Penguins, Playoffs Game Five of Eastern Conference Semifinal, lost 3–2 OT)

Regular Season Games with NYR: 68

Playoff Games with NYR: 8

Finnish-born left winger Lauri Korpikoski was the Rangers' first-round pick and 19th overall in the 2004 NHL Entry Draft.

Korpikoski was a highly skilled player who made his NHL and Ranger debut in the 2008 Stanley Cup Playoffs. The native of Turku, Finland, scored his first goal in the playoff game, but the Rangers were eliminated.

Photo by Keith Allison via Wikimedia Commons.

First-Round pick of Rangers in 2004 Draft.

He made the team out of training camp for the 2008–09 season. He scored his first regular season goal in a win over New Jersey in late November.

Korpikoski played 68 games and scored six goals, but was traded to the Arizona Coyotes after the season.

Jeff Toms

NYR Debut: January 16, 2001 (vs. Philadelphia Flyers, won 4–3)
Regular Season Games with NYR: 53
Playoff Games with NYR: 0
Also wore: #32

Left winger Jeff Toms was drafted by New Jersey in 1992, but he never played a game with the Devils. However, he did play for the New York Islanders and completed the New York-Metro Area "trifecta" with the Rangers.

Toms was claimed off waivers from the Islanders in January 2001. He played parts of two seasons with the Rangers.

Toms scored three of his eight career goals with the Rangers in one game. In January 2002, he scored his only career hat trick in a win against the Boston Bruins at Madison Square Garden.

In March 2002, the Pittsburgh Penguins claimed Toms off the waiver wire.

Johan Witehall

NYR Debut: January 30, 1999 (at Detroit Red Wings, won 3–2)
Regular Season Games with NYR: 28
Playoff Games with NYR: 0

Johan Witehall was an outstanding goal scorer and playmaker for seven seasons in Sweden before being selected by the Rangers as an eighth-round pick in the 1998 NHL Entry Draft.

Witehall played four games with the Rangers in the 1998–99 season, and spent most of his time with the Hartford Wolf Pack of the AHL. Witehall represented Hartford in the 1999 AHL All-Star Game.

Witehall spent parts of three seasons with the Rangers before being claimed off waivers by Montreal in January 2001.

Joby Messier

NYR Debut: February 1, 1993 (at New York Islanders, 4–4 OT tie)

Regular Season Games with NYR: 25

Playoff Games with NYR: 0

Also wore: #8 and #28

Joby Messier was a second cousin of Hall of Famer Mark Messier, and had a modest three-year career with the Rangers.

Messier was a sixth-round pick in the 1989 NHL Entry Draft.

After the 1994–95 season, Messier was signed by the New York Islanders as a free agent, but a knee injury cost him the entire 1995–96 season. Messier was involved in a horrific auto accident that resulted in a fatality in August 1996, which essentially ended his playing career.

Don Jackson

NYR Debut: October 11, 1986 (at Pittsburgh Penguins, lost 6–5 OT)

Regular Season Games with NYR: 22

Playoff Games with NYR: 0

Don Jackson was a hulking defenseman who knew how to use his size, yet stay out of the penalty box.

At 6-foot-3 and 210 pounds, Jackson could move bodies around.

The native of Minneapolis, Minnesota, was acquired by the Rangers in a multi-player trade with Edmonton in October 1986.

Jackson was a two-time Stanley Cup winner with the Oilers. He played 22 games with the Rangers before retiring after the season.

The following players played less than 20 games with NYR:

Roman Lyashenko - center

NYR Debut: March 13, 2002 (vs. Boston Bruins, lost 3–1)

Regular Season Games with NYR: 17

Playoff Games with NYR: 0

Also wore: #19 and #28

Darren Van Impe - defenseman

NYR Debut: October 13, 2001 (at Ottawa Senators, 2–2 OT tie)
Regular Season Games with NYR: 17
Playoff Games with NYR: 0

Ray Markham - center

NYR Debut: November 13, 1979 (at New York Islanders, lost 10–5)
Regular Season Games with NYR: 14
Playoff Games with NYR: 7

Bruce Bell - defenseman

NYR Debut: October 19, 1987 (vs. Washington Capitals, lost 4–2)
Regular Season Games with NYR: 13
Playoff Games with NYR: 0

Ryane Clowe - left wing

NYR Debut: April 3, 2013 (vs. Pittsburgh Penguins, won 6–1)
Regular Season Games with NYR: 12
Playoff Games with NYR: 2

Krzysztof Oliwa - left wing

NYR Debut: October 9, 2002 (at Carolina Hurricanes, won 4–1)
Regular Season Games with NYR: 9
Playoff Games with NYR: 0

Chad Johnson - goaltender

NYR Debut: December 9, 2009 (vs. Philadelphia Flyers, lost 6–0)
Regular Season Games with NYR: 6
Playoff Games with NYR: 0

Photo courtesy of Mark Rosenman.

One of the many backups to the King.

Rudy Poeschek - right wing

NYR Debut: February 11, 1988 (vs. Washington Capitals, lost 5–3)
Regular Season Games with NYR: 4
Playoff Games with NYR: 0
Also wore: #41

Barry Richter - defenseman

NYR Debut: April 5, 1996 (vs. Philadelphia Flyers, won 3–1)
Regular Season Games with NYR: 4
Playoff Games with NYR: 0

Terry Virtue - defenseman

NYR Debut: November 26, 1999 (at Florida Panthers, lost 6–2)
Regular Season Games with NYR: 1
Playoff Games with NYR: 0

#30: "THE KING"

Henrik Lundqvist

NYR Debut: October 8, 2005 (at New Jersey Devils, lost 3–2 OT)

Regular Season Games with NYR: 742

Playoff Games with NYR: 128

Henrik Lundqvist has won the most games as a goaltender in Rangers' franchise history. When it's all said and done, Lundqvist may be the greatest netminder in franchise history.

Lundqvist was the Rangers' seventh-round pick (205th overall) in the 2000 NHL Entry Draft, but he quickly proved that he should've been an earlier pick.

The Swedish-born goaltender played in his home country until 2005, when he opted to go to the NHL and play for the Rangers. A labor dispute

Photo courtesy of Mark Rosenman.

The KING.

caused the NHL owners to lockout the players. As a result, the league cancelled the entire 2004–05 season.

While NHL players were sidelined and attempted to play elsewhere, Lundqvist was shining in his native country, coming off three straight Honken Trophies, the Swedish Elite League's Vezina Trophy. He was also named the "nation's greatest player" and "most valuable player," so the Rangers were anxious to see what they had in training camp.

Veteran Kevin Weekes was vying for the starting job, but Lundqvist would be the number one. In his first season, Lundqvist won 30 games and began a streak of seven consecutive seasons (only to be interrupted by another labor dispute) where he won 30 or more games.

In his first six seasons, Lundqvist finished in the top ten in voting for the Vezina Trophy. He finally won it during the 2011–12 season, when he won a career-high 39 games with a 1.97 goals against average (GAA).

Early in his career, Lundqvist had some tough times in the playoffs. In 2009, the Rangers blew a 3–1 series lead to the Washington Capitals. Lundqvist gave up 11 goals in the final three losses, including the series-winner late in the third period of Game Seven in Washington. The Rangers and Lundqvist lost a five-game series to the Capitals in 2011, but things began the change the following season.

Lundqvist was stellar in beating the Ottawa Senators, 2–1, in Game Seven of the Eastern Conference Quarterfinal. All three goals were scored by midway in the second period, so Lundqvist had to make some incredible stops over the course of the final 30 minutes to preserve the lead.

For a third time in four seasons, the Rangers played the Capitals and the series once again came down to a seventh and deciding game. This time the game was at Madison Square Garden, and Lundqvist was brilliant in finally beating Washington, 2–1.

The teams played again in the 2013 playoffs. The Rangers trailed the series three games to two, but Lundqvist pitched a shutout in a 1–0 win in the Game Six victory at the Garden, and duplicated the feat in Game Seven with a 5–0 win in D.C.

Lundqvist was becoming known for his success in Game Sevens, and it continued in the 2014 playoffs as the Rangers eliminated the Philadelphia Flyers in the opening round.

The Rangers made franchise history in the next round against Pittsburgh. The Penguins took a three-games-to-one lead after a 4–2 win in Game Four.

The Rangers had never rebounded from that kind of deficit before, but they rode the back of their goaltender to pull off an unprecedented achievement. Lundqvist gave up three goals in the final three games and made 35 of 36 saves in a 2–1 win in Game Seven, as the Rangers pulled off an incredible comeback to stun the Penguins.

The Rangers went on to defeat the Montreal Canadiens in six games in the Eastern Conference Final. Lundqvist blanked the Canadiens in a memorable 1–0, series-clinching win at the Garden. The Rangers came up short against the Los Angeles Kings in the Final, but Lundqvist did all he could and was still brilliant in defeat.

The playoff magic continued in 2015, when the Rangers again rallied from a 3–1 series deficit. This time, the Capitals were victimized by the Rangers' resilience as Lundqvist came up big again in a seventh game. The Rangers beat Washington, 2–1, in overtime on Derek Stepan's game-winning goal, but it was Lundqvist who added to his legacy with another seventh game victory.

In March 2014, Lundqvist beat the Ottawa Senators and won his 302nd game to pass Mike Richter as the winningest goaltender in Rangers' franchise history. In February 2017, Lundqvist became the fastest goaltender in NHL history to reach 400 wins.

John Davidson

NYR Debut: October 10, 1975 (at Atlanta Flames, won 2–1)
Regular Season Games with NYR: 222
Playoff Games with NYR: 30
Also wore: #0 and #35

Many Ranger fans know John Davidson as a broadcaster, but he was also a solid goaltender who led one of the great upsets in franchise history.

Davidson was acquired by the Rangers in a multi-player deal with the St. Louis Blues in 1975. He was the fifth overall pick of the Blues in the 1973 NHL Amateur Draft.

Davidson made 56 starts in the 1975–76 season, his first in New York. For the bulk of his eight seasons with the Rangers, Davidson was the starting goaltender, though he wasn't a workhorse as he shared the duties with goalies Doug Soetaert, Wayne Thomas, and Steve Baker.

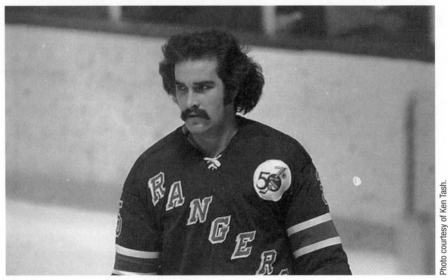

Photo courtesy of Ken Tash.

JD led magical run to Stanley Cup Finals.

Davidson's shining moment came in the 1979 Stanley Cup Playoffs.

The Rangers beat the Los Angeles Kings and the Philadelphia Flyers rather easily in the first two rounds, and then faced their up-and-coming cross-town rival, the heavily favored New York Islanders, in the Stanley Cup Semifinal.

The Rangers led the series three games to two, with Game Six scheduled for Madison Square Garden.

Davidson was on top of his game in Game Six as he stopped 21 of 22 Islanders' shots to preserve a 2–1 win and one of the more unlikely upsets in Stanley Cup Playoff history. When the buzzer sounded, an iconic picture of Davidson emerged with both of his arms outstretched toward the sky, signifying the momentous victory as the Rangers advanced to the Final against the eventual champion Montreal Canadiens.

As he got older, Davidson's playing time lessened each season. In 1981–82, the Rangers were grooming a young, eighteen-year-old goaltender named John Vanbiesbrouck, and Davidson knew his career was nearing an end. He was also dealing with a back issue that afflicted him in his later years and eventually forced his retirement in 1983.

After he retired, Davidson went on to a successful career as a broadcaster on Ranger telecasts for twenty years.

Gilles Villemure

NYR Debut: November 20, 1963 (vs. Boston Bruins, 1–1 tie)

Regular Season Games with NYR: 184

Playoff Games with NYR: 13

Also wore: #1

Goaltender Gilles Villemure spent a lot of time in the Rangers' minor league system before finally getting a chance to stick with the big club in the 1970–71 season.

Villemure signed with the Rangers in 1962 and played a total of 499 minor league games with the Rangers. Going into the 1970–71 season, the Rangers decided to have a second goaltender share the duties and lessen the load on Ed Giacomin.

Villemure won 22 games while Giacomin won 27. The move paid off, as the duo won the Vezina Trophy.

Villemure spent his off seasons as a harness racing driver/trainer. When he joined the Rangers, Villemure was able to get work as a driver at Roosevelt Raceway.

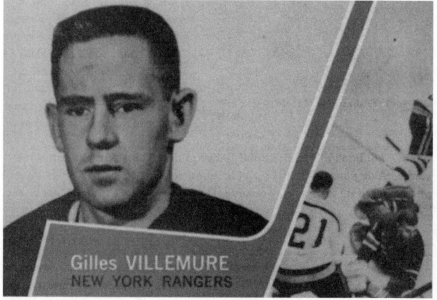

Gilles VILLEMURE
NEW YORK RANGERS

Hockey card from the public domain.

Spent his off-seasons as a driver at Roosevelt Raceway.

In the 1974–75 season, the Quebec native won 22 games, but was already thirty-four years old. After the season, in October 1975, the Rangers traded Villemure to the Chicago Black Hawks.

Larry Melnyk

NYR Debut: December 21, 1985 (at New York Islanders, won 5–4)
Regular Season Games with NYR: 133
Playoff Games with NYR: 22

Larry Melnyk was a stay-at-home defenseman who came to the Rangers in a trade with the Edmonton Oilers in December 1985 for center Mike Rogers.

Melnyk was a solid back liner and adept at moving the puck out of his own end.

The native of Saskatchewan played parts of three seasons with the Rangers before being traded to Vancouver for defenseman Michel Petit.

Glenn Healy

NYR Debut: October 7, 1993 (vs. Tampa Bay Lightning, won 5–4)
Regular Season Games with NYR: 113
Playoff Games with NYR: 7

Glenn Healy was one of the best back-up goaltenders that the Rangers ever had.

Healy was a veteran goaltender who joined the Rangers after spending seven years with the Los Angeles Kings and New York Islanders.

Healy was claimed by Anaheim in the 1993 NHL Expansion Draft, and then claimed by Tampa Bay in phase two of the Draft. Healy never played a minute for Tampa Bay, as the Lightning traded him to the Rangers in June 1993.

Healy, who had an ebullient personality, backed up starting goaltender Mike Richter and played 29 games in his first season with the Rangers. Healy's timing couldn't have been better as he joined the Rangers in time for the 1994 Stanley Cup Championship.

In the 1995–96 season, Healy played 44 games as Richter suffered through an injury-plagued season.

Healy played one more season with the Rangers before finishing out his contract and becoming a free agent.

Mike Dunham

NYR Debut: December 16, 2002 (vs. San Jose Sharks, won 2–1)
Regular Season Games with NYR: 100
Playoff Games with NYR: 0

American-born goaltender Mike Dunham made his NHL debut with the New Jersey Devils in 1996. After two seasons in New Jersey and five more in Nashville, Dunham was traded to the Rangers in December 2002.

Dunham replaced the injured Mike Richter, who was suffering from post-concussion symptoms, and played 44 games in the 2002–03 season. His playing time increased to 52 games in the 2003–04 season and he posted a record of 16–30. Following the season, Dunham became a free agent.

Chris Nilan

NYR Debut: January 28, 1988 (at Philadelphia Flyers, won 5–2)
Regular Season Games with NYR: 85
Playoff Games with NYR: 8

Right winger Chris Nilan was the epitome of an NHL enforcer, but he could also play some hockey.

In January 1988, the Rangers were looking to add an enforcer to the roster so they acquired Nilan from the Montreal Canadiens. The 6-foot energetic winger would play well at Madison Square Garden with the die-hards. He was known as "Knuckles," as he would never hesitate to drop the gloves and get into an altercation with an opponent.

Grant Ledyard

NYR Debut: January 6, 1985 (vs. New Jersey Devils, won 5–4 OT)
Regular Season Games with NYR: 69
Playoff Games with NYR: 3

Defenseman Grant Ledyard signed with the Rangers in 1982, making his debut in 1984. The native of Winnipeg played parts of two seasons with the Rangers before being traded to the Los Angeles Kings in December 1985. Ledyard went on to play 18 seasons in the NHL.

Kirk McLean

NYR Debut: October 5, 1999 (vs. Ottawa Senators, lost 2–1)
Regular Season Games with NYR: 45
Playoff Games with NYR: 0

The saying goes that, if you can't beat 'em, join 'em.

Kirk McLean was the goaltender for the Vancouver Canucks when they lost the 1994 Stanley Cup Final to the Rangers. In July 1999, McLean signed a free agent contract with the Rangers.

McLean backed up Mike Richter for two seasons, the final two of his NHL career, retiring after the 2000–01 season.

Cesare Maniago

NYR Debut: January 8, 1966 (vs. Chicago Black Hawks, won 6–4)
Regular Season Games with NYR: 34
Playoff Games with NYR: 0

Goaltender Cesare Maniago played with five NHL teams in his career. The Rangers were his second stop in June 1965, when he was acquired from Montreal as part of a multi-player trade.

Maniago played parts of two seasons with the Rangers. After the 1966–67 season, he was claimed by the Minnesota North Stars in the NHL Expansion Draft.

Don Simmons

NYR Debut: November 10, 1965 (vs. Boston Bruins, tie 2–2)
Regular Season Games with NYR: 22
Playoff Games with NYR: 0

Goaltender Don Simmons spent a significant part of his Ranger tenure in their minor-league system. He was a first-team WHL All-Star in 1967, as he led the league with 38 wins. Simmons played in parts of three seasons for the Rangers. He retired after the 1968–69 season.

Terry Sawchuk

NYR Debut: October 26, 1969 (vs. Montreal Canadiens, lost 8–3)

Regular Season Games with NYR: 8

Playoff Games with NYR: 3

Hall of Fame goaltender Terry Sawchuk finished his fabulous 21-year NHL career with the Rangers. Unfortunately, his life was finished as well.

Sawchuk was acquired in a trade with Detroit in June 1969. Following the 1969–70 season, Sawchuk and teammate Ron Stewart got into a scuffle after both had been drinking. The Hall of Famer died from internal injuries suffered in the altercation.

#31: GOALIES PATROL

Steve Weeks

NYR Debut: April 2, 1981 (at New York Islanders, first round playoffs, won 10–3)
Regular Season Games with NYR: 94
Playoff Games with NYR: 5

Goaltender Steve Weeks, who was the Rangers' eleventh-round selection in the 1978 NHL Amateur Draft, was projected to be a backup goalie.

After completing his collegiate career at Northern Michigan, the Ontario native turned pro and joined the Rangers' New Haven affiliate in the AHL. Weeks wasn't exactly spectacular (14–17, 4.13 GAA) in the minors, but made his debut in the postseason when he relieved starter Steve Baker in Game Three of the 1981 "preliminary round" against the Los Angeles Kings.

Head coach Herb Brooks named him the starting goaltender for the 1981–82 season and Weeks responded with a 23–16—9 mark and a 3.77 GAA, as the Rangers made the playoffs. In the Patrick Division Final against the defending Stanley Cup Champion New York Islanders, Weeks struggled as he gave up 11 goals in the first two games, including a 7–2 rout in Game Two. The twenty-three-year-old was benched for the remainder of the series and his playing time decreased in the 1982–83 season.

In September 1984, the Rangers traded Weeks to the Hartford Whalers.

Dan Blackburn

NYR Debut: October 10, 2001 (vs. Washington Capitals, lost 5–2)
Regular Season Games with NYR: 63
Playoff Games with NYR: 0

Dan Blackburn was a promising goaltender who was the Rangers' first-round choice and the 10th overall pick in the 2001 NHL Entry Draft. Unfortunately, Blackburn was victimized by bad luck and his career was curtailed by a serious shoulder injury.

Blackburn made his mark by dominating the WHL for two straight seasons. After winning the WHL Playoff MVP in 1999–2000, Blackburn led the league with 33 wins and was the "Goaltender of the Year" in 2000–01.

The eighteen-year-old made the Rangers after an outstanding training camp and preseason, playing in 31 games and winning 12. When he made his debut, Blackburn was the fourth-youngest goalie to appear in an NHL game.

Blackburn played the entire 2002–03 season with the Rangers, but suffered nerve damage in his shoulder before the start of the 2003 training camp and was never the same.

Blackburn underwent exploratory surgery in 2004, but the injury never healed. Blackburn retired in 2005 at the age of twenty-two.

Alex Frolov

NYR Debut: October 9, 2010 (at Buffalo Sabres, won 6–3)
Regular Season Games with NYR: 43
Playoff Games with NYR: 0

Russian-born left winger Alex Frolov was the 20th overall selection of the Los Angeles Kings in the 2001 NHL Entry Draft. He is also the only non-goaltender to wear #31 as a member of the Rangers.

Frolov played seven years with the Kings before signing with the Rangers as a free agent in 2010. He played in 43 games and scored seven goals before returning to Russia to play in the KHL in January 2011.

The following goaltenders played less than 15 games with NYR:

Guy Hebert

NYR Debut: March 9, 2001 (at Washington Capitals, lost 5–3)
Regular Season Games with NYR: 13
Playoff Games with NYR: 0

Rob Zamuner

NYR Debut: January 16, 1992 (vs. Calgary Flames, won 6–4)
Regular Season Games with NYR: 9
Playoff Games with NYR: 0

Recorded an assist in his first NHL game.

Peter McDuffe

NYR Debut: December 10, 1972 (vs. New York Islanders, won 4–1)

Regular Season Games with NYR: 7

Playoff Games with NYR: 0

Jason Muzzatti

NYR Debut: October 9, 1997 (at Calgary Flames, 1–1 OT tie)

Regular Season Games with NYR: 6

Playoff Games with NYR: 0

Hardy Astrom

NYR Debut: February 25, 1978 (at Montreal Canadiens, won 6–3)

Regular Season Games with NYR: 4

Playoff Games with NYR: 0

Corey Hirsch

NYR Debut: January 19, 1993 (at Detroit Red Wings, 2–2 OT tie)

Regular Season Games with NYR: 4

Playoff Games with NYR: 0

Vitali Yeremeyev

NYR Debut: December 27, 2000 (at Carolina Hurricanes, lost 4–3)

Regular Season Games with NYR: 4

Playoff Games with NYR: 0

Alex Auld

NYR Debut: March 6, 2010 (at Washington Capitals, lost 2–0)

Regular Season Games with NYR: 3

Playoff Games with NYR: 0

Curt Ridley

NYR Debut: December 19, 1974 (at Boston Bruins, lost 11–3)

Regular Season Games with NYR: 2

Playoff Games with NYR: 0

Also wore: #35

Jean-Franois Labbe

NYR Debut: April 5, 2000 (vs. Montreal Canadiens, lost 3–0)

Regular Season Games with NYR: 1

Playoff Games with NYR: 0

#32: THE MOST SIGNIFICANT GOAL IN RANGER HISTORY

Stephane Matteau

NYR Debut: March 22, 1994 (at Calgary Flames, 4–4 OT tie)

Regular Season Games with NYR: 85

Playoff Games with NYR: 32

It was becoming clear during the 1993–94 season that the Rangers had a real chance to end their 54-year drought without a Stanley Cup Championship.

Head coach Mike Keenan was not totally convinced, however, and felt the team needed a little tweak to be ready for the grind of the postseason. On March 21, 1994, the Rangers acquired wingers Brian Noonan and Stephane Matteau from the Chicago Blackhawks in exchange for promising, young right winger Tony Amonte and a minor leaguer.

Matteau was a twenty-five-year-old checking winger who also showed he could score some goals. Little did anyone know that this unassuming 6-foot-4, 220-pounder would go on to score the most significant goal in Rangers' franchise history.

STEPHANE MATTEAU
NEW YORK RANGERS ▼

Matteau! Matteau! Matteau!

Topps trading Cards used courtesy of The Topps Company Inc.

Matteau finished the regular season with four goals and three assists in 12 games for the Rangers, but his time would come in the postseason. In his very first game with the team, Matteau gave a portent of things to come when he scored the tying goal with 14 seconds left in the third period against the Calgary Flames.

The Rangers cruised through the first two rounds of the playoffs and were tied at one game apiece against the New Jersey Devils in the Eastern Conference Final. In Game Three, Matteau scored at 6:13 of double overtime to give the Rangers a 3–2 win and a 2–1 series lead. But for Matteau, the best was yet to come.

The series went to Game Seven at Madison Square Garden. With 7.7 seconds remaining in the third period, New Jersey scored the tying goal, sending the game to overtime. Matteau had not logged much ice time during the game so, when it went to a second overtime session, he was one of the fresher players on the ice.

The tension at the Garden was immeasurable with what was at stake.

A little over four minutes into the second overtime, the Rangers were on the attack in the offensive zone. Matteau played the puck on the left wing and swooped in around the net where he was able to stuff the puck past the left leg of Devils goaltender Martin Brodeur. Rangers' radio announcer Howie Rose's famous call of "Matteau! Matteau! Matteau!" was born and the Garden went absolutely ballistic.

Matteau had one assist in the Final, but his legacy was already written when the Rangers went on capture their first Stanley Cup Championship in 54 years.

Matteau played parts of three seasons with the Rangers. Nineteen months after he scored his momentous goal, he was traded to the St. Louis Blues for right winger Ian Laperriere.

Kevin Miller

NYR Debut: December 23, 1988 (at Washington Capitals, 2–2 OT tie)
Regular Season Games with NYR: 103
Playoff Games with NYR: 1
Also wore: #26

Michigan-born center Kevin Miller was the Rangers' tenth-round pick in the 1984 NHL Entry Draft. Kevin is one of three brothers (Kip and Kelly, who also played for the Rangers) to play in the NHL.

Miller was projected to be a steady two-way forward in the NHL. After completing four collegiate years at Michigan State, he joined the Rangers' Denver affiliate in the IHL. He split the 1988–89 season between Denver and the big club, playing 24 games in New York.

Miller spent parts of three seasons with the Rangers. He had one full season in 1990–91, where he played 63 games and scored 17 goals. After that season, Miller was traded to the Detroit Red Wings in March 1991.

Mike Eastwood

NYR Debut: February 8, 1997 (at New York Islanders, won 5–2)
Regular Season Games with NYR: 75
Playoff Games with NYR: 15

During a 13-year NHL career, center Mike Eastwood made a "pit stop" with the Rangers.

Eastwood was acquired in a trade with the Phoenix Coyotes in February 1997, and played parts of two seasons. He scored a total of six goals in 75 career games in New York.

In March 1998, Eastwood was traded to the St. Louis Blues for center Harry York.

Antti Raanta

> **NYR Debut:** October 19, 2015 (vs. San Jose Sharks, won 4–0)
> **Regular Season Games with NYR:** 55
> **Playoff Games with NYR:** 3

Finnish-born goaltender Antii Raanta was a solid backup to Henrik Lundqvist for two seasons.

Days after winning the 2015 Stanley Cup with the Chicago Blackhawks, Raanta was traded to the Rangers. In his very first game with the Blueshirts, Raanta stopped all 22 shots he faced in blanking the San Jose Sharks at Madison Square Garden.

Raanta was more than a capable backup, as was demonstrated when he filled in for an injured Lundqvist in the latter part of the 2015–16 season. Lundqvist was dealing with neck spasms, and it showed in the playoffs against Pittsburgh. Raanta played in three games of the five-game series loss.

Early in the 2016–17 season, Raanta temporarily took over the starting job for a struggling Lundqvist. In December, he had a stretch of three shutouts in six days. Two days after Raanta blanked his old team, the Blackhawks in Chicago, he made it back-to-back shutouts when he shut down the New Jersey Devils. Raanta then made it three of four games where he didn't allow a goal when he shut out Dallas four days later.

Raanta did not play in the 2017 playoffs. In June 2017, he was traded, along with center Derek Stepan, to the Arizona Coyotes for their first-round pick and young defenseman Anthony DeAngelo.

Sergio Momesso

> **NYR Debut:** March 1, 1996 (vs. Buffalo Sabres, 3–3 OT tie)
> **Regular Season Games with NYR:** 28
> **Playoff Games with NYR:** 11

Sergio Momesso was a member of the Vancouver Canucks' team that lost to the Rangers in the 1994 Stanley Cup Final, so the team got a first-hand look at what they were getting when the left winger was acquired in a trade with Toronto in February 1996.

The 6-foot-3 winger knew how to use his body and also how to use his stick to score goals.

He played 28 games in parts of two seasons with the Rangers. In November 1996, the Rangers sent Momesso to the St. Louis Blues to re-acquire right winger Brian Noonan.

Mike Hurlbut

NYR Debut: November 19, 1992 (at Philadelphia Flyers, lost 7–3)
Regular Season Games with NYR: 23
Playoff Games with NYR: 0

In the 1988 NHL Supplemental Draft, the Rangers had the fifth overall selection and used it to draft local kid, Mike Hurlbut.

The Massena-born defenseman spent most of his Rangers' tenure with their minor league affiliates, but he got into 23 games in the 1992–93 season. In September 1993, Hurlbut was traded to the Quebec Nordiques for defenseman Alexander Karpovtsev.

The following played less than 20 games with NYR:

Corey Millen - center

NYR Debut: January 3, 1990 (vs. Washington Capitals, won 2–1)
Regular Season Games with NYR: 19
Playoff Games with NYR: 6
Also wore: #23

Gordie Dwyer - left wing

NYR Debut: December 16, 2002 (vs. San Jose Sharks, won 2–1 OT)
Regular Season Games with NYR: 17
Playoff Games with NYR: 0

Bob Crawford - right wing

NYR Debut: March 12, 1986 (vs. Calgary Flames, lost 3–2)

Regular Season Games with NYR: 14

Playoff Games with NYR: 7

Sean Pronger - center

NYR Debut: November 27, 1998 (at Pittsburgh Penguins, 2–2 OT tie)

Regular Season Games with NYR: 14

Playoff Games with NYR: 0

Tony Feltrin - defenseman

NYR Debut: November 29, 1985 (at Washington Capitals, won 5–2)

Regular Season Games with NYR: 10

Playoff Games with NYR: 0

Dale Weise - right wing

NYR Debut: December 18, 2010 (at Philadelphia Flyers, lost 4–1)

Regular Season Games with NYR: 10

Playoff Games with NYR: 0

Michael Haley - center

NYR Debut: March 5, 2013 (vs. Philadelphia Flyers, won 4–2)

Regular Season Games with NYR: 9

Playoff Games with NYR: 2

Harry York - center

NYR Debut: March 25, 1998 (vs. Ottawa Senators, lost 3–2 OT)

Regular Season Games with NYR: 7

Playoff Games with NYR: 0

Dave Pichette - defenseman

NYR Debut: November 7, 1987 (at Los Angeles Kings, lost 5–4)
Regular Season Games with NYR: 6
Playoff Games with NYR: 0

Dan Clark - defenseman

NYR Debut: December 20, 1978 (vs. Buffalo Sabres, won 6–3)
Regular Season Games with NYR: 4
Playoff Games with NYR: 0

Johan Holmqvist - goaltender

NYR Debut: October 27, 2000 (vs. Pittsburgh Penguins, lost 4–1)
Regular Season Games with NYR: 4
Playoff Games with NYR: 0

Stephane Brochu - defenseman

NYR Debut: November 15, 1988 (at Philadelphia Flyers, 3–3 OT tie)
Regular Season Games with NYR: 1
Playoff Games with NYR: 0

#33: GOALIE CAM

Cam Talbot

NYR Debut: October 24, 2013 (at Philadelphia Flyers, lost 2–1)

Regular Season Games with NYR: 57

Playoff Games with NYR: 2

With his 6-foot-3 frame, goaltender Cam Talbot could cover much of the net without even having to move.

Talbot caught the eye of some scouts when he played collegiately for the University of Alabama at Huntsville from 2007–10. After his third season, Talbot signed with the Rangers as an undrafted free agent.

Talbot made his official debut during the 2013–14 season. In March 2011, Talbot was recalled to dress as Henrik Lundqvist's backup, but did not get into the game. Working with goaltending

Won 33 of his 57 as backup to the King.

Photo by Lisa Gansky from New York, NY, USA via Wikimedia Commons.

coach Benoit Allaire, Talbot led all first-year goaltenders with a 1.64 GAA. In November, Talbot recorded his first career shutout when he blanked the Canadiens in Montreal. It was the first shutout by a Ranger goaltender in Montreal since 1967.

When Lundqvist was struck in the throat by a puck during a game in February 2015, Talbot took over as the starting goaltender and thrived in the position.

The twenty-seven-year-old net-minder started 24 consecutive games and posted a 17–4–3 record to help the Rangers secure the President's Trophy.

Talbot played 57 games and won 33 of those in his two seasons with the Rangers. After the 2014–15 season, Talbot was traded to the Edmonton Oilers in a deal for draft picks.

Tony Amonte

NYR Debut: April 11, 1991 (vs. Washington Capitals Playoffs, Game Five, lost 5–4 OT)
Regular Season Games with NYR: 234
Playoff Games with NYR: 15
Also wore: #31

Right winger Tony Amonte was a fourth-round pick of the Rangers in the 1988 NHL Entryt Draft.

Amonte compiled an impressive collegiate career for Boston University. Two days after a heartbreaking triple-overtime loss to Northern Michigan in the 1991 NCAA Championship, Amonte signed with the Rangers.

Amonte acquitted himself very well when he made his NHL debut in the 1991 Patrick Division Semifinal against the Washington Capitals. In two games, he had two assists.

The Massachusetts-born Amonte made the team out of training camp and burst on the scene with an incredible rookie season in 1991–92, scoring 35 goals (one shy of the Rangers' rookie record) and finishing second in the voting for the Calder Trophy.

He followed up his first season with 33 goals and 43 assists for 76 points during the 1992–93 season. It appeared Amonte would be an integral part of the team that was a Stanley Cup contender in the 1993–94 season, but he had a down season (16 goals in 72 games) and the Rangers used him as bait in a key trade.

In March 1994, the Rangers traded Amonte to the Chicago Blackhawks for wingers Brian Noonan and Stephane Matteau.

Bruce Driver

NYR Debut: November 6, 1995 (vs. Calgary Flames, won 4–2)
Regular Season Games with NYR: 220
Playoff Games with NYR: 26

Defenseman Bruce Driver faced the Rangers as an opponent many times in his 12-year career with the New Jersey Devils. After winning the Stanley Cup with New Jersey in 1995, Driver signed with the Rangers as a free agent.

Driver got off to a good start in his Rangers' career. In his very first game, Driver had two assists including the primary assist on Mark Messier's 500th career goal. He scored three goals with 34 assists for 37 points in his first full season of 1995–96.

Driver's numbers began to tail off in his last two seasons with the Rangers. He was thirty-five years old during his final season of 1997–98 and still played 75 games. After the season, Driver retired from hockey.

Andre Dore

NYR Debut: March 7, 1979 (vs. Colorado Rockies, won 5–3)
Regular Season Games with NYR: 139
Playoff Games with NYR: 10
Also wore: #2 and #27

The Rangers selected 6-foot-2, 200-pound defenseman Andre Dore in the fourth round of the 1978 NHL Entry Draft with the hope of adding a physical defenseman to their blue line.

Dore was up and down between the minors and the NHL during his Ranger career, which featured two tenures. He was promoted late in the 1978–79 season, and appeared in two games. The next two seasons, Dore played a total of 17 games with the Rangers but finally got his break in the 1981–82 season when he took on more of a regular role with the team.

In January 1983, the Rangers traded Dore to the St. Louis Blues for right winger Vaclav Nedomansky and goaltender Glen Hanlon. In October 1984, the Rangers claimed Dore off waivers but, a year later, traded him to the Philadelphia Flyers as compensation for head coach Ted Sator.

Bob Froese

NYR Debut: December 23, 1986 (vs. New Jersey Devils, lost 8–5)
Regular Season Games with NYR: 98
Playoff Games with NYR: 6

Bob Froese served the Rangers as the backup goaltender to John Vanbies-brouck from 1986–90.

Froese began his career with the Philadelphia Flyers, but was traded to the Rangers in December 1986.

The highlight of Froese's Rangers career came on January 19, 1989, when he blanked the St. Louis Blues in a 5–0 win on the road. Fittingly, #33 made 33 saves in the only shutout of his Ranger tenure.

Early in the 1989–90 season, Froese suffered a shoulder injury that would limit him to 15 games and end his career. He retired after the season.

Marc Savard

NYR Debut: October 3, 1997 (at New York Islanders, 2–2 OT tie)
Regular Season Games with NYR: 98
Playoff Games with NYR: 0
Also wore: #10

Marc Savard was a promising offensive center who was selected by the Rangers in the fourth round of the 1995 NHL Entry Draft.

Savard won the Lars-Erik Sjoberg Award as the best rookie, and made the team out of training camp in 1997. He was sent back to the minors after playing 28 games, as he struggled with the NHL game.

Savard scored nine goals with 36 assists for 45 points in 70 games during the 1998–99 season. In June 1999, he was traded to the Calgary Flames.

Dave Karpa

NYR Debut: October 5, 2001 (at Carolina Hurricanes, lost 3–1)
Regular Season Games with NYR: 94
Playoff Games with NYR: 0

Dave Karpa was a physical, stay-at-home defenseman. After ten years in the league, he signed with the Rangers in 2001 as a free agent.

Karpa lasted parts of two seasons with the Rangers. His first was in 2001–02, when he played 75 games. In the 2002–03 season, Karpa spent time with the Rangers' AHL affiliate in Hartford before retiring after the season.

Gilles Gratton

NYR Debut: October 6, 1976 (vs. Minnesota North Stars, won 6–5)

Regular Season Games with NYR: 41

Playoff Games with NYR: 0

Goaltender Gilles Gratton ended his modest two-year NHL career with the Rangers in 1976–77. Gratton played three years in the WHA before joining the St. Louis Blues in 1975.

Gratton appeared in 41 games for the Rangers and posted an 11–18–7 record. He retired after the season.

The following played less than 20 games with NYR:

Mike Mottau - defenseman

NYR Debut: October 26, 2000 (at Philadelphia Flyers, lost 3–0)

Regular Season Games with NYR: 19

Playoff Games with NYR: 0

Also wore: #4

Andre Deveaux - center

NYR Debut: October 31, 2011 (vs. San Jose Sharks, won 5–2)

Regular Season Games with NYR: 9

Playoff Games with NYR: 0

Jamie McLennan - goaltender

NYR Debut: March 13, 2004 (at Florida Panthers, lost 3–2 OT)

Regular Season Games with NYR: 4

Playoff Games with NYR: 0

Milan Hnilicka - goaltender

NYR Debut: October 14, 1999 (vs. Pittsburgh Penguins, lost 5–2)

Regular Season Games with NYR: 2

Playoff Games with NYR: 0

#34: THE "BEEZER"

John Vanbiesbrouck

> **NYR Debut:** December 5, 1981 (at Colorado Rockies, won 2–1)
>
> **Regular Season Games with NYR:** 449
>
> **Playoff Games with NYR:** 38

With their fourth-round pick in the 1981 NHL Entry Draft, the Rangers took an eighteen-year-old goaltender from Detroit, Michigan, named John Vanbiesbrouck.

Vanbiesbrouck, aka the "Beezer," played four games with the Rangers in his first two seasons but became the starting goaltender for the 1984–85 season. Vanbiesbrouck was known for being very adept with the stick, as evidenced by his franchise record for career assists (25) by a Ranger goaltender.

In 1985–86, Beezer had a breakout season with a league-leading 31 victories, as he became the fourth goaltender in Rangers' franchise history to win the Vezina Trophy. In the 1986 Stanley Cup Playoffs,

Beezer was fourth Blueshirt to win Vezina Trophy.

Vanbiesbrouck was up and down but the Rangers did advance to the Stanley Cup Semifinal.

The Detroit native was never able to duplicate the success of the 1985–86 season in New York. Vanbiesbrouck won 20 or more games four more times and finished top ten in the voting for the Vezina three times.

Vanbiesbrouck was the starting goalie for the Rangers until Mike Richter came on the scene in the 1989–90 season. (Richter made his NHL debut in the 1989 playoffs; see Chapter Thirty-Five.) The writing was on the wall, as the plan was to eventually have Richter take over the starting job.

In June 1993, the Rangers traded Vanbiesbrouck to the Vancouver Canucks but he was left unprotected in the expansion draft and was claimed by the Florida Panthers.

Jason Strudwick

NYR Debut: October 5, 2005 (at Philadelphia Flyers, won 5–3)
Regular Season Games with NYR: 124
Playoff Games with NYR: 5

Defenseman Jason Strudwick was signed by the Rangers twice as a free agent.

In 2005, Strudwick was going into this ninth NHL season when he signed with the Rangers for the first time. The 6-foot-4 defenseman was solid in the zone and was an adept shot blocker.

Strudwick played 65 games in his first season and scored three goals with four assists. After the season, he signed on to play in Switzerland but returned to the Rangers as a free agent in March 2007.

Strudwick played parts of two more seasons in New York before playing out his contract after the 2007–08 season.

Aaron Voros

NYR Debut: October 4, 2008 (at Tampa Bay Lightning, won 2–1)
Regular Season Games with NYR: 95
Playoff Games with NYR: 4

At 6-foot-4, left winger Aaron Voros was signed by the Rangers to add a physical presence.

Voros' first season with the Rangers was 2008–09, when he played 54 games and accumulated 122 penalty minutes. He also scored eight goals with eight assists.

In his second and final season with the Rangers, Voros was second on the team with 89 penalty minutes. In July 2010, he was traded to Anaheim for defenseman Steve Eminger.

Bryan Berard

NYR Debut: October 5, 2001 (at Carolina Hurricanes, lost 3–1)
Regular Season Games with NYR: 82
Playoff Games with NYR: 0

Rhode Island native Bryan Berard was attempting a comeback when he signed with the Rangers for the 2001–02 season. Berard had suffered a serious eye injury when he was clipped by a high stick during a game in March 2000. This would have been a career-ending injury for most, but Berard was determined to return to the NHL.

In October 2001, the Rangers took a chance on the veteran defenseman and signed him to a one year, free agent contract. Berard played one full season with the Rangers and played out his contract to sign with the Boston Bruins.

Peter Popovic

NYR Debut: October 9, 1998 (vs. Philadelphia Flyers, lost 1–0)
Regular Season Games with NYR: 68
Playoff Games with NYR: 0

Peter Popovic was a huge defenseman who played one season with the Rangers. At 6-foot-6 and 243 pounds, Popovic used his enormous size and long reach to clear his own crease.

In September 1999, Popovic was traded to the Pittsburgh Penguins for defenseman Kevin Hatcher.

John Mitchell

NYR Debut: November 25, 2011 (at Washington Capitals, won 6–3)
Regular Season Games with NYR: 63
Playoff Games with NYR: 18

The Rangers acquired center John Mitchell from Toronto for a draft pick in February 2011. Mitchell spent some time with the Rangers' Connecticut Whale AHL affiliate before joining the team for the 2011–12 season.

The Ontario native played one season with the Rangers, scoring five goals in the regular season but did not dent the score sheet in 18 postseason games.

Vaclav Nedomansky

NYR Debut: October 6, 1982 (vs. Washington Capitals, lost 5–4)
Regular Season Games with NYR: 35
Playoff Games with NYR: 0

By the time right winger Vaclav Nedomansky joined the Rangers in 1982, he was already thirty-eight years old.

Czech Republic-born Nedomansky did not come to North America until he defected in 1974. He played four years in the WHA and then signed with the Detroit Red Wings.

The Rangers acquired Nedomansky and goalie Glen Hanlon from St. Louis for defenseman Andre Dore.

The following played less than ten games with NYR:

Jason LaBarbera - goaltender

NYR Debut: October 14, 2000 (at Pittsburgh Penguins, lost 8–6)
Regular Season Games with NYR: 5
Playoff Games with NYR: 0

Jim Mayer - right wing

NYR Debut: February 27, 1980 (vs. Los Angeles Kings, won 5–4)
Regular Season Games with NYR: 4
Playoff Games with NYR: 0

Jamie Ram - goaltender

NYR Debut: February 3, 1996 (at Colorado Avalanche, lost 7–1)
Regular Season Games with NYR: 1
Playoff Games with NYR: 0

#35: AMERICA'S CUP

Mike Richter

NYR Debut: April 9, 1989 (vs. Pittsburgh Penguins, playoffs, lost 4–3)

Regular Season Games with NYR: 666

Playoff Games with NYR: 76

Two weeks after he graduated high school, the Rangers chose American-born goaltender Mike Richter with their second-round pick in the 1985 NHL Entry Draft. It turned into one of the best picks in franchise history.

Richter is one of four goaltenders in franchise history to win a Stanley Cup, and his #35 is one of seven retired (for eight players) by the team.

Before joining the Rangers, Richter played with the University of Wisconsin and for the United States. He was the starting goaltender for team USA in the 1989 Winter Olympics in Calgary.

Richter made his NHL debut amidst controversy in the 1989 Patrick Division Semi-

His stop of Pavel Bure's penalty shot may be biggest save in Ranger history.

final against the Pittsburgh Penguins. After losing the first three games, general manager and acting head coach Phil Esposito decided to start Richter in goal over veterans John Vanbiesbrouck and Bob Froese. It was a daring move by Esposito, who fired head coach Michel Bergeron with two games remaining in the regular season, but it unfortunately backfired.

Richter's inexperience came to the forefront as he gave up three goals in the first 11 minutes of the game. He was able to settle down, but still gave up the game winner as the Rangers lost 4–3 in a four-game sweep. After the loss, Esposito was fired and Neil Smith was named to replace him.

In the 1990–91 season, Richter began sharing time with Vanbiesbrouck as the Rangers began grooming him for the starting job. He played 45 games and had 21 wins, finishing third in the vote for the Vezina Trophy as the top goaltender in the league.

After the 1992–93 season, the Rangers traded Vanbiesbrouck, making Richter the number one and he thrived in the role. In 1993–94, Richter won a franchise-record 42 games as the Rangers captured the President's Trophy, but he saved his best for the postseason. Richter was named an All-Star, with the game being held at Madison Square Garden. Richter earned the MVP award in a game that was won by the Eastern Conference, 9–8.

Richter won 16 games in winning the Cup with a number of highlights along the way. He shut out the New York Islanders in the first two games to key a four-game sweep. Richter had another shutout in the next series against Washington and again in Game Two of the Eastern Conference Semifinal against the New Jersey Devils.

In Game Six, Richter "stood on his head" and kept the Rangers in the game as he kept the deficit at two goals so Mark Messier could complete his historic hat trick and send the series to a seventh game.

In that do-or-die game, Richter was brilliant as he nearly shut out New Jersey again, but the Devils tied the game with 7.7 seconds left in the third period. The extra time didn't seem to faze the Ranger goaltender, as he made some brilliant stops in a little over 24 minutes of overtime.

In Game Three of the Final against Vancouver, Richter made one of the great saves in franchise history. The native of Abington, Pennsylvania, stopped Canucks' star winger Pavel Bure on a penalty shot. Many observers pointed to the save as the turning point in the series.

Richter went on to play nine more seasons with the Rangers. His last was in 2002–03, as multiple concussions forced him to retire. When Richter hung up his skates, he had 301 wins which, at the time, was the most in franchise history. (It was later broken by Henrik Lundqvist.)

In February 2004, he became the third player in Ranger history to have his number hoisted to the rafters at the Garden.

Steve Baker

NYR Debut: November 28, 1979 (vs. Minnesota North Stars, 4–4 tie)
Regular Season Games with NYR: 57
Playoff Games with NYR: 14

Steve Baker's Rangers career started with a bang but fizzled in the end.

Baker debuted in the 1979–80 season and won nine of his first ten games. The Boston native's playing time diminished from 1980–83, as he split time

Won 9 of his first 10 games as Ranger.

in the minors. After playing three games in the 1982–83 season, Baker finished his playing career in the minors.

Ron Scott

NYR Debut: February 2, 1984 (at Calgary Flames, lost 8–1)

Regular Season Games with NYR: 16

Playoff Games with NYR: 0

Also wore: #31

Ron Scott spent parts of four seasons with the Rangers and totaled three wins. After the 1987–88 season, he played out his contract to become a free agent.

#36: "ZUCC"

Mats Zuccarello

NYR Debut: December 23, 2010 (vs. Tampa Bay Lightning, lost 4–3 SO)
Regular Season Games with NYR: 383
Playoff Games with NYR: 60

Mats Zuccarello is one of the most popular players in franchise history. The Norwegian-born right winger was signed as an undrafted free agent in 2010.

The 5-foot-7 Zuccarello has won over the Ranger fans with his energetic, in-your-face style of hockey. When Zuccarello scores a goal or gets an assist, the crowd at Madison Square Garden will chant a shortened version of his name, as "Zucc" can be heard resonating throughout the arena.

Zuccarello was a star in Norway who played sparingly in his first two NHL seasons. When the NHL locked out the players in September 2012, Zuccarello signed to play in the KHL. He returned to the Rangers in March 2013 to finish out the season.

Photo by Lillehammer 2016 Youth Olympic Games from Norway via Wikimedia Commons.

ZUCCC

It was no coincidence that Zuccarello's breakout season in 2013–14 was the year the Rangers made it all the way to the Stanley Cup Final.

Zuccarello scored 19 goals with 40 assists for 59 points, but he took his game to another level in the postseason. In 25 playoff games, Zuccarello scored five goals with eight assists for 13 points.

In Game One of the Eastern Conference Final against the Montreal Canadiens, Zuccarello had a goal and two assists in a 7–2 win. He then made history when he became the first Norwegian-born player to reach the Stanley Cup Final. In the double-overtime loss in Game Two against the Los Angeles Kings, Zuccarello had a goal and an assist.

In the 2015–16 season, Zuccarello set career highs with 26 goals and 61 points. On October 30, 2015, Zucc was a one-man gang as he scored all three goals and his first career hat trick in beating the Toronto Maple Leafs at the Garden, 3–1.

Zuccarello continued to be a consistent postseason performer in 2017. In the series-clinching Game Six of the first-round series against Montreal, Zuccarello scored two goals—including the game winner—in a 3–1 triumph.

In seven seasons with the Rangers, Zuccarello has scored 86 goals and 176 assists for 262 points.

Glenn Anderson

NYR Debut: March 22, 1994 (at Calgary Flames, 4–4 OT tie)
Regular Season Games with NYR: 12
Playoff Games with NYR: 23

When the Rangers acquired right winger Glenn Anderson from the Toronto Maple Leafs in March 1994, he was considered one of the final pieces that the team needed to make a run at the Stanley Cup.

Anderson was acquired at the 1994 trade deadline in exchange for high-scoring and popular right winger Mike Gartner. The Hall of Famer had already won five Cups with Edmonton, and had scored the game-winning goal in overtime four times in his playoff career. Head coach Mike Keenan felt Anderson was a better fit than Gartner, and Anderson wasted no time in making an impression with his new team as he scored two goals in his first game with the Rangers.

Anderson's addition paid dividends in the 1994 Eastern Conference Final against the New Jersey Devils, when he scored his first Ranger playoff goal in the series-evening 4–0 win in Game Two.

In the Final against the Vancouver Canucks, the Rangers once again dropped the first game. In Game Two, Anderson scored the game-winning goal in a 3–1 win to even the series at a game apiece. The British Columbia native scored a second consecutive game-winning goal in a 5–1 win in Game Three.

The Rangers went on to capture the Cup in seven games. After the season, Anderson played out his contract and became an unrestricted free agent.

Matthew Barnaby

> **NYR Debut:** December 15, 2001 (vs. Buffalo Sabres, won 4–2)
> **Regular Season Games with NYR:** 196
> **Playoff Games with NYR:** 0

Matthew Barnaby was a well-traveled NHL player when the Rangers acquired him in a trade with the Tampa Bay Lightning in December 2001.

Barnaby did not score a point in 29 games with the Lightning, but contributed 21 points in 48 games after joining the Rangers.

Barnaby went on to play two more seasons with the Rangers. He won the "Steven McDonald Extra Effort Award," as voted by the fans, in 2003. Toward the end of the 2003–04 season, Barnaby was traded to the Colorado Avalanche.

Rumun Ndur

> **NYR Debut:** December 23, 1998 (vs. Carolina Hurricanes, won 1–0)
> **Regular Season Games with NYR:** 31
> **Playoff Games with NYR:** 0

Defenseman Rumun Ndur was born in Nigeria, but moved to Ontario. He was a third-round pick of the Buffalo Sabres in 1994.

The Rangers acquired the 6-foot-2 Ndur on waivers from Buffalo in December 1998. He scored his only Ranger goal in a 1–1 tie against Washington at Madison Square Garden in March 1999.

The following played less than ten games with NYR:

Todd Charlesworth - defenseman

> **NYR Debut:** March 17, 1990 (at New York Islanders, lost 6–3)
> **Regular Season Games with NYR:** 7
> **Playoff Games with NYR:** 0

Benn Ferriero - center

NYR Debut: January 26, 2013 (vs. Toronto Maple Leafs, won 5–2)
Regular Season Games with NYR: 4
Playoff Games with NYR: 0

Pierre Sevigny - left wing

NYR Debut: October 26, 1997 (vs. Mighty Ducks of Anaheim, 3–3 OT tie)
Regular Season Games with NYR: 3
Playoff Games with NYR: 0

Jeff Nielsen - right wing

NYR Debut: February 19, 1997 (at New Jersey Devils, 2–2 OT tie)
Regular Season Games with NYR: 2
Playoff Games with NYR: 0

Alexei Vasiliev - defenseman

NYR Debut: April 5, 2000 (vs. Montreal Canadiens, lost 3–0)
Regular Season Games with NYR: 1
Playoff Games with NYR: 0

David Wilke - defenseman

NYR Debut: October 14, 2000 (at Pittsburgh Penguins, lost 8–6)
Regular Season Games with NYR: 1
Playoff Games with NYR: 0

#37–58: ROLE PLAYERS

#37

Paul Broten

NYR Debut: December 17, 1989 (vs. Montreal Canadiens, lost 2–0)

Regular Season Games with NYR: 194

Playoff Games with NYR: 24

The Rangers selected American-born right winger Paul Broten in the fourth round of the 1984 NHL Entry Draft. Broten comes from a hockey family, as his brothers Neil and Aaron also played in the NHL.

Broten's best season with the Rangers was 1991–92, when he scored 13 goals with 15 assists for 28 points. In October 1993, Broten was placed on waivers and claimed by the Dallas Stars.

Mikael Samuelsson

NYR Debut: November 6, 2001 (vs. Minnesota Wild, won 3–1)

Regular Season Games with NYR: 125

Playoff Games with NYR: 0

Right winger Mikael Samuelsson became the answer to a trivia question when he was acquired in a trade with the San Jose Sharks in June 2001. Who did the Rangers send to San Jose to obtain Samuelsson? The answer is Stanley Cup champion left winger Adam Graves.

Samuelsson was under some pressure to produce. He appeared to be on his way when he had a two-goal game to beat Colorado in late November 2001, but only scored four more goals for the rest of the season. In the 2002–03 season, Samuelsson scored eight goals in 58 games before being traded to Pittsburgh as part of a multi-player deal in February 2003.

George McPhee

NYR Debut: April 5, 1983 (at Philadelphia Flyers, Playoffs, Game One Patrick Division Semifinal, won 5–3)

Regular Season Games with NYR: 109

Playoff Games with NYR: 29

Also wore: #21

Left winger George McPhee was listed as being 5-foot-9 and 170 pounds, but he played much bigger than that during his career.

McPhee signed with the Rangers as an undrafted free agent in July 1982. The native of Guelph, Ontario, was known as a feisty winger that never backed down.

During the 1984–85 season, McPhee scored 12 goals with 15 assists for 27 points, but also led the team with 139 penalty minutes. According to hockeyfights.com, McPhee was in 12 fights during that season.

McPhee played parts of four seasons with the Rangers before being traded to the Winnipeg Jets in September 1987.

Brent Fedyk

> **NYR Debut:** October 9, 1998 (vs. Philadelphia Flyers, lost 1–0)
> **Regular Season Games with NYR:** 67
> **Playoff Games with NYR:** 0

Right winger Brent Fedyk was playing minor league hockey for two seasons before he signed with the Rangers as a free agent in August 1998.

Fedyk was a nine-year veteran who had three seasons of 20 or more goals. In his one season with the Rangers, he scored four goals.

Norm MacIver

> **NYR Debut:** October 9, 1986 (vs. New Jersey Devils, lost 5–3)
> **Regular Season Games with NYR:** 66
> **Playoff Games with NYR:** 0

Defenseman Norm MacIver made his name as an outstanding collegiate player. In four years at the University of Minnesota-Duluth, MacIver had 152 assists and finished as a finalist for the 1985–86 Hobey Baker Award.

MacIver played parts of three seasons in New York before being traded to the Hartford Whalers in December 1988.

Tim Sweeney

> **NYR Debut:** October 20, 1997 (vs. Carolina Hurricanes, won 4–2)
> **Regular Season Games with NYR:** 56
> **Playoff Games with NYR:** 0

Right winger Tim Sweeney was drafted out of high school by the Calgary Flames in the sixth round of the 1985 NHL Entry Draft. Sweeney was twenty-three years old when he made his NHL debut with the Flames in 1990.

The Rangers signed Sweeney as an unrestricted free agent in 1997.

In 56 career games with the Rangers during the 1997–98 season, Sweeney scored 11 goals with 18 assists for 29 points. He retired from the NHL after his one season with the Rangers.

Daniel Lacroix

NYR Debut: October 5, 1993 (vs. Boston Bruins, lost 4–3)
Regular Season Games with NYR: 30
Playoff Games with NYR: 0
Also wore: #32

Left winger Daniel Lacroix was selected by the Rangers in the second round of the 1987 NHL Entry Draft.

Lacroix was a scorer in junior hockey but became a grinding, defensive forward in the NHL. He played parts of three seasons over two stints with the Rangers. In August 1994, the Rangers traded Lacroix to Boston but reacquired him off waivers from the Bruins in March 1995. After the 1995–96 season, Lacroix played out his contract and became a free agent.

Ryan VandenBussche

NYR Debut: December 13, 1996 (at Buffalo Sabres, won 3–0)
Regular Season Games with NYR: 27
Playoff Games with NYR: 0

Right winger Ryan VandenBussche had one of the longest names in franchise history—and one of the shortest tenures.

VandenBussche signed with the Rangers as an unrestricted free agent before the 1995–96 season. He played parts of two seasons with the Rangers and a number of minor league games before being traded to the Chicago Blackhawks in March 1998.

The following played less than ten games with NYR:

Tony Tuzzolino - right wing

NYR Debut: February 11, 2001 (vs. New Jersey Devils, OT tie 1–1)
Regular Season Games with NYR: 6
Playoff Games with NYR: 0

#38

Michael Sauer

NYR Debut: March 24, 2009 (vs. Minnesota Wild, won 2–1)
Regular Season Games with NYR: 98
Playoff Games with NYR: 5
Also wore: #56

Michael Sauer had a promising career cut short by a controversial hit.

The St. Cloud, Minnesota-born defenseman was a second-round pick of the Rangers in the 2005 NHL Entry Draft. In his rookie season of 2010–11, he scored three goals with 12 assists for 15 points. Sauer was fourth among NHL rookies with a plus-20 rating in 76 games. His all-around game was never more evident than in a late regular season contest in March 2011 against Boston. Sauer scored the game-winning goal, added an assist, and was credited with a team-high five blocked shots to lead the Rangers past the Bruins, 5–3.

On December 5, 2011, Sauer's career came to an end during a game at Madison Square Garden against the Toronto Maple Leafs. Sauer's head was down and Maple Leafs hard hitting defenseman Dion Phaneuf leveled him with a forearm that sent him to the locker room with a concussion. Sauer never played another game, as he continued to struggle with post-concussion symptoms.

Ronald Petrovicky

NYR Debut: October 12, 2002 (at Pittsburgh Penguins, lost 6–0)
Regular Season Games with NYR: 66
Playoff Games with NYR: 0

There was symmetry to right winger Ronald Petrovicky's Ranger career.

The native of Slovakia was claimed by the Rangers from Calgary in the 2002 NHL Waiver Draft. A year later, he was claimed from the Rangers by the Atlanta Thrashers in the 2003 NHL Waiver Draft.

Terry Carkner

NYR Debut: October 15, 1986 (at Chicago Blackhawks, 5–5 OT tie)
Regular Season Games with NYR: 52
Playoff Games with NYR: 1

Defenseman Terry Carkner debuted in the 1986–87 season and won the Rangers' Fan Club's Rookie of the Year Award. Carkner played in 52 games and had two goals and 13 assists for 15 points. After the season, he was traded to Quebec with left winger Jeff Jackson for left winger John Ogrodnick and defenseman David Shaw.

Jeff Bloemberg

NYR Debut: February 20, 1989 (vs. New Jersey Devils, won 7–4)
Regular Season Games with NYR: 43
Playoff Games with NYR: 7

Jeff Bloemberg was a 6-foot-2 defenseman who knew how to use his size without being dirty. Bloemberg was a fifth-round choice of the Rangers in the 1986 NHL Entry Draft. He played parts of four seasons with the Rangers before being left unprotected and claimed by the expansion Tampa Bay Lightning in the 1992 NHL Expansion Draft.

The following played less than 25 games with NYR:

P.A. Parenteau - left wing

NYR Debut: October 28, 2009 (at New York Islanders, lost 3–1)
Regular Season Games with NYR: 22
Playoff Games with NYR: 0

Jarko Immonen - center

NYR Debut: April 6, 2006 (vs. New York Islanders, won 3–1)
Regular Season Games with NYR: 20
Playoff Games with NYR: 0

Bryce Lampman - defenseman

NYR Debut: March 9, 2004 (at Atlanta Thrashers, won 2–0)

Regular Season Games with NYR: 10

Playoff Games with NYR: 0

Also wore: #26 and #33

Sylvain Blouin - left wing

NYR Debut: November 18, 1996 (at Calgary Flames, lost 5–3)

Regular Season Games with NYR: 7

Playoff Games with NYR: 0

Also wore: #30 and #32

Chris Kenady - right wing

NYR Debut: November 13, 1999 (vs. Boston Bruins, lost 5–2)

Regular Season Games with NYR: 2

Playoff Games with NYR: 0

Also wore: #29

#39

Doug Weight

NYR Debut: April 13, 1991 (at Washington Capitals, Playoffs, Game Six Patrick Division Semifinal, lost 4–2)

Regular Season Games with NYR: 118

Playoff Games with NYR: 8

Center Doug Weight was a second-round pick of the Rangers in the 1990 NHL Entry Draft. The Michigan-born Weight made his name at Lake Superior State University. In two collegiate seasons, he scored 50 goals with 94 assists.

Weight made his debut in the 1991 Stanley Cup Playoffs. In 1991–92, he played 53 games as a rookie and scored eight goals with 22 assists for 30 points.

The next season, Weight appeared to be on his way to a productive career in New York. The 5-foot-11 pivot man had 15 goals and 25 assists for

40 points in 65 games, but the Rangers stunned the twenty-two-year-old by trading him to the Edmonton Oilers for left winger Esa Tikkanen.

Dan LaCouture

NYR Debut: February 12, 2003 (at Florida Panthers, won 3–1)

Regular Season Games with NYR: 83

Playoff Games with NYR: 0

Left winger Dan LaCouture came to the Rangers as part of a seven-player trade with the Pittsburgh Penguins in February 2003.

The Massachusetts native played parts of two seasons in New York, including his final season of 2003–04 when he finished the season with a minus-13 rating.

Joel Bouchard

NYR Debut: December 11, 2002 (vs. Chicago Blackhawks, lost 4–3)

Regular Season Games with NYR: 55

Playoff Games with NYR: 0

Also wore: #74

Joel Bouchard had two separate tenures with the Rangers. He joined the first team by signing as an unrestricted free agent in August 2002. After playing 27 games, the defenseman was traded to the Pittsburgh Penguins for Dan LaCouture (see above).

Bouchard scored only five goals in the 2002–03 season, but two of those were game winners.

Dan Cloutier

NYR Debut: January 3, 1998 (at Washington Capitals, won 3–2)

Regular Season Games with NYR: 34

Playoff Games with NYR: 0

Also wore: #34

Goaltender Dan Cloutier had an impressive career in junior hockey so the Rangers made him their #1 pick and the 26th overall in the 1994 NHL Entry Draft.

Cloutier won 43 games over a two-year period for the Sault Ste. Marie Greyhounds of the OHL before he was chosen by the Rangers.

Cloutier made 16 saves in winning his NHL debut in the second half of the 1997–98 season. He won his first three career starts but only won one more game the rest of the season. In 1998–99, Cloutier was up and down while playing in 22 games where he posted a 6–8–3 record. After the season, he was traded to the Chicago Blackhawks.

Vladimir Vorobiev

NYR Debut: January 12, 1997 (vs. New Jersey Devils, won 3–0)
Regular Season Games with NYR: 31
Playoff Games with NYR: 0

Vladimir Vorobiev came over from Russia in 1996 to join the Rangers and pursue a career in the NHL. The right winger was known as a dynamic play-maker in the Soviet Union.

Vorobiev debuted with the Binghamton Rangers in 1996, and got off to a fast start after his Ranger debut in January 1997. In his first ten games, Vorobiev scored four goals with five assists for nine points, including a four-point game (one goal, three assists) in a tie with the Edmonton Oilers.

During the 1998–99 season, Vorobiev scored 65 points in 65 games for the Rangers' AHL affiliate in Hartford. In March 1999, he was traded to the Edmonton Oilers.

The following players played less than 15 games with NYR:

Peter Laviolette - defenseman

NYR Debut: November 8, 1988 (at New York Islanders, lost 4–3)
Regular Season Games with NYR: 12
Playoff Games with NYR: 0

Nicklas Jensen - right wing

NYR Debut: December 8, 2016 (at Winnipeg Jets, won 2–1)
Regular Season Games with NYR: 7
Playoff Games with NYR: 0

Shawn McCosh - center

NYR Debut: January 30, 1995 (vs. Ottawa Senators, won 6–2)
Regular Season Games with NYR: 5
Playoff Games with NYR: 0

Brad Smyth - right wing

NYR Debut: April 14, 1998 (at Washington Capitals, lost 3–1)
Regular Season Games with NYR: 5
Playoff Games with NYR: 0
Also wore: #8

Drew Bannister - defenseman

NYR Debut: October 18, 2000 (at Chicago Blackhawks, won 4–2)
Regular Season Games with NYR: 3
Playoff Games with NYR: 0

Brendan Bell - defenseman

NYR Debut: October 22, 2011 (at Edmonton Oilers, lost 2–0)
Regular Season Games with NYR: 1
Playoff Games with NYR: 0

Brodie Dupont - center

NYR Debut: January 22, 2011 (at Atlanta Thrashers, won 3–2 SO)
Regular Season Games with NYR: 1
Playoff Games with NYR: 0

Alexandre Giroux - left wing

NYR Debut: March 25, 2006 (at Tampa Bay Lightning, lost 4–3, SO)
Regular Season Games with NYR: 1
Playoff Games with NYR: 0

Steve Larouche - center

NYR Debut: December 15, 1995 (at Buffalo Sabres, lost 5–4)

Regular Season Games with NYR: 1

Playoff Games with NYR: 0

Todd Marchant - center

NYR Debut: March 18, 1994 (vs. Chicago Blackhawks, lost 7–3)

Regular Season Games with NYR: 1

Playoff Games with NYR: 0

Trent Whitfield - center

NYR Debut: January 17, 2002 (at New Jersey Devils, lost 6–4)

Regular Season Games with NYR: 1

Playoff Games with NYR: 0

#40

Michael Grabner

NYR Debut: October 13, 2016 (vs. New York Islanders, won 1–0)

Regular Season Games with NYR: 76

Playoff Games with NYR: 12

Right winger Michael Grabner signed with the Rangers as a free agent in July 2016, and immediately paid dividends. Grabner was signed for his defensive prowess and excellent work on the penalty kill, but he scored 27 goals to spark the Rangers to a surprising 48–28–6 record.

Grabner scored a hat trick in late October to lead the Rangers to a 6–1 win over Tampa Bay at Madison Square Garden. Grabner's best game was in early January when he led the Rangers to a come-from-behind win over the Columbus Blue Jackets.

The Rangers trailed 4–1 in the second period of that game, but Grabner scored three of the next four Ranger goals including the game winner with :17 seconds left in the third period.

Photo courtesy of Mark Rosenman.

His first season with Rangers exceeded all expectations.

Grabner played 76 games in the regular season and added four goals and two assists for six points in 12 postseason games.

Erik Christensen

NYR Debut: December 5, 2009 (at Buffalo Sabres, won 2–1)
Regular Season Games with NYR: 132
Playoff Games with NYR: 5
Also wore: #26

Erik Christensen was a journeyman center who spent parts of three seasons with the Rangers. In December 2009, the Rangers claimed the Edmonton, Alberta, native off the waiver wire from the Anaheim Ducks.

Christensen's best season was 2010–11, when he scored 11 goals with 16 assists for 27 points. In February 2012, Christensen was traded to the Minnesota Wild.

The following players played less than 30 games with NYR:

Jussi Markkanen - goaltender

NYR Debut: October 11, 2003 (at Columbus Blue Jackets, lost 5–0)
Regular Season Games with NYR: 26
Playoff Games with NYR: 0

Dennis Vial - defenseman

NYR Debut: October 13, 1990 (at Washington Capitals, won 5–2)
Regular Season Games with NYR: 21
Playoff Games with NYR: 0

Roman Hamrlik - defenseman

NYR Debut: March 7, 2013 (at New York Islanders, won 2–1 OT)
Regular Season Games with NYR: 12
Playoff Games with NYR: 2

Brandon Mashinter - left wing

NYR Debut: February 19, 2013 (vs. Montreal Canadiens, lost 3–1)
Regular Season Games with NYR: 10
Playoff Games with NYR: 0

Chris Holt - goaltender

NYR Debut: December 3, 2005 (at Washington Capitals, lost 5–1)
Regular Season Games with NYR: 1
Playoff Games with NYR: 0

#41

Jed Ortmeyer

NYR Debut: November 15, 2003 (at New Jersey Devils, lost 5–0)
Regular Season Games with NYR: 177
Playoff Games with NYR: 13

Omaha, Nebraska, native Jed Ortmeyer signed with the Rangers as an undrafted free agent in May 2003. The twenty-four-year-old right winger finished four solid collegiate seasons with the University of Michigan, but was bypassed in the NHL Draft.

In the 2005–06 season, Ortmeyer played on a line with center Dominic Moore and left winger Ryan Hollweg, nicknamed the "HMO Line." The threesome brought energy and played "in your face" hockey in a season where the Rangers finished with 100 points.

Ortmeyer played one more season with the Rangers before playing out his contract.

Steve Richmond

NYR Debut: January 18, 1984 (vs. St. Louis Blues, won 6–2)
Regular Season Games with NYR: 77
Playoff Games with NYR: 4

Defenseman Steve Richmond was signed as an undrafted free agent in June 1982. The Chicago native played four seasons for the University of Michigan and parts of three seasons with the Rangers.

The 6-foot-1, 205-pound defenseman played a physical game, as evidenced by 110 penalty minutes in 26 games during his first season with the Rangers. Richmond played in 51 games in the next two seasons. In December 1985, Richmond was traded to the Detroit Red Wings for defenseman Mike McEwen.

Stu Bickel

NYR Debut: December 20, 2011 (at New Jersey Devils, won 4–1)
Regular Season Games with NYR: 67
Playoff Games with NYR: 18

At 6-foot-4, Stu Bickel was far from being labeled an offensive defenseman but, in his first three NHL games, had four assists. After that, he had five more assists for his entire Ranger career.

Bickel was acquired in a trade with the Anaheim Ducks in 2010 before making his NHL debut with the Rangers. Bickel was asked to provide a physical presence and did just that. In his first season of 2011–12, Bickel

NEW YORK RANGERS BY THE NUMBERS

was third on the team with 12 fighting major penalties. After playing with Hartford in the 2013–14 season, Bickel signed with the Minnesota Wild as a free agent.

Eddie Mio

> **NYR Debut:** December 19, 1981 (at Pittsburgh Penguins, 3–3 tie)
> **Regular Season Games with NYR:** 66
> **Playoff Games with NYR:** 16

Following a career in the World Hockey Association, goaltender Eddie Mio joined the Rangers for the 1981–82 season.

In 1982–83, Mio was the starting goaltender, as he played in 41 games. In June 1983, Mio was part of a multi-player trade with the Detroit Red Wings. Mio, along with center Ron Duguay and right winger Eddie Johnstone, went to Motown for defenseman Willie Huber, right winger Mike Blaisdell, and left winger Mark Osborne.

The following players played less than 15 games with NYR:

Simon Wheeldon - center

> **NYR Debut:** March 19, 1988 (at Toronto Maple Leafs, won 4–3)
> **Regular Season Games with NYR:** 11
> **Playoff Games with NYR:** 0
> **Also wore:** #33

Mike Siltala - right wing

> **NYR Debut:** November 17, 1986 (at New Jersey Devils, lost 3–2)
> **Regular Season Games with NYR:** 4
> **Playoff Games with NYR:** 0

Peter Fiorentino - defenseman

> **NYR Debut:** October 23, 1991 (vs. Los Angeles Kings, won 7–2)
> **Regular Season Games with NYR:** 1
> **Playoff Games with NYR:** 0

#42

Artem Anisimov

NYR Debut: February 3, 2009 (vs. Atlanta Thrashers, lost 2–1 SO)
Regular Season Games with NYR: 244
Playoff Games with NYR: 26

The Rangers used their second-round pick in the 2006 NHL Entry Draft to select Russian born center Artem Anisimov.

Anisimov came to the United States in 2007 and played 74 games with the Rangers' AHL affiliate in Hartford. In 2008–09, Anisimov scored 37 goals with 44 assists for 81 points. That earned him a shot with the NHL club in 2009 for one regular season game and one playoff game.

In the 2009–10 and 2010–11 seasons, Anisimov did not miss a game and totaled 30 goals and 42 assists for 72 points.

In his final season of 2011–12, Anisimov broke out in the post-season. In 20 games, he scored three goals with seven assists for ten points.

Was part of blockbuster trade for Rick Nash.

Photo by Herman Von Petri via Wikimedia Commons.

Anisimov's career was on an upswing but the Rangers used the twenty-four-year-old as part of a major trade. In July 2012, the team sent Anisimov and center Brandon Dubinsky to the Columbus Blue Jackets for high-scoring winger Rick Nash.

Dylan McIlrath

NYR Debut: December 12, 2013 (vs. Columbus Blue Jackets, won 4–2)
Regular Season Games with NYR: 38
Playoff Games with NYR: 1

At 6-foot-5, defenseman Dylan McIlrath was the 10th overall selection of the Rangers in the 2010 NHL Entry Draft. Drafted for his size, McIlrath also put up some offensive numbers in the minors.

He joined the team for two games in the 2013–14 season and played only one game in 2014–15. The Rangers were becoming disappointed in the way he was developing.

McIlrath played 34 games in the 2015–16 season and scored two goals with two assists, but he had his "Ranger moment" on February 14, 2016, against the Philadelphia Flyers at Madison Square Garden. The teams met eight days previous in Philadelphia. In the first period, Flyers' tough guy Wayne Simmonds hit Rangers captain Ryan McDonagh with a sucker punch that resulted in a concussion. It took just fifty-nine seconds into the first period of the rematch for McIlrath to answer Simmonds for taking out his captain. After a stoppage in play, McIlrath and Simmonds sized each other up and came to blows. McIlrath got some good shots in and, when they were separated, the crowd let the young defenseman know that they appreciated his effort.

McIlrath was traded to the Florida Panthers in November 2016 for defenseman Steven Kampfer.

Brendan Smith

NYR Debut: March 2, 2017 (at Boston Bruins, won 2–1)
Regular Season Games with NYR: 18
Playoff Games with NYR: 12

Brendan Smith was an excellent addition at the 2017 trade deadline. The defenseman was acquired from the Detroit Red Wings in February 2017 for draft picks.

Smith made his presence felt right away and became one of the Rangers' steadiest defenseman down the stretch of the 2016–17 season and playoffs.

The following players played less than ten games with NYR:

Photo by Muéro via Wikimedia Commons.

Has become a steady force on Blueline since coming over from Red Wings.

John Tripp - right wing

NYR Debut: January 8, 2003 (vs. Carolina Hurricanes, won 5–1)

Regular Season Games with NYR: 9

Playoff Games with NYR: 0

Paul Fenton - left wing

NYR Debut: November 2, 1986 (vs. Winnipeg Jets, lost 5–4 OT)

Regular Season Games with NYR: 8

Playoff Games with NYR: 0

Also wore: #25

Dave Marcinyshyn - defenseman

NYR Debut: February 26, 1993 (at Calgary Flames, 4–4 OT tie)

Regular Season Games with NYR: 2

Playoff Games with NYR: 0

Brandon Segal - right wing

NYR Debut: January 19, 2013 (at Boston Bruins, lost 3–1)

Regular Season Games with NYR: 1

Playoff Games with NYR: 0

#43

Martin Biron

NYR Debut: October 21, 2010 (at Toronto Maple Leafs, won 2–1)

Regular Season Games with NYR: 46

Playoff Games with NYR: 0

Veteran goaltender Martin Biron completed his 16-year NHL career with a four-year stint in New York.

Biron joined the Rangers for the 2010–11 season. Unfortunately, his season was cut short by a fractured collarbone that he suffered during practice in February 2011.

Backed up the King for three seasons.

Photo courtesy of Mark Rosenman.

Biron backed up Henrik Lundqvist for three seasons before retiring after playing two games in the 2013–14 season.

The following players played ten games or less with NYR:

Steven Kampfer - defenseman

NYR Debut: February 28, 2017 (vs. Washington Capitals, lost 4–1)
Regular Season Games with NYR: 10
Playoff Games with NYR: 0

Jason MacDonald - right wing

NYR Debut: December 12, 2003 (at Buffalo Sabres, won 3–1)
Regular Season Games with NYR: 4
Playoff Games with NYR: 0

#44

Ryan Hollweg

NYR Debut: October 5, 2005 (at Philadelphia Flyers, won 5–3)

Regular Season Games with NYR: 200

Playoff Games with NYR: 14

Left winger Ryan Hollweg was an offensively skilled player in junior hockey, but became more of a defensive forward when he joined the Rangers in the 2005–06 season.

Hollweg became a regular on the Rangers' fourth line with center Blair Betts and right winger Colton Orr, and played three seasons in New York as a physical, checking forward.

In March 2007, Hollweg was involved in a memorable confrontation with New York Islanders winger Chris Simon (see Chapter Seventeen).

The Rangers traded Hollweg to the Toronto Maple Leafs in July 2008.

Lindy Ruff

NYR Debut: March 8, 1989 (vs. Buffalo Sabres, lost 2–0)

Regular Season Games with NYR: 83

Playoff Games with NYR: 10

Lindy Ruff came to the Rangers after playing parts of ten seasons with the Buffalo Sabres. Ruff was a tough, gritty defenseman who was well respected by his peers.

Ruff was traded to the Rangers from the Sabres in March 1989. He played parts of three injury-plagued seasons for the Rangers, including his final season of 1990–91.

Per Djoos

NYR Debut: October 16, 1991 (vs. New Jersey Devils, won 4–2)

Regular Season Games with NYR: 56

Playoff Games with NYR: 0

Defenseman Per Djoos was an offensively gifted player who didn't really fit the NHL style. Djoos could skate and move the puck, but was more effective on the larger rinks in Europe.

Djoos was traded from the Detroit Red Wings to the Rangers in March 1991. In the 1991–92 season, he had 18 assists in 50 games. For most of the 1992–93 season, Djoos played for the Rangers AHL affiliate at Binghamton. After the season, the Swedish-born defenseman returned to play in Europe.

Matt Hunwick

NYR Debut: October 11, 2014 (at Columbus Blue Jackets, lost 5–2)

Regular Season Games with NYR: 55

Playoff Games with NYR: 6

Photo by Lisa Gansky from New York, NY, USA, via Wikimedia Commons.

Scored game winner over Panthers in March 2015.

American-born defenseman Matt Hunwick was a solid two-way player for the University of Michigan.

Hunwick played one season in 2014–15. His best game came in March 2015 when he scored the game-winning goal and added an assist in a 2–1 win over the Florida Panthers.

The following players played less than 25 games with NYR:

Justin Falk - defenseman

NYR Debut: October 12, 2013 (at St. Louis Blues, lost 5–3)
Regular Season Games with NYR: 21
Playoff Games with NYR: 0

Josh Green - left wing

NYR Debut: December 14, 2002 (at Toronto Maple Leafs, lost 4–1)
Regular Season Games with NYR: 18
Playoff Games with NYR: 0

James Latos - right wing

NYR Debut: March 1, 1989 (vs. Toronto Maple Leafs, won 7–4)
Regular Season Games with NYR: 1
Playoff Games with NYR: 0

Terry Kleisinger - goaltender

NYR Debut: October 12, 1985 (at Hartford Whalers, lost 8–2)
Regular Season Games with NYR: 4
Playoff Games with NYR: 0

Billy Tibbetts - right wing

NYR Debut: December 16, 2002 (vs. San Jose Sharks, won 2–1)
Regular Season Games with NYR: 11
Playoff Games with NYR: 0

Corey Potter - defenseman

> **NYR Debut:** October 7, 2008 (vs. Calgary Flames, lost 3–0)
> **Regular Season Games with NYR:** 8
> **Playoff Games with NYR:** 0

#45

Dale Purinton

> **NYR Debut:** April 9, 2000 (vs. Philadelphia Flyers, lost 4–1)
> **Regular Season Games with NYR:** 181
> **Playoff Games with NYR:** 0
> **Also wore:** #5

Defenseman Dale Purinton was an unheralded draft pick of the Rangers who made it to the NHL. Purinton made it to New York on his energetic and gritty play, but was also a very good puck handler.

Purinton, who was chosen in the fifth round of the 1995 NHL Entry Draft, made his way through the Rangers' minor league system to make his debut in the second half of the 1999–2000 season.

The native of Fort Wayne, Indiana, had his best overall season in 2002–03. Purinton set career highs with three goals and nine assists for 12 points. He also led the team with 161 penalty minutes.

In parts of five seasons with the Rangers, Purinton accumulated 578 penalty minutes.

Dmitri Kalinin

> **NYR Debut:** October 4, 2008 (at Tampa Bay Lightning, won 2–1)
> **Regular Season Games with NYR:** 58
> **Playoff Games with NYR:** 0

After eight seasons with the Buffalo Sabres, Russian-born defenseman Dmitri Kalinin singed with the Rangers as a free agent for the 2008–09 season.

Kalinin was a 6-foot-3 defenseman who had the size, speed, and skill to be an offensive threat. The twenty-eight-year-old scored one goal during his Rangers' tenure. In March 2009, he was traded to the Phoenix Coyotes for left winger Nigel Dawes, right winger Petr Prucha, and defenseman Derek Morris.

Steve Valiquette

NYR Debut: March 27, 2004 (at Philadelphia Flyers, won 3–1)

Regular Season Games with NYR: 39

Playoff Games with NYR: 2

Also wore: #40

Goaltender Steve Valiquette was acquired by the Rangers via a trade with the Edmonton Oilers in March 2004.

Valiquette played two games for the Rangers before he signed to play in Russia during the lockout season of 2005–06. When the NHL resumed, Valiquette signed with the Rangers as a free agent.

The Ontario native played parts of the next four seasons with the Rangers. In 2007–08, Valiquette had a pair of shutouts and finished with four in his Ranger career.

After his playing career was over, Valiquette became a broadcaster. He is currently a studio analyst for Ranger games on the MSG network.

Arron Asham

NYR Debut: January 20, 2013 (vs. Pittsburgh Penguins, lost 6–3)

Regular Season Games with NYR: 33

Playoff Games with NYR: 10

Right winger Arron Asham signed a two-year, free agent contract with the Rangers beginning with the 2012–13 season. Asham was a physical forward who scored two goals during parts of two seasons with the Rangers.

Asham's memorable Ranger moment was in the seventh game of the 2013 Eastern Conference Quarterfinal. Asham scored the first, and what became the game-winning, goal to help the Rangers to a series-clinching 5–0 win.

The Rangers got off to a slow start in the 2013–14 season, so management shook up the roster. Asham was one of the casualties and was placed on waivers. He finished the season and his career with the Hartford Wolf Pack of the AHL.

The following played less than 25 games with NYR:

Jody Shelley - left wing

NYR Debut: February 14, 2010 (vs. Tampa Bay Lightning, won 5–2)

Regular Season Games with NYR: 21

Playoff Games with NYR: 0

James Sheppard - center

NYR Debut: March 4, 2015 (at Detroit Red Wings, lost 2–1 OT)

Regular Season Games with NYR: 14

Playoff Games with NYR: 13

Magnus Hellberg - goaltender

NYR Debut: December 20, 2015 (vs. Washington Capitals, won 7–3)

Regular Season Games with NYR: 3

Playoff Games with NYR: 0

#46

Marek Hrivik

NYR Debut: February 21, 2016 (vs. Detroit Red Wings, won 1–0)

Regular Season Games with NYR: 21

Playoff Games with NYR: 0

Slovakian-born left winger Marek Hrivik made his NHL debut during the 2015–16 season, but it wasn't until the following season that the Rangers began to see why they initially had interest in him. Hrivik was lighting up the score sheet for the Rangers' AHL affiliate in Hartford during the 2016–17 season. In 56 games, he scored 40 points (16 goals, 24 assists), and so he joined the Rangers for 16 games, recording two assists.

#47
Rich Pilon

NYR Debut: December 1, 1999 (at New Jersey Devils, lost 3–2)
Regular Season Games with NYR: 114
Playoff Games with NYR: 0

Defenseman Rich Pilon was a fixture with the New York Islanders for parts of 12 seasons before he was claimed off waivers by the Rangers in December 1999.

Pilon played parts of two seasons before playing out his contract in April 2001.

The following players played less than ten games with NYR:

Pat Price - defenseman

NYR Debut: March 8, 1987 (vs. Calgary Flames, lost 7–4)
Regular Season Games with NYR: 13
Playoff Games with NYR: 6

Steve Nemeth - center

NYR Debut: November 29, 1987 (vs. New York Islanders, won 3–1)
Regular Season Games with NYR: 12
Playoff Games with NYR: 0

Barrett Heisten - left wing

NYR Debut: October 5, 2001 (at Carolina Hurricanes, lost 3–1)
Regular Season Games with NYR: 10
Playoff Games with NYR: 0

Mike Green - center

NYR Debut: March 9, 2004 (at Atlanta Thrashers, won 2–0)
Regular Season Games with NYR: 13
Playoff Games with NYR: 0

#49

Dan Fritsche - center

NYR Debut: October 13, 2008 (vs. New Jersey Devils, won 4–1)
Regular Season Games with NYR: 16
Playoff Games with NYR: 0

Ilkka Heikkinen - defenseman

NYR Debut: December 5, 2009 (at Buffalo Sabres, won 2–1)
Regular Season Games with NYR: 7
Playoff Games with NYR: 0

Greg Moore - right wing

NYR Debut: November 21, 2007 (at Tampa Bay Lightning, won 2–1)
Regular Season Games with NYR: 6
Playoff Games with NYR: 0

#51

Fedor Tyutin

NYR Debut: February 14, 2004 (at Philadelphia Flyers, lost 6–2)
Regular Season Games with NYR: 250
Playoff Games with NYR: 24

The Rangers chose eighteen-year-old Russian-born defenseman Fedor Tyutin in the second round of the 2001 NHL Entry Draft. Tyutin was projected to be a combination of size (6-foot-2) and skill.

After being drafted, Tyutin elected to play junior hockey, where he scored 19 goals with 40 assists for the Guelph Storm of Ontario Hockey League during the 2001–02 season. In 2003–04, he joined the Hartford Wolf Pack of the AHL.

The Rangers promoted Tyutin in February 2004, playing 25 games and scoring two goals with five assists. After playing in Russia during the 2004–05 season (that was cancelled by a lockout), Tyutin returned to the Rangers for the 2005–06 season and scored a career-high 25 points.

Tyutin developed into a solid, NHL defenseman and was showing that he could also produce in the postseason. In the 2007 playoffs, Tyutin had five assists to help the Rangers sweep the Atlanta Thrashers in the Eastern Conference Quarterfinal.

After playing 82 regular season games in the 2007–08 season and all 10 postseason games, Tyutin was traded to the Columbus Blue Jackets for right winger Nikolai Zherdev and center Dan Fritsche.

Photo by Michael Miller via Wikimedia Commons.

#53
Tim Erixon - defenseman

NYR Debut: October 7, 2011 (at Los Angeles Kings, lost 3–2 OT)
Regular Season Games with NYR: 18
Playoff Games with NYR: 0

Traded to the Columbus Blue Jackets for right winger Nikolai Zherdev.

Son of former Rangers' left winger Jan Erixon (see Chapter Twenty).

Derek Morris - defenseman

NYR Debut: March 5, 2009 (at New York Islanders, won 4–2)
Regular Season Games with NYR: 18
Playoff Games with NYR: 7

Layne Ulmer - defenseman

NYR Debut: April 3, 2004 (at Washington Capitals, won 3–2)
Regular Season Games with NYR: 1
Playoff Games with NYR: 0

#55
Igor Ulanov - defenseman

NYR Debut: October 5, 2001 (at Carolina Hurricanes, lost 3–1)
Regular Season Games with NYR: 39
Playoff Games with NYR: 0

Christian Backman - defenseman

NYR Debut: February 28, 2008 (at Carolina Hurricanes, won 4–2)
Regular Season Games with NYR: 18
Playoff Games with NYR: 8

Marty McSorley - defenseman

NYR Debut: March 16, 1996 (at Montreal Canadiens, lost 4–2)
Regular Season Games with NYR: 9
Playoff Games with NYR: 4
Also wore: #36

Chris Summers - defenseman

NYR Debut: March 29, 2015 (vs. Washington Capitals, lost 5–2)
Regular Season Games with NYR: 6
Playoff Games with NYR: 0

David Liffiton - defenseman

NYR Debut: April 11, 2006 (vs. New York Islanders, lost 3–2)
Regular Season Games with NYR: 3
Playoff Games with NYR: 0

#58

Christian Thomas - right wing

NYR Debut: February 23, 2013 (at Montreal Canadiens, lost 3–0)
Regular Season Games with NYR: 1
Playoff Games with NYR: 0

#61–68: HIGH SCORING 60S

#61

Rick Nash

NYR Debut: January 19, 2013 (at Boston Bruins, lost 3–1)
Regular Season Games with NYR: 315
Playoff Games with NYR: 73

Going into the 2012–13 season, the Rangers were in need of a goal scorer. The season would be cut short by a lockout but, in July 2012, the Rangers acquired high-scoring right winger Rick Nash from Columbus in a blockbuster trade that sent wingers Brandon Dubinsky and Artem Anisimov, along with defenseman Tim Erixon, to the Blue Jackets.

Nash had a solid first season in New York, with 21 goals and 21 assists for 42 points in 44 games. In the playoffs, he struggled to score only one goal in 12 games.

Nash started fast in the 2013–14 season, but suffered a concussion following a hit from San Jose Sharks defenseman Brad Stuart and missed 17 games. Nash scored 26 goals in the regular season but, again,

His 32 even-strength goals in 2014–15 led the NHL.

struggled in the playoffs. The Rangers went to the Stanley Cup Final, but Nash scored only three goals in 25 games. His defensive game was improving, but he was brought in to score big goals.

The 2014–15 season was Nash's best in New York. He was third in the league with a career-best 42 goals and was the team's MVP. Nash also had a productive postseason, with five goals and nine assists in 14 games.

The 6-foot-4 winger tailed off in the 2015–16 season, as he was plagued by injuries. Nash missed 22 games due to back spasms and was dealing with a knee and groin injury for much of the season. In November 2016, Nash reached a milestone by scoring his 400th career goal against the Vancouver Canucks at Madison Square Garden.

Nash's name was mentioned in trade rumors throughout the 2016–17 season, but he finished with 23 goals in 67 games.

In five seasons with the Rangers (through 2016–17), Nash has scored 127 goals with 97 assists for 224 points in 315 games.

Pascal Dupuis - left wing

NYR Debut: February 15, 2007 (at Carolina Hurricanes, won 4–1)
Regular Season Games with NYR: 6
Playoff Games with NYR: 0

Left winger Pascal Dupuis scored one goal in his Rangers' career, which came in his very first game with New York.

#62

Carl Hagelin

NYR Debut: November 25, 2011 (at Washington Capitals, won 6–3)
Regular Season Games with NYR: 266
Playoff Games with NYR: 73

Speedy left winger Carl Hagelin was a sixth-round pick of the Rangers in the 2007 NHL Entry Draft.

The Swedish-born Hagelin played three seasons collegiately at the University of Michigan before joining the Connecticut Whale, the Rangers' AHL affiliate, in 2011.

Hagelin continued to play for his native Sweden in international competition (including the 2014 Winter Olympics) before joining the NHL club for the 2011–12 season.

Photo by Sarah Connors via Wikimedia Commons.

Had series-clinching goal over Penguins in 2014–15 playoffs.

Hagelin's greatest asset was his blazing speed. He became the first Rangers' rookie since Steven Rice in 1992–93 to tally four points in his first four NHL games. Hagelin scored his first goal in his second NHL game against the Philadelphia Flyers, and added a two-goal game against Buffalo in early December. The twenty-three-year-old finished his first season with 14 goals and 24 assists for 38 points and a fifth-place finish in the voting for the Calder Trophy.

Hagelin played all 48 games in the lockout-shortened season of 2012–13, and had a breakout season in 2013–2014 with 17 goals, but he really shined in the 2014 Stanley Cup Playoffs. In 25 postseason games, Hagelin scored seven goals with five assists for 12 points.

In the epic comeback against Pittsburgh in the Metropolitan Division Final, Hagelin scored the game-winning goal in Game Six. Hagelin had two goals and three assists in the series as the Rangers rallied from a three games to one series deficit.

In Game Four of the Eastern Conference Final, Hagelin had the primary assist on Martin St. Louis's game-winning goal in overtime. Hagelin also added a goal and an assist in the Final against the Los Angeles Kings.

In the 2014–15 season, Hagelin played all 82 games and scored 17 goals. In the playoffs, he had his last moment as a Ranger when he scored the series-clinching, Game Five-winning goal in overtime to oust the Penguins for a second straight season.

After the season, Hagelin was traded to the Anaheim Ducks but eventually landed with Pittsburgh, where he won back-to-back Stanley Cup Championships.

#63

Anthony Duclair

> **NYR Debut:** October 9, 2014 (at St. Louis Blues, won 3–2)
> **Regular Season Games with NYR:** 18
> **Playoff Games with NYR:** 0

After scoring 50 goals for Quebec of the Quebec Major Junior Hockey League, left winger Anthony Duclair was being touted as the next great Ranger forward.

Duclair was an offensively gifted player who ended up with one goal in his Ranger career. After the season, he was part of a multi-player trade with the Arizona Coyotes that brought back defenseman Keith Yandle.

Photo by Lisa Gansky from New York, NY, USA, via Wikimedia Commons.

Was traded for Keith Yandle.

#67

Benoit Pouliot

NYR Debut: October 3, 2013 (at Phoenix Coyotes, lost 4–1)

Regular Season Games with NYR: 80

Playoff Games with NYR: 25

Benoit Pouliot acquitted himself very well in his one season with the Rangers. The twenty-seven-year-old left winger, who was signed as a free agent, played 80 games and scored 15 goals with 21 assists for 36 points. In the 2014 playoffs, Pouliot had five goals and five assists in 25 games.

Chritoval Nieves - center

NYR Debut: November 15, 2016 (at Vancouver Canucks, won 7–2)

Regular Season Games with NYR: 1

Playoff Games with NYR: 0

#68

Jaromir Jagr

NYR Debut: January 24, 2004 (at Ottawa Senators, lost 9–1)

Regular Season Games with NYR: 277

Playoff Games with NYR: 23

In January 2004, the Rangers acquired one of the greatest players in the history of the National Hockey League when they traded right winger Anson Carter to the Washington Capitals for right winger Jaromir Jagr.

The Czech-born Jagr made an immediate impact with the fans in his Madison Square Garden debut, as he scored a goal with two assists in the Rangers' 5–2 win over the Florida Panthers.

Jagr cemented his Ranger legacy in the 2005–06 season when he set a franchise record with 54 goals to break Adam Graves's 1993–94 record of 51. Jagr also set a single-season, team record for the most points (123) and the most assists (69) by a right winger in a single season. He also set team marks for most power play goals (24), and tied the record for the most game-winning goals (9) in one season.

Photo by Michael Miller via Wikimedia Commons.

Holds franchise record of 54 goals in one season.

In his three-plus seasons in New York, Jagr showed he was also durable as he missed only two regular-season games.

In Jagr's final season of 2007–08, he scored 25 goals with 46 assists for 71 points.

#70-97: GETTING A "PHIL" OF HIGH NUMBERS

#70

Mackenzie Skapski

NYR Debut: February 20, 2015 (at Buffalo Sabres, won 3–1)

Regular Season Games with NYR: 2

Playoff Games with NYR: 0

In the sixth round of the 2013 NHL Entry Draft, the Rangers drafted goaltender Mackenzie Skapski.

Third-youngest Ranger goalie to post win in debut.

Photo courtesy of Mark Rosenman.

Skapski was an outstanding goalie in junior hockey, playing in the Western Hockey League for the Kootenay Ice. He joined Hartford for the 2014–15 season and posted a 10–4–2 mark over his last 16 starts.

In February 2015, the twenty-year-old was called up to get his first NHL start against the Buffalo Sabres. Skapski stopped 24 of 25 shots and became the third-youngest goaltender in franchise history to get a win in his debut, as the Rangers scored a 3–1 victory.

Skapski was so good his first time around that he got another chance in the same venue less than a month later. This time, Skapski was even better and made 20 saves in posting his first NHL shutout.

#71

Mike Rupp

NYR Debut: October 7, 2011 (at Los Angeles Kings, lost 3–2 OT)
Regular Season Games with NYR: 68
Playoff Games with NYR: 20
Also wore: #17

At 6-foot-5 and 235 pounds, center Mike Rupp was signed as a free agent in 2011 to provide a physical presence for the Rangers.

Rupp played 60 games in the 2011–12 season. His presence was felt in the 2012 Eastern Conference Final against the New Jersey Devils. Late in Game Four, the Cleveland-born forward threw a punch at Devils' goaltender Martin Brodeur. Rupp received a four-minute roughing penalty and a ten-minute misconduct.

Scored Rangers first goal in Winter Classic, and then gave the Jagr Salute.

Photo by Michael Miller via Wikimedia Commons.

Rupp's second season with the Rangers lasted eight games. He was receiving less and less ice time and was eventually traded to the Minnesota Wild in February 2013.

#73

Brandon Pirri

NYR Debut: October 13, 2016 (vs. New York Islanders, won 5–3)
Regular Season Games with NYR: 60
Playoff Games with NYR: 0

Center Brandon Pirri was signed to a one-year contract by the Rangers with the idea of enhancing the power play. He couldn't have gotten off to a better start.

In his first game with the Rangers, Pirri had a power play goal and an assist to help the Rangers open the 2016–17 season at Madison Square Garden with a 5–3 win over the New York Islanders.

Pirri played 60 regular season games, but did not appear in the postseason.

#76

Brady Skjei

NYR Debut: December 15, 2015 (at Edmonton Oilers, lost 3–0)
Regular Season Games with NYR: 87
Playoff Games with NYR: 17

The Rangers made Lakeville, Minnesota-native Brady Skjei their #1 pick and the 28th overall in the 2012 NHL Entry Draft.

Skjei was projected to be a solid, NHL defenseman and took some big strides toward becoming that player during the 2016–17 season.

Skjei played seven games late in the 2015–16 season and was in the line-up for the five-game series loss to Pittsburgh in the 2016 playoffs.

The twenty-two-year-old played 80 games in the 2016–17 season and scored five goals with 34 assists for 39 points. Skjei played all 12 postseason games, including Game Two of the second round against the Ottawa Senators when he had the first two-goal game in his playoffs career.

#77

Phil Esposito

NYR Debut: November 7, 1975 (at California Golden Seals, lost 7–5)
Regular Season Games with NYR: 422
Playoff Games with NYR: 30

On November 7, 1975, the Rangers stunned the hockey world by completing a blockbuster five-player trade with the Boston Bruins.

Hall of Fame center Phil Esposito and defenseman Carol Vadnais went to the Rangers in exchange for Hall of Fame center Jean Ratelle, Hall of Fame defenseman Brad Park, and defenseman Joe Zanussi.

The thirty-three-year-old Esposito was the leading goal scorer in the NHL over the previous six seasons, and was a two-time Stanley Cup winner in Boston. The Rangers were in the midst of overhauling their roster, so "Espo" was brought in to provide leadership as well as goal scoring.

Part of biggest trade in Rangers history.

Photo courtesy of Ken Tash.

Esposito continued to be a consistent goal scorer with the Rangers. In his first season of 1975–76, Esposito scored 29 goals in 68 games. On November 4, 1977, he scored his 600th career goal, becoming the first to do so in a Ranger uniform.

His totals steadily increased over the next three seasons, capped off by his 42-goal season during the 1978–79 campaign.

Esposito's leadership qualities paid off in the 1979 postseason. The thirty-six-year-old scored the game-winning goal in overtime to key a two-game sweep of the Los Angeles Kings in the preliminary round.

In the team's Stanley Cup Semifinal upset of the New York Islanders, Esposito scored the game-winning goal in Game Three that gave the Rangers a 2–1 series lead. He added another goal as the Rangers went on to upset their heavily favored rival. Esposito added two more goals in the five-game loss to Montreal in the Final. He finished the postseason with eight goals and 12 assists for 20 points in 18 games.

Esposito had his last big season in 1979–80, when he scored 34 goals. After playing 41 games in the 1980–81 season, he decided to retire.

After his playing career ended, Esposito served as a broadcaster, a general manager, and a head coach of the Rangers.

#80

Kevin Weekes

NYR Debut: October 5, 2005 (at Philadelphia Flyers, won 5–3)
Regular Season Games with NYR: 46
Playoff Games with NYR: 1

Goaltender Kevin Weekes signed a free agent contract with the Rangers in 2004 but, because the season was cancelled, did not make his New York debut until 2005.

Weekes played parts of two seasons with the Rangers. After the 2005–06 season, he played out his contract and became a free agent.

Nik Antropov - center

NYR Debut: March 5, 2009 (at New York Islanders, won 4–2)
Regular Season Games with NYR: 18
Playoff Games with NYR: 7

#81

Marcel Hossa

NYR Debut: October 5, 2005 (at Philadelphia Flyers, won 5–3)
Regular Season Games with NYR: 164
Playoff Games with NYR: 14

Left winger Marcel Hossa has always played in the shadow of his brother, Marian, a three-time Stanley Cup winner and All-Star.

Marcel Hossa was acquired by the Rangers from Montreal in September 2005. Hossa played parts of three seasons with the Rangers, scoring 21 goals with the team. In February 2008, he was sent to the Phoenix Coyotes as part of a multi-player trade.

Enver Lisin

NYR Debut: October 2, 2009 (at Pittsburgh Penguins, lost 3–2)
Regular Season Games with NYR: 57
Playoff Games with NYR: 0

Right winger Enver Lisin scored six goals with eight assists for 14 points in 57 games with the Rangers.

#82

Martin Straka

NYR Debut: October 5, 2005 (at Philadelphia Flyers, won 5–3)
Regular Season Games with NYR: 224
Playoff Games with NYR: 24

At 5-foot-9 and 180 pounds, left winger Martin Straka was considered small by NHL standards but played bigger than his size during a 15-year career. Straka's final two seasons were spent with the Rangers after he signed as a free agent in 2005.

Straka was a consistent goal scorer throughout his career, and that was no different when he came to New York. The Czech-born winger scored 22 goals in his first season of 2005–06. He had four games where he scored two or more goals, including a hat trick in a 5–1 win against the New York Islanders late in the regular season. Unfortunately, Straka was scoreless in the Eastern Conference Quarterfinal as the Rangers were swept by the New Jersey Devils.

In 2006–07, Straka scored 29 goals, including eight on the power play, while adding 41 assists for 70 points. In the playoffs, he was much better this time around and scored two goals with eight assists for ten points in ten games.

Straka's goal totals dipped to 14 in his final Ranger season of 2007–08, but he once again had a strong postseason. In the Rangers' five-game series win over the New Jersey Devils in the Eastern Conference Quarterfinal, Straka had a goal and the lone assist on the game-winning goal in Game Four. In Game Five, he had two assists as the Rangers closed out the series with a

5–3 win. Straka added two goals in the five-game, semifinal loss to Pitts-burgh that ended the season and his NHL career.

After the season, he decided to return to play in the Czech Republic.

#84

Corey Locke - center

> **NYR Debut:** March 30, 2010 (at New York Islanders, won 4–3)
>
> **Regular Season Games with NYR:** 3
>
> **Playoff Games with NYR:** 0

#86

Wojtek Wolski

> **NYR Debut:** January 11, 2011 (vs. Montreal Canadiens, lost 2–1)
>
> **Regular Season Games with NYR:** 46
>
> **Playoff Games with NYR:** 5

Left winger Wojtek Wolski made his name in Ranger lore during his second game. After being acquired from Phoenix in a trade for defenseman Michal Rozsival in January 2011, Wolski scored the only goal of the game on the power play as the Rangers topped the Vancouver Canucks, 1–0, at Madison Square Garden. Wolski became the fourth player in Rangers' history whose first Rangers goal came in a 1–0 game (Bill Cook, Taffy Abel, and Bill Boyd all did it in the franchise's first 11 games in 1926).

Wolski played 46 games in parts of two seasons with the Rangers. In Feb-ruary 2012, he was traded to the Florida Panthers.

Josh Jooris - center

> **NYR Debut:** October 17, 2016 (vs. San Jose Sharks, won 7–4)
>
> **Regular Season Games with NYR:** 12
>
> **Playoff Games with NYR:** 0

Jeremy Williams - right wing

> **NYR Debut:** October 24, 2010 (vs. New Jersey Devils, won 3–1)
>
> **Regular Season Games with NYR:** 1
>
> **Playoff Games with NYR:** 0

#87

Donald Brashear

> **NYR Debut:** October 2, 2009 (at Pittsburgh Penguins, lost 3–2)
> **Regular Season Games with NYR:** 36
> **Playoff Games with NYR:** 0

Big, bruising left winger Donald Brashear played for five NHL teams during his 16-year career, but his last stop was in New York. The 6-foot-3, 237-pound native of Bedford, Indiana, signed a free agent contract with the Rangers for the 2009–10 season. He split time between the Rangers and the Hartford Wolf Pack of the AHL. Following the season, Brashear was traded to the Atlanta Thrashers but did not play a game for them before retiring at the end of the season.

#88

Eric Lindros

> **NYR Debut:** October 5, 2001 (at Carolina Hurricanes, lost 3–1)
> **Regular Season Games with NYR:** 192
> **Playoff Games with NYR:** 0

After missing out the first time around, the Rangers finally acquired Eric Lindros in 2001.

Lindros was a highly-coveted prospect who was chosen #1 overall by Quebec in the 1991 NHL Entry Draft. The eighteen-year-old refused to play for the Nordiques, so they were forced to trade him. Quebec held Lindros's rights until the 1992 Draft, when they engineered a trade with the Rangers—or so the team thought. The Philadelphia Flyers claimed they also had a deal for Lindros, and filed a complaint with the NHL. Apparently, the Nordiques agreed to two trades so the league hired Larry Bertuzzi, an independent arbitrator and a Toronto lawyer, to rule on the trade.

Bertuzzi ruled in favor of the Flyers, so the Rangers would not be able to have Lindros wear their uniform until more than nine years later. Lindros would have an injury-plagued career with the Flyers, as he suffered seven reported concussions.

The Rangers acquired Lindros in August 2001 from Philadelphia for three players and a draft choice.

The 6-foot-4 center played three seasons with the Rangers, including the only injury-free season of his career in 2002–03, when he played 81 games.

In the following season of 2003–04, Lindros played in 39 games but suffered the eighth concussion of his career. After the season, he became an unrestricted free agent and went on to play with Toronto and Dallas before retiring in 2007.

Ken Hodge

> **NYR Debut:** October 6, 1976 (vs. Minnesota North Stars, won 6–5)
> **Regular Season Games with NYR:** 96
> **Playoff Games with NYR:** 0

Veteran right winger Ken Hodge became an unfortunate victim of circumstance when he came to the Rangers in 1976.

Hodge will be forever known as the player that the Rangers received in a trade with the Boston Bruins, which turned into one of the worst in franchise history when they sent promising young right winger Rick Middleton to Beantown.

The twenty-two-year-old Middleton (see Chapter Nine) was a dynamic and skilled forward who was starting to come into his own. Hodge skated on a high-scoring line with Phil Esposito and Wayne Cashman in Boston, and was a former 50-goal scorer and two-time Stanley Cup winner.

The Rangers felt reuniting Hodge and Esposito would enhance their offense. They felt they had other young prospects in their system and could afford to give up Middleton, who was ten years younger than Hodge.

The trade didn't sit well with the die-hard fans, who felt the Rangers gave up too much. As it turned out, they were correct.

Middleton scored 402 career goals during a 12-year career in Boston, while Hodge felt the wrath of the fans despite scoring 21 goals in his first season in New York. Hodge retired after the 1977–78 season.

#89

Pavel Buchnevich

> **NYR Debut:** October 13, 2016 (vs. New York Islanders, won 5–3)
> **Regular Season Games with NYR:** 41
> **Playoff Games with NYR:** 5

The Rangers drafted Russian-born left winger Pavel Buchnevich in the third round of the 2013 NHL Draft. It was a risky pick in that it was not known if Buchnevich would ever leave Russia to play in the NHL.

Buchnevich was projected as a highly skilled player who saw the ice well and was a tremendous passer and playmaker.

Buchnevich, twenty-one at the time, made the opening-day roster. He scored his first NHL goal in early November, which was the first of four straight games with a goal. With his early success, it appeared the young Russian was on his way.

A back injury and a lack of confidence from head coach Alain Vigneault limited his production and ice time (eight goals in 41 games), but the Rangers are looking for bigger and better from him in the future.

#91

Markus Naslund

> **NYR Debut:** October 4, 2008 (at Tampa Bay Lightning, won 2–1)
> **Regular Season Games with NYR:** 82
> **Playoff Games with NYR:** 7

In 2008, the Rangers signed veteran left winger Markus Naslund. The thirty-five-year-old was a consistent goal scorer throughout his career which included three seasons with 40 or more.

Naslund acquitted himself very well in his one season with the Rangers. He played an entire 82-game season and scored 24 goals with 22 assists for 46 points. In seven postseason games, Naslund had a goal and two assists. He retired after the season.

Evgeny Grachev - center

> **NYR Debut:** October 29, 2010 (vs. Carolina Hurricanes, lost 4–3)
> **Regular Season Games with NYR:** 8
> **Playoff Games with NYR:** 0

#92

Michael Nylander

> **NYR Debut:** October 5, 2005 (at Philadelphia Flyers, won 5–3)
> **Regular Season Games with NYR:** 160
> **Playoff Games with NYR:** 14

Michael Nylander was an exceptional playmaker who signed a free agent contract with the Rangers in 2004.

Nylander had 56 assists and scored 23 goals for 79 points in 81 games in his first Ranger season of 2005–06.

He continued to show his consistency in 2006–07, when he scored 26 goals with 57 assists for 83 points. In the 2007 playoffs, Nylander scored a hat trick in Game Three of the Rangers' four-game sweep of the Atlanta Thrashers in the Eastern Conference Quarterfinal. In Game Three of the Conference Semifinal, Nylander had the primary assist on Michal Rozsival's game-winning goal in double overtime.

Was exceptional playmaker for Rangers.

Photo by nrbelex via Wikimedia Commons.

Nylander played out his contract after the season.

#93

Petr Nedved

NYR Debut: January 20, 1995 (vs. Buffalo Sabres, lost 2–1)
Regular Season Games with NYR: 478
Playoff Games with NYR: 10
Also wore: #10

Center Petr Nedved had two tenures with the Rangers.

In July 1994, the Rangers acquired the twenty-two-year-old pivot man from the St. Louis Blues in exchange for winger Esa Tikkanen and defenseman Doug Lidster. Unfortunately, Nedved never really played up to his full potential during both of his Ranger tenures.

During the first go-round, Nedved played one lockout-shortened season, scoring 11 goals in 46 games. After the season, he was traded to the Pittsburgh Penguins in exchange for left winger Luc Robitaille and defenseman Ulf Samuelsson.

Nedved was re-acquired from Pittsburgh in a trade for right winger Alexei Kovalev in November 1998.

Nedved went on to play parts of six more seasons for the Rangers. His best was in 2000–01, when he scored a team-leading 32 goals with 46 assists for 78 points.

Photo by Handshakes between CZE and SVK 2014 Winter Olympics via Wikimedia Commons.

Led team with 32 goals in 2000–01 season.

Keith Yandle

NYR Debut: March 2, 2015 (vs. Nashville Predators, won 4–1)

Regular Season Games with NYR: 103

Playoff Games with NYR: 24

The Rangers needed help on the power play at the 2015 NHL trade deadline and so completed a multi-player trade with the Arizona Coyotes for defenseman and power play specialist Keith Yandle. (Yandle finished the 2014–15 season second in the league in power play assists.)

Yandle was an offensive defenseman who had 42 assists during his one, full season with the Rangers in 2015–16, which led the team.

After the season, Yandle was dealt to the Florida Panthers. During his Ranger tenure of 103

Photo courtesy of Mark Rosenman.

Brought in to be power play QB, Yandle had 25 points on the power play in 103 games.

games, the native of Boston, Massachusetts, scored two power play goals and had 23 power play assists.

Mika Zibanejad

> **NYR Debut:** October 13, 2016 (vs. New York Islanders, won 5–3)
> **Regular Season Games with NYR:** 56
> **Playoff Games with NYR:** 12

In order to acquire twenty-three-year-old center Mika Zibanejad from the Ottawa Senators, the Rangers gave up reliable twenty-nine-year-old center Derick Brassard. Not only did they get a younger player, but also acquired a right-handed center. Brassard was left handed, and the roster was overloaded with left-handed forwards.

Zibanejad had an injury-plagued first season with the Rangers in 2016–17. In late November, he broke his ankle after sliding into the boards at Madison Square Garden, and was out for nearly two months.

Zibanejad returned in late January and finished his first season in New

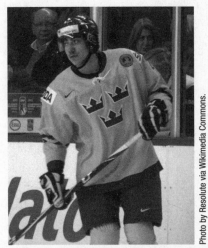

After a regular-season injury, Mika showed why Rangers traded for him with strong a postseason.

York with 14 goals and 23 assists. In 12 postseason games, he scored two goals with seven assists for nine points.

#94

Derek Boogaard - left wing

> **NYR Debut:** October 9, 2010 (at Buffalo Sabres, won 6–3)
> **Regular Season Games with NYR:** 22
> **Playoff Games with NYR:** 0

Five months after he played his last Ranger and NHL game, Derek Boogaard died of an accidental drug overdose. After his untimely death, an examination of his brain revealed Boogaard, who was an "enforcer" during

Photo courtesy of Mark Rosenman.

The game's ultimate enforcer, died of an accidental drug overdose.

his playing days, had an advanced case of CTE (Chronic Traumatic Enceph-alopathy).

#96

Emerson Etem - right wing

NYR Debut: October 15, 2015 (at Montreal Canadiens, lost 3–0)
Regular Season Games with NYR: 19
Playoff Games with NYR: 0

#97

Matt Gilroy

NYR Debut: October 2, 2009 (at Pittsburgh Penguins, lost 3–2)
Regular Season Games with NYR: 142
Playoff Games with NYR: 5

Photo courtesy of Mark Rosenman.

Hobey Baker winner, Bellmore native played 142 games for Rangers.

Boston University defenseman Matt Gilroy was the 2009 Hobey Baker Award winner, emblematic as the best collegiate player in the country. He was born in Bellmore, New York, and signed with his hometown team in 2009.

In his first season of 2009–10, Gilroy played 69 games and scored four goals with 11 assists for 15 points. He signed on with Tampa Bay for the 2011–12 season.

In January 2013, Gilroy signed a one-year deal to return to the Rangers for the remainder of the season. He played out the deal and signed with Florida the next season.

#99: THE GREAT ONE LANDS ON EIGHTH AVENUE

Wayne Gretzky

NYR Debut: October 5, 1996 (at Boston Bruins, 4–4 OT tie)
Regular Season Games with NYR: 234
Playoff Games with NYR: 15

The Rangers have had some all-time great players wear their sweater over the years, but on July 21, 1996, they signed the player who many consider the greatest player of all time.

Wayne Gretzky was thirty-six years old when he signed a free agent contract with the Rangers, missing only 12 games during his three-year tenure. In joining the Rangers, Gretzky was reunited with some of his former teammates with the Edmonton Oilers, including Mark Messier, Adam Graves, and Jeff Beukeboom.

In the 1996–97 season, his first in New York, Gretzky put up some typical numbers with 25 goals and 72 assists for 97 points. In the 1997 playoffs, the Ranger fans

The Great One retired a Ranger.

Photo by Håkan Dahlström via Wikimedia Commons.

saw some of that "ol' Gretzky magic." In the second period of Game Four of the Eastern Conference Quarterfinal against the Florida Panthers at Madison Square Garden, Gretzky scored a natural hat trick and the Rangers held on for a 3–2 win.

The explosion occurred in a six minute and twenty-three second span. The first was on the power play which tied the game at one. Three minutes and thirty-nine seconds later, Gretzky scored on a slap shot that beat Panthers goaltender and former Ranger John Vanbiesbrouck (see Chapter

Thirty-Four). Less than three minutes after that, Gretzky capped off the rare feat with a pretty move as he faked a shot, gave himself more skating room, and then fired a slap shot past Vanbiesbrouck to complete the hat trick. Afterwards, Gretzky pointed to his wife in the stands and skated to the bench to hug Messier. The Rangers would fail to make the playoffs in Gretzky's final two seasons.

After the season, Messier signed a free agent contract with the Vancouver Canucks, but Gretzky continued to be productive in 1997–98 with 23 goals and 67 assists for 90 points.

In his final season of 1998–99, Gretzky played 70 games and scored nine goals with 53 assists for 62 points.

On April 16, 1999, Gretzky announced that he would be retiring after the season. The Rangers were not going to the playoffs, so his final game would be at Madison Square Garden two days later against the Pittsburgh Penguins.

The final game featured lavish ceremonies and tributes from around the hockey world. Before the game, the Rangers presented Gretzky with a new Mercedes while highlights of his career were shown on the video board.

During the game, every time that Gretzky touched the puck, the crowd cheered. Pittsburgh beat the Rangers in overtime, 2–1, but Gretzky did have an assist. When the game was over, Gretzky tried to "soak it all in" for one final time. While the fans stood and cheered, Gretzky skated slow and deliberately around the ice.

Gretzky's modus operandi during his career was to be the first one dressed after a game but, after his final game, he didn't take off the uniform right away.

Gretzky finished his Rangers' career with 57 goals and 192 assists for 249 points in 234 games.

#104: A BADGE OF HONOR

The three-digit number was never worn by any New York Ranger in a game. However, it was worn by every player on January 13, 2017, at Madison Square Garden, during the pre-game warmups against the Toronto Maple Leafs in honor of the late Detective Steven McDonald. More than the material that the jerseys were made of, Steven McDonald has been part of the fabric of the New York Rangers since 1987.

"The Steven McDonald Extra Effort Award" is given every year to the New York Ranger player who, as voted by the fans, "goes above and beyond the call of duty." The award, which has been given annually since the 1987–88 season, is named after New York City Police Detective Steven McDonald, who was shot and injured in the line of duty on July 12, 1986, and passed away on January 10, 2017.

Photo courtesy of Mark Rosenman.

Rangers honor # 104.

SEASON WINNER:

Years	Player
1987–88	Jan Erixon
1988–89	Tony Granato
1989–90	Kelly Kisio
	John Vanbiesbrouck
1990–91	Jan Erixon
1991–92	Adam Graves
1992–93	Adam Graves
1993–94	Adam Graves
1994–95	Mark Messier
1995–96	Mark Messier
1996–97	Brian Leetch
1997–98	Wayne Gretzky
1998–99	Adam Graves
1999–2000	Adam Graves
2000–01	Sandy McCarthy
2001–02	Sandy McCarthy
2002–03	Matthew Barnaby
2003–04	Jed Ortmeyer
2005–06	Henrik Lundqvist
2006–07	Jed Ortmeyer
2007–08	Brandon Dubinsky
2008–09	Ryan Callahan
2009–10	Ryan Callahan
2010–11	Brandon Prust
2011–12	Ryan Callahan
2012–13	Ryan Callahan
2013–14	Mats Zuccarello
2014–15	Cam Talbot
2015–16	Mats Zuccarello
2016–17	Mats Zuccarello

ACKNOWLEDGMENTS

Mark:
Over the last ten years of doing SportsTalkNY, I have read hundreds of books. I, like many others, do not always take the time to read the acknowledgements. Having gone through the process of writing three books now, I have a greater appreciation as to how important these pages are to the ones preceding it, for without the names I am about to list, there would have been no book to read.

First and foremost, as always, is my amazing wife Beth who is always there as an endless source of encouragement, love, and support. My children, Josh and Liana, who by the joy and passion in which they approach everything they do in life inspire me to do the same.

My late parents, Morris and Estelle, who allowed me to buy every sports book whenever there was a book fair at school and always encouraged me to pursue my passions.

My sister, Cheryl, and my late sister, Suzie, who always set great examples for their little brother.

I would like to thank the following members of the press who welcomed me into their work space with open arms and showed me the ropes, including but not limited to: Ken Albert, Christian Arnold, Amanda Borges, Larry Brooks, Matt Calamia, Rick "Carpy" Carpinello, Jim Cerny, Scott Charles, Russ Cohen, Charles Curtis, Brett Cyrgalis, Stan Fischler, Bob Gelb, Zach Gelb, John Giannone, Denis Gorman, Andrew Gross, Sean Hartnett, Patrick Kearns, Allan Kreda, Don La Greca, Dave Maloney, Gil Martin, Joe McDonald, Joe Micheletti, Pat Leonard, Brian Monzo, Ira Podell, Sam Rosen, Seth Rothman, Ashley Scharge, Adam Skollar, Arthur Staple, Katie Strang, Joe Socca, Justin Tasch, Chayim Tauber, and Steve Zipay.

Thank you to the New York Rangers PR department, John Rosasco, Ryan Nissan, Lindsay Hayes, and Michael Rappaport, for all their help during this project and over the past ten years—this project would have never happened without you.

Thank you to the WLIE SportsTalkNY interns Jonathan Ottomanelli and Ryan Sherman, who were a huge help in transcribing hours and hours of interviews and importing stats into a usable database.

A note of gratitude to the scores of authors who have appeared on WLIE 540 AM SportsTalkNY, who have inspired me over the years, as well as our loyal sponsors Leith Baren, Neil Cohen, Robert Solomon, David and Andrew Reale, and my co-host AJ Carter, as without them none of this would have been possible.

A stick tap to the staff at Skyhorse Publishing, and in particular Niels Aaboe and Jason Katzman, who allowed Howie and me to complete our Hat Trick with them.

A special shout out to my friends Rob Stein and Steve Kassapidis, who I shared many years of season tickets with, including the one that will last a lifetime!

Last but not least, my writing partner in this project, Howie Karpin, as writing a book with Howie is like playing on the line with Wayne Gretzky.

Howie:

As has been a tradition with all my books, I have to start with acknowledging the support I get from my family.

My wife, Kathy Karpin, has been with me the whole way and it's been quite a ride. Danny Karpin and Jake Karpin, my two boys who I couldn't be more proud of.

My sister, Carol Shore and her husband, Barry who has always been like a real brother to me. Their support over the years has been immeasurable. My nieces Wendy and Sharon and their families and we will always remember and have Melanie Shore in our hearts.

Mark acknowledged the wonderful people that we share the press box with but let me add my two cents. I've known and respected John Rosasco for a long time. The Rangers have always treated me well and that started with John a long time ago and it continues to this day with Ryan Nissan and his professional staff. I grew up with the Rangers and have had the privilege of covering the team for the past 35 years.

Thank you Kenny Albert for "the opening face-off" for this book.

Covering Ranger games at the Garden has been a wonderful experience thanks to people like Sam Rosen, Joe Michelletti, Dave Maloney, my good buddies Don LaGreca and John Giannone (who helped me move into a new apartment in 1984) along with my long time colleagues in the press box including Larry Brooks, Rick Carpinello, Jim Cerny, Andrew Gross, Ashley Scharge, Arthur Staple and Steve Zipay, just to mention a few.

Howie Karpin